Craft
OF THE
WILD
WITCH

About the Author

Poppy Palin is the author and illustrator of several books on her work as a wildwitch and spiritwalker, including the *Waking the Wild Spirit Tarot*. As a trained artist, she illustrates for other green-spirited books and magazines, and is a sacred tattooist specialising in one-off designs for transformative purposes. Poppy is a qualified, experienced teacher and lecturer.

To Write to the Author

If you wish to contact the author or would like more information about this book, please write to the author in care of Llewellyn Worldwide and we will forward your request. Both the author and publisher appreciate hearing from you and learning of your enjoyment of this book and how it has helped you. Llewellyn Worldwide cannot guarantee that every letter written to the author can be answered, but all will be forwarded. Please write to:

Poppy Palin
℅ Llewellyn Worldwide
2143 Wooddale Drive
Woodbury, MN 55125-2989

Please enclose a self-addressed stamped envelope for reply,
or $1.00 to cover costs. If outside U.S.A., enclose
international postal reply coupon.

Craft
OF THE
WILD
WITCH

Green
Spirituality
&
Natural
Enchantment

Llewellyn Publications
Woodbury, Minnesota

First Edition
Fifth Printing, 2013

Cover images © Digital Stock
Cover design by Ellen Dahl
Editing by Jennifer Gehlhar
Interior design by Karin Simoneau

Library of Congress Cataloging-in-Publication Data
Palin, Poppy, 1966–
    Craft of the wild witch: green spirituality & natural enchantment / Poppy Palin.
        p. cm.
    Includes bibliographical references.
    ISBN 13: 978-0-7387-0577-4
    ISBN 10: 0-7387-0577-2
        1. Witchcraft. I. Title.
    BF1566.P25 2004
    133.4'3—dc22   2004049066

Llewellyn Publications
A Division of Llewellyn Worldwide Ltd.
2143 Wooddale Drive
Woodbury, MN 55125-2989
www.llewellyn.com
Llewellyn is a registered trademark of Llewellyn Worldwide Ltd.
Printed in the United States of America

This book is for my loving parents, Margaret and Denis, who do not always understand what I do but always support me nonetheless. With my eternal gratitude for their selfless giving.

CONTENTS

ACKNOWLEDGMENTS

I would like to thank the extremely gifted artist Davey Kendall for his generous support when I was writing *Craft of the Wild Witch*; he has been a true and dear friend to me.

My thanks also to the Llewellyn team who believed in my unusual approach enough to back me, especially my wonderful editor Jenny Gehlhar.

And my gratitude to all those who work tirelessly for our creature kin, protesting outside the hellish laboratories, farms, and cruel corporations that deny animals the respect and freedom they deserve. I wish to express my thanks to everyone who has ever saved a fox from the hounds or a guinea pig from a life of torture behind bars. Bless you.

PREFACE

There is lyricism and mystery, simple wisdom and profound realisation, great comfort and life-changing power in the wild witchery I will be discussing in this book. It is witchcraft for those of us who yearn to express our own inherent spirituality in a joyous, meaningful manner, not within temples or churches but out in the landscape and within the deepest fathomless places in our own souls . . . places that echo the furthest reaches of the starry-veiled cosmos. It is a way to understand our own wild heart, our soul nature. I will explain how our soul nature finds a perfect elemental expression on wind-buffeted granite outcrops and in deep still green water alike. The understanding of our true soul nature will come as unexpectedly as the warmth to be found in midwinter sunlight, as tenacious as the twisted tree that blooms and grows despite its exposed position, as moving and awe-inspiring as the sound of a single swan's wingbeats that are heard as it makes its way home alone across the moors. It is a magical path for those of us with poetry in our souls.

Some of us may feel like we are revisiting a lost part of ourselves, fulfilling an incessant longing within us. Or we may feel like we've found a new way to express who we feel ourselves to be, inherently, while honouring our native land and its spirits. However wild witchcraft affects us as individuals, its core message is always the same; it represents all that is steadfast and true in a modern world that can often seem chaotic and cruel if we have no anchor, no real sense of purpose. The essential message of wild witchcraft is found under cinnamon leaves, where the bright scales of hidden creatures shine, found in the fronds of glistening weeds swaying in brackish depths, in the swell and surge of massing thunderheads, and in the dazzling sparkles of sunlight dancing on a summer sea; there is beauty, magic, and meaning in the world if we only try to find it.

This is a magical book that combines instruction, ideas, and inspirations to help find all that is precious and real in the world by personal experience. It is, therefore, a guidebook that teaches by example and encourages exploration. By learning to read nature's language for ourselves, we can develop a living relationship with the land and regain a sense of inner orientation based in a living green spirituality. Via communion with the mysteries we encounter in the wild heart of our being, and through the simple enchantments we undertake to both honour and mirror them, we are refreshed at a soul level and more able to respond to the demands of modern society.

For those up to the challenge, the way ahead is lined with wildflowers, nodding in gentle summer breezes, uplifting our spirits, and affirming our wild ways.

WALK THIS WAY

Whispering voices come to me,
Silvered like leaves on the willow tree,
Wafting down lanes in my memory . . .

To truly know whether this path is the right one for us we must consider what it means to be a wildwitch. In essence, this is one who gently and ingeniously works as a spiritweaver, seeking guidance from the unseen realms in order to work with the gossamer strands of fate for positive purposes. This is done with complete reverence for nature and natural cycles. A wildwitch seeks to honour the land on which they live, experiencing life as an endless circling dance of enchantment and devotion, finding magic in the mundane and inspiration in the midst of modern existence. In this way, seeing a dusty dandelion push up between cracks in city pavement is just as moving as watching a heron take flight while its pale reflection dances in the river beneath.

With this acknowledgement of the enchantment to be found in the everyday, a wildwitch would consider making a healing soup for an old friend as much of a magical act as casting a more formal spell for the same purpose. This is done by imagining the friend's illness washed away as the vegetables are cleaned, the disease being eradicated as they are chopped, and health and happiness being restored while chanting a prayer and rhythmically stirring the soup. All these acts become part of a wholesome sympathetic magic.

For those who walk the way of wild enchantment, veils of separation begin to lift and everything becomes alive with possibility. This wild way—the life path of a wildwitch—is animistic and holistic in that it gives reverence and relevance to all energetic beings, seen and unseen, making it both Earthy and ethereal, a beautiful burgeoning blend.

We are all the magical creators of new ways of being and, if we so choose, we may be the regenerators of the ancient mystery, which has been hiding in glade-shade dapples and gathering power under dark stone in cool, green depths. We each hold within us the memory of the sacred seed-fire of existence and we can let it burn in our bellies, allowing it to pulse through our willing fingers, moving from rich, moist darkness into incandescent light. We can live lives of natural enchantment in a world filled with soulful beings and spirits.

The Way

To be a wildwitch it is important to understand that we are part of a way; it is a way that unfolds and is bright with soul treasure, purpose, and meaning. It is not, therefore, a straight, well-trodden road with junctions, signposts, road markings, and people travelling in a parallel manner. It is a winding track that may feel, by turns, dangerous, delightful, or confusing. Like all walks along overgrown country routes, we may be called on to be resourceful when walking the way of a wildwitch—having to deal with the spiritual equivalent of fast-moving streams to cross, brambles to push through, or clouds of irritating insects to fend off. The way of a wildwitch is full of surprises and requires us to be up for a challenge. There are no maps, only a guidebook such as this.

Wild!

The wild element refers to the spontaneous, reverent response we have to the majesty and symmetry found in the natural world—it is an impulse we have within us to be a flowing, growing part of everything. Such a response occurs when we act naturally, with immediacy and congruence. Wildness can be both potent and gentle, uniting the strength and wit of the owl with the delicacy and dexterity of the harvest mouse. Our wildness is akin to the galloping of a horse across a deserted beach, whose unrestrained leaping and prancing echoes the sparkling waves pouncing on the sand. The act is full of breathtaking elemental intensity, yet lyrical and shimmering.

Wildness has scant regard for petty snobberies and the cultivated social expectations of others; by its very nature it is without artifice. We can learn to express the untamed aspects of our being by looking at the lifestyle of others around us. For example, the fox has little need to try and be anything other than a fox. The thought of a fox dying his fur or behaving in a deferential manner for the sake of conforming to some social norm or to be impressive is ludicrous and rather distressing. It would be the very antithesis of his wild nature.

The wild path is for us if we are willing to be seen as "different" whilst never courting attention. It is a way for those of us who place more store on personal integrity than social standing. This said, wildwitches value their own personal creative expression more highly than any symbol of status. It may be well to be prepared for the world at large to start seeing us as mildly eccentric at best and slightly cracked at worst! Wild witchery may not enhance our respectability but it will certainly make us more able to smile at another person's assumptions and prejudices.

Are we afraid of being seen as cranky or crazy? We would all do well to remember that to be "touched" with psychic vision in some Native American societies is to be blessed by the hand of the Great Spirit. Prophesy and vision are seen as gifts. This is a far cry from the images of crazed folk it conjures up for the majority of Westerners today.

To follow the wildwitch's path we do need to put aside other people's opinions and standards. We are working with the Earth and we have to accept that this is not everybody's priority at this time. We need to be confident and centred in what we know to be true and meaningful. This takes a strong person who does not need to have reinforcements from external sources or even acknowledgement. It can seem, on occasions, a lonely place to be but we need only remember that we have a whole host of sentient beings around us at every moment of every day—ranging from our houseplants to the four-legged companions who share our homes to the spirits who walk with us, those who never tire of supporting us from the wings of the stage of life. A sense of loneliness is for those who see the world as a dead place full of inanimate things, possessions, and dumb soulless creatures. We may walk a solitary path through the wildwood of the heart in some respects but we know that nothing we ever do is in isolation. This is not a way for the egotist who desires to blaze a singular trail and wield power for powers sake. The power we experience in the wild craft is very real and we must be aware of our personal motives, needs, and wants from the outset.

Secrets

There is poetry to be found in every interaction and as wildwitches we are able to appreciate the secrets to be found behind each fluid motion, each harvest and planting, and each swirl in a snail's shell as it lays in the centre of our palm. We are able to acknowledge that all beings, and all aspects of creation, are our teachers; they are as unique and filled with potential as we are. It is our eventual connection with Otherworlds and our uncanny ability to see (with our psychic sight) that allows for secrets to be unveiled. These secrets include hidden realms as well as otherworldly beings and the truths they can share with us to help us on our mission to find inspiration in every untamed corner and every bright shadow. Our simple spellwork is accomplished by journeying to the more subtle levels of existence that many still choose to discount. We dance with the elements as our willing partners and, as spiritweavers, we work wonders with the ether.

Guides

The path toward wild enchantment is organic and, like planting a seed, needs only a little fundamental groundwork to bloom and grow under its own natural impetus. Wild witchcraft is, even with the essential structured ground rules in place, a way for those who like to be free, natural, and open. It is certainly possible to have a respect for sound principles while enjoying a magical spiritual life that is vibrant with unbridled living mystery.

We can obtain guidance from the unseen levels, once we become conversant with the techniques, but we can also learn how to approach everything with a sensible degree of caution from books such as this one. In the days when we had the oral tradition we would have learned through inherited wisdoms passed down from our predecessors in the form of story, chant, and symbolism. It would have been a much more regulated way of approaching the craft. Now we have the books written by those who have walked before us to act as mentors, books written by those we have never met in the flesh but whose work helps us to discern our own truth and meaning.

Whether our guidance comes from authors, otherworldly spirits, or personal mentors, we must learn a formal basis to our craft in order for our work to be successful. It would be foolish to expect an untrained artist to pick up a pencil and sketch an imaginative, yet technically brilliant masterpiece! Within this book there are rules for safe and effective practice. All of them can be adapted to the individual's way of working as long as the core meaning is not lost. None of them will limit us, only keep us within the limits of our expertise at any one time.

This brings us to a second point. Keep in mind, one may be a fine artist with much training but if there is no real feeling for the subject matter, if one finds it deadly dull and uninspiring, then the artistic work will be a pretty sham, reflecting only learned ability and having no dynamic soul energy. So it is with wild witchcraft. We may have all the right moves in theory, and look as if we are doing the job, but our results will have no glow, no life of their own, no real affecting quality, and little effect if our acts are not heartfelt. If they do not affect us, they will not have an effect in the world.

So we know roughly what sort of character it takes to make the first steps on the wild path. It will suit the self-motivated, the nonconformists, the people happiest out-of-doors, where they can feel the soft summer rain on their skin; and the open and questing souls who already have a very deep sense of the sacredness of all things. It will suit those who feel awe at the beauty and mystery of nature, those who yearn to find a thoughtful and creative expression of their own nature with respect to the circle of all beings. But is that all it takes? Do we need special skills, inborn gifts—like psychic sight—in order to walk the path? The answer is both yes and no!

Natural Witch

The seeing and the knowing, the uncanny and yet wholly natural aptitudes or abilities of the wildwitch, are both inherent and learned. We will look at these terms in more detail throughout the book. Suffice it to say now that "seeing" refers to psychic sight and a "seer" is one who is sensitive to things beyond the natural range of perception. Once we realise our abilities to see, our subsequent understanding of the importance to embrace and practise our psychic abilities within the wildwitch way is referred to as the "knowing." To say that seeing and knowing are both inherent and learned is to say that it is vital to have that empathic, sensitive, and perceptive element as a spark within ourselves before developing it into a fully fledged skill. Again, we are referring to a blend of things, not a strict definition. No, we do not need to be born a clairvoyant with accurate mediumistic skills and have a heritage that boasts a long line of seers, but we do need to have an innate aptitude for exploring feeling, sensation, and vibration. We will need an inner gift that is hard to define; one that expresses itself in compassion, motivates us to be empathic, and encourages us to truly perceive all that is expressed around us. As wildwitches we simply need to be open to feelings, to have a sensitivity that enables us to pick up external and internal impressions. In other words, it is important that wildwitches are able to be sensitive but not vital that they be naturally sensitive. We can be receptive and ready to learn the seeing without being able to spontaneously do it already.

By "defined psychic gifts" I am referring to a wide range of psychic abilities. To illustrate the point, we may have had a long history of hunches but do not consider ourselves to be anything as grand as psychics. This would mean we are adroit at sensing the atmospheres of situations and people and, perhaps, could even be attuned enough to sense changes in energetic patterns as they shift on the web of life. This would be revealed in an instance such as knowing when to avoid a certain road home, even though we use it every night, only to later discover that a truck jack-knifed across that same road the very time we would have been driving along it. It may also be revealed in repeatedly knowing when a friend will phone unexpectedly, or what someone will say next. We may not consider these to be special talents but if we trust our intuitions nonetheless, we are naturally perceptive.

Another indicator of innate perceptiveness is strange symbolic warnings that are revealed either in dreams or with visible waking portents. We may receive such a warning in a dream that leaves us knowing when a close friend or relative will die, or in a vision that shows us when a major disaster will occur. Perhaps we display signs of being disturbed by atmospheres in houses. Such signs include feeling shivers up the spine or finding hairs on the body standing on end. Maybe we have a knack for detecting smells or sounds with no visible cause. Common examples of these include sweet perfume or insistent knocking. We could even have seen things that others have not, such as shapes and forms, fleeting glimpses of figures passing us, sensations of presences no one else seems to detect. We may be able to see a nimbus of coloured light around a person and know if they are suffering any illness due to irregularities in their auric field. Perhaps we have distant memories of other lives that we can recall spontaneously, or a real flair for accurate divination.

These few examples are far from the exhaustive list that exists. They are common events that we may relate to but have never given a second thought. Many people write off such events or experiences as odd incidents, embarrassing talents, mere coincidences, or even curses. In actuality, having such experiences is probably an indicator that we are receptive with the sort of openness that is needed to successfully walk the wild way.

If we were born with defined psychic gifts then it is highly appropriate for us to carry on along the wild path but then I would advise caution if psychic talents exist without the essential capacity to be moved by the living, breathing, nonhuman world around us. To see we need first to feel. Our feelings are valuable indicators of who we are inside. We may express these feelings through our hobbies or jobs, becoming carers, nurturers, and enablers, as well as naturalists, gardeners, or lecturers in specialist subjects with a distinctly green flavour. Such feelings would rise up within us when we witness a harvest moon rise; when we see the first plants thrust up through frosty ground; when we hear a blackbird's song rise up through the smoky autumn twilight; when we catch a deer leaping, or witness a young hare boxing at shadows. We may experience wonder, a profound sense of ourselves being affected, which then takes us beyond daily experience to a level of transcendent exultation, bringing both tears of gratitude and a deep inner peace. To be a wildwitch it is vital that we have had such experience, knowing the bittersweet pain of rapturous appreciation for creation—having our hearts hurt because of it, feeling full to the brim with it. There is no course on Earth that can educate us on how to feel these things; they are innate responses and they, perhaps above all else, make us able to practice an unpretentious, impassioned, but controlled wild craft.

There is a much-used saying that "witches are born, not made" and this I have to agree with, to a point. There must be a little raw material, an essential wild soul energy, that enables us to work at the craft. It is necessary to have that inherent "witchyness," something not easily defined but that roughly translates into the world as a certain ethereal quality. Natural witches are no more special or chosen than natural swimmers or natural actors, they just have that inner starlight.

A born witch is one who has both the capacity to see, in potential or at present, and the responsiveness to feel. Witches can be made—trained, instructed, guided—but unless the necessary inner lyricism and the faculty for feeling is in place, they can never be wild because they will not be being true to themselves or who they were born to be. We cannot force a square peg into a round hole, nor can we make someone best suited for a dedicated career in conventional scientific research take on the lifelong green mantle of a wildwitch.

A natural seer is one who has always, since childhood, experienced some level of spirit communication, manifestations, or waking visions, and has been party to information that is not general knowledge. Such seers may be accomplished and fulfilled wildwitches if they can relate their fabulous skill to the wider world beyond human concerns. It is one thing to see people's dead relatives in order to bring comfort and deeper understanding to the living; to predict the birth of a boy; or to channel excellent and accurate information from discarnate beings; but again, if we have no real connection with the very planet that allows such activities, then our witchery will lack spark, for it has no connecting tissue to the wider, wilder aspects of being incarnate on Earth. Also, if we can only ascribe spiritual qualities and attributes to humanity then we are going to be ineffective. This brings us to our next point.

Animism

Wildwitchery is an animistic practice. Like the modern forms of popular shamanism, it witnesses and celebrates the life force in all beings, from the "wise ones of the bark" (trees) to a tiny dove-grey pebble worn smooth by the ocean. To honour the planetary host, which is benevolent enough to sustain us while we live our lives; to acknowledge all those who dwell close to us in fur or feathered skins, or in Fey or elemental forms; these are the real motivations that transform being a psychic in the modern world to being a creative and responsive wildwitch, one with purpose and motivation. At this point we can look beyond the realms of humanity and embrace the diversity and inter-connectedness of all creation.

What makes this way different from others is that we are weaving strands together, bringing our willingness, our enthusiasm, our sentient selves, and our latent aptitudes to bear in one expression of green spirituality. It is not solely about being a clairvoyant seer. Nor is it purely about loving Earth without any interaction with spirit. Through our green spirituality we have a hope to awaken the dormant human ability to sense the common life force in all things; by doing so, we hope to eventually reunite everyone with an awareness of the land's aliveness. Without this awareness we are ever poorer and Mother Earth, and all our fellow inhabitants, are in danger. It is for the wildwitches today to address this aching need by using learned and inherent skills, and the life-enhancing, spirit-conscious craft of enchantment.

It is for us to weave strong, shining threads into a patchwork of magic. To create beauty that comforts and offers a practical purpose, we stitch whilst dreaming of a better tomorrow. Our work is made from jewel-rich scraps garnered from the past as well as those embroidered with hope for the future. As the needle moves in and out of our lovingly created patchwork we may rock and hum, invoking for unity and harmony, seeing each fragment of colour as a field—some barren, some glowing golden, some green and luxuriant—all coming together, bringing a wild harvest for all to share. If we are willing to concentrate on each individual piece of fabric, while understanding the whole design, and if we are willing to give our thanks for being part of the dance of life while humbly acknowledging our role in bringing all aspects together, then we are able to answer the calling of the wildwitch.

Be wise, be wild, be blessed, and follow the magical path that leads off the beaten track.

Chapter One

THE MAGICAL LIFE

Sun-warmed bark under work-rough hand,
Dry grass swaying on the shifting sand,
Worn-smooth stone wreathed in dew-clad strands . . .

*I*s it possible to live a life of natural enchantment and, if so, does that mean we are practising a wild kind of witchcraft? Wildwitchery is all about a weaving of celebration, invocation, visualisation, and our heartfelt intent into our familiar practices. We weave while respecting and recognising the spirit inherent in each part of creation and the ebb and flow of the seasons.

The wildness gives our practice an unpredictable element, making sure we are ready even in the midst of the most tedious aspects of life, like doing the laundry or cleaning, to interact with our surroundings magically. When we work magic we weave the wild energy of everything from seasonal energy to spirit energy into our everyday deeds. It is this ongoing work that results in our life of natural enchantment. The "witchyness" comes into the equation by means of our starlight vision—our ability and will to perceive these energies—which allows us to understand and connect with all that is considered to be mysterious and hidden.

The word "craft" used in wild witch*craft* is about intentionally translating that magical spark into grounded and ordinary tasks, consciously bringing enchantment into our household chores, childcare, handiwork, relationships, and leisure pursuits. Our craft ensures that we have the skill—that we know how magic works and have a familiarity with safe procedures—and the knowledge—particularly of energetic influences, spiritual attributes, and seasonal meanings—we need for the work we will be doing. It is true that spellcraft can be practised under a full moon in robes but it can also be worked whilst baking bread, shelling peas, watering plants, combing hair, or painting a room. A wildwitch can create formal spells in a controlled way but chooses to do so not as an isolated, occasional act but as a part of an integrated magical life in which every thought or deed can become an act of devotion or enchantment. The key is to see the potential for each moment to be magical and each act to be a sacred experience.

With complete commitment, awareness, and a sense of fulfilling a vital role in our modern world, a wildwitch's whole life can become an unfolding, ongoing spirit song of dedication to healing, harmony, and wholeness. Wild witchcraft is, therefore, not only something that we practice when the occasion calls for it but something that we live from minute to minute. Because of this, there are no ordinary, dull moments, only a seamless flow, a merging of magic into life.

Maintain Balance

Wild witchcraft is a balance of Earthly (manifest) appreciation and spiritual (ethereal) understanding; an interaction that is both simple and effective. We are all souls that need to develop and grow, but we are also humans that need to find meaning in life. If we are interested in the wild craft we should first consider if our souls are energetically compatible with a path that empowers through a love for the Earth and that works with the waxing and waning tides of life for magical, healing purposes. This is but one of many ways to walk toward truth. The wild way will resonate profoundly with us if we are willing to commit to a process that not only strengthens and nurtures us as spiritual beings but also gives us an opportunity to act for the environment and our fellow creatures in an active, physical sense. It is a way to live well.

It is important that we can feel comfortable with the idea that this balance exists in the outside world and is found within us; we are a balance of the eternal and the corporeal. Even though the corporeal seems more solid at this moment, it is actually the more transient of the two expressions; souls last beyond a lifetime whereas bodies do not! For wildwitches, there can be no separation between ourselves and the rest of creation; likewise, there can be no separation between the inner and outer expression of a wildwitch's own self. One always affects the other. Consequently, we will work from the perspective of the interconnectedness of all creation, with ourselves as valuable (although not superior) parts of it. To acknowledge the life force in ourselves and all fellow beings on a daily basis is known as an Earth-honouring green spirituality.

What we know to be physical and what we understand to be spiritual is the basis to spellweaving, green spirituality, and wild witchery. We respect the differences between the physical and the spiritual levels of existence while realising that they cannot be separated and defined in a black and white sense; they are interwoven, interdependent aspects of being. Our lives can glow with the interplay of fixed and mutable energies, the solid and ethereal realities that make up the weft and warp of the wholeness of existence. Our role as wildwitches is to weave the thread back and forth between the levels of being for the purpose of magical transformation and to note the patterns, textures, and hues that reveal themselves to us in this process.

Earthwalk

We may find that the role of the wildwitch and our own nature are interlinked, entwined and bound by promises made long ago or by understandings gained in the time before time. With this possibility, we are acknowledging our existence as both a temporal and temporary human being and as an eternal spiritual essence finding human expression. Consequently, it may seem entirely natural to weave magical understanding into the very fabric of our daily existence, to become an enchanter or enchantress, and to see ourselves as actively *being* enchantment. Indeed, our wild craft requires such commitment. By applying such dedication we will be putting both human heart and eternal soul into our wild craft for the duration of this incarnate life. And, perhaps, beyond.

We shall refer to the duration of our present incarnation as the "Earthwalk." When balancing the manifest and ethereal, it is important to end the separation between human existence on this planet and our generous host, Earth Mother. Our Earthwalk suggests a specific partnership, a relationship between manifest beings and Earth, which is a complex living organism that chooses to support the continued existence of all physical beings. The whole ethos of walking as a wildwitch revolves around this end to apartness; it is vital that we state both verbally and symbolically, as often as we can, without contrivance, how we honour our connection to the planet Earth.

Seeing and Knowing

In order to truly lead a balanced way we must awaken our starlight vision, which we briefly mentioned in the introduction. To do this, we must combine intuiting and feeling (sensing the ethereal) with education and hands-on doing (practical, manifest application). Once again, to sense the ethereal is "seeing" and to understand the ethereal is "knowing." Therefore we could say that, as wildwitches, we continually exercise the seeing, the knowing, and the physical magical practices we learn by study-ing the wild craft. The physical magical practices include working with healing herbs, utilising symbolic objects, and practising divination with specific tools. It is important to remember that there should always be an appreciation of both the physical presence and the unseen resonance of all that we do.

One such way wildwitches work in perfect balance with the seen and unseen is by making the divisions between the nebulous and the solid less clear. We can do this by working with pure sound, scent, and colour in our magic, or by using word sounds and patterns in chant. The most common of these methods is daily enchantment. Wild enchantment relies on spoken affirmation and repetitive rhyme, hence the "chant" in en*chant*ment, meaning to use verbal incantation for magical purposes. We may also use simple statements for affirmation of our intent at any given stage during our wild witchcraft. Throughout this book there will be adages in quotations that may help us to focus on and reaffirm our more general and universal intent as wildwitches. The first of these sums up what we have talked about above: "We mend, tend, and blend."

Our desire to blend the realms of existence, both the widely considered "seen" (manifest) and intentionally or inadvertently "unseen" (ethereal/spiritual), ever closer together is for the good of our own magical development, but will ultimately ripple out to benefit the whole of creation, bringing greater balance and harmony into daily life. In other words, as we know ourselves to be living representatives of the natural way—holding within us the same flame of life force that animates the birds and the rivers, the distant star and the grain of sand, the millionaire and the beggar—we understand that whatever we do to ourselves applies to all of creation by direct association. We know that we can no longer see pollution or destruction as "externals" because they may be caused by us. By healing our own ailments through inner work and magical practice, we can reflect this rebalancing and healing outward and onward. The maxim "As within, so without" is relevant here as it means that what we find to be true and valid within the microcosm of our own lives is inevitably reflected as a universal principle, and vice versa, with beautiful simple symmetry.

Also, what wildwitches acknowledge to be authentic and valid in a spiritual sense becomes reality in the manifest levels, each aspect feeds the other. By having heartfelt faith in the connection between our own self and the universal whole of creation, we draw the two aspects ever closer into balance. This is the basis of wild magic. Our acts of faith, which sparkle with raw elemental energy, are woven into the tides of life and the seasons of the natural world. We blend our seeing with the knowledge of what we must physically do and then all of our spells and prayers are focused with this understanding as a basis. When we have faith in our truth—when we feel it and give it our energy, and use our practical knowledge and skill to enhance it—then it becomes a truth in the world. Just as the preparation and cooking of a soup can be dedicated to our work and infused with intent, so can we act simply and focus powerfully to bring about positive change in a myriad of other creative ways.

For the Good of the All

Acknowledging the wildwitch's ability to bring about manifest magical change is a liberating experience but also a responsibility to be taken very seriously as it could easily be misused. "For the good of the All" (the "All" being all encompassing, all that is) must always be our primary motivation. In a spiritual way with no absolutes in terms of tenets, this one heartfelt plea serves as an inspirational principle to work by. To understand what may be for the good of the All, we always need to first consult with our companion spirits in a safe astral place. We will discuss companions and astral place in detail later. For now, it is important to know that our companion spirits can give us "the overview" (the bigger picture or wider perspective of existence). This allows us to look beyond our own human dilemmas and enables us to witness the interconnectedness of all that is seen and unseen. It is a gift bestowed on us by the spirits so that we may see how our actions affect the whole and how the whole affects us. In our own search, we also aim to one day see all of humanity look beyond to the interconnectedness that currently awaits recognition.

To many witches this honourable aspiration is revealed in a popular maxim: "And it harm none." There is something to be said about this phrase. Although its intentions are perfectly valid, it is sometimes inevitable that someone will consider themselves hurt in the process of change that is for a greater good. The whole ethos is never to deliberately hurt anyone or anything, but it is realistic to acknowledge that to work for the highest benefit of creation we must sometimes put a few noses out of joint. It must be understood that we never would do this with a malicious intent. It is perfectly possible that an oil company could consider itself hard done by if we all switched to using bicycles and woodburning stoves tomorrow, yet our intention would be to help Mother

Earth, not to harm the individuals of the company. As we are all connected, some repercussions may be considered inescapable.

Perhaps it is more appropriate to think of an environmental adage: "Think globally, act locally." With this in mind, we can specifically acknowledge how we can effect change in the wider world with our homespun gifts of green magic. It all begins with us and our small yet potent gestures; the stronger our belief in our connection to the All, the more we are able to influence it. This faith in the interconnectedness of all that is seen and unseen also strengthens us. How can we not be strong? We are directly linked to the same life force of vast and enigmatic planets, cascading waterfalls, and lions bringing down their prey on sun-baked savannahs. We acknowledge elemental power and therefore acknowledge the power within our own wild self.

Because of our deep personal understanding and experience of the interconnectedness of all life, the harder it becomes for us to separate out our witch time—the time we put aside for inner work, spellweaving, or divination—from the rest of daily existence. The holistic viewpoint attained in wild witchcraft makes it nigh on impossible to act as someone who compartmentalises their life into "witchy" and "nonwitchy" activity. Unless we weave our beliefs and creative magic into all that we do, we are not living well, nor are we walking our truth as wildwitches. In other words, wild witchcraft is not just something that we do but something that we are. The wild way gives us the insight and ability to weave spells by wish and will, with love and care.

The Greening

The wild way also offers an opportunity for us to work as otherworldly emissaries. Our craft prepares us to go out on a limb to bring the beauty and inspiration of the unseen levels long since hidden from the majority of human eyes into manifest existence. If we are prepared to take the first steps on the wild path, then we need to be committed to this idea that the "lost" worlds, the enchanted realms that once were much closer to the human experience, can be brought back into our level of perception. We are speaking here of the lost worlds of Faery. Reweaving the shining magic of the Faery folk (Fey) into our own more basic mode of operation is a life's work. We may see little reward in terms of money or kudos for this work but it will generate untold wealth and satisfaction. Our work will enrich and empower us on far deeper levels than financial gain or social praise. Like all ways of the wild craft, reweaving Fey magic is a daily experience.

Even though it is a life's work, it cannot just be referred to on high days and holidays. It gives definition and form to all our days and colours our experience of the world.

On a wildwitch's path this work is the "Greening," meaning to bring magic back to life with the energy of verdant resurgence, which may be found in the Fey or unseen realms. Even though these realms are hidden from the sight of most mortals, the wildwitch can experience them safely as an intermediary between them and the far denser realm that we inhabit from day to day. We may journey in a trance state to these realms and bring to light the enchantments found in our otherworldly interactions, reintroducing the glorious magics of mythic folktales into the modern world. We embark on such a trance journey so that we may again dance with dragons and dally with colourful capering minstrels for the sake of inspiration and pure joy. Through such a trance journey, we may delve into the greenwood of our unfettered imagination and, led by the luminous, wonderfully mischievous sprites of our childhood dreaming, access the living realms that surround us in full colour, shimmer with vibrant energy, and that are hidden from us only because of our own unwillingness to acknowledge anything that isn't immediate, solid, and accepted as the norm.

The Greening is therefore an emotive metaphor for a more wholesome, natural, and infinitely more affecting way of experiencing life. It is important that the concept moves us as potential wildwitches. When this feeling is coupled with motivation, our trained ability to focus our will, and our understanding of interconnectedness, then we have the basis for a real living way, a way that empowers us while ensuring we are both responsible and respectful.

Fey Spirits

Through interaction with Fey spirits we are filled by their simple grace and can be representatives of their energies, sparking with their latent power. We may make the veil between the unseen levels and the twenty-first-century world more transparent so that there may once again be peace, harmony, and vibrant creativity on the land. The more we interact with the Fey the more this process will flow into existence. The possibility of a Greening for Mother Earth and all of her denizens—be they otherworldly, Fey, or flesh and blood, the leafy-boughed and mineral-moulded alike—becomes as real as we envision it to be. Our envisioning, be it part of a daydream or a trance journey, is at the root of our power. To envision is to access soul imagery for the purpose of greater knowledge and deeper understanding. When we envision, we enliven our dreams and give birth to bright imaginings. We also see more than meets the human eye, we look into the beyond.

Uniting the elemental realms of the Fey with the manifest levels of humanity serves the purpose of healing Mother Earth especially well as the Fey are nature personified, subtle yet influential and radiant beyond measure or reason. However, to say that Fey folk are "nature spirits" is to limit them to only one guise. They actually came to Earth, poetically speaking, on "the backs of the stars" in a time before human domination of the planet. Rich in paradox and glamorous beyond our human knowing, they defy any attempt to label or define them. They are generally happy to guide us if we accept them for the faces that they choose to show to us, and happy to lead us if we are not vigilant. The Fey are pure natural energy and only take form for our human benefit as we need a physical shape to recognise them. They can pluck imagery out of the collective human conciousness and present themselves in the standard pointed cap and boots of our fairytales. It suits their nature to "dress up" in the form of red-capped pixies and willowy, watery sprites. They love to entertain, bemuse, and sometimes cause alarm by the ever-shifting guises they choose to wear for us.

The Fey are both the star-born Shining Ones and the Children of the Earth's Greening. They are incredibly powerful and numinous yet innocent, playful, and full of earthy humour. To help bring back their magic is to help keep Earth alive and thriving.

Mother Earth

Working with the Fey is but one resource we have to help bring about the Greening. Perhaps first we can acknowledge the living land and all her inhabitants as allies in the work. We share a common aim.

Although we may not always have a spiritual home on this planet and we too may have a soul birthplace in the stars, we have chosen to be present for an Earthwalk now at a time when we are needed here. How are we needed? Well, not only to bring about the Greening, a spiritual resurgence of beauty and enchantment to replace the pall of destructive greed that endeavours to grip the planet, but also to work in a more physical way by recycling, gardening organic food, and campaigning for more ethical treatment of animals, people, and the land. All of these acts, from writing a letter of protest to investing time and energy in an allotment of land, can be imbued with magical intent. Every positive gesture has the potential to become a spell. When we envision a healed Earth and work toward that outcome, weaving our imagination and our actions together with magical intent, we practice a wild craft.

Mother Earth deserves willing representatives prepared to champion her cause on all levels; all pertinent green issues can be woven into our craft. Therefore, it is central to our wild work to be able to make a sincere and deeply felt pledge to support Mother Earth, in any way we can. Put most simply, we can show our intent by walking gently on her, with affection and respect, and acknowledging her as a beneficent and immensely powerful being in her own right. To clarify, she does not need our healing, she goes through her own cycles of growth and dying and may choose to shrug us off her verdant shoulders, like fleas off the back of a dog, at any time. However, we are her guests at this time. Rather than being fatalistic and selfish, it is far more appropriate to respond to our generous host with kindness and caring.

Trance Journey

We just briefly mentioned trance journeys in our discussion on the Greening. We spoke of travelling to meet the Fey and, indeed, our trance journeys are the most valuable way to interact with the unseen levels of being. We achieve this by entering a light meditative state. Soon we will look at our wild journeys more closely.

A trance journey is the most obvious expression of a wildwitches inner work. It is not a physical outward journey but a journey into deeper inner mystery. That deep mystery within leads us to all that is immanent. We can specifically focus inward on the purpose of our Earthly level of existence. We can then journey to bring about desired change in the manifest world, for what we do in the inner realms is reflected in the world and vice versa. "As within, so without."

Generally, we trance journey in order to converse with spirit companions safely, meet with our animal helpers, call up troublesome presences to be banished, and to find inspiration and information pertaining to our craft.

We will learn specific reasons to trance journey soon. For now it is important to understand that when we journey we enter another way of being. The places we journey to our very different than ordinary reality. As with all aspects of wild witchery it is the intent and symbolism we use manifestly that helps us to journey to otherwordly places.

Wild and Alive

Wild witchcraft gives life lustre and meaning; it is never an obligation or something that we turn to only when we feel in need of a boost, support, or entertainment. One cannot contain the migration of birds in a box, nor can we grow healthy sunflowers in a cupboard. All things need space to spread their wings and the conditions for growth. Our craft is a living thing in itself, a never-ending ramble through the wildwood of our being, a fascinating exploration, a learning curve. Therefore it cannot be put away, artificially contained, or given sporadic stimulus.

Our craft is alive when it is expressed on a train journey as we create a spontaneous, repetitive, healing chant in our minds for the owners of the passing farmsteads. Our intent for the chant may be to cease chemical spray use on the crops for the better health of the All. The rhythm of the train forms the measure of the chant. It is also expressed when we buy a paper bag full of wonderfully irregular and muddy parsnips at the local organic market whilst making a heartfelt plea: "As we support the need for wholefood with our purchase, so may all food be uncontaminated again for the sake of the Mother and all her children." Each apparently average moment has magical potential within it; yet, it is also expressed at the dark moon when we sit in deliberate contemplation, weaving a preplanned spell to banish our fears with paper and pen, fire and water. Whether we act spontaneously with sacred intent or whether we plan a more formal rite, the magic exists just the same.

To be a practising wildwitch one must live the life. This cannot be stressed enough. To reduce the way to a handful of random acts, however well our intentions may be, is the equivalent of damming a healthy freshwater stream and working with a trickle rather than a steady musical flow. We can still drink the water, and it will still refresh us for a time, but the energy it contains has been lessened and the life it supports has been restricted.

Religion or Spiritual Way?

Wild witchcraft is not a religion. Religious ways hold seekers within preordained human frameworks. Wild witchcraft aims to free, not restrict, individuals and the whole. As with all things in the wild craft, as in nature, there are cycles and spirals linking all in a non-hierarchical, magical continuum. Even the root of the Latin word *religare* (religion) means "to tie" and therefore it is wholly inappropriate for a way that claims to be unrestrictive.

As wildwitches we do not wish to subscribe to a way that makes us feel omnipotent or dominant, nor do we desire to belong to a chosen clique above the rest of society (or above other magical spiritweavers who do not share our qualifications or ideology). Being a wildwitch is not about "power over" or even solely "power within," but is more like being a part of a "power circuit," where everything involved is equally important and we are acting as receivers and transmitters while engaging in the vital energetic process of interaction and exchange.

As wildwitches it is important that we know ourselves and are honest about our own inclinations. The reason we do this is not to become self-obsessed or to consider ourselves special or exalted, rather to be better able as healed, whole beings to do what needs to be done at this time, for the good of the All. Therefore, we cannot package our craft up and get it out on Sunday evenings, the rest of the week reverting to being people who are impervious to subtle energies. We are either open and connected, or resistant and unready to engage. Unlike other practices, it will not satisfy us to perform one act of worship, or attend one ceremony per week.

To some, even having a title such as "wildwitch" may seem separatist and elitist. However, titles are important in our current stage of evolution because, as humans, we need some sense of who we are and what we do. For example, labels—like plumbers, cakemakers, and dentists—can be useful to identify those we can approach with a problem or need. These terms do not describe who people really are, but only reveal the manner in which they choose to express their skills and make a living in the world. It would be a little strange to suggest that someone had the soul of a plumber, but by this title we can acknowledge a human skill. To have an awareness of the difference between what we do in the manifest sense and who we are internally and eternally is important. What we do in the world is not the sum total of who we are as it denies a spiritual level to being incarnate. However, what we do in the world may well reflect who we are inside if we have chosen our career or vocation well. Perhaps in time we will feel no need to call ourselves anything, simply being on the path, openly and with grace, will be enough.

Soul Nature

It is more appropriate to view ourselves on a personal path than to think of ourselves following an already existing path designed by a pre-existing religion. With this in mind, the title "wildwitch" may actually be more than a temporary Earth title. For some of us, it may be a soul label. If this is the case, the witchcraft we practice will reflect our soul nature. When we practice witchery without applying ourselves, body and soul, we are simply using learned skills. At the same time, to practice a sincere and natural form of wild witchcraft is no more impressive than practising good dentistry and it is certainly just as useful, even if mainstream society hasn't recognised this yet. It will be a marvellous day when those with the seeing and the knowing are considered as vital to a healthy society as all the healthcare professionals, shoemakers, farmers, and so on. Without actively courting acceptance and craving respectability, we can all do our bit to work toward this day by being as down-to-earth (as befits our practice) and as open as possible. Although we often work alone and in secret, dealing directly with the eternal mysteries, we need not foster drama that can often lead to what we do as being sensationalised as some dark art or trivialised as pantomime. By being our-selves, true to our magical soul nature, we can be revealed as balanced members of a society that desperately needs what we have to offer.

At present, we live in testing times—the spiritual or unseen dimension has been either shunned in favour of immediate material gain or buried under layer upon layer of human fear, need, and greed. Humanity is very adept at couching a spiritual mes-sage in dogma, gilding it with a veneer of superiority, and layering on pomp and cere-mony, all of which obscures the original meaning. When the material overshadows the spiritual it is easy for all ethereal truth to get lost in the desire to possess, dominate, and control information in a very temporary human sense. Hence, truth becomes reli-gion, yet another monolithic Earthly structure that removes us from experiencing and witnessing the Otherworlds for ourselves at a deep personal level. As wildwitches we stay true to our very personal and independent soul nature despite the clashing funda-mentalist approaches to spirituality that the churches and society pressure us with on a regular basis.

Spiritual Way

As we have just explained, the wildwitch's soul is driven by instinct and guided by self-knowledge, personal spiritual connection, and hands-on experience, whereas religious people tend to operate within the preordained perimeters of a third party's making. To follow such a religion, one does not need to have direct experience of the central char-acter or theme. In wild witchcraft there are no central characters in terms of figures to be worshipped, only spirits that are encountered in very personal situations and with whom we have committed and intimate relationships.

It is all too often assumed that by saying we have a spiritual impulse we mean we have a religious allegiance; it is entirely possible for us, as individuals with a strong sense of conscience and a positive internal morality, to self-regulate our own experience of what is holy. It seems ludicrous to suggest that all apple trees should look to one authority for commandments on how they should grow and it is similarly unnecessary for the wildwitch to need such a restrictive code to live by. To have faith in the cycles of nature, in ourselves, in the guiding spirits, and in the universal energies is all we need to walk along our wild spiritual way.

This is not to say that we should revile or undermine other paths that claim religious status, for any road may take us a little closer to truth. The healing and nurturing aspects of all religious disciplines must surely be beneficial and acknowledgement of spirit, in any form, is certainly worthwhile. However, the divisive and dogmatic approaches of religious groups may be seen as entirely unhelpful in a world already burdened with ideas about supremacy and dominance. Further segregation, based in non-negotiable doctrine, is unnecessary in our age. Such beliefs lead to further suspicion, separation, and violent conflict and are entirely in opposition to the wildwitch's firsthand spiritual approach, which favours unity and peace whilst encouraging freedom of expression.

This is yet another reason why it is important to relate to our self-imposed labels with a sense of the poetic rather than with a need to be marked out as part of a regulated body or clan that has a need to be acknowledged as remarkable, absolute, or correct. To be empowered we do not need to be elevated or set apart. It is an acknowledgement of ourselves as vibrant and worthwhile cells in a functioning whole that is more desirable. Wildwitches see themselves as a part of creation, fulfilling a natural role—one more pure, true note in the symphony of life—no more and no less than this. If we know who we are in soul terms then we can walk our wild way more effectively within this whole.

Nonconformist of Yesterday

Some feel that it is important to remember that there is an age-old enmity between a certain monotheistic religion and witchcraft in general, in terms of the Western world. This is due to the past subjugation, ill treatment, and murder in the Middle Ages of anyone who did not conform to "the one true way" of medieval Catholicism and post–Reformation puritanical Protestant behaviours. Conforming meant sublimation of the personal will to the men who controlled both church and state, on pain of death. Because of the unpleasant nature of this period of history, it is easy for most people to get carried away with righteous passion and indignation, believing that the desire to eradicate the influence of witchcraft, and all subsequent crimes against those accused as witches, were validated because of the genuine evilness of the craft. On the other hand, when we know witchcraft is not inherently evil, it is easy to be intolerant of the organised religions that once sought to exterminate fellow magical practitioners and to be resentful, if not downright hostile, toward Christianity in general.

For vast swathes of our society today, the medieval woodcut imagery of the menacing hook-nosed harridan with her broomstick and strange familiar spirit is still how witches are perceived. The propaganda of the emotive witch hunts that occurred in the Middle Ages is so influential that witches are still frequently dismissed as ludicrous, hideous figures with no relevance to real modern life. One may also detect a frisson of uneasy fear at their mention. Clearly this image has no correlation to the thousands of people who claim to practice a form of witchery today. And it probably had no real bearing on those who practised a form of nature spirituality in the past. So were those accused of witchery in those terrible times really witches at all?

Usually, those branded as witches were simply nonconformists. To be a nonconformist was a crime punishable by degradation at best, and torture, hanging, or burning at worst. This was legalised via the Papal Bull of 1484, which sanctioned "inquiry" based on the wholly abhorrent *Malleus Maleficarum*. This is a book named "Hammer of the Witches," but aimed to hammer anyone who was not orthodox, not in active support of the church, or any who were considered to be religious heretics or antisocial.

The persecutions of the Middle Ages were just as frequently about money, power, and misogynistic hatred as they were about any green-spirited or folk beliefs among the populace. It was often the widow or lone, elderly woman sitting on some property, which a greedy landowner coveted, who met an untimely demise; it could easily have been the wife that talked back to her husband or failed to bear a healthy child; or the poet, the fool, or the dissident. To keep the people poor, both in terms of knowledge and influence, and to keep the women subservient and without hope, dependent spiritually as well as financially, were the core aims.

As the majority of those practising any form of folk art from midwifery to herbalism were poor, uneducated, and by and large women, there are no real written records of just who was doing what for us to consult. In fact, the majority of what was considered to be "solid documentary evidence" used to label one as a witch was actually derived from the sensationalist, blatantly falsified reports written by those who sought to eliminate witchcraft. These reports were accepted as official despite the obvious prejudices at work. Although we can observe remnants of folk customs and pagan ways in most regions today, witch hunts were widespread, resulting in precious little evidence of the real day-to-day practices and beliefs of the so-called witches of the past whom we associate with nature-based celebrations.

There have always been those who walk between the worlds, the healers and seers going quietly about their gentle arts, living simple, magical lives in close harmony with the land and serving the community in unique and inspiring ways. In the Middle Ages, these people may have been no part of an organised witch cult; perhaps they had never even seen another magical practitioner save their own hereditary teacher. We will never know for sure. What we do know, is that they were picked off, one by one, thousands of them, and all because they failed to fulfil a social, economic, or ethical criteria set by the all-powerful church and state.

And what of those folk who did practice their earthy witchery? Can we claim to have a direct knowledge of their spiritual ethos? Again, the truth is lost to us as written records are not forthcoming. Using guesswork, it is probable that the primary sort of witchcraft practised was hereditary, the oral tradition serving as a means of recording and transmitting; solitary, due to the isolated nature of many country dwellers; and steeped in the local lore of the area, as most poor folk had little opportunity to travel far beyond the nearest village. Their festivals and celebrations would have been guided by intuition and continual observance of nature's shifting patterns, as there would have been little reliance on calendars and clocks to regulate the annual high and holy days. These hereditary witches would independently work their craft by discovering the qualities of a particular full moon, reading omens, and listening to inner voices in equal measure and with no hard and fast rules, as flexible yet structured as nature herself.

Nonconformist of Today

Perhaps as wildwitches we would recognise this lilting and deeply experiential craft of our ancestors as akin to our own. But our frames of reference are so vastly different—we cannot pretend to come from an age without cars, mass market books, the Internet, and specialist shops—that it is stretching the definition of tradition to say that we have a direct lineage from rural practitioners of the Middle Ages and earlier. Therefore, to take up a hereditary crusade on their behalf seems somewhat presumptuous, as who knows what they would make of our ways today.

We can only empathise with the plight of those who died for their beliefs, whatever they may have been, remember them as our brave ancestors, hopefully honour them in our own earth-based practices, and strive to ensure that freedom of spiritual expression is the norm for future generations. This includes showing tolerance of those who choose to follow monotheistic religious paths. Harbouring any resentments about incomprehensible massacring at this stage in our journey will not serve our need to bring deeper understanding, concord, and equanimity.

The very people making accusations of witchcraft in the Middle Ages were often as ignorant and fearful as those arrested for their real, or more often imagined, crimes against the church. It was a time of great confusion, mistrust, and debilitating panic. The prevailing air of hysteria probably meant that as long as someone else was being accused, another was safe, and this surely must have led to spurious accusations in order to be left alone. The doctrine of the dominant religion of the time was steeped in images of torment and we can only assume that it was dreadful climate to exist in, from any perspective. It is easy to revile those who sought to warp the spiritual truths of their religion in order to inflict a reign of terror, yet, hard as it may be to comprehend, some of those involved believed passionately that they were doing the right thing. Within their frame of reference they were acting out of love and saving the souls of those they murdered by purifying the bodies with fire. It was believed that by burning the bodies of the sinful, the souls of those sinners would be acceptable before God.

One of the most beautiful tenets of true Christian belief, as taught by the mythic Jesus, is to have compassion for an adversary. Perhaps it would be beneficial for us to express this by feeling an immense pity, as well as the lingering shock and distaste, for those who acted in a brutal fashion during the witch hunts. If we can be gentle with the mistakes and oversights of others, then we are better equipped to know how not to do things in our personal lives as well as how to proceed on our Earthwalk with love and forgiveness.

Why is it important to look at this issue? Well, it always crops up in our explorations of what it means to use the label "witch" and how we feel about the idea of religion and religious allegiance. We are bound to encounter people who wish to bear grudges and have enemies and so it is valid for us, as fledgling wildwitches, to see how we feel about the issue. When our choice to walk the wild way is questioned, it is for us not to rally against such religious structures, rather to explain that we are concerned for the world in terms of spiritual nourishment and that we are simply doing our best to make sure our own lives reflect the relevant principles we hold dear. To reflect on our common goals and similarities and to focus on how we wish to develop and grow does far more to strengthen our connections to the All than to continue dwelling on what is wrong with another's way of seeing the world.

If we are sure of our purpose as spiritweavers and fulfilled by our work as wildwitches, then we have precious little need to focus on thoughts of revenge or hate. Also, if we have a healthy respect for our own abilities, we can recognise that our negative thoughts, if given enough of our energy, can influence the web of life around us and cause harm. Our aim is never to use our abilities for selfish, wanton, greedy, destructive, or intrusive ends. A tall order perhaps but something to aspire to in a realistic way.

To spread a positive spiritual regard that fosters joyful renewal for the one we have most respect for, Mother Earth, and all her children is our primary concern. Without her, we could not have an Earthwalk in order to learn, grow, and experience. Her well-being must be placed at the heart of all our work. Therefore we may never practice cursing, ill wishing, or harmful "hexing" as to hurt even one of her inhabitants is to act against her and to introduce yet more angry, bitter, and vindictive energy into a world overcrowded with such detritus. It would go against all we hold dear. In the same way we know we are reflections of the All, so do we acknowledge every other living being as such. For example, we may be afraid of spiders but if we accept that they are divine expressions walking in a different way to us, then we cannot simply obliterate them for our own sake. Nor can we curse them for offending us. It is a huge responsibility, a life-changing realisation, but once we have fully taken on board that in effect whatever we do to any part of the All, we do to ourselves, we begin to live well.

Wild Solitude

Finally, we will look at our practice compared to other witchcraft. The wild practitioner is a solitary one. This is to say we do not work with other humans but in essence we are never alone in our craft, for we work with spirits and the forces of nature. This is not due to any prejudice toward covens—an integral part of most witchcraft—as they are certainly places to gain much in the way of magical support and energetic input, yet the intrinsic nature of those of us drawn to wild witchcraft dictates that we would find it to be restrictive to contain our free-flowing way of relating—which is based in a very individual experience of the sacred—within a structured group situation. Indeed, the whole idea of structure may cause us wildwitches a few problems, being that generally we feel more comfortable with spontaneity and accessibility, and prefer to practice the craft at any time the mood comes upon us.

The structure found within covens may even remind us of the religious ways that we discussed earlier. In fact, within the coven structure there are official roles, most notably the high priestess and priest who have earned the right, through experience and application, to act as spokesmen at any rite. They are taking on the responsibility to channel divine energies on behalf of their group, which consists of people who act as support for this sacred action. In wild witchcraft this would not be appropriate, as personal and direct interaction with energies is essential and to have anyone else, no matter how knowledgeable or capable, acting as a channel on our behalf would seem entirely frustrating and completely unnecessary.

Obviously within the coven there are levels of operation and these restrict individuals from moving beyond a certain grade of responsibility, even when one has proven to be of a sufficiently high standard at the work. When we work alone there has to be a great deal of self-regulation and self-knowledge and direct communion with companion spirits, who will guide our judgements, in order for us to perform at suitable levels. Indeed, wild witchcraft as a solitary experiential pursuit requires a certain amount of falling down on the job, at least at first. But again, the nature of those who deeply wish to practice a solitary, earthy, wholly unrehearsed craft will be those who enjoy hands-on learning and who are motivated and disciplined enough to carry it out with success, and perhaps even with a certain degree of style.

So it is that the wild craft is largely practised alone or with one or two like-minded people who may come together informally to celebrate particular occasions or to mark the seasonal cycles. Anything other than this complicates what is essentially an informal way of being and not a ritualistic manifestation of spiritual belief. The very simplicity of this unpretentious craft is more akin to embroidery than religious ceremony; one needs to be focused on the act with a certain degree of skill and a developed sense of what makes a beautiful piece of work. It is a calling, an art, and a heartfelt way that can never be explored or expressed adequately in the formal setting that any group requires. Coven witchery is important in its own right but it is not what this work is about.

We may not adhere to a religion or the structure found in covens, preferring a gently unfolding way based in personal experience, but we need not condemn those who do. That is not the intent behind our discussion on religion or religious people. As long as we seek what is holy and enduring, searching for truth and union within the heart of our being, then we will find it in a way that is appropriate for us at this time.

Worship or Reverence?

Wild witchcraft is centred in our daily experience of the sacred. It is a continuous honouring of life and the divine life-force energy that animates each aspect of being. Yet with this ongoing sense of interaction, with energy that is eminent and imminent, do we need to worship? Can we praise creation by living magical lives or do we need to use a more formal manner in reference to a deity?

As wildwitches following a spiritual way we have a profound respect for the universal energies, Earth powers, spirit companions, and archetypal beings we encounter, but we do not deify them. Nor do we feel the need to be overly deferential or sycophantic in their presence. To encounter such spirits in an honest, earthy way we only need be awe-inspired and fired with a passion that burns deep in the very root of us. There is a real sense of working with these forces of nature as supportive partners rather than needing to placate, beseech, or overtly adore them as is customary in the devotee-godhead relationship. Respect is the key rather than out and out obediance as there is no need to feel subservient or to petition for favours if we honestly regard ourselves as functioning, valued, and unique parts of an integrated whole. We can feel empowered by our own sense of connection and by our own understanding of the dance of life rather than relying on a distant and unbalanced relationship that views people as needing to placate and appease a deity in order to get by in life.

Beyond Worship

We measure our relationship with the divine not in terms of religious rites but in terms of how much praise and acknowledgement we find within us at any given moment. It is a spontaneous and immediate response, an integral part of our craft. And the wild craft we are discussing is not Wicca, which is often taken as the only form of modern witchcraft. In Wicca, there are God and Goddess forms to be worshipped. Having a Goddess of equal if not superior power to a God in modern Wiccan belief obviously helps those long conditioned by patriarchy to overcome a limiting, unbalanced world view. Yet, perhaps we can celebrate the male and female principles and energies without deifying them. As wildwitches, balance and egalitarianism is the aim. This said, in wild witchcraft there are no Gods or Goddesses; instead, such great beings are archetypes, representatives of universal principles in human form, beings who once again deserve to be respected and acknowledged. They are unique and powerful spiritual essences with whom we may respectfully work to achieve specific tasks.

Reverence for All

As wildwitches, we see each tiny scuttling beetle and each perfect yet vulnerable daisy as beautiful, individual expressions of life-force energy, just as we see ourselves. If we are expressions of this energy then we are a part of it, as is the greatest and the smallest created beings. We all share the same essence as the Creator, or the source energy of life. We are all expressions of the divine. It is hard to perceive a separate deity figure when this is your perspective.

A wildwitch would find it difficult to build a hierarchy based on one aspect of creation being better than another. Who may equate the attributes of a wren to those of a mountain and judge one lacking? Are both not successful, succinct ways of revealing the sacred? With this in our hearts, we find no real need to elevate any one spiritual being above ourselves. Nor do we hold our own being in higher importance than any other. It is a truly egalitarian way, one built on the understanding that we are all vital strands in the weaving, serving an express purpose; we are complementing and supporting each other as teachers, guardians, and companions on this life journey.

There is an exchange of ideas and energies that arises from this way of relating. It means that we both give and receive openly and do not use any other being as a "resource," a thing to be tapped into at will to enhance learning. Nor do we surrender our autonomy or deny the responsibility we have as sentient beings. When we engage on this level, we have access to previously inaccessible information; the powerful unseen beings and elemental forces freely offer their spiritual guidance. And what do they receive in return? Not worship but our promise, as fellow beings, that we will express their will, their way, and their wisdom to the world. We are incarnate and they are not. We can make manifest change while they are not able to express themselves in a way considered substantial. We have the means of making a difference while on Earth whilst they may be given little credence in the modern frame of reference. Yet for all the disregard they are accustomed to experiencing in human realms, they have that which is most valuable to us: greater access to truths, to that which is hidden from our mortal eyes at present. They are once removed from this dense level of being and consequently become our link to the mysteries beyond the mist of human vision. They have the overview.

Our allies in spirit are the best friends we can ever have with their giving of unconditional love, nonjudgemental stance, and far-sighted outlook. We can loosely catagorise these spirit friends as follows:

Elemental: primal and pulsing representatives of air, fire, water, and earth

Ancestral: those who once walked the Earth as we do now but who have chosen to act as Earth-linked watchers, guardians, and wisdom keepers

Fey: the Muse-filled myriad of shape-shifting, independent beings who dance in the realms once removed from (or parallel to) our own

Nature: the spirits who exist in nonhuman forms but who live amongst us, for example, the four-legged and winged, the bark-clad and the many-petalled

We have an entirely symbiotic relationship with these friends. We act as their hands and mouthpieces in the world and they whisper in our ears and nudge us into action, always with the sense of humour, verve, and illuminating insight that we can so often lack whilst engaging in the Earthwalk. They may have a valuable viewpoint that is not in the slightest bit human, yet be willing and able to translate it into something we can grasp by means of symbolic and poetic feeling. Their communication rises like the glistening salmon, spraying us with a thousand rainbow droplets of understanding. It pushes and prods at us like a frisky goat, snagging our skirts like brambles and burrs, winding into our hair with bindweed twine, exploding around us with seeds of truth like a dandelion clock. With extraordinary moments of synchronicity, which come to be both common and marvellously unexpected, they teach us, lead us, and support us.

They do not demand nor do they punish us, though they may trip us up like a particularly gnarled tree root when we are too self-absorbed to notice the rest of nature around us. We do not make them offerings in the hope that they will change our lives; seeking their favours with sacrifices would be highly inappropriate. Instead they cooperate with us and we bring them gifts of thanks as is fitting in a one-on-one relationship based in trust and an unsentimental love.

Undoubtedly there are those spirits that, being further removed from our Earthly level, have immense and awesome power and as unfamiliar energies uninhibited by any remotely humanly recognisable shape, have the ability to make us fall to our knees gasping. The universe is full of vast, unidentifiable, swirling collections of energy, great beauty, and superhuman attributes. There are those whom we could deem gods as they are so entirely unknowable and unfathomable; those of brilliant intensity who dwell far from the dense human realms; those whom we may only glimpse or sense but never truly encounter, as to do so would truly "blow our minds." We may relate to them when we ourselves are discarnate and "in spirit," but when we are on our Earthwalk, we are limited by very human senses and synapses that simply could not cope with the energetic overload presented by these purely etheric beings.

Reverence for the Creator

The further a being moves from having a solid form, the more energy it has. We can understand this if we consider that steam is far more energetic than a glass of water, in terms of its molecular action. Similarly, the further we travel from solid, human life on a little planet, both in terms of "real" space and in spiritual dimensions, the less we have to relate to. As regards to our example, we can contain water, quantify and experience it, with far more ease than we can steam. Things that we cannot relate to well, unknown things of great and unpredictable power, can either be intensely frightening or completely mesmeric; or both, a combination often attributed to a deity. All creations share the same source, be they the inert sloth hanging from a branch somewhere on a small, blue-green planet or a huge undulating lifeform that moves through the seas of space and time, rippling with glorious lights. And that source is *the* Source, a great, unifying, all-encompassing spirit, the root of all that is: the Creator energy.

As part of creation, we are a part of that unknowable, ultimately mysterious Creator. It parented us with a mixture of compassion, detachment, and curiosity. Like children, we need not raise our parent up on a platform and give it subservience when a healthy acknowledgement, profound respect, and ongoing attitude of gratitude expresses the love much more profitably. We can relate to the parent by a name but we need not make it a god.

The universe is not, as we have already suggested, humancentric. Therefore, why should the Creator be human? The ultimate universal Creator is unknowable to our human minds, yet omnipresent in terms of our human lives today. It is the great mystery that cannot be unravelled but that is present in all creation. We can express our joyful appreciation (rather than worship) when we respond to each of the Creator's gifts, each born of that sacred source energy. These gifts are both found within us and within our fellow travellers, seen and unseen, on the winding road of life. Every interaction is an encounter with the Creator energy and each interaction is, therefore, a blessing to be counted.

Wild Energies

As wildwitches, we do not work with deities but we do work practically with energies. Etheric energy shapes and sustains the entire universe. It is the subtle yet potent force that connects us to the universe and all that resides therein. We may choose to work with particular types of energy for the course of our lifetime and, as wildwitches, will feel drawn toward a particular spiritual resonance that results from a sacred interplay between the natural world and the human psyche. For many of us, there will also be a strong Fey element to those energies in spiritual form that we feel close to. The energies we work with show themselves as representatives of nature, as green-spirited, insightful, and magical beings tempered with the human need for interchange and colloquy.

Again, we are not discussing deities here but rather spiritual avatars of certain Earth-based principles. Still, they are not the elemental, ancestral, Fey, or nature spirit friends we spoke of earlier. There are many spiritual beings who embody the traits that appeal to the soul nature of the wildwitch and who can aid us to develop as humans while we're on our Earthwalk. We may find that if such beings resonate with us we may work with them and perhaps even see them manifest in nature as we go about our daily tasks. They are not our gods but rather our spiritual mentors, those who we can look up to but not feel the need to coerce with fervent prayers.

Such spiritual avatars serve us by their willingness to impart knowledge and we serve them as committed translators of their messages. As they embody qualities so needed in the world today, the commitment to listen to them and bring their teachings into the everyday of our existence is an easy task. They are known by many names and it is only when we begin our work and seek guidance through the methods described in this book, that we will encounter our own avatars. Again, they are not our companion spirits or familiars (we will look at these in chapter 4) but they can still guide us.

We need not believe in these spirits, for belief limits and confines us, rendering us unable to see beyond the limits of that which we have prescribed as true. Yet we can have an open-ended, free-flowing faith in our ability to encounter genuine, independent, spirit energies. We can let go of our need to believe in another being and simply have faith that what we experience in a spiritual context is valid. When we have learned the skills involved with the wildwitch's work, we can blend our intuition with solid, grounded practice to ensure that this faith can flourish.

How we experience these avatars and what our personal way of seeing them happens to be at any particular time is not a rigid thing. Instead, our personification of them is filtered through our limited human understanding at any given time. Such energies shine like the sun and wax like the moon; they cannot be permanently defined for they are free of bodily governance and aligned only to the spirit powers of nature. They are of the Earth's mystery; not Earthly yet Earthed. The nature of the green-spirited avatar is mutable, not fixed, and bound freely for eternity.

When spirits are functioning for the highest good, they are without any ego-based needs and so do not mind being known by the names we give to them. As long as we perceive their symbology and receive their valuable messages, the truly evolved and beneficent green-spirited beings we encounter will happily walk the wild way with us as unseen counterparts, wearing any archetypal mask or going by any name that fits. It is the energy exchange that is valuable to the spirits and they fully appreciate the human need to have appropriate labels and imagery. It is enough for us to psychically receive a pure energetic vibration of who they are and translate it into the world; so that this can be done successfully, they will appeal to us in a host of familiar, deeply resonant forms.

If this is hard to understand at this stage, remember that we are dealing with enigmatic, eloquent, emotive allegory. We are not talking about bricks and mortar in our world but the numinous, nebulous foundations of magic, that which can be best expressed in poetic terms. We do not need to completely unravel the mystery to grasp its meaning. Part of what fires us up and motivates us on our Earthwalk is the quest for understanding, the desire to have an ultimate revelation about the meaning of it all, yet we may never resolve the riddle whilst we are incarnate—we just enjoy trying! How can we hope to pin down and categorise our otherworldly counterparts when we still know so little about our own human nature and that of the greater universe? If something works for us and stimulates us, feeding us at a soul level, filling us with feelings that can be beyond words entirely, then it is valid.

What follows are inspirational descriptions of spirit avatars who may dance the dream of the Greening alive with us in trance and through our daily magic. The descriptions act as a taster to bring to life the possibilities that lie ahead for us if we choose to walk the wild way; they are, we will observe, full of paradoxes. They provide the aspiring wildwitch with a real sense of how we relate to these ethereal beings and they may reveal who we would be best advised to seek out as valued spiritual associates. It is useful to remember that just as the tree is green in summer so is it bare in winter, and just as fruit is ripe on the bough in fall so was it once a seed in the spring. So it is with us, we are all many things—baby, lover, parent, old person—yet none of these descriptions add up to the sum total of who we are. The natural world is complex and ever-changing yet bound by cycles and perfect in its simplicity; there is no reason why our nature-spirited companions should be any different!

The first we will look at is Jack-in-the-Green, a verdant, vibrant male energy. As wild witchcraft is about balance and harmony, it is always vital to remember that both male and female energies are needed. We could say that Jack represents the divine male principle as regards to nature-based spirituality while the second example, that of the Moon Mother, is obviously a representative of the divine feminine. Remember, these examples are just a taster and we will look at our spirit mentors, their qualities, and their relation to sacred archetypes in much more depth in chapter 4.

Jack in the Green

We meet him in so many unexpected places, wearing so many guises. He reveals himself as the trickster, hiding behind the moon-pale eyes and charcoal-grey hood of the jackdaw, that consummate stealer of all things that sparkle. He brays out the foolish laughter of the canny jackass or tumbles like the playfully intelligent jackanapes. He is a little boy of nursery rhyme and fairytale who appears witless—falling down and breaking his crown, selling his cow for beans—but who turns out to be sharp and keen. Just when we think we experience him only as the loveable buffoon, then we see him anew in every children's heroic tale, as Jack the Giant Killer, a figure to look up to and admire.

He is the wild card and we never know quite how to take him. Two-faced Jack tricking us, slapping us on the back while taking our measure, incorrigible as could be. We may fear his unpredictable nature yet we are compelled to interact with his ebullient and inspirational spirit nonetheless.

We may encounter him as a forest-dwelling sprite, firing his elf arrows straight and true from his green and shadowy lair. His fox eyes glint as he steps from a pool of purple shade, aiming and shooting for the sake of honour and justice. Then he takes flight, slender and strong, bounding over fallen trees and ducking under branches, giving a tantalising glimpse of strangely pointed ears as his hood falls away from his silky hair. Is he a skulking exile? A willing outlaw, proud and defiant in his rebellious stance? Hero or villain? Hidden man or wild woodling boy? A greenwood king and a ragamuffin knave, a prince of thieves and a noble elf clad in grey—he is all of these.

In truth he is both the hunter and the hunted, eternally dancing between light and darkness, crowned by glossy leaves of oak and bound to no man's law. He is in both the crazy baying of the hounds and the surging blood of the stag, as well as the singing of the bow that shoots arrows of desire to pierce flank and heart alike.

He can make himself known, walking among the people if he chooses. He is present at Mayday celebrations; a man dressed in verdant foliage, shrouded in a sheath of mystery, peering out at us with almost inhuman eyes. Wearing a framework of wicker and dressed thickly with vegetation, he cavorts and capers willingly. He expresses all that is natural and free whilst hiding his true face under layer upon layer of leaves. He stands as a willing representative of the Greening of the land; he and the festooned maypole sharing the same common source, for not only is he the hidden archer but he is also the rising passion of the waxing year—upfront, full of vigour, and dancing in eternal, paternal circles. Fecund and sexual yet gentle, playful, and generous. Untamed yet honourable. Jack is the mystical, mythic forest, and he is the forest made into man.

Ever the jester ready with a belly laugh, eternally the enigmatic, fathomless cunning man. He leaps and lands on the earth in boots of softest leather. Is he Lord of the Dance or a prancing idiot? Facing us squarely he defies us to categorise him. He grins broadly, his twinkling eyes barely hiding a steely strength.

He stands now as the challenger as well as the defender. He is the dying lord of a winter's turning, whose place is assured on the seasonal round as much as his leafy, bawdy counterpart. He takes up his age-old, forever-fresh stance willingly, prepared for the struggle between the light and dark, the past and future, all that is yet to be. He holds the balance even as he steps lightly into the arena, ready to take on his most arch rival, his most beloved foe . . . himself. The guiser, wilful and virile, merry even in his final stand, for he knows he must fall, and fall he will, with grace. He faces his counterpart whose breath is the slow sigh of autumn, which must as ever be felt before the chill thrill of winter's kiss enchants the land once more. With a steady hand he rolls the bones of his own fate; ever the brave one, always the conjurer.

At harvest time Jack is sacrificed as part of the eternal returning (the eternal cycles found in the natural way of being, such as death and rebirth, the dying and the Greening of the land). He is ploughed into the earth and becomes potential tilth for the good seed. His promise, expressed in the wild dance of summer, peaking as the sun reaches its zenith, now pours forth like a benediction onto the land. His legacy, therefore, is assured, for when it is his time once more, he will be the first thrust of a green blade from an earth that still seems frozen. He makes the vow each year, renews it with his own essence, accepting his role as the wood-spirited goodfellow who will be elf-shotten and, for a time, forgotten. But the arrows that fall on him like bright rain ensure that even as he falls he will rise again. For Jack is a symbol and he is symbiotic with the land. His land. Our land. He is Mother Nature's lover, her son, and heir, but he is also a part of her as Father Nature.

In the dark days of winter he is sparkling Jack Frost—still leaping, a bag of bones wrapped in a tattered cloak—whose icy fingers send a thrill down our spines. He is as unseen as the seed in dark soil, yet as full of potential. We know him even when he does not walk in our world; we feel his flight and fight as the fire in our bellies, which drives us on to make a stand, to lend a hand. He is paradoxical, both the skilled archer and he who is to be cut down by the shining arrows of those who know that he must die; he who encourages us to shoot our own arrows of desire in truth, with honor, for the good of the All.

Jack, like all heroes, like all mysteries, is whatever we want him to be; or perhaps, whatever we need him to be in a time when Mother Earth requires strong, brave individuals to stand and fight for her. He teaches us that being an outcast is acceptable if that's what it takes, and to never be ashamed of our part in protecting nature. He is a perfect muse, advocating that we follow our own truths against the odds of modern, tame life, expressing our own creativity with ease and applying ourselves to all we do with renewed vigour. He is an inspiring figure for both men and boys, giving permission for them to be both strong and vulnerable, immensely playful and garrulous, yet capable of expressing their masculinity in physical acts of passion. Never cruel but always quick; always mischievous but never destructive; Jack is a friend we can look up to, a hero we can aspire to, a myth we can relate to, and a presence we can invoke for both protection and motivation.

He is part of a future vision of hope. He stands for all of us: for our children's futures and for the sake of all life on the planet, which he has sworn to guard with his life's green blood. He is a poetic resurgence, a legendary champion, and a hazy form at dawn and dusk; tumbling and spinning, his bubbling laughter is an echo of our own potential to live life to the fullest.

Moon Mother

Who is the stranger on the shore, the Dark Queen who sighs like the receding tide, whose salty life-blood pounds like the ocean in our ears?

Why, she is the enigmatic daughter of a thousand lost nights, each one illuminated by the pale silvered glow of her counterpart, her bright face: Lady Luna. Mother Moon, haunted by moths, is the bringer of the seeing of witches, vision in velvet places, and sanguine sorceries. She is the She who inspires the diviner, prompts the prophet, gives meaning to the meaningless. By the grace of her bone-white hand we are lead deeper and deeper into the heart of understanding, into the dripping caverns of dreaming.

It is she who pulls the veils of night aside, holding us close as we ride the wave of intuition into the cave of devotion. Rushing at us, lapping at us, hissing and foaming like a mad woman, she strokes wyrd-stone of our destiny smooth and offers us her secret treasure. Pearls of wisdom, strung together with our own pain and washed up in a shimmering circle, are linked by her silver crescent clasp as she reaches into the abyss and grasps enchantment. Driftwood and all the lies we have ever told are beached on her white sand and coveted; reworked into something beautiful, something eternal. She, the crow-footed, sharp-eyed harbinger of sorrows, scavenges and fashions all there is of us into the glittering of the darkness.

As she works on us, she rattles with death trinkets and glistens with sweat, leaping by her dying fire embers in her wild priestess hair of floating sky. She continues forging us until we are flashing star fire.

Mother of the Moon, the wise woman who waits for us, is a transformer and a mender of hearts with her cauldron of inspiration. She is a mermaid-mirror to show us horror, a blanched face in the deep floating widow's weeds, yet she will rise up full of renewed vigour to take our pain. She will take it and she will weave it into a filigree of the finest pewter, removing the tarnish, creating something we may wear with pride, a badge of honour.

She is cold and brilliant, distant and unknowable, and yet she is our Mother and her love is like no other; it brings us home to ourselves while she looks on with eyes flashing, impassive, wholly devoted to all that we seek, for she seeks it too. There are two of her, one above and so one reflected below in the waters of life; one of her is walking with us while the other watches, luminous, ominous, impervious.

As the moon spins seductively around Earth and Earth turns away in her own slow dance, so does the Moon Mother wax and wane in our lives, pulling us, drawing us, and letting us go. Ever the fickle mistress yet more true to our witch nature than any other, wreathed in mysteries of mist yet revealed, naked and unashamed, this pale candle of a woman with eyes of obsidian and a backbone of sparkling granite is our Mama. She knows us, she moves us, she illuminates our craft constantly even when she averts her face. She cannot leave us even when she hides, she promises to return, a slender sliver in a cobalt sky, so we may be renewed, stripped back and reworked in a new image. Old moon, new moon, dark moon, cold moon. As she turns, so do we become more fully ourselves.

She is reflected in rock pools of imagination, in subterranean wells of inspiration; found in our most profound magical meditation, we may drink down her image and find refreshment. Her face is at once the most beautiful and the most terrible for she is both Hag Queen and gentle spinster; a matriarch for all seasons of the night. She is a mystical patron who will spur us on if only we accept the deep, chill draught of her elixir: a witches brew that has been filtered through hidden places, flowing through the earth like a silver snake.

Tangled in burnished starfish, the Shining Dark One of the waves lifts us up as an offering, casting us onto black rocks. Should we fear her strong, woman energy? Actually, her milk-white arms lift us, delivering us from ourselves and pulling us free of the slimy clinging weeds of our fears. We may be in awe of her and have an honest respect for her. We may have faith in her, for she grants to us the gift of sight even as she blinds us with her sorcerous power—taking us within, spitting us out. Clarifying and purifying by heart trials and soul tests, she is the ruler of our emotions and sails through the night in a spray of wistful wishes, leaving in her wake a silver locket in the shape of a heart, which bobs on the green water, moving toward us.

What would we find if we released the catch on this locket? Dare we open it to release her magic? Her magic is ours, bound free by the powers of light and darkness; within it lies the eternal gift of the seeing and the knowing, humming like a tiny gleaming seed in the shadows, waiting to be sown in the fertile soil of our spirit selves.

These two representatives of the energies of sacred polarity and of nature's cyclical, often paradoxical, dance are ever present to inspire and guide us. We may find the Moon Mother or Jack-in-Green energies symbolically in the rotting of the leaves or in the humour and pathos of the tiny wren attempting to feed the cuckoo that has usurped her own chick's position in her nest. We may see their aspects in our own lives, both in the quixotic and the prosaic, and in our own cycles of growth and dying back. They are always to be found in our trance journeys, if we seek them, and they will certainly help us bring renewed vigour and deeper meaning to our daily wild craft. If we feel suitably inspired by working with such vibrant energies then perhaps it is time that we began looking at the wildwitch's work in earnest.

The Work Behind the Craft

In the following chapters we will begin the process of learning how to apply practical techniques to our everyday appreciation of the natural world. First, we must understand the work we will be doing: by heightening our awareness of the spiritual aspect of existence, we give a greater depth, clarity, meaning, and mystical relevance to our human lives. The prescribed methods we will learn in order to do this are tried and tested and place the individual's psychic safety and security as the highest priority. Once we understand the means of protecting ourselves, surely we may design methods that best suit us as individuals. Alongside personal spiritual development, Earth healing, and growing magical confidence, we should always place vigilance and protection in paramount importance on our path.

When we begin our work as wildwitches we are not about to blithely skip off into a realm of sweetness and light—such behaviour is reserved for those who pass on from this mortal coil!—rather, we are preparing to purposefully walk with spirit into an enchanted realm that has its own dangers as well as delights. It is easy to become intoxicated with the first rush of spiritual success and glibly think that we no longer need the ground rules. Experimenting and pushing personal boundaries within our witchery is one thing but blatantly ignoring the astral or otherworldly signposts that help us to keep within a safe framework is another. The framework is not rigid, it bends with us to a degree, but it exists as a structural guideline in the same way that general safety procedures exist for crossing a road.

We cannot go into a busy street on a Saturday afternoon and think we are above using standard procedure for dealing with heavy traffic. Nor can we enter into our wild craft with the attitude that we can fly free without any sense of ground control or air traffic information! So the work we will be doing relies heavily on simple, effective rules that will enhance, not hamper, our progress and ensure we always come back from our journeys in one piece. We will look at many protective procedures in chapter 3. For now, it is important to recognise safety procedures as an integral part of our work.

So, how do we begin our quest to heighten our spiritual awareness? It is important at this time to reiterate that wild witchcraft is just as likely to be practiced sheltering alone in a rocky outcrop on a misty moorland, or at the kitchen table, as it is to be performed with bell, book, and candle. The actual work is a blend of seeing, knowing, and physically *doing*, but this is preceded by observation, sensation, and interaction.

Observation

Observation includes looking at the natural world all around us, building up the ability to read omens and portents in patterns, which can include cloud formations, bird behaviours, wind direction, the mood of cattle, etc. Reading omens is a self-defined activity, though it can be based in local folklore if it feels appropriate. For the wildwitch, it is always best to blend our own learned experience of how patterns affect our lives with the more established wisdom of the ancestors. The viewpoints of our ancestors are now archived wisdom and the quirky riddles that make up "old wives" superstitions. It should be noted that just because these viewpoints are antiquated, this doesn't make them more valid. As we are the ancestors of the future, our experience is just as valid.

When observing omens it is best to steer away from reading too much into modern affectations. It is all too easy to let superstition rule and to become quite obsessed with such things as, for example, the sequence of car number plates. However, a sign can be observed in the way paper blows across a street in much the same way that leaves blow across a street. Basically, we must use discretion when observing omens and remember that real omens are of the wider world and not necessarily revealed in manufactured ways. Also remember that wild witchcraft is about the subtle interchange between the natural world, the spiritual levels, and our human experience. To focus overly on any one aspect is to become an unbalanced practitioner.

We can also observe our personal responses to tides: ebbs and flows, including how a dark moon or a particular weather cycle affects us, and seasonal comings and goings in the natural world, including animal hibernation, the leaves turning to russet and umber, and the first blossoms bursting forth. It really doesn't matter whether we are observing from the viewpoint of a cityscape or a farm; what does matter is that we are engaging with the environment and tuning in to what is happening in nature. This is a step to remove the layers of separation that deaden us and a move toward feeling as if we are a functioning part of a beautiful whole. The key is to relate what we observe to how we, and other beings, directly experience what we observe.

To observe with any degree of success we must open up to how these eternal cycles and random events make us feel. We must work toward putting an end to that very modern human malaise, that of feeling like a spectator, one who sees nature as a picturesque backdrop for human enjoyment. The sensation of having a sheet of glass between ourselves and the world is a common one, perhaps engendered through our stultifying life-through-a-lens approach in society. We witness all manner of violence, tragedy, destruction, and even other peoples sexual mores through the filter of a screen. We even view the world as if it is "outside" while we are somehow apart and "inside," looking through a pane of glass. Some of us can spend entire days going from one bubble to another, always separated from the natural world by the windows in our homes, offices, shops, and modes of transport. This once-removed reality we experience ultimately leads to desensitisation. Is it any wonder we have trouble relating to the natural world?

Observation is the first step to effectively reverse the process of desensitisation. It makes us more effective as both wildwitches and as fully awakened humans. By actively engaging in observation we re-establish our connection to all that is and strip away everything that inhibits us from feeling like we're an active part of nature.

Sensation

To be successfully engaged in the process of observation we must be fully sensate, that is, all of our senses must be fully open at all times. As we observe we can ensure that we do not only see what is happening around us but we can note our deep responses to what we see. Although we may be able to utilise our ability to see successfully and can, to a greater or lesser degree, smell, taste, and hear what we witness, we are not responding until we can know it in our own energy matrix. That is, until it touches us and affects us on a deep soul level. To be moved by what we observe, for good or ill, is central to wild witchcraft. It is no use experiencing things only on a superficial or intellectual level.

To truly make untamed magic we must be personally involved and filled with ecstasy, passion, empathy, and the lilting refrain of occasional, deep melancholy. As we walk the wild path, to be "fully sensate" also means being deeply aware on a spiritual level—our sixth sense must come into play as a developed ally. This is the area, if we can segregate our integrated practice into bite-sized chunks, that covers the seeing and the knowing. To become more adept at this valuable aspect of our witchery and to witness life on a much more profound level, we must actively work at tuning in to how we feel by means of meditation and trance journeys. We travel within in order to connect to everything that is without, effectively removing our attentions from the manifest world in order to connect with the less tangible energies that give this world animation and meaning.

By combining the element of air (through breathing), the employment of several visual "cues" (statements to precede your actions: "I will pass through a woodland glade and climb a hill"), and a preordained purpose, we can participate in otherworldly journeys in a light trance state. These three aspects, needed in order to trance journey effectively, are simple yet require focus. For example, we all breathe from moment to moment, but how many of us are even aware of it, let alone grateful? And how deep or satisfying are the breaths we take? We can develop our ability to focus by drawing deeply from the element air, being fully aware of its power. By means of very uncomplicated techniques we can work with air to bring about a calm state. This area of our practice does require some basic learning but once we have given time and energy to our practice, applying the techniques in all life situations, it becomes second nature.

Similarly, the visualisation aspect of the work will eventually become second nature. People often say that they cannot engage in trance journeying and working with the Otherworlds as they simply cannot see; their ability to engage with imagery is somehow inhibited. It is easy to become intimidated at the beginning of a process. This book aims to make the learning side of what we do as wildwitches as down-to-earth and lyrical as is appropriate for such a homespun craft. This said, the psychic centre of the mind's eye is in operation every time we imagine, fantasise, and daydream. It is activated when we think of a pot of jam and see an appropriate image of it. It is further enhanced when we remember the smell and taste of jam.

Once we relax ourselves and are prepared to travel beyond our daily human lives, into a deeper, eternal resonance, we need direction. This is formed once we discover our purpose for travelling. Often, the purpose to travel into these otherworldly realms is to gain guidance from treasured spirit companions. We may travel to ask for healing, to gain an insight into a specific issue, or to meet a particular spirit pertinent to the work we are undertaking in the manifest world. We may simply travel to find inspiration. The juxtaposition between our spirit travelling and our work in the world is always emphasised: we travel to the Otherworlds in order to enhance our worldly craft.

A trance journey is not a means of escape. We need a reason to journey. If we trance journey in an undisciplined way—to day trip or escape reality—we are opting out of our Earthwalk obligations. Indeed, it is not easy to stick with a discipline such as a specific trance journey for healing or insights when we could be wandering in a flight of fancy. Although the craft is wild, it certainly respects necessary boundaries. Whilst being free it also emphasises courtesy, consideration, care, and above all, personal responsibility. We cannot opt out of our Earthwalk. The trance work is a way of enhancing an incarnation, not evading all it entails. When we acknowledge ourselves as wildwitches we have certain profound obligations, which gives our Earthwalk deeper meaning, and so the temptation to "go on an astral holiday" is lessened but obviously must still be recognised and discouraged.

By means of walking in the world with our senses opened like a flower in full bloom we are able to improve our trance work. Likewise, our work as wildwitches will become more effective. Thus we begin to experience subtle emanations when out walking in the country and when we are journeying in a trance state we find we can really smell the wildflower's heady scent. One level feeds the other, as ever, and enriches our experience as humans. Why live in a world that functions solely on the premise of solid objects providing the only reality, living a life that has no meaning except for in those solid terms, when it is possible with a little application and a whole heaping measure of joy to live in a world of texture, fragrance, vibration, and nonphysical impressions?

Interaction

This includes the manifest work that we do, the magical meat of our practice. The majority of this is spellweaving but it also includes prayer, celebration, and divination. To interact as a wildwitch means that we see each practical act as being full of enchantment and we can make certain transactions more meaningful by use of ceremony. Ceremony here does not mean the highly formal and regulated rites found in religious practice, rather a spontaneous moment of deep concentration. The level of concentration is reached by the help of physical objects that have been imbued with particular qualities that are significant to the purpose of the project. Such objects may be as natural as a blade of grass or a fallen oak branch. For ceremonial work, we cast a circle with the assistance of the elemental energies that guard each quarter (or compass direction) as well as invite our own companion spirits to offer their protection and guidance. Then we perhaps use a combination of poetry, song, chant, or prayer to create a particular outcome (for example, enhanced creativity).

In other words, we use the aforementioned physical objects to focus our attentions whilst in our circle. Simply put, these "props" are manifest representations of what we are trying to achieve with our enchantment and by using them we remember the always present blend of the seen and the unseen in wild witchcraft. For example, a pebble with a painted symbol could represent the strength we need at a given time and after the rite we may carry it with us to a particular interview or stressful situation. We gain courage from its resonant presence. A homemade doll (often known as a poppet) adorned with a scrap of cloth, a hank of hair, nail clippings, and a photograph of a sick person can be used in a healing rite. Or, a particular coloured candle can be inscribed with the appropriate runes and anointed with a compatible essential oil whilst we invoke for whatever it is that needs to burn brightly in the world. As the candle flame burns so is that energy released. *Note:* With all such ceremony we must first obtain full permission from anyone else involved.

Magic is ethereal yet it has Earthly correspondences. It is woven into our daily lives yet it is also special. It can be done formally in the sacred circle, the eternal round that symbolises the cyclical nature of creation, or it can be as simple and everyday as repeating a chant every time we pass over a bridge of a local river. More so, this can be done on the way to and from work, ensuring that as the river flows on, unpolluted and full of life, so will a friend's troubles be washed away and health and happiness will return. The chant could be as basic and purposefully rhythmic as:

River flow, in health flow on,
And strongly flow, go on and on,
Off to the sea to swell, go well,
And take with thee my friend's worry,
Take it now to the deep blue sea,
Oh river bright, take it with thee!

As the chant is recited the steady beat and repetitiveness are emphasised to give it power. The river can be visualised as a golden force, flowing on strongly. Perhaps, with such a simple sympathetic magic, it would be appropriate to take something from the willing friend that represents specific ailments or difficulties. This item would then be thrown into the river, joined with its energy, as the chant is recited with feeling. This offering could be a scrap of paper with a meaningful word inscribed on it by the person or a stale crust of the person's bread to represent all that is old and unwanted in his or her life. The organic nature of such representative acts is vital; throwing plastic into the river would be highly inappropriate. And the object must be symbolic, not necessarily literal; there would be no need to cast in a shoe if a friend had recurring foot problems!

In this example we interact with the river, making magic in the landscape. At home we may interact with found objects in a ceremonial sense, giving, for example, feathers or acorns a particular significance. Such objects can represent whatever it is that we wish to work on in magical terms just as well as a powerful landscape. We cast spells with the help of found and natural objects but also use widely accepted and trusted tools such as pendulums, tarot cards, or any other homespun, personal means of predicting and assessing the energies around us. To interact is to acknowledge and utilise what we have as humans. We give ordinary objects and everyday situations a spiritual resonance and meaning for the express purpose of weaving fate, for the good of the All. This must always be approached, from a wildwitch's perspective, with full consent of the object or place. As we consider all beings and environs to be enspirited, or animated with life force, then we cannot simply go imposing our will upon all we encounter. In other words, we must interact with the pebble and river to see if it is appropriate for their own energies to be included in the spell or rite. This is an act of respect, just like when we ask permission of a sick friend to perform a healing rite. It is an especially pertinent issue when we work out of doors.

We also interact when we celebrate in a ceremonial sense. On a daily basis, there is so much to celebrate in nature and in our lives of green-spirited enchantment, but sometimes it is fulfilling to enact a particular rite for the sake of marking a season, a moon phase, or a personal life milestone. Within the protection of the sacred circle, we then can chant our praises and thanks by working with found objects that best represent our focus. Such objects may be, for example, corn at the time of harvest or a white bowl of spring water at the full moon. We would then appropriate the energies, being fully present in the seasonal moment and open to all guidance and pertinent impressions thereof.

As wildwitches, we correlate the external energies we become sensitive to with our environs. All of the myriad manifestations of nature's bounty become allies with whom we can work. They are partners who are willing to be representatives. Ours is a very symbolic way of expressing our feelings, one that relies heavily on the cooperation of Mother Earth and all of her children. We may be solitary but we are never alone in our endeavours.

What we do as wildwitches is bound together by all that is beyond us, within us, and sustaining us; as well as by the spiritual (or inner) work that heightens our senses in order for us to observe more astutely, feel more keenly, and act in very manifest ways with more effectiveness. We must observe, we must sense, and we must *do* in the world all while maintaining a blend of these factors in equal measures. There are no shortcuts. The results we achieve and the satisfaction we feel is dependent on our application. The work is rewarding and it is woven into everything that we do but it is work nonetheless and should never be seen as a glamorous quick fix to impress or to solve things at the flick of a switch.

This is a wild craft rooted in the earth, not a fast-track modern panacea. In the Western world we are used to all that is instant, and instantly gratifying. Here we revert back to a pace that is more akin to the gentle pulse of nature, Earth's own heartbeat. Therefore the results we see will be more measured and sustaining. We are of this Earth but not of the modern world. Not to say that what we do is harking back to some mythical age, rather we are tuning in to the flow of the current age—we are tuning in to all that lies beneath transient human attributes and affectations.

How to Commit to the Way of the Wild

We may, at this stage, feel that it would be appropriate for us to make some sort of gesture or a vow to honour our decision to walk on the wild side. Commitment and dedication can be tied up in a "wildwitch's promise," which gives us a direct experience of a simply crafted spell of sorts.

This is not the same as an initiation, though wildwitches may choose to undertake an initiation further in their journey to deepen their commitment. This is simply a gesture. It serves as a way to understand how energies work and how we associate our interaction with the unseen (and our faith in it) with all that we can see. Yet it also stands as a beautiful and singularly profound statement of intent, a timely reminder of who we are. It is a way of stepping between the worlds; a declaration that draws us ever closer to the wild, uniting us with the wonderful spirit mentors of whom we all have waiting for us. This is important, because we will often ask those mentors to help us in the dance of life. It is the first evocative line of an ongoing life poem. To promise ourselves to the wild way we can weave several strands, as follows:

The Promise (The Purpose)

The promise is unseen word magic in which we have faith. A green-spirited wish. It sends our aspirations, dreams, and prayerful bidding up to the stars. It is spoken with spirit and filled with our heart's desire. It represents the ethereal aspect of our wild way.

The Token (The Manifest Representative)

A manifest object that reflects our vow in the world. Something that can be worn, buried, or hidden. A physical way to recall our promise. The way to ground the magic in our current reality, an "earthing" device that gives us a physical means to focus on our intent. The physical aspect of the wild craft.

The Intent (Our Sacred Energy)

This binds the aspects together by wish and will. The intent is the will. In this example, it is a way to focus the energy of the promise into the object. It also is a way of projecting that energy (outside of both human wish and manifest object) into the universal whole. It is both a binding and a releasing agent. Why? Because we intend it to be so. We need our spells to be "bound free," to exist both in us and outside of us at the same time.

The Secret (Enchantment)

As with all things spiritual, and particularly in terms of the green spirituality we discuss here, there are many paradoxes. We see here, the riddle of something existing both as an encapsulated energy and also as a dissipated one. In basic terms, as children we understood without question that a frog could also be a handsome prince. Until the prince is kissed by the right person, his manifest appearance is a frog. A similar childhood belief is that Cinderella could be transformed into a pumpkin if she stayed out after midnight. In both examples, an encapsulated and dissipated energy coexist in one being. The frog is still a prince, even though it doesn't look that way. Such was our childhood belief in the straightforward law of magic, which transcended logic. It is an excellent idea with this wild craft to have a little of that magical childhood innocence about our practice. Magic is beyond the mundane while also being in it. Actually, frogs and pumpkins are pretty ordinary physical manifestations! We will come across many more interesting things on our wild path.

Enchantment is not quantifiable, yet we know it exists. As wildwitches, we know that the manifest level and the spiritual realms intertwine and reflect each other; therefore, we know that what we make known here (within) will travel and resonate there (without). Even if we can't see our energies, we have our magical representative to remind us of that single moment when we let the energies fly free. The unseen energies remain within and without. In spellweaving we have a formula:

We say our piece, we represent our piece, and we send yet keep our piece.
Then we keep our peace!

This last line reminds us that power is held in silence. To discuss what we have done is to weaken the energy it has been given, it leaks away every time we discuss it. The work is primarily about energy and energy transference, after all. Our energy of personal intent makes our spellwork live, it weaves it into the universal energy matrix.

We are all creators, we alone hold a sacred strand of life's tapestry that is uniquely ours. We all have power and we have creativity—there are no exceptions! As wildwitches, we express this through natural enchantment and green spirituality. Let us now continue to look at our dedication to this path.

Our Promise

This is going to be very basic and gentle, just an affirmation in an appropriate setting. It is fitting for a new beginning (or a renewal), it is an initial statement of intent and not a great ritual act, though both can be powerful. It really is up to us how much we can give to it personally.

Before we engage in anything with a magical intent, which involves "opening up" to energies, it is vital that we employ the most basic level of spiritual and psychic protection. For this, we simply visualise ourselves standing within a glowing golden egg, the gold shimmering and pulsing like a beautiful living organism. Then we state out loud or to ourselves: "I am standing within a protective egg of golden light, let none come within my safe psychic space."

For the protection procedure to be effective, we must make our statement, have faith in it, and see the physical representation of protection, such as the egg. We will learn more advanced protective techniques and we will come to understand why protection is so important as this book progresses. We will also learn that once we have created something "etherically" (like the golden protective egg) we must continue to "feed" it if we want it to go on existing. For this mild exercise, that of making a promise, we are not engaging in a lengthy, energetically powerful journey, so it is sufficient to visualise our egg strongly at the beginning of the rite. It will remain in situ for the duration of the work and simply fade away afterward.

The first step in making a promise is to select a day that seems appropriate. At this stage, we will assume that we have little or no prior knowledge of what would make a day appropriate (in terms of seasonal, lunar, or other energies) and so we will rely purely on what feels right to us as individuals. This can be an exercise in tuning ourselves in to how we feel in order to experience the natural energies around us; our choice is not dependent on any specific academic or accepted reference points. There are no rights or wrongs to how things feel at this level. We simply pick a day that has a certain rightness about it. We don't base our decision solely on social, home, and work timetables (although such considerations matter, clearly, as manifest factors) but do look on a blank, monthly wall calendar. First we spend time just looking at each date, trying to allow ourselves to sense the day of the month that feels good to us.

Next we will need an approximate time of day. For this, we simply choose the time we love best; the time when we feel most empowered, awake, and creative. If we have no real preference, then twilight or dawn are particularly beautiful and resonant times to dedicate ourselves to the craft, being as they are full of magical potential and mild, wild mystery.

Now we have chosen a day and an approximate time. Next we will need to choose a location. A lovely idea is to take a short walk of intent, which is part nature ramble and part ceremonial procession. Here we will begin our observation and sensing as soon as we step outside to follow a preplanned route. We must continue to sense, see, and smell as we physically journey to a place where we may find the peace and inspiration to express a heartfelt vow. We should have our walk end at a place that has a bench or natural log seat. If we live by the sea, we could end on the sand, facing the water. Wherever we end up on our walk, the place where we pause to make a promise should not be too densely peopled. We cannot plan for solitude but to knowingly go to a well-loved tourist spot during a public holiday seems to be a surefire way to court company! Conversely, we shouldn't find somewhere so isolated that we feel unsafe.

It is an excellent idea for us to be in a particularly elemental place if we can manage it and as long as we do not tire ourselves out in the process; for instance, a walk to a hilltop, waterfall, or woodland glade would be particularly beneficial. Elemental places have a surplus of green, life-force energy and are ideal for such work. Think about a wildwitch's promise and all its verdant possibility, its wind-whipped and briar-tangled mystery, its sun-kissed, moon-bathed delights. Now, pick an appropriate spot.

Alternatively, if we feel that the weather is too unpredictable, or if a physical ailment prevents us from undertaking this walk, then we can create a space within our home that can become, temporarily at least, private and peaceful. Having physical manifestations of wild, natural energy around us is essential when we make a vow of green-spirited authenticity. Representatives of the current season are appropriate. These items may include fallen green branches or blossoms, nuts or seeds, or even homegrown fruits or vegetables. In the wild craft, it is not always appropriate to cut flowers or living branches, so we should try to find "windfalls," if possible, at least until we can communicate fully with the essence of plants to ask permission to take anything from them. We should also pander to our open senses and get as many good smells—warm earth; cool, wet local rock; wild hedgerow herbs—in our vicinity as is feasible.

Now, what will we say and how will we represent our promise in the world? We will need a written or memorised vow and a symbolic token that we could perhaps wear, at least for a time, until we feel confident enough in our new role as wildwitches. A true wildwitch feels no real need to declare his or her affiliations to the world by means of flashy symbolic jewelry, but simple, discreet talismans can be very reassuring on the path.

We will keep our written vow, our silver-tongued word magic, heartfelt and open, succinct yet flowing. We may not have any particular experience or skills in bard-craft, but we can still make a meaningful spell if the soul is there. It can be a simple, formal statement but will be far more "alive" if we let go of any inhibitions and simply say what we want to say. There is no one that will judge our literary skills! Once we decide what to say, we will then "voice" (sing, chant, speak, or deeply vibrate/hum) the message out loud or in our mind. The only priority is the resonance. To start, we can create a short piece that sends the appropriate energy into the ether. Sending our energy is all important, having faith in that is paramount. If we believe in what we say, then it will be so. Here is an example vow:

I, child of Earth and being of spirit,
Now sing the stars of my intent,
And pour forth from my heart's own wishing,
My will is strong and won't be bent!

As I feel my feet upon the Mother,
I raise my voice unto the sky,
And I state that I will walk the pathway
Of the wise and of the wild!

Hear me now, oh nature's spirits,
Be with me now my unseen friends,
Know I will work to bring the Greening,
I will work for best of ends!

Hear my wild, green witch's promise,
To mend, to tend, to grow, to love,
With hand on heart and feet on earth,
As it is below and so above!

For the Mother, for every tree, for all of us,
So may it be!

We should write a vow with personal sentiments; it will be a lot more specific and personal than the given example. We could vow to recycle, to help animals, to do spells for the sick, or any combination of specific acts to which we feel drawn. We could make it very general or try to pinpoint our real calling. There is no one way to promise ourselves to the wild way.

When we have finished our recitation, perhaps we could roll up our vow and bind it with a green ribbon or piece of wool. This can be kept hidden but read when we feel the need to connect with who we are. All of us lose a sense of purpose somewhere along the path, no matter how well connected we think we are, and it is nice to have that initial heartfelt vow to reflect back on in times of self-doubt or worry.

It is certainly appropriate to enact what we say while we recite the promise. We may repeat the promise up to nine times or any multiple of three, three being a marvellous magical number. In turn, we touch the earth, our chest, forehead, and finally our lips to honour the connection of our heart, mind, and soul to the land. *Note:* The number three is significant for its natural energy. It is the number traditionally used in folk and fairytales (for example, granting three wishes); it appears in Christianity, most notably as the Holy Trinity; it appears in the three phases of the moon, which is linked to the maid, mother, and crone stages of a woman's life; the dynamic triangle of mind, body, and spirit; the relationship between man, woman, and the child they create; the powerful triple spiral symbol, the pattern often seen in rock art such as that found on Newgrange Passage Tomb in Meath County, Ireland, which suggests the cycles of life: birth, growth, and death. As we can see, three is a marvellous number.

Since the elements are the mainstay of our manifest life, it is always good to surround ourselves with the elemental forces when performing any sort of magical act. This said, it is a good idea to have ready a small bowl of spring water, a candle flame for fire, an incense stick for air, and a bowl of soil for earth. *Note:* Spring water is preferable as it suggests we have made the effort to find water as it rises from the earth naturally; it fits with the wild way more than simply turning on a tap. We place all of our elemental representatives around us in a way that feels appropriate but we do surround ourselves with them, encircling and aligning ourselves with elemental power.

After we voice our promise we can dedicate our chosen token to the wildwitch's way. It is appropriate to touch the token to the four elemental aspects before we wear it. It is acceptable to use the same elemental representatives we surrounded ourselves with a moment ago. As we speak our intent to meld the token with the elemental energies, we touch the token to the respective element: pass the token through the smoke, around the flame, in the water, and in the dirt. If we are dunking our object in water and soil, we may want a soft cloth at hand. We then hold our object in our hands and focus on it, melding with it, giving it magical relevance. We imagine it is glowing with magical light. We ask it to work with us as we promise to honour all it stands for. As we dedicate our item to our wild way, we may say something along the lines of:

This object I do dedicate,
To my life's work and to my fate,
For I am a wildwitch through and through,
And this is my symbol, potent and true.

Blessed by soil, spirit of sustenance,
Blessed by air, spirit of inspiration,
Blessed by fire, spirit of courage,
Blessed by water, spirit of creativity,
Bound by spirit, set free by spirit . . .

So may it be, wild and free,
For the Mother, for every tree.

We must be aware now, as we complete the first real manifest act on our path, that our symbolic object has a spiritual resonance, that it has been imbued with a life of its own. The more we interact with it, holding it and relating to it with respect, the more it will shine as an independent representative of our pure intent. We must treat it with honour and work with it to reaffirm our vow on a daily basis. Our relationship may be outgrown one day, being that the spiritual path is an organic process, not a dead end, but as long as we sense an energetic interaction with it, we can continue to acknowledge it as a potent symbol.

* * *

This marks the end of our view of the world as a space full of inanimate, unspirited objects and the dawn of a new way as a wildwitch, a way that gives all creation respect and acknowledgement as being spiritful. When we have declared our promise and consecrated our token, then we may like to sit in quiet contemplation for a few moments, giving thanks for the opportunity to express ourselves in this way. We can still the mind to see if any impressions, images, or communications come to us. All too often we pray, ask questions of the universe, and generally make mental requests, but never give the chance for an answer. If we have faith that there will be one, if it is appropriate, then it is only polite to wait! Again, this may not be instant, we are working in otherworldly time, not the frantic pace of modern life.

When we have finished, we do not go back to how we were before, but try to remain in this enhanced state. We have our object to remind us of our chosen path. However, to end the proceedings we should bring our awareness back to the manifest level, in other words, we must "ground" ourselves in our current, Earth reality. We will look at grounding in greater detail in our discussion on protection in chapter 3. For now, we can ground ourselves after making our promise by simply concluding our walk or by leaving our room and then making a note of what we did, whilst having a cup of something to drink and a light snack. It is a good time to start a journal of everything we did and when we did it so that we can keep a record of our progression as wildwitches and note the future effectiveness of our actions. This discipline can also serve as a tool for grounding us in the manifest levels as we physically write our thoughts on the paper. At the same time, it focuses us on the detail and sensations of the work. Keeping a journal acts as a wonderful blend of the manifest and the spiritual.

The wildwitch promise acts as an excellent introduction to the key concepts of the wild craft; the value of a promise is immeasurable no matter how simple we choose to make it. We are now in a position to continue with the craft. It may not be possible to teach the art of the wildwitch as it is truly instinctive, reflecting a way of self-expression that is probably already familiar to us. What follows in this text is, perhaps, a way of fanning the flame that already flickers within and a chance to make that flame safe so that we may be warmed, but never burned.

Chapter Two

STRONG ROOTS,
LENGTHENING BRANCHES

Swan feather falls as swan flies on,
Buttercup catches the setting sun,
Shadow swallows silver now the dream's begun . . .

*I*n this chapter we will begin working with the cycles of nature within the spinning, gyrating dance of life. It may seem obvious to state that nature is made up of circles and not straight lines but it serves us well, as we enter into the sacred round of our magical life, to really look at this afresh and feel it as an observable truth. Not only is nature made of curves and spheres but she is based in pattern, repetition, revolution, and interconnectedness. It is very easy for us to retain a little of our conditioned linear social responses to the natural world even when we, as sylvan-spirited seekers, have accepted on some level the cyclical nature of being. To shake ourselves free of the remaining fetters that we experience in the modern Western frame of reference we must reconnect with the whirling truth of the endless ancient spiral of creation.

But how can we do this? How can we truly look beyond that first understanding of nature's roundness and her gently meandering rotations? First we can try to find evidence of straight lines in nature! We can go on a special walk to an area rich with wildlife, or to a place of special geographical interest, or even out into our own gardens and yards if we are fortunate enough to have access to a patch of earth. There we can lie on our bellies, looking at tiny shells, pebbles, petals, or beetles, or we can look up and see the cumulus clouds, the birds of prey riding thermal currents, or the flitting passage of a tiny blue butterfly. We can see how nature herself behaves and how she shapes herself when she is unrestricted. We can compare this to how man's influence cuts across her natural curvature with its paths, hard-edged litter, intrusive boxlike structures, and field margins.

We can approach the question from another tangent and look at the round patterns within nature through the all-important combination of firsthand observation and secondhand book learning. We can do this by first really looking. We can recognise shapes and forms in natural settings. We can take this a step further by examining the way leaves of a potted herb grow; perhaps we can do this with a magnifying glass in order to witness the structural make-up of these familiar allies that share our land. To look under a microscope would also be interesting, revealing a new perspective on the beautiful and simple make-up of a leaf at a more intricate level. We could have a look at a hive and find out how the bees cooperate within their fantastic interrelating combs, or visit a reconstructed human settlement to see how the traditional dwellings, such as roundhouses or yurts, were constructed to unite with the landscape.

Through our observations, we can note, in a very personal and experiential manner, that creation is a blend of surging, billowing, wheeling movement, and repeated, harmonious, structural pattern. This could be perceived when we watch the drift of incense smoke in our own homes. Such smoke reveals the eloquent expression of nature's spiralling, twisting, repeating movement. It could be considered when we watch fish swimming in a local pond, noticing both their graceful undulating motions and their shimmering, interlocking coat of scales. The pond is an ideal environment to watch the concentric ripples that occur after the surface is disturbed, or to see bright bubbles rising; both are fluent expressions of the rings and rounds of being, of the eternal interaction between one energy and another. Ripples clearly illustrate how each encounter between one way of being and another, be that unseen or manifest, creates a noticeable rhythmic effect.

We can expand our awareness of the deep composition of life further by reading about how cells make up an organism or how flowers are structured internally. We can also review the studies others have done on such seemingly diverse areas as tribal settlements and fractals. This helps us fully realise how within nature, and therefore within us all, there is a need for purposeful pattern and interdependency. We will repeatedly see one aspect of physical existence fitting up against another with seamless ease, with perfectly curved elegance.

Once we are aware of the roundness found in all aspects of existence, we can add in a deeper understanding of the cyclical movement of nature. This can be seen in her constant rising, falling away, and swelling again. For instance, observe the lifecycle of a star, the precipitation-evaporation cycle of water, or the migratory patterns of swallows.

It could as easily be witnessed in our own moods within a month, a year, or even a day. It is the process—departures and returns, ebbing and flowing, rising and falling—that we are addressing. We want to focus on how these cycles make us feel, how they respond to us (our actions), and how we respond to them.

Once we recognise the natural cycles in everything around us, our next step is to combine our immediate daily experience, which is near and familiar to us, with study and observation of the most distant or challenging elements in creation, those that are far from our ordinary experience. This is when we start to truly look beyond our first understanding of nature's roundness. If we look at our own lives and at the beings that share our daily space and compare the basic patterns and rhythms, we can see relationships between ourselves, the revolutions of an unknowable planet, and the ways of all life, right down to the creatures of the deepest sea. We are all bound by the laws of cellular structure, from death and rebirth to rest and activity. To hone in on something tangible and close to home is just as valid to the wildwitch as focusing on a distant, perhaps more impressive, object. Both are connected by the energies we witness and work with. We study the microcosm within the macrocosm to better understand the bigger picture.

When we begin to tune in to the inherent structure of nature, an understanding that the tribal or ancestral people understood in their blood and bones, it eventually becomes jarring to witness anything that goes against this graceful pattern. This re-sensitising (or re-wilding) of our spiritual and rational selves to the land, the wider universal way, and the rhythmic expressions of all that we witness, serves to heighten our awareness and open our hearts further to the profound lyricism of a simple cyclical way of being.

With a genuinely questing attitude we can correlate what we see with what we know and add in what we feel in a spiritual and heart-centred sense. Through observation and learning we can bring together our own holistic vision of a truly nonlinear universe. By actively doing our own research and then living our own lives in a cyclical way as often as possible, we can help strip back ingrained human assumptions with our new understanding of how to look beyond what is frequently presented as truth.

A Straight Line World

If we think and see in straight lines then it makes perfect sense to keep progressing toward bigger and "better" until we reach the end of the line. The whole ethos of straight-line thinking suggests that we can have dominion over each other, for in a linear world there are surely those at either end of the measuring stick, the winners and the losers. The whole notion of winning, of reaching the finishing post at the other end, seems to be the only purpose of linear living.

Linear thinking leads us to believe that we can have full control over our own environs and our bodies, making no reference to the subtler emanations or natural cycles that affect us. When we see nature as a living whole that has nothing to do with financial worth or ownership, then it is hard to continue on a linear path. Furthermore, when we experience the universe as a spiritful and interconnected place, it is impossible to think that we can march toward material success single-mindedly, as we know that many subtle influences and interactions affect our journey. Even the idea of boxed-up lives within regular-walled dwellings can seem to be faintly ridiculous when we truly begin to interact with the roundness, the inclusive and gently complementary ways of natural existence.

Thinking in a straight line also denies any spiritual aspect to existence and puts the emphasis on the fact that we are "winning" when we engage in the race (or game) of climbing to the top. The top is a metaphorical mountain made of jobs, houses, cars, etc., and pays no heed to the less tangible reality that we are incarnate. Consequently, within this structure, taken at its harshest, there is no sympathy for those who become ill, those who are elderly, or those who come by misfortune such as flood or theft. There is certainly no empathy or even time for those who see with psychic vision or look beyond ordinary reality. When climbing to the top of a ladder it is "every man for himself" and it is casually accepted that there will be casualties who just couldn't make it. There is a rejection of the interlocking interdependency that creates a harmonious structure and no heed to the gentle rhythms that take us through life in a spiral motion. There is no place for anyone who walks with spirit. As wildwitches, with a common aim that is for the good of the All, it serves us well to reject all such linear thinking that encourages a separatist lifestyle.

In a world of such one-track lives, is it any wonder that the majority of us find it so hard to grasp an infinitely unfolding universe? A universe that is seemingly involved in continually rippling onward in all sorts of dimensional directions at once, a universe that expands just for the sake of it? Wildwitchery is born of this same universal motion and sets no store by the graded linear approach. Instead it sets store by creating for creation's sake, just as a velvety-faced, jewel-bright pansy flower thrusts its little petals toward the sun without a care, without the need for praise or even acknowledgement.

Pansies, like all beings who remember their true nature, do not need to "win" or conquer. They just *be*. So it is well for those of us who walk the wild path to remember our own true nature and to simply *be*. In other words, unfold with dignity. Through the wild craft there is no need to aquire or even to achieve as long as there is growth through joy, understanding, and experiencing on a deep soul level.

Dance the Round Truth

Wildwitches can learn to disengage from the prevalent undercurrent of mainstream Western society not by rebelling or proselytising, but by directly observing, studying, and then walking our truth in the world. That is, honouring our own vision of a sacred whole by being caring green-spirited workers of nature magic. Live by example. The energies that we express freely in the world will affect the world. A wildwitch understands that everything is made of living energy and our living energies are everything! To understand the interconnectedness of all life is the key.

At this point we have probably found evidence of straight lines near and far from our everyday lives. Our next step is to acknowledge our own personal ways of physically operating on Earth that may in fact be encouraging the dangerous and debilitating separation from the circle dance of life. The towering office structures made of straight lines and compartments, which have conditioned air and perhaps no view of the sun; the endless boxy housing complexes swarming in oddly irregular, rectangular ways over the land while dividing it up; the fenced-off landscape; the locked car with windows up and music loud to drown out the external noise of both traffic and birdsong—all of these things are normal to us. All of them cause us to feel separate.

What we say may also be encouraging separation. We can probably think of some of our own seemingly innocent phrases that sneak into daily conversation and make an assumption, at a more guileful level, about how we live and how we experience life. An example of this would be the phrase "the property ladder." As if our having the privilege of a shelter equates to nothing more than an ongoing linear climb to acquire a bigger, more impressive dwelling for the sake of social status or material possession alone.

It is well for us to note any insidious little sayings and assumptions that serve to keep us in that old and restrictive structure. They reinforce, by indirect means, our separation from the cycles of life. They make human beings feel as if they have gone against all of nature's old-fashioned ideas and have somehow gained a mastery over the lilting refrains of nature's turning, bringing a false sense of reality and security. As if we could conquer nature—or would even want to! We *are* nature.

Where in the natural world may we find a regular straight line or boxy structure? Certainly the dwellings of our fellow creatures, from the nest to the burrow, do not reveal such designs. In fact, there are few natural straight lines in nature. Even those few that occur appear to be in harmony with nature. In the straightest tree limb there are knots and swirls of bark making irregular features, elliptical, rounded, or roughly spear-shaped leaves with curved edges, and within the most regular tree there are concentric rings of living wood. Such straight lines in nature have a repetitive beauty. A tree trunk is rounded, not squared; bark consists of interdependent segments, not uniform strips.

In crystals hewn from the living Mother Earth there appear to be straight lines—the quartz has a structure of repeated linear forms—but what happens when we look at these structures more closely? We do not see many parallel lines in a random configuration, but what we do see is interlocking shapes that build on regular patterning, a beautiful cellular miracle. It is good to remember that even within the straight crystalline form of quartz there are rainbows to be seen when it is exposed from the hidden places that formed it. And what rainbow travels across the sky like a jet, leaving a purposeful trail in its wake? In man's world there is a need to get from A to B. During a journey, the destination is all important. People zip and zoom and take the most direct route, with no concern for what must be cut across. Also, most people gaze on the world through squared panes of glass. Windows have no rainbows, they are flat and serve only as shields between what society deems "ours" and what is "out there." This is a false delineation. It is vital to engage as often as possible with that which is patently not of this manufactured realm but with all that is pure and unrestricted by such human mores. The rainbow, that marriage of flowing water and curving light—like the land, like every physical atomic essence of our being and the universal being—follows the curve, is part of the round that wildwitches aim to join.

Leylines appear to be straight, too. However, while they travel across the land in lines they are actually comprised of undulating Earth energy and are not rigid or static. For example, the Michael and Mary leys that run through Glastonbury flow through each other in a serpentine fashion, hence the use of "dragon line" as another name for leyline.

In our modern world we have not even tried to echo nature's fecund roundness or to fit in with the landscape. Instead, we have endeavoured to make our presence felt over it for social or economic reasons. Our linear lines have no such cellular depth, they are not based in interrelated harmony, in interwoven mystery, but more in human priorities, like financial viability and cost effectiveness. The grandeur we seek has none of nature's grace and humility.

Even if we cannot leave our steel and glass complexes, we can engage with the plant beings that share our space. And if there are no leafy beings in our environment then we could ask why! If we are able to get outside, we can make each day a pilgrimage, acknowledging butterflies on bobbing heads of purple buddleia by the busy roadside. Even if we cannot get out into the landscape, we can still engage in trance journeys and rise on a Faerytide of flowing fervent feeling, revelling in all that is the exact opposite of the calculated and sterile human environment we may find ourselves in.

When we still live in a culture that deems it acceptable to keep our animal companions in peculiar little oblong caskets with squared wire mesh ventilation, or perhaps worse, to cage a bird in a manner that does not allow for flight, then it is bound to be a hard journey in terms of ridding ourselves of all these accepted means of separation. Even if, for the present, we must live in the standard shelter that society offers, looking through windows and dweling in boxed dimensions, we can have an awareness of a more rounded and healthy lifestyle that awaits. All the while, we can strive to break down the spiritual, mental, and emotional barriers around us. To change perception, attitude, and how we experience the sacred in daily life is enough, we need not exhaust ourselves by attempting to demolish structures when the attitudes will remain in their wake. Still, unless we change our perspective, we will be at risk of repeating the process.

We are living as part of a mystic spiral, an all-embracing ring of life, and this is expressed in a whirling myriad of ways, from the blink of an owl's eye to the glossy brown seed, from a single trembling fertile drop of spring rain to the shimmering strands of a spider's web in the fissure of a rock. Our inner and other worlds are rounded, connected, and cyclical. We live within a sacred hoop and at the same time we are a part of it. As wildwitches we celebrate this on a daily basis.

And we will not forget it.

Dance of the Earth and Sun

It is impossible to begin to describe the Earth's dance, the Earth's own circle dance as revealed by the seasonal round, without including and focusing on the power of the sun. We do not always consider the sun to be an overly valid part of our practice as witches. To the majority of people, witchcraft is more aligned with darkness, moonlight, and secrecy. Our wild craft is all encompassing and pays full respect to the vast and awesome being that gilds our days and helps bring us from the aspects of life that are hard and unyielding to days that are lush and thriving.

We do not worship the sun but we give that heavenly body a suitable credence. The sun is often referred to as our brother or grandfather for all of his cheery presence and direct support, yet we may know the sun as another living being without ascribing names, roles, or even gender. It is a matter of personal choice and will not affect our practice, but calling such an important body "it" seems denigrating. However, as long as we embrace his living energy as a vital part of our way then we are honouring both the role he occupies and accepting him as a living being.

It is valuable to remind the reader here that, in this work, poetic analogy is used to give a deep resonance. Please do not feel obliged to adopt the terms used here, for the sun or otherwise, in your own practice. In fact, be imaginative and create your own. This book is an inspirational guide, not a gospel!

For the purpose of our work here, I will relate to the sun as "he" and as both the benevolent, caring male partner and the virile and flamboyant bringer of incandescent passion. The Earth's dance involves a partnership, after all. As Earth Mother spins gracefully around her great companion, he keeps up a steady stream of supportive yet intense energy. This energy encourages her to turn a personal pirouette, which moves her into light from darkness and round again, and also allows her to experience fruition to dying and on to germination once more. He performs his own sedate yet sensual dance of rotation. The sun's time of performing an entire turn is approximately one Earth month. It takes him this amount of time because he is a ball of gas, not a solid being, and, because he is so vast, his central area moves faster than his pole regions. Therefore his entire revolution is between the twenty-sixth and thirty-fourth days of the month.

Through Earth Mother, the sun experiences what it is to give life; through him, she experiences what it is to receive. The energy is earthed in a creative way, in a seasonal procession of unbridled beauty and wild diversity. As wildwitches, we can share Earth Mother's experiences as we move through the wheel of the year and through the lesser cycles of her own daily personal revolutions. We can feel within ourselves, through our deepening spiritual connection and profound observations, the fluctuations in energy that occur in any period of twenty-four hours. It is important to understand that even when it is overcast we still experience the blessing of the sun's energy cycles.

Even though the sun's energy fluctuations are powerful influences over the land, the natural resonance of this energy at any given hour may be far removed from the human expectations placed upon those same times. For instance, we may not personally be able to rise with the lark and go to bed as the sun sets. We might even feel out of balance unless we rise late and take to our beds after midnight. We may need an afternoon nap when society dictates we should be in the office or productively engaged. We may find our best work is done late in the evening when society decrees that we should be winding down. In short, our personal energies may not tie in with what human ways expect of us; we may find our energies wax when society decrees that they should be waning.

Societal pressures aside, there are clearly certain times when it is pertinent to connect with daily energies for specific magical purposes. Our work must always resonate with the energies associated with the time of day and with our own energies. If we have simply relegated magical acts to a time before tea or between programmes on the television (with little thought on the energetic resonance), then the act loses a great deal of power. As wildwitches, we aren't truly experiencing our connection to Earth or the sun if we become creatures in a rut, acting by rote and out of some sense of duty, and our incarnate experience of the magical Earthwalk will no longer be spontaneous, joyous, and free. Resorting to parody out of a sense of obligation is not wild! There is no point in forcing ourselves to feel the energy of a specific time of day, but we need to at least understand that there may be periods within the daily cycle that are best suited for certain acts of enchantment.

Midday is clearly a time of full-on, upfront power. As such, it sits opposite on the wheel of the daily Earth dance to night's hidden but no less potent vibration. Midday has a hot and thrusting power; night has a deep mystical influence. The aromatic smells of these times are exotic and sensuous. The two other main daily emanations, dawn and twilight, are more subtle, they are also opposites yet are connected by their wafting melodies. Dawn has the air of renewal and growth; twilight has the atmosphere of reflection. The fragrant smells of the flowers, just awakening or tucking in for slumber, are light and joyous.

Dawn

As regards to the subtle energies of sunrise, it is appropriate to feel the dew on our skin at dawn and to watch the daisy petals gently unfurling at first light. It is during this time that we are mildly thinking about renewal. We can reserve our more vibrant and urgent renewal concerns for the midday. Sunrise, and the opposite waning energy of twilight, are certainly inspiring and evocative times, but these times are not imbued with the most magical "oomph." It clearly suits the more gentle magical touch to lie on the cool wet grass and gaze up at the rain-washed sky as a watery sun emerges, a sun that turns a stream to a rill of gold as the birds thrill the spirit with their sweet rising voices. Due to the subtle influences of this time, it is actually a unique experience to feel magical rebirth and personal energetic restoration in the morning. Only if we are able to feel awake and refreshed at an early hour is it positive to receive the sun's blessing at dawn.

Actively getting involved with the natural rhythm of the land in a manifest way is just as important as connecting with the unseen subtle energies. Remember, we always need to blend the spiritual with the manifest aspects of being. Playing a simple wind instrument like a recorder or whistle is a wonderful way to pipe in the new day with the birds at sunrise, as is singing a melodious enchantment about the return of love to your life as an accompaniment to the joyful bird chorus. We are never simply humans sitting in the landscape, performing our set piece; we are wildwitches interacting, observing, being spontaneous enough to let go of previous expectations, and going with the flow of the moment, feeling it authentically and letting it be translated through us. We are a part of nature and can get involved!

The subtle energy at dawn not only affects our thoughts on renewal, but in fact, whatever we find at midday in the brightest rays, we have as a more pale and lucent reflection at dawn; passion is muted to love, creativity to inspiration, desire to wistful dreaming. The energy of the sunrise is about returns and is ideal for prayers around the theme of the Greening. Other magical themes include the further merging of magic into the mundane, the re-emergence of the Fey into the manifest, the revival of an Earth-honouring culture, and the resurgence of love and kinship with all nature. A very simple prayer for the dawn could be:

> *As the light grows the stronger,*
> *So shall my love grow the brighter in the world,*
> *And in my love may all love be found,*
> *Burgeoning in the light of a new day.*
> *As the lark ascends and the blackbird gives voice to new joy,*
> *So may it be!*

Remember, we are dealing with soul poetry here and each time of day must evoke a certain response in us in order for us to align the magic with the energies effectively. Whether we are wide-eyed in wonder or moved to the core we must *feel* whatever we do.

Midday

At noon, when the sun is at its zenith, we may want to release a charm for increased creativity or invoke for passion in our lives through a wild dance on a sun-blessed hilltop. At midday we are simply echoing the sun and Earth in their positions and are working with full-bodied, peak-powered magic concerning physical strength, endurance, desire, personal performance, and optimum self-expression. It is obvious that doing a sombre banishing spell would not fit in with the fiery positive pulse of the moment, yet a green-spirited magical act based in an ardent artistic or amorous energy would be completely appropriate. With this in mind, we can chant something like:

> *Fire in my belly,*
> *Sun in my eyes,*
> *Spinning under noonday skies,*
> *I lift my hands to seize this moment,*
> *Ablaze with power my magic's potent!*
> *Fire above and fire below,*
> *As the sun shines my enchantment glows!*

Anything done with vigour and ardent intent such as wild drumming or stamping of feet will add to the pounding energy that echoes the pulsing of the Earth's green blood at peak strength when it responds to the hot full kiss of noon. This is the time to really shout out our desires in the passion of the moment, celebrating this eternal union between fire and earth in our magical lives.

Twilight

Just as dawn and midday have their correspondences in our work and to each other, relating as they do to love and desire, renewal and a vital resurgence, so it is that twilight and midnight are also silvered reflections of one another. Midnight is the time of deep magic and profound insight; twilight is the misty-eyed and soulful moment of yearning and remembering.

The time around twilight and dusk is veiled and full of whispered secrets and sighs. It is gentle nightfall, shrouded and silent yet pulsing with primal power. Now the glittering firmament is slowly revealed, beguiling us and seducing us into forgetting all that is trivial and of human concern. It is the time to focus on the eternal, philosophical questions, and deeply spiritual matters. At twilight, we may feel mildly disturbing shivers of anticipation, thrills of unknown, and possibly unsettling pleasure.

Twilight is a marvellous time for wildwitches who desire to strengthen otherworldly connections and gain deeper understandings of Earth's more secretive denizens. Spirit conversations along these topics could focus around the need for a more profound level of understanding of the hidden aspects of being. We may contact the Fey and speak with the night creatures who inhabit a shadowy nonhuman world. We may use poetry to cast green magic relating to inspiration, as twilight suits flowing lyrical invocations. We could express this as something like:

> *Oh Shining Ones who slip between the realms,*
> *Clad in your mantles of mist and wreathed in moon-berry mystery,*
> *Hear me now as I call to you in the voice of the lone hawthorn,*
> *Hung with tinkling silver bells, shrouded by the veils that separate us.*
>
> *Children of the amaranthine, dancing ones of the white apples,*
> *Hear me and draw closer, for I wish to hear your poetry,*
> *I long for your inspiration in my life,*
> *And to feel your timeless beauty in my own Fey soul.*
>
> *Hear me now if it pleases you and dance closer!*
> *By elder blossom at midsummer and the tears of the weeping willow,*
> *By your grace and by my fascination, I ask that this may be!*

It is vital here to note that the Fey will not be commanded and will probably get quite irate, if not very troublesome, if we choose to be as foolhardy as to summon them by force. A prettily worded and polite request is far more pleasing to them.

Twilight is the time of the weaver of fate who sits on the edge of the worlds whilst being connected to the rhythms of life and all the beings. To be a walker between the worlds at this time is to work with the energies of the day and the night.

Midnight

Nightfall is the time when we may commune with our spiritual companions for the purpose of gaining universal insights. That is to say, we gain guidance that does not relate to the personal but to the wider conciousness, the great eternal spiritual questions. Therefore, it is the best time to speak with those who have passed over, for the simple purpose of gaining reassurance that human relations are lasting. On a practical level, night is the time when most of humanity sleeps and so the extraneous buzz of human activity, voices, and electronic gadgets is lessened and a more pure and resonant level of communication may be reached.

As mentioned earlier, some of us may feel the need to practice our communing with spiritual companions at any convenient time of day. We may only ever practice spells at night when we have the required level of privacy. We may consider it to be suitable, or convenient, only to use poem, prayer, and chanting in the middle of the afternoon, while walking the dog in the woods. This is absolutely fine as long as the act of enchantment does not become habitual and without meaning. From time to time it may be good to try something new, to tune in to a different time of day, or to break with routine. We can try doing our meditation in the evening or at midnight, just to ensure that we haven't become stuck in our ways. It is important to remember that we have different energies from different times of the day to use to our advantage. Here we will look at that time after twilight, the dead of night. It is possible to experience profound night-terrors in the darkness—where there is fear there is real power.

As the burned apricot skies of twilight pass away into the indigo darkness, the one segues into the other; subtle enchantments of dusk's meditative energy move with a fluid motion into more hidden mysteries, more intense experiences, more deeply felt interactions. Night is a time for invoking the moon-blessed power of the sight and starlight vision in order to heighten our perception beyond our current limited human faculties, for the good of the All. It is a time for journeying into deep inner space and making soul prayers for bright night blessings. We may intone a night prayer that has this resonance:

As the light grows dimmer,
And darkness creeps into the hidden recesses of my soul,
May I turn from the lights of temporary human life,
And look within, to the dark and eternal,
To the ancient well that reflects star patterns within me,
And so may my fear be dispersed in that void.

As my fear recedes so shall my vision flare brightly,
As my fear is swallowed by velvet night so shall I know myself more fully,
As my vision expands so shall I see what I must do,
In truth, revealed, so shall my fear fade,
In truth, revealed, so shall my fear recede!

By all that is luminous, held by all that is endless,
So may it be!

This is the time to use candle magic to full effect, to reclaim the lost power of the hidden witches who worked by flickering tallow torches. It is a time to use all the wonderful props that enhance the mood of mystery, including leaping shadows from lanterns, swirling incense smoke, and wreathing, wavering reflections in dark mirrors.

Dance of the Moon

As with all aspects of the wild craft, opposites are acknowledged to maintain balance. Since we just discussed the energetic influences of the sun, we will now look at his opposite and complementary energies that are found in the moon. The moon, as we are about to discuss in poetic terms, is a wildwitch's energetic guide. She is our patron. As with the sun being male, so can we see the moon as either a cold, dead lump of rock, which just happens to orbit Earth, or we can see a living being whose lunar effect is felt on all the watery, emotional, female aspects of Earthly existence and refer to her in the feminine. With her feminine influence over all that flows on Earth, she most notably inspires the female menstrual cycle. Approximately every twenty-eight days the woman bleeds and every twenty-eight days the moon completes a cycle. Here we reveal a wildwitch's way of looking at the moon's ensouled presence; she becomes a being of immense power to us, at once dispassionate yet unceasingly generous with her gifts.

As we touched on her attributes in the description of the Moon Mother in the previous chapter, so let us expand our poetic understanding now. The moon, the She, is the Mistress of Near-Misses, the luminescent face of a lonely velvet space, hiding in storm clouds with silver linings; playing her role as both lucky sixpence and ravishing temptress; hiding or revealing her face of mystery and enchantment under a raven's glossy wing of night. She is of inspiration and doom, granting a boon or bringing devastation at sea. She is like a half-remembered destination, reminding us of home. She is hauntingly familiar yet at the same time completely cold, remote, and alien to us.

She is more than two-faced, flaunting the image of a fickle female. She is also unerringly constant. She doesn't care in a human sense, she is without sentiment, once removed, and haughty. Still, her gifts are of the most profound kind and without them we are just husks going through the magical motions. As Queen of Tides she lets the cool pearlescent essence of mystery flow into our veins. She gives us the ability to live life more fully by imbuing us with the ability to see with psychic vision and feel with honest emotion. Her caring is felt in her bestowing upon us this blessing. With her blessing, we may see a moon-washed world of infinite and overwhelming beauty; consequently, our practice then becomes celestial, otherworldly, and fantastical. Once we have crossed the boundaries of fantasy and reality, she offers us her luminosity so that we may have the clarity to work wonders.

She is the Harbinger and Bringer of the Sight. Bright shadows crawling hear her calling. Immeasurably powerful, her influence is felt in our bodies, minds, and spirits as she, magnetic and compelling, pulls us closer toward her silvered energy. Her dreams—nebular, milky, and swirly—shape our dreams with all that is fleeting, all that we reach out to and long to catch and keep as a moonbeam in a jar. She touches us, yet she is night's dweller and moves in eloquent silence, alone. Holding cobwebs of years, she is the ancient one. Shrouded by Earth's turning and blocked from the sun, her surface seethes with the ashes of kisses, for she was once, and will be again, the epitome of the full-bodied, creamy-skinned enchantress. Veiled in swathes of night, she induces madness with her beauty, or invokes the most stunning artistic responses in her name: poetry and music like waves, outpourings onto paper and canvas, encounters with strings and keyboards.

Just as some people find driving rain exhilarating whilst it renders others miserable and moody, so do the moon's phases have markedly different resonances on us as individuals. There are obvious symbolic qualities as regards to each phase and we will all find them more or less energetically compatible with us as wildwitches. There is no correct way to feel influenced by a full moon, although the energies that are involved are constant. It is only our responses that differ. As regards to our magical lives, the ebb and flow of our working, we must have an awareness of these qualities. However, as with all of the practice discussed so far, we must also have an understanding based in our experiential relationship with the moon and her journey around Earth. In other words, while we can read the poetic descriptions of the symbology involved in the lunar cycle and gain understanding, we also have to spend time actually feeling, observing, and interacting with the moon to know how we truly may work with her power. Again, journal notes can build up a rounded picture of our findings over several months or years. Our observation of the moon is yet another ongoing process in our quest to live wild enchanted lives.

In order to express the cycle, we can journey through the three main phases, realising that within this fluid motion there are many lesser phases and that this is an ongoing round, which flows continually with no real beginning or end.

New Moon

Rising tide, waxing.

From the first bright fingernail of light to appear in a velvet sky, it is the time of beginnings and renewals; it resonates strongly with the period of February 1 to March 21 and has the same quickening energy of dawn. The whole feeling is of budding, beginning, and moving toward a blossoming as the waxing of the moon continues. It is just as feasible to align what we wish to bloom and grow in the world with the moon's cycle as it is appropriate to work with the cycle of the sun. Also, just as we plant and nurture concepts and thoughts in early spring, so can we allow our dreams to grow with the moon as she waxes. Of course, as the moon is about intuition, it is far more appropriate to align her with mystical understanding and visions, whereas we would align the energies of the sun with more practical matters. Earth and sun are associated with mud and bone, mildew and loam, while the moon has a more subtle refrain to sing by, her power is in strands of spun gossamer thread, immensely strong yet apparently ghost-pale and fine.

The new moon is a time of maiden energy, touched with the joy of youthful questing, and enlivened with tentative, tremulous experience. This energy can change the world whilst being as delicate and as precious as a violet. The moon maiden is fleet of foot and graceful. Her eager eyes gaze from a lean and hungry face as her thoughts race. This pale one is not wan, she is lit by a powerful inner radiance. She will do as she pleases and will not be bound by convention. She is a wilful, beautiful white filly racing along clifftops, riding the wind.

There is no hard and fast rule, but we could say that the new moon is the dancer of a new clarity for our vision, a new phase for our psychic ability, a new blossoming of our imaginings, and a fresh start for our creative dreaming and healing. While the seasonal procession, marked at springtime, is more appropriate for matters that are more firmly anchored in the world—for matters that require sun, air, and water to feed it, as well as the fire of passion to give it life—we may still use earthy props for our new moon magic: seeds and frothy white blossom, silver and white candles, a chalice of sacred spring water. All of these things aid our focus on the ethereal and the directing of subtle magical power for the purposes of spiritual renewal.

Since the new moon maiden is a dream of hope, inspiration, and the bright promise of all new spiritual beginnings, an appropriate prayer could reflect new dreams and ideas.

Soul Song to the New Moon Energy

Sky dancer, of exquisite poise and perfection,
Sliding with serenity through the endless grace of night's blessing,
Hear my wildwitch calling! Feel my inner yearning!
And may I be made new in your bright returning!

May I ride with you on your silent journey,
May I rise with you, feel my power rising,
May I grow with you, feel my power expanding,
May I glide with you, find that I am moving,
Onward and outward in my magical progression
As you flow through my life on your own procession.

Newness, returning, for peace and harmony,
Enhanced by the sky dance,
So may it be.

Full Moon

High tide, peaking.

As the new moon waxes, the energy concerned rises symbolically through the seasons, from April to May. The full moon's energy aligns with the time of the summer solstice; it represents the zenith, a culmination. Therefore, the most powerful time of the year to make magic concerned with completion, success, and fertility is the full moon in June. The correspondent time, in terms of the sun and Earth dance, is midday (early afternoon)—the time of high-powered and positive celebratory magic.

To continue with the analogy of the Moon Mother, we see her at full moon as a full-bodied woman, mature and brimming with creative juices, fertile and ripe. Her delight is found in experience, in touch and union, in wild self-expression. Her cool, bare feet glide over the warm, pulsing earth; her long slim fingers trail sensuously over the velvet fuzz of a peach, caressing each burning blue star in the firmament as she reaches up, enjoying the contrast in sensation. She has fire in her swelling belly, stretching it taut, and the passion within her makes her long for water. She draws the tides to her for comfort, dowsing her ardour, revelling in the surge and becoming, in her fertile imagination, the highest, most powerful wave and the gentlest eddy. She catches a glimpse of her round, serene face in a rock pool and catches the new and old lines of experience etched between nose and mouth. She has no fear of change for she is full of hot, wet laughter, brimming with salty tears, and bursting with flowing emotional experience. Why should she fear? She is no longer young, but she is not adversely affected by this physical change in herself; she loves who she has become.

She is queen of emotion and ruler of sensation; blessed with heights and depths of feeling. She wants to share but knows that she must be distant, so she silently pours out her gift of vision into the night. Onto her sleeping children, she is emptying herself into the darkness, decanting all of her fertile mystery into the world. She spills it out, milky and soothing, giving birth to memory and feeling. Those who honour her receive it and do not let it drain away unseen, unfelt, or unacknowledged. Her inspiration is taken deep within us. She looks on, she sees all, and then she moves on. Our Earth turns. And somewhere sonatas, seascapes, serenades, and sculptures are created. Somewhere, a dream comes to fruition.

Remember at this time what true "lunacy" is: passionate, crazy power of full-moon energy allowed to run amok. It is vital that we acknowledge this power and channel it appropriately for healing, creative, and loving purposes and, of course, to increase the gift of vision. The full moon is a wonderful time to pray for a heartfelt desire and, if the desire is altruistic, then all the better for the energy to flow through us and onward. We become enhanced as we channel the power and send it in a new direction.

At the time of the full moon, we may invoke for all that is munificent and rounded, for full-flowing and clear psychic sight. Again, to represent the energies involved in a manifest sense we can align our wild magic with the visual aspect of the seasonal or moon phase. This allows our personal perceptions of the moon to mesh with the more universal energies so that we can gain specific clues for what work we should currently focus on during our magic. Even if we do not receive a clue for a specific cause to work toward, we can always focus our intent on more general concerns that are appropriate for a full moon (or whatever energies we are working with at the moment). The lovely, full, luminous face of Lady Luna so eloquently says that we can always focus on everything requiring illumination, all that needs to be brought to fruition and fullness, and all that represents full-bodied love and beauty.

Soul Song for the Full Moon Energy

Glorious Mother, your gaze is upon me,
Great Mother Moon, your power is with me!
Mystical Mother, your force radiates,
And fills me with radiance, beauty, and grace.

I am lit within by your lambent love
And I am heart-blessed by your vigil above,
I am open and filled with your great mystery,
And so filled with promise of what I may be.

May you shine in my darkness,
May you shine on through me,
Fill me with witch light and bright potency,
I am opened, your channel, and so may it be,

For every river flowing down to the sea,
For every river, so may it be!

Dark Moon

Ebbing tide, waning.

Here is the season of sorcery. The dark moon is a real wildwitch's time; it has not the obvious beauty of the full moon but it holds a great deal of wild power. It belongs to the waning time of October 31 and sees its culmination at winter solstice—the time between times. Because the moon is hidden from us (although obviously still present) it is a time of delving into the occult side of being. It is during this time that we may find ourselves diving for pearls of wisdom in the inky blackness of ourselves.

Dark Moon Mother is of bats and mice, of the empty womb filled only with whispering secrets. In old age, her physical eyes may be growing dim but her pin-sharp and penetrating inner sight compensates. She has the gift of reflection, the twilight boon that enables her to look back on her youth, and the fruits of her full-bodied middle age, which provide her with deep understanding, compassion, and contentment. She will share this inner peace willingly if only we approach her. Her laughter sounds like the snapping of twigs and the breaking of bones—because of this, most fear to come close, turning away in trepidation from her pale and watery, yet deeply disconcerting gaze. Those who do approach find her extending a withered hand, happy to allow her sacred knowledge to pass on and on through a profound connection.

If we can see beyond her surface, the wrinkled, withered body, the dry and papery skin rustling, then we will hear her words. Words like pungent aromatic smoke from resinous woods, which burn brightly in November; words to charm us and make our heads spin. Her breath has a hint of apple cider and her voice is of the dying, from the dead. As we approach, she may cast off her hood and reveal a smile like a rip in the very fabric of our being. She has our face, she has no face at all. And if we look into the eyes of that grinning skull, deep into the empty sockets, we may fall into our own being, into the womb where we may be reborn.

And all will shift to dust around us and we will find the essence of time slipping through our fingers. Primal, precious, and endless, Dark Moon Mother is everything and nothing, everywhere and nowhere, and she is our power.

If the Dark Moon Mother has a message, it is this: "I ask that you know me . . . for I am your own." In other words, here is a time for really looking within—for owning what is ours in terms of negative emotions and thought patterns, such as fear, anger, hate, and loneliness—and banishing negatives by transmuting them in the cauldron of night. Just as we practice transformative dark magic—not in the sense of evil, only in the sense of mysterious and shrouded—at the waning time of year, so may we work now to cleanse ourselves. As ever, moon magic is more concerned with the nebulous and ethereal, and so thoughts and feelings can be transmuted by means of inner work. Again, in the act of spiritual self-exploration we may trance journey to find answers, and we may work with other visionary techniques and divination tools to gain further deep insights. Visual props for magic at this time may help us focus. Again, such props can be a combination of seasonal symbols and physical representatives of the moon energies we are currently working with in our magic.

We may be leaping ahead of ourselves to begin discussing exactly what we may do, as such techniques have not yet been discussed in detail. Suffice it to say at this stage that inner work is best performed at this time. It is an inward time that, paradoxically, connects us outward. It forges connections to the cosmos and to greater universal wisdom as well as revealing concealed, personal spiritual truths.

Soul Song for the Dark Moon Energy

Grandmother, Dark Mother, ancient mama mine,
Give me the wisdom and the power to divine!
May I find the riches in your dripping hidden places,
And hold the mirror of my truth to all my own dark faces.

Let me find in solitude the silence of the spell,
And banish all that stops me now from living my life well.
May I cast out my demons, may I sing my song in peace,
May I see what haunts me so that it may be released!

Reveal to me my terror so that I can look beyond,
And remove the fear that mutes so my tongue is never bound.

Crone Mother, night lover, old Mother Moon,
May I be a witch with sight and sing the wildest tune,
May I sing it in the blackest place, the dark night of the soul,
And by your gift of vision may I find my spirit home.

Behind the sun, so may it be,
By standing stone and twisted tree!

Dance of the Seasons

As the sun, that dynamic, explosive, vibrant body of energy and living being of fire, and the moon, that silvered, solitary, woman of many faces, interact with Earth Mother on a daily basis (as she turns her face away and reveals it again), so does the dance continue on another level, that of the seasonal cycle. It is an endless procession that leads the beings of Earth and Earth's living body through the sacred round of death and rebirth, transformation and desolation.

It may be important to note here that climate change—wrought by a combination of our human thoughtlessness and Mother's own desire for change, which she experiences at intervals through her own incarnatory process—can affect how we feel and perceive the seasons and therefore can affect how we practice our wild craft. The feeling of a seasonless world has been a common one in England as of late, with one long experience of grey and mild conditions predominating. However the climate feels to us at present, we may still honour the energies behind the weather we experience as Earth is still orbiting the grand body of the sun, whether that is obvious to us or not.

Just as a specific time of day evokes a strong energetic resonance, so do moods invoked by weather create flux and flow within us. Bright sunlight may be an anathema to some, an elixir to others, or mist and damp may send shivers up the spine of one while making another feel low and dismal. To observe the affect that these atmospheric changes have on our spiritual and physical selves is very beneficial.

Certainly high- and low-pressure fronts and systems influence our moods, regardless of our preference for sun or shade. As wildwitches, we feel subtle fluctuations in mood and elemental temperament keenly and such physical energetic manifestations as pressure can certainly make or break us in magical terms. High pressure obviously means clear skies and lends itself to clarity, crispness, and brightness, while the low-pressure front in a weather system may cause heavy, oppressive, and introspective sensations. Clearly we can align ourselves to such unpredictable changes in our energetic environs by being spontaneous in attitude and attuned to our psyche so that we may attribute mood swings to worthy causes. For example, it may be easy to attribute a feeling of dour or ominous energy to the place we are in, or to the person we are with, but we should acknowledge when these feelings are really the weather having an affect on our subtler energies.

To work in the moment and create enchantments that flow into the atmosphere of the day is certainly preferable to remaining rigid in the face of ever-moving atmospheric influences. In magical terms, a gusty day may be appropriate for whipping old habits or cares away, a rainy one for washing harmful influences down the drain, a foggy one for clearing anything that obscures clarity in trance vision. Simple and spontaneous acts are part of our wild craft. It is just as well for us to be informal; every one of us, at least once in our magical life, will encounter gale-force winds and torrential rain when we have planned an elaborate outdoor ceremony! Nature is unpredictable therefore we must be open to change.

Weather fluctuations aside, we will now look at the core energies of the seasonal festivals as we follow Earth around the sun in the age-old annual dance. Here it seems appropriate to use specific dates as it helps us to align with the points of most concentrated energy. The dates give us the traditionally observed festival, or holy day (holiday), and act as guidelines. The dates are flexible markers in that intuition tells us the best moment to celebrate a culmination of the appropriate seasonal energy, which may last for a period rather than just a day. The energy of a season may seem to peak at a particular point, but we will only feel this if we are sensing, experiencing, and in some way magically acting out the energies involved.

October 31: Time of Mists and Sighs

Also known as All Hallows Eve, Halloween, Samhain.

October 31 is a time of mystery and of a particularly resonant wild magic. Some may even say that this time lends to dangerous magic. Witches have always been associated with Halloween in popular culture and there is (for once!) some truth in this association. In the public consciousness, darkness, familiar spirits in the guise of black cats, cauldrons, jack-o-lanterns carved like grinning skulls, and the image of the moon are all linked to the idea of witchcraft. This connection with darkness and death is all for good reason.

All things have a season and this is the wildwitch's hour and the time most sacred to those who walk the way of green enchantment. This date marks the end of autumn and the coming of winter in a slow season of woodsmoke and drifting low cloud. It is a festival for all that is past. A time to go within and travel through the veils of separation between the worlds to access lost wisdoms, gain ancestral blessings, and to feel the ghosts in our own lives shifting and settling.

It is a time of working with the revealers, the spirit energies of the old, wise women and men who can guide us deeper into the realms of our deep selves and profound spirit beings. The archetypes of the cunning wizard, he who is the shadow hunter, fit well into our meditations as do visions of the Dark Lady as crone, a spirit woman who appears well past her physical prime but who is filled with the wisdom of age. It is a journey into the cauldron of transformation, into the mystic primal forest of consciousness, into the womb of existence (with the wise ones as our guides); it is a timely experience. The Queen of dim and dusky Mysteries and the Lord of Night's Calling haunt our smoky autumn dreams.

The seeing and the knowing are used; in fact, the sight is acknowledged, valued, and relied upon. All that is hidden is sought out, the lost is laid to rest. Divination—using apples and hazelnuts, sorted fruits of ancient wisdom—is practised as hearth-fires flicker with meaningful pictures. In black basins, water reflects our face back at us as the other-self image we held in other lives. Separation is actively challenged as the connection between the seen and the unseen is respected and the craft of connecting with the secrets of the Otherworlds is revered. Predictions are made and prophesies are given freely to those who seek them.

The land is wreathed in sighs, cloaked in mysteries of mist. A nameless yearning fills those wild-spirited ones who have a little sweetly singing Fey blood still in their veins. It is a time guarded by the heron as he eyes the damp landscape balefully, taking to the skies in a fluid motion with a mournful cry. With him our secret magic flies into forever, lost to humankind for another long year.

Lowering lilac skies filled with a drifting miasma that is part smoke, part spirit, inspire us to write introspective poetry or compose melancholy music. Crisp bright days surprise and delight us even as we smell the earth's damp chill beneath our feet. We may sense the night closing in early, the moon seeking a place in the sky with the sun as we kick through leaves of umber and saffron on our way home. It is a time of contrasts between the subtlety of swirling mist and the starkness of dark bark, the richness of the ruby leaves and the fleeting shadows of the past.

The single, upright charcoal finger of a scarecrow stirs the air as the remaining fields are burned. Arms outstretched, with a face stitched on sun-bleached sack with bindweed twine, the crow-god of lowly odds stares blindly at the dying year. The very rooks, crows, jackdaws, and magpies that he is meant to scare circle impatiently, noisily. The birds are croaking their defiance loudly, looking for all the world like charred and tattered revenants flapping in the strange yellow light of a fading October afternoon. Gently dreaming pyres gutter and splutter in stubble fields as the crows finally swoop and land, appearing as the darkling seeds of shadow-fires, with ancient wisdom in their oil-slick eyes. The black birds are the harbingers of the season, the outcast spirit companions of witches who do not fear them but know them as black and shining kin. At this deeply magical time of year, they are the flyers between the worlds, spirit messengers to be valued and recognised.

The land longs for the warmth that has left it whilst craving the slumber that lies ahead in the dark and lonely womb of winter. There is a sense of contemplation and introspection—it is a time of dreaming and inwardly preparing for what we are to actively do in the future. Life is waning, observing a gentle slide into quiet inertia, and we are experiencing a gathering-in of all we are, of all that is. As creatures snuggle in beds of leaf litter and bracken so do we curl up in our homes, content to address our spiritual inner needs and reflect on all that has been, giving thanks for our ability to address mystery, showing gratitude for all that has passed in the last cycle. It is a time for acknowledging where we have been and knowing where we are but not a time for forward motion or activity. Now is the season of letting go, of resonant and meaningful contemplation. We know this, as the land deems it so—the trees drawing down their sap, the plants dying back, the little four-legged ones going to ground.

We can banish our own fears at this time, symbolically sending them to the ground, to be transformed into new hope in the spring after they have been transmuted by the power of the dying year's mystery and purified by winter's chill touch. Suitable wild magic would be, for example, writing what we wish to see recede from our lives on a piece of recycled unbleached paper in the dark juice of old blackberries; then hiding it inside a hollow tree so that it may rot down and be swallowed up by the energies of the dying year, by the sodden and leaf-littered soil. Then in the spring an offering of thanks could be made to the tree for swallowing up what was outworn in our lives. To ask the permission of both blackberry bush and tree is, of course, vital. In the case of the offering, a dialogue could be established over the dark months of winter to ascertain what the tree would like as a gift.

This is a suitable spoken enchantment for seasonal spiritwork. It involves contact with the Wise Ones (our ancestors in the spirit realms) for the purpose of receiving clear guidance.

Black crow, turn back, hollow root,
Bare branch shiver to my reedy flute.
I ask for the wisdom of the long-dead mute,
I am calling to the Wise!

Wings beat time to the ghost-owl's drum,
Foxes bark as their night-blood hums,
Wild is the darkness that we become,
I am calling to the Wise!

Grandmother, Grandfather, hear my plea,
Step through the bright mist and speak with me,
Bring me the blessing of the things you see,
From your realm beyond the stars.

For that which is lost and that which is found,
That which is rotting in the hallowed ground,
That which whispers yet makes no sound,
I am opening my heart.

By withered apple, by rich black loam,
May you bring me wisdom from your spirit home!

December 21: Time of the Glittering Ground

Also known as Yuletide, midwinter, winter solstice.

This date marks "the longest night," when daylight hours are scarce and darkness is the better friend of our waking hours. But even as we mark this, we observe the pattern shifting as the wheel of life turns steadily, inexorably onward. After this day the balance will shift and the Spirit of Light will reclaim a little of his territory every passing day. Thus many on a green-spirited wild path may choose to rise early to witness a chilly dawn and hail the still weak but ever-victorious energy of the sun as he tips the balance from darkness into light within the pattern of our days.

The seasonal energies now are dormant, inert, waiting; never dead, only sleeping; resting and withdrawn. The cauldron of death and rebirth seethes under a seemingly still surface, looking empty and barren yet hiding the potential of new life and growth just as the earth keeps the cold seed's secrets. It is the time before a new moon but after a dark moon, when all is suspended on the quiet wave. For now there is inactivity, yet in nature's cycle this cannot remain ever so. It is but a phase.

At this time, the wheel has turned and we have gone within just as Earth has withdrawn her energy, just as all beings of bark, leaf, and stem, and those of fur, slippery skin, and shining scale, have gone to ground, deep inside, slumbering. All of nature lies asleep under a blanket embroidered with stars of frost, a gift from the spirit of Jack who, nimble and quick, moves amongst us in the dark hours, casting his lonesome, achingly beautiful spell on the land. He reminds us of his icy fingers trailing over garden and hillside alike, marking them with arcane sigils that speak of his promise to be reborn with the spring as our verdant champion.

Mother Nature herself has settled down under her quilt stitched from skeletons of leaves and patched with the wistful dreams of her children. She may seem dead, her energies depleted and departed, yet she is only sleeping. She may seem oblivious to the cold that affects her children who walk on her frozen surface, yet it is hers alone to dream the dreams that bring us peace and hope for an awakening. Her fantasies bloom in the fertile dark of her winter's dreaming, foretelling when we will see the first shoots push up through the ground that seems as hard as iron, and feel the singing in our souls that heralds the quickening of the land.

It is a time of scarcity. Yet, there is a wealth of glittering prizes to be admired in the hedgerows, webs sparkling with hoarfrost hang between each trembling, stripped-back branch. glossy holly leaves shine and their brilliant crimson berries glow. Wreaths of dark emerald and bright blood red tell of the vibrancy of life even at this time of apparent inertia and speak of the spiritual and physical marriage between the landscape and those who walk upon that land. It is a green blood bond. We make wreaths to remember this, binding the green and the red with gold ribbon, symbolic of the light we seek in the darkest days, an acknowledgement of its sure return.

It is a season of harmonious unity, generosity, and rest. We, like the little creatures, huddle close to loved ones, counting our blessings and drowsily dwelling on what we have. We celebrate this abundance at Christmas gatherings when we share our Yulelog's blazing warmth; we eat foods we have previously and diligently prepared and stored; taste wine from summer fruits or autumn spices, savouring and remembering. We have worked hard and now deserve to enjoy what we have managed to achieve for ourselves, for all creation. There is peace and equanimity, perhaps a healing of old conflicts within families—a communion marked with the giving of gifts. We may converse with those closest to us about our achievements, of what nourishes and sustains us, and perhaps we imagine what may come to be when the light fully returns into our lives. To symbolically represent these concerns we may light candles to remind us that soon there will be bright blessings of longer days once more. We bless the sun's eternal returning and ask for the brightly flaring return of a certain energy into our own lives.

If we walk the wild way we have much to celebrate and to be thankful for in both physical and spiritual terms. It is an excellent time to offer prayers of thanks for an abundance in our lives. We could raise our voices in a spirit song of heartfelt prayer, asking that as we are fed and sustained by Mother Nature's generous bounty in the darkest hours, so may those who are less fortunate find sustenance, comfort, and joy. An appropriate vow for Earth and all her children could be something like:

> *If I have a surplus, may I pass it on.*
> *May the sharing return as the weak winter sun,*
> *May it grow stronger until it has won,*
> *And the day of the selfish be over and done,*
> *Like night fog I pray hunger fades and is gone,*
> *May abundance return like the weak winter sun.*
>
> *May the hunger for justice be all that remains,*
> *May we all count our blessings and break hunger chains,*
> *May we make human chains down the white country lanes,*
> *May we honour connections and take on nature's pains,*
> *May the whole of the world sing this heartfelt refrain,*
> *And as the ice breaks may we break hunger chains.*
>
> *By all that is generous, all that is giving,*
> *So may this be felt in the land of the living.*

February 2: Time of the Quickening Pulse
Also known as Imbolc or Candlemas.

This marks a seasonal celebration of the Earth's first stirrings. Mother Nature yawns, stretches, and makes as if to rise. Jack's green fingers are reaching out and upward from under the wintry quilt he has shared with his Queen of the Land and he makes to throw off the blanket of snow that has covered him with a sudden impulse to shake off his inertia. They both wait, these spirit denizens of the Greening, with one eye open, reaching out, yet still concealed. Their arms are outstretched and, with one quick push, they break Earth's ringing with sharp bright fingers of brilliant living green. Here and there the shock of these first shoots begin to flower delicate blooms against a backdrop of purest white snowdrops and darkest brown earth. The bare earth is barely glimpsed under a frosted mantle.

The snowdrops are a sign of inspiration, the shoots and buds that may appear at this time are signs to us that anything is possible, that we too can create new and fresh ideas, images, and practices. The tiny nodding snowdrops confirm that we should be filled with a fresh optimism and purpose yet be aware that at this stage all is tender and precious and can easily be trampled if we are not sensitive.

The overriding energies are positive and full of hope. It is a time to pray for beautiful new beginnings and for a cleansing of all that is harmful and hateful from the land. Our prayers should be simple and pure. For example:

> *Through the dark earth new hope is rising,*
> *In the dark of human souls all hate is melting,*
> *As gentle as snow falling we call for Earth healing,*
> *As the spring waters rise so does pure feeling,*
> *And all upon this land there is a clearing,*
> *Of pollution and greed . . . now disappearing!*
> *For the sake of peace and purification,*
> *So may it be in every nation!*

We may not have much physical evidence of the Earth's awakening but if we listen and open ourselves to the resonance of the land we can feel the gentle shift, the potency of preparation. All creatures seem to be sensing Earth's realised dream of returning and there is expectancy in the chill air. Our plumes of breath mingle and the rising birdsong accompanies the barely perceptible sound of the stirring sap.

It is a time for really focusing on a new dream, for working with Earth Mother to bring a new ideal, a new vision, into this year's eternal dance. It is a time within the cycle of "becoming," a time when we can perceive the most minute changes in the energy of the land—those first unexpected vibrations of her thrusting upward motion, the intent of hopeful innocent renewal. We may now contemplate on many questions relating to the coming year: What do we want to see in this coming year? What do we hope to achieve on a personal and universal level? How may we take our own pale and pure hope, as complex as a snowflake and surely as delicate and unique, and fashion it into a spell for the future?

By thinking of seeds growing restless in the deep hidden places, by linking in with their concealed potential, which gently thrums intuitively within their tiny core, we can attune to what it is that we need to do. Once we discover what we need to do, we can make a promise to complete the task. Like a new moon sailing across an ocean of deep violet sky there is much that reveals the fullness that is to come from a pale promise. With each passing day during the season, the energy increases, growing from a sliver of silvered hope to a fat crescent of wild desire. The sun is regaining his strength too, and his rays are becoming more penetrating, giving the Earth a longer kiss; it is a kiss with a little more warmth, which makes icicles drip and frozen streams melt and flow faster. Our own personal desire to fulfil a promise will grow accordingly. We may begin to think of ways to flow faster and we may even find green magic that suits this time of hope and promise. We could start by making a wishlist consisting of three wishes of hope for the coming cycle. During every festival to come, we could light a candle and focus upon one of the wishes. Or, we could create a theme for the coming year and then decide how it will be expressed magically and physically in our own lives. The theme could be life without cruelty. This could involve adopting an animal from a shelter, writing articles, giving money to antivivisection charities, giving away all leather goods, or changing our diet. Our aim is to use every gesture and act as a way of invoking for change. We could also choose an area of land close to where we live and vow to not only keep it free of litter but to observe the changing face of wildlife and plant beings who dwell on it in the course of a year. We can work with it for inspiration and creative projects and get to know its spirits.

Even as we plan and dream, finding new impetus and inspiration, all is still shivering and trembling. Barely perceptible at first, the stirring in us and Mother Earth grows steadily stronger, filling our short days and long nights with the thrill of anticipation.

March 21: Time of the Hatching Dream

Also known as Oestara / Eostre, Easter, spring equinox.

This date marks the time when day and night are of equal lengths before the sun wins out and claims back the greater share of our waking hours. It is the first day of spring. It is affiliated with the ancient goddess of fertility, Oestara (Eostre); hence the tradition of Easter eggs. It is also recognised as the time of Jesus's apparent resurrection.

Now is the time when we actually witness the Earth rising, refreshed and renewed, finding the energy to throw off the tattered remainder of a blanket woven from introspection and hung with tinkling crystals of ice. Mother Nature and her young companion, Jack-in-the-Green, burst forth, filled with delight that they can once again fulfil the promise of the Returning. He is leaping, eager and proud, and where he lands, wild primroses bloom in pale profusion, scattering their creamy yellow caress over the land. Mother Nature wriggles her shoulders in glee and the hares dance upon them, rabbits tumbling down the living slopes of her swelling body.

And brought forth on the tide of their rising come the pretty crocuses and flowering coltsfoot. The wild places erupt in a swaying, dancing sea of gold as daffodils thrust their way up and bow their heads in gratitude. The sap is moving up and gladly through the heart of pale green wood as the fragile eggs laid in darker days begin to crack, revealing sticky life within.

The energies are slender, flaxen-haired dancers, moving moons of maidenly grace, bringing the teasing promise of fertile blessings. They are coquettish energies in contrast to the cheeky, infinitely chirpy resonance of Green Jack, who bounds and prances like a newborn lamb testing out shaky limbs, then madly celebrating his newfound youth and exuberance. The land is filled with giggling, babbling energy, with wild and wonderful abounding joy.

We can spin and play like creatures on the hillsides and in the woodland. Newly emerged, we can test out new ways of being, as well as new thoughts, songs, and creations. We can plan which seeds to plant, both in our lives and in the land. We can rededicate ourselves to a path that has been revealed again, after the long grey days and snowy embrace of winter, and renew any promises made. We can begin to make any dreams reality. It is a time to take all that was incubating over winter, a spirit seed, a piece of comfort in the cold and barren times, and really give it life, filling it with all the real delight of a green resurgence.

May 1: Time of the Blossoming Blood

Also known as Beltaine, May Day, a holy day, the first day of summer.

Here is the celebration of a strengthening sun and longer days upon us! The essence of this time is romance and loving union, of wild blood surging and passionate relationships blossoming. This season is about creation, not only in partnerships but in individual ways, referring to all projects and ideas created lovingly. It is about being wildly enthusiastic about something, someone, or indeed life itself. And how can it not be when the creatures around us are mating, building homes, feasting on lush grass, and singing out their pleasures? It is also about the precious re-greening of a wild way of being, the regeneration of all we hold dear. All the radiant energy we need to pour into our vision is available to us at this time, humming with life like the first bee to emerge into the sunlight.

The energies are rising to a fever pitch of joy, though there is still a grace and gentleness to nature's behaviour. It is a time of intuitive patterns, of dancing old dances as our souls remember them, of playing out ancient roles while walking in the world decked in fresh young leaves, crowned with a diadem of new dew-damp wildflowers. It is a radiant time.

The Lady of the Moon, seductive and ripe, yet not quite full, is wooed by her Bright Lord, he who burns with the sun's renewed ardour and vigour. Both will be made greater, more fecund and complete, by the coupling. Even as these two celestial energies play out their eternal roles so do we experience Jack in his most playful yet romantic role, as he seeks to embrace the Queen of May, cream-thighed and flowering in a marriage-bed of nettles. Their union, surrounded by swirling floating blossom, witnessed by a crazy daisy dancing in a shower of spinning petals, is echoed in the courtship dance of stag and doe. Wide-eyed with wonder and baying with triumphant pleasure, the soft and sensuous merge together with the hard and vigorous. Intuition and strength, fire and water, creativity and practicality, all merge and entwine like the red and the white on the Maypole of folklore; stomping and vivacious as the youthful stallion, curving and dipping like a swan, proud as the young oak, and lithe as the willow. At this time, there is a wonderful blend of raw and sexual with exquisite and sensual. We could sing a prayer lustily, stamping our feet and swaying:

Dancing blood within my veins,
Cast off all that now restrains,
Pulsing petals, waxing, open,
Spell of separation now be broken!

Thrum and thrust, pink, white, and green,
Now be felt and now be seen,
Lightening, brightening in my hands,
As it's felt in me so in the land,

For union felt like a rising tide,
May love and power in us reside!
For the marriage of the Green Ones and the land,
Heart and soul be hand in hand!

And the potent yet subtle fertility dance goes on, for the good of the All. This is the time of the bluebell's blessing, when the woodland is alive with yellow and lilac. It is the season of a greenwood marriage, which we can echo as we take manifest and spiritual commitments to all that we are passionate about, and really intertwine our passions into our daily lives. As bud-clad branch becomes leafy bough, so it is that we experience a real thriving, a spurt of impetus, inspiration, and magical purpose. Mind, body, and spirit are married in a bright burst of briar rose and hawthorn petals spill and spin around us like confetti. We wind our fingers with strong new gypsy grasses and, as the wild-spirited ones who vowed to serve the Greening, we plant late seeds, clear up litter from a riverbed, do a sponsored walk for a local animal charity, write an article on local wildlife, or stop eating nonorganic produce. Our marriage is of the worldly with the otherworldly, enchantment with action. We fall in love with what we do, with who we are, as well as with each other.

We may undertake trance journeys to align ourselves with the resurgent energies and travel to meet the Fey as they dance their own untamed reel within the ancient boundaries of a stone ring on a high moor. We may observe them, our elemental kin, hidden in a glade of young, slender, silver birch trees, whose tear-shaped leaves pour down around their strange, sinuous figures like cool green rain. We may chance upon fox cubs, with the brightest eyes and black-button noses, sunning themselves on a ridge, playing rough and tumble with sisters and brothers, pouncing catlike from behind clumps of dandelions, and springing in the long dry grass.

It is the time of the Greening of the land and of a resurgence for the spirit. It is only for us to echo these things in practical ways in our daily lives. Under a cerulean-blue sky chased by scudding clouds, we may feel the pounding of the life force in the veins of the land beneath our bare feet and go running into the arms of our own heartfelt vision.

June 21: Time of the Deep Green Kiss

Also known as Litha, midsummer, summer solstice.

During this time, the days are at their longest. This is midsummer, the height of summer. It can also be called Litha (opposite of Yule), which is a Scandinavian term that was once used for the months of June and July. Litha has become a popular term for this midsummer festival, which Christians celebrated on June 24 as St. John's birthday. This is also the time that marks, as with the winter equivalent, a point before a change in the energetic tide. With the summer solstice we observe a peak, the opposite of winter's trough, and we know that from this point on there will be a waning. It is a good opportunity to celebrate what is given to us, the bounty of sun-kissed summer life, at the moment of climax as the sun reaches its annual and daily zenith at midday.

The energies of this wonderful, positive time are at their peak of glowing, healthy strength and fertility. As we are discussing a seasonal round, it is important to see how one energy seamlessly segues into another. It is obvious that from union comes a gift of fulfilment: Easter to Beltain is about paring up and mating, or beginning a creative work; Litha is the full-blown rose, the round belly, and the time when it becomes apparent that all will soon come to fruition at Lammas. The land is impregnated with a joyous, writhing, serpentine vitality and all creatures are blessed with a glorious surge of ebullient life force. Our own zest and vigour can be matched with the land. Even if we do not feel too great personally, we can align ourselves with that reassuring energetic resonance that comes from being aware of the seasonal procession. In the simple acknowledgement of the returning patterns in nature, we are able to tune in and draw comfort and magical strength from what we see, feel, and experience all around us.

As young buzzards twirl and tumble above us, showing off their skills, calling us into the heart of wild being with their plaintive cries, we are touched by a madness, an overwhelming gladness to be alive. Reeds whisper as we pass them, gossiping in the afternoon sun; water rats plop lazily into the water and white mouths open as the milky fish pop up to swallow juicy flies; elderflower blossoms foam and froth. The lazy hazy atmosphere tangles us in mistle-thistle kisses that are marsh-meadow sweet, and we may wallow in the contentment found in warm sunshine. Clover pink and languorous the land lies, met by sleepy cornflower skies swirled with crazy bees a-bumble. Even a walk along a roadside sees us greeted by delicate wild poppies who nod their drowsy greeting, their papery scarlet petals barely fluttering in a soft, warm breeze. If we pluck them they simply fall apart. Just as with wild magic, the poppy has to be left to grow and fulfil its cycle. It should not be rudely uprooted and moved out of time and place.

Life at this time is cow-fat and pendulous, the energies are rounded. The energetic representatives of this time are the pregnant Earth Mother about to give birth, in full bloom, watering her marigolds. She is empathic, compassionate, generous, and grounded, as soft as meadowsweet. Her partner is the All-Father, a mature and virile man, certain of his own part in the dance; he is protective and paternal, yet fiercely independent and full of vigorous good humour.

There is a sense that all creation is living fully at this time. To make the most of that energy available we can have mass celebrations, incorporating music and dance performed in the open air. We can go on shared picnics in meadows and explore exciting unfamiliar places. We could wander in fields by day and by night, admiring the strangely moving, deeply beautiful crop-glyphs that have formed as if by magic in the fields of corn. These crops are swirled and flattened in arcane patterns that speak to the soul of artistic perfection and of mystical significance. They echo the patterns of nature and of humanity's relation to the land, to spirit, and to the universe. Whatever their meaning, crop markings allow people to connect with the land, whether under luminous skies spangled with clear-blue starlight or on balmy evenings filled with birdsong and clouds of tiny insects.

It is a time to celebrate out of doors as often as possible. Joyfully dance while singing a simple chant of celebration with others, in a round. For example:

> *I stand in the circle of life this day,*
> *Blessed beyond all measure,*
> *I dance in the circle of the All this day,*
> *Surrounded by nature's treasure,*
> *By wild rose fire I am now blessed,*
> *By beings of fur and feather,*

May the feather on my life path now fly free,
And fly into forever!

Seasonal wild magic during this time should concern living life to the full and being thankful for all that fulfils us. Therefore, simple green-spirited spells could be performed while focusing on the energy, golden like the sun, at the centre of a wild rose as we visualise ourselves as fully opened, vital, beautiful, and untamed. We can eat wild strawberries and be dedicated to experiencing the sweet, red, wild heart of being. Or we could gather hedgerow (not roadside) elderflowers (with a prayerful intent, as always asking permission of the tree) and make a light, sparkling cordial with sugar, lemon, and white-wine vinegar. As we stir and tend the brew, we can sing praise to it of our gladness, of our delight at being a part of something so utterly magnificent as nature in full bloom. We can bottle it up in green bottles marked with swirls of bright energy and share the resulting drink with friends in weeks to come as a celebration of life, friendship, and kinship with nature.

August 2: Time of the Abundant Promise
Also known as Lammas or the feast of Lugh.

Lammas derives from a Saxon word and relates to the loaves we associate with the harvested grain of the season. Lugh (Lughnassadh) was a Celtic fire god who gave his life in sacrifice at this time to ensure a continued good harvest. It is the first harvest festival and denotes a whole season of gathering in.

The first fruits of our year's harvest are showing in our lives just as the blackberries appear on twisted bramble limbs in the busy hedgerows, still reddish but swelling to ripening. Even as the sun begins to decline in strength, gradually we see the rich jewel-like beauty of the rosehips, sloes, elderberries, and haws coming into being. The colours emerge slowly, magically, as the vibrant yellow-green of what once was the heart of their blossom loses its verdant hue and mellows in the gentle, warm, late summer breezes. Nature is still active but slowing her pace. Butterflies still fly, alighting on late privet flowers, sending the heady scent of vanilla wafting out to hang heavy in the air down country lanes.

The peak of light and life has passed but darkness and death are nowhere to be seen as yet. Earth Mother stretches like a cat under the benevolent sun's rays and Father Sun kisses her softly, still with plenty of warmth. He has past his prime and is no longer showing off, resplendent in a cloak of leaping flame, he is more content now within himself, sure of his role and sated. His is the colour of goldenrod and tansy.

Ants are swarming and flying in the towns by day, the sonorous afternoon heat bringing them out to perform their annual dance. In the park, horse chestnuts swell inside their still green prickly cases and tiny windfall apples litter a path in an overgrown garden. Children, enjoying their summer break from school, feed on juicy plums and fat peaches, sweet syrup running down their chins; while adults break seed-bread together and discuss their achievements thus far, supping on recently brewed homemade elderflower wine or hedgerow cordial. Feeling loved and well fed, we may send our loving thoughts and energy out to those who do not have such abundance or such community: to the starving and the sick, to the lonely and dispossessed.

A simple prayer for Lammas, time of abundant promises, may be:

> *My simple wooden cup is full,*
> *And love is spilling over,*
> *I cup my hands to receive grace,*
> *I am in clover.*
> *Let thoughts of joy take swallow's wings,*
> *Let all perceive them,*
> *May they touch upon those in most need,*
> *Let them receive them.*
> *Sweet as hay, golden as corn,*
> *Bounty be shared, joy be reborn!*

There is a buzz of well-being at this time, summer is not yet done but is already offering up the first signs of bounty for a season well spent. It is a time to join hands and give thanks for what we have managed to bring to bear so far, knowing that there is one last phase before the energy truly begins to wane. We may use the last of this sun-blessed vibrant summer energy to push our dreams and projects on one step further.

As an act of natural enchantment it would be fitting to make a small pouch from recycled fabric in a rich, subtle colour that is suitable for such a mellow, ripened season. Into this pouch we could place anything we feel to be symbolic of the first fruits of our year's journey, symbols of any project we are involved in, or any creative idea or work. Along with this, we could add some of the first hedgerow fruits that we see, dried and dedicated to the union of our wildwitch's work and the natural, fruitful progression of the land. We could make a woven tie from tall meadow grass to close it, and as we weave we could pour all the warm, lingering dynamism of the time of year into our hands, ensuring that the work we do, and our link with the land, is blessed by this magical energy. We could wear this around our necks, or about our person, until the seasonal wheel turns again. It can be a reassuring reminder in the dark days of winter that new life and a fresh harvest will come around once more.

September 21: Time of Changing Winds

Also known as Mabon and autumn equinox.

This is the second harvest festival. The autumn equinox speaks of days of equal length to nights, and so of divine balance, waiting, hanging, and being centred and poised before the energy shifts and wanes.

Here we experience a gathering in—of gifts both physical and spiritual, a reaping of what has been sown in the fields, and in our lives. Earth Mother has been spending the cooler days and shorter nights making a patchwork quilt and this she casts lovingly over a land that now feels a chill after dark. It is a marvellous quilt, made of ploughed fields, once golden and green, now fallow or full of stubble. Colours are both rich and subtle. There is nothing obvious or blatant about this season.

There is a bronzing of the land as leaves, grasses, and petals all experience the touch that turns them from amber to russet, sapping their strength and making them drift away, curl up, retreat back. Dark berries shine wetly in long showers; glistening, their plum-black and glowing scarlet is a striking contrast to the slow withering that occurs around them. Ivy attracts maddened wasps who, drunk on fat, windfall apples, know that there time is almost done and that even they, in their zingy coats of yellow and black, will fade back into the dying, drying year.

Father Nature has strands of grey in his beard and silver in his nut-brown hair. Strings of glossy conkers hang around his lined neck and his pockets are full of sycamore seed treasures, acorns, and the fruits of wisdom given by the hazel tree, whose leaves were once baby-soft and downy, now turning tough and hairy. Father Nature swings his staff of ash and feet begin to crunch through the leaves, leaves already passed away from the tree that bore them, making patterns on Mother Nature's quilt of land. He sniffs the air and feels the wind of change, as does the squirrel and the wren, both bobbing and weaving, preparing for the inevitable return of winter.

Earth Mother yawns, her quilt now spread, and she reclines, not yet exhausted but drifting into sleep nonetheless. She is pulling her strength back into the core of herself, withdrawing as thoughts turn to heart and hearth. She is still beautiful, with brambles in her fading, tangled auburn tresses, yet there are heavy lines around her eyes, her gaze is distant, and her pose is weary. Still, she finds the strength to open her arms as the creatures draw their own harvest in and her cracked rosehip lips smile to see their industry of gathering and storing. All life is on the wane.

We may now ponder: What has grown and what is to wane in our lives?

*   *   *

Remember, there are no real rights or wrongs about how we feel seasonal, archetypal, or spiritual energies. There is no need to rehearse and recite what has been given here, although, the suggestions offered here will work well for us as witches just beginning a wild way. This chapter has been designed to offer both an awareness of the cycles and a poetic understanding of them.

In the next chapter, we will continue with this blending of our spiritual journey with a manifest understanding. We will learn how to travel safely into the otherworldly realms while maintaining both an awareness of, and a relationship with, our physical surroundings and the inherent energies of the moment.

From this point on, it is hoped that something of the lyrical nature of wildwitchery, as shared here, will penetrate deeply into all that we practice.

Chapter Three

WILD LANDSCAPES OF THE SOUL

Sapling shifts under shimmering sky,
Glamorous glimmer in a mystery's eye,
As the world unfurls to a heron's cry . . .

If we are going to walk our talk effectively in the world as wildwitches, then we need to walk with spirit, working directly (and perhaps consciously for the first time) with the unseen. This cannot be taken lightly, although there should be much joy in it. In this chapter, we will be discovering how to work with energies efficiently and how to safely communicate with spirits. We will build on the understanding that wild witchcraft is an enduring blend of interacting with the unseen and manifest levels of existence. We will look at specific reasons we work with the unseen and then explore the different methods that will be part of our practical outer work.

When we say "inner work" we are speaking of the work that is concerned with turning our gaze away from the everyday events of our worldly lives and directing it toward the hidden; it refers to things that are not of the world in a mundane sense. It is introspective and reflective work that allows us to go within ourselves, to the places where we may find our own truths. We can often do inner work by means of the same trance journeys we undertake for more universal, magical purposes. We also engage in inner work when we visualise, prayerfully contemplate, and cast enchantments. In fact, any work that involves being psychically opened to energies or using the mind's eye to see is inner work. The importance of the inner work that supports our practical applications will become clearer as we progress through the methods that will help develop our skills.

Firstly, lets get back to the basics. In order to make soulful—and therefore magical—connections, we need to get ourselves well and truly connected. That is to say, before we can continue on our romantic journey into the passionate heart of wild enchantment, we must first root ourselves firmly in Earth Mother. Though we wish to travel to otherwordly places, we must never forget that we have chosen to be part of an Earthwalk. As the "living wood" that makes the link between the land and the beyond, we must have a strong and secure foundation in order for our "sap" (will and wish) to travel through us. We must safely move out and onward to bring the Greening into the collective conciousness. Likewise, any spiritual insights we gain from reaching out beyond ourselves and our current manifest realm need to be able to flow downward and become grounded, bringing healing and teaching to the manifest realms. As wildwitches we are like our mentors, the trees—our sap is the life-force energy filtered through the rich loam of our Earth magic. We can learn to pull this energy up or draw it down. Like the trees, we have a resinous inner knowing at a deep cellular level, if only we care to remember it.

It is true to say that we would only have a poor appreciation of the awesome strength and breathtaking beauty of a tree if we had no actual grasp of its structure, of its inner workings. When the leaves turn to russet and saffron in October, we would just think of it as a cute trick. Likewise, if we had no knowledge of sap and roots we might think that it is incredibly clever of a big tree to stand upright, unsupported. Our relationship with the tree and our insights into the connection we experience with it would be shallow compared to the resonance knowledge can bring. In order to have the full, unbridled joy of working with energies and the unseen we need to spend some time learning the rudiments first, gaining some understanding of the structure and inner workings of all things.

In another analogy pertaining to our work, there can be no illumination in a lightbulb if it is disconnected from the power source. Energy cannot be transmitted without a circuit. To become connected, to make a circuit, we must know how to protect ourselves from the energy involved. We know that holding a live wire is unadvisable. Well, spiritual energy, as electrical energy, needs to be understood and respected in order to work with it safely and effectively. If we are to become a conduit that achieves a gentle radiance through spiritual practice then we need to know how best to earth and insulate ourselves so that we do not burn out.

Protection

Such regulated matters as energetic protection need not be tedious; a sense of the poetic permeates all that runs through our integrated magical lives. Once we become opened to the possibility of green magic in our daily routines, we begin to understand that all acts, however mundane, can be imbued with wild power or sacred intent. Like following a recipe, the perfect dish is only achieved by adhering to instructions, at least until the cook becomes so familiar with the dish that improvisation on the theme is appropriate. Progressing straight to the real juicy bits of a wildwitch's work without covering protection is like skipping a vital part of the preparation in a recipe, the resulting dish may be unpalatable at best and give us a stomach upset at worst. In time, protection just becomes part of the flow of our practices and can be made as beautiful as the individual sees fit to make it. For now, it is best to stick to the tried and tested methods—structured recipes that guarantee safe and palatable results.

Although the wild newcomer may be familiar with the basic recipe for witchcraft, and may understand terms such as "spellweaving" or "journeying," the whole area of personal psychic protection is often omitted from contemporary books and work- shops. The topic may even seem like an extraneous quirk of this book, an unnecessary discussion that may be skipped in favour of the more familiar and glamorous aspects of witchery. It is not clear why protection finds little coverage as part of witchcraft. Per- haps it is not considered an immediate enough topic for people of our "instant" society. Perhaps it is assumed that such an audience demands to be wooed with fast-track ways of gaining access to wonders untold. Perhaps to cut to the chase on how to weave spells for love or wealth is far more entertaining than the slow plod through the process of protection. Whatever the reason, to approach our wild witchcraft without taking the time to employ protection would be doing those genuinely willing and able to make a commitment to a magical life a grave disservice. If safety still seems unnec- essary to us, then we should read on to be aware of the risks, at least.

This brings us to our first point of safety and that is to address human consumption. Sounds simple, but it is an important point. It is best not to engage in eating or drink- ing too heavily before a session of inner work. There are two reasons for this, firstly our body will be engaged in the process of dealing with its new intake of sustenance and therefore possibly seek to distract us with digestive burblings and bloated feelings; secondly, the symbology of becoming "stuffed" before such work puts far too much emphasis on the bodily manifest realm when we are trying to open up to the beyond.

Drinking alcohol before inner work is absolutely not advisable as it impairs judgement and attracts the wrong kind of energies; to be intoxicated is not the right energetic signal to emit. It suggests an incautious and irreverent attitude. I personally have had the experience of being so incautious while staying in an old and decidedly disturbed hotel. Myself and another witch, even though we had indulged in a few drinks, decided to open up and tune in to the energies in a corridor that felt particularly energetically unpleasant. I was rewarded for my recklessness by having my coat vanish from my lap where I had placed it, followed by the most painful migraine headache. We were simply not up to the job in hand and I got what I deserved for messing about when I should have known better. I no longer touch any alcohol, as I find I would rather be ready to engage with energies than be inebriated. Many "sensitives" find that they cannot easily tolerate alcohol anyway. It goes without saying that mind-altering drugs should be avoided by those serious about working magically. All drugs open us up to the very real energies of the lower human astral realms in an undisciplined and random way, and leave us vulnerable.

It may be considered overly cautious (or tame instead of wild) to state that before we can truly be open enough to weave fate, walk with the spirits, and make magic we must address an issue such as eating and drinking. In fact, at this point we may still find it unnecessary to protect ourselves at all. Lets look at another example. A field of scarlet poppies seems truly wild and yet without the basic structured formulae—seeds having dark earth to germinate in, water and sunlight to feed them—there would be no flowers dancing in a gentle June breeze. Any gardener placing a cloche over precious seedlings when they know (or intuit) that the frost is coming is only being sensible. This is a form of protection—there is nothing particularly wild about a bunch of dead plants. Likewise, there is nothing to be said for a blasé approach to being opened to energies. The psychic equivalent of frost can wither the most enthusiastic, unprotected witches and perhaps put them off their magical path, which is an unnecessary shame.

Our witchcraft is not sophisticated, but rather earthy and authentic. Therefore, we must consciously try not to dispense with a glossy veneer of freedom (in other words, we should aim to not put on a glamorous act), for this is really an act of shallow irresponsibility and brings temporary glory. We are not tethering ourselves by ensuring we have a root in the ground, rather empowering the whole flowering plant of our craft in order for our work to reach its full potential. Being grounded enough to let the truth fly free, and knowing it as truth by means of a system of protection, is essential. What may seem like a time-wasting hindrance at the start of our journey is the very thing that allows us to traverse the wildest regions without a care.

The universe, seen and unseen, is unpredictable and full of surprises. It is not regulated solely by what humans consider to be law and order. When working with the unpredictable, it is best to be prepared in a very positive way. As wildwitches, we will be aiming to respond to situations, not react. To respond smoothly and effectively means we must have a calmness and security that comes from preparation and part of that preparation is in knowing how things work. Like the gardeners who make preparations based on what the unpredictable weather may do, we must prepare to avoid acting rashly once weather has already struck. And, like electricians, we need to know about the energy we engage with and acknowledge that we need certain tools at hand for potentially hazardous work. And, like explorers, we need to have a backpack full of sustenance and, if necessary, the right weapons to see us through the unknown terrain.

In short, we need to be told what to expect and how to get the best out of what we are about to do.

What to Expect

Without wishing to sound alarmist, the unseen realms, or the energetic levels of nature, are not one-dimensional places of light, purity, and good intentions. There are indeed unicorns and dragons, elves and beings of incredible generosity and wit; yes, the unseen realms are full of paradox and whimsy, but they are also full of trickery of a more malicious and lasting kind. It would be wrong to lull prospective green-spirited witches into a false sense of security by telling them that the universe is a uniformly pleasant place full of well-meaning sprites and angels. Everything a human being can imagine, and much more, can actually inhabit the beyond. So, yes, there are smiling avatars bestowing blessings and good Faeries ready to help us but there are also those who masquerade as such beings whilst in reality being the psychic equivalent of a verruca. One could consider our psychic protection like the sandals we wear to ensure we do not catch such irritating warts while walking around a public pool.

There are vampires and villains, cheats and liars, allies and heroes "in spirit" just as in the incarnate forms of life. How is it possible to say this? Isn't the human manifest world full enough of such nastiness? Surely the astral, etheric, and otherworldly levels must be far nicer places to visit and work with? Read on . . .

Thought and Deed

It is the very human aspect of manifest existence that causes the majority of difficulties in making trance journeys. To achieve clear and accurate spirit guidance, we must work with the levels closest to Earth and it is here that we find a direct reflection of all the corrupt human thoughts that could exist. Thoughts have their own energy, especially if they are dwelled on repeatedly, and so they can become energetic detritus moulded by human wish and will from the "clay" of the human astral levels. Thoughts can, and do, take on form. Some people deliberately structure these thoughtforms to do their will in a parody of magical work that involves influencing other people without their consent or knowledge. Still other people inadvertently create spiritual monsters by their constantly brooding on a particular malevolent subject.

Is human society overall a place of sweetness and goodwill or a place generating fearful thoughts, rampant competitiveness, misdirected anger, and feelings of resentment? Just imagine the levels of thoughtforms, and the nature prescribed to them by their human creators, generated by one city in one year alone! These thoughts form a once-removed miasma that is unseen from the manifest realm, a miasma that influences the subtle levels of our existence on Earth. Earth is their matrix and they are kept in our orbit by their human connections. Trained wildwitches can detect and deal with such influences. If we choose to do our work without discipline, then we are as much prey to such energetic ghouls as anyone else. In order for these thoughtforms to stay "alive" (or in existence), they need to feed off our energy and to do this they promote the very fear, depression, or violent anger they were fashioned from in the first place. They interfere with our subtle energies, if we let them, in order to generate feelings in us that they find tasty. They are not independent beings, they were manufactured and they need our support in terms of energetic input. Without such food from us, they deflate and fade away.

To gain sustenance they use trickery and pretend to be other than what they are. They may simply slip into our presence when we are unaware and interfere with our energetic matrix. They pose a significant threat to our psychic and spiritual well-being, so an initial safety step is to know the places where such thoughtforms dwell.

Where Thoughtforms Fly Free

If we work in a group or in close proximity to others then we need to be protected from extraneous thoughts and psychic material that is clearly not ours. It will only distract us if we pick up on another's wish or will, or even the mental recitation of a shopping list. When we are "open" (available for spirit dialogue and contact), we cannot just be open to some things and not others. We must be wholly able to receive images, information, or energetic material that will assist us with our work.

The only hope we have to filter out what is not ours is to be protected so that the only thing that may come close to our astral space is of a positive energy and out for our highest good. It doesn't mean that other things won't try to get in, it just means we will be ready for them—ready and able to block out any human energetic interference from our own current level of existence in the busy manifest realm. Here are some examples of when we may like to use protection so that we can remain open but not be bombarded with extraneous energies and negative human thoughts.

Sacred Sites

This includes some churches and graveyards, especially the older ones deliberately built on power spots by those Christians with an understanding of mysticism and geomancy. Any human-built sacred site where there is much human visitation and interaction has potential to harbour unwanted energy. This is due to people inadvertently invoking all sorts of spirits who come masquerading as gods. There is often no knowledge of how to ascertain what is genuine and what is false and so it is wise to protect ourselves against anything that has been previously conjured up; usually this will be a poor excuse for a powerful being. Not everyone is as vigilant as we hope to be and therefore caution is advisable.

In places where people pray or invoke, especially if the people are distressed or highly undisciplined in their approach, the sort of dross that may turn up will hang around, waiting for more easy prey to feed off energetically. Also, ardent prayer, if desperate, can stir up a similar psychic atmosphere and leave a residue. Prayer, if it is repeated and all consuming, like repeated thoughts, can create forms that come from the depression or bitterness in which they were created. Sites out of doors and in exposed places will not be so susceptible to this as the land herself and the spirits who guard the place will deal with the majority of unclean visitors—most external transient human energy will simply blow away. Confined constructed spaces are far more receptive and retentive, especially if made with stone, which is a great storer of energy.

Monuments to human spiritual connection may seem like ideal, or even very obvious, places to work our craft. We must accept that in such spaces we will not be able to have the intimate relationship with the land that we need in order to practice our craft unhindered. Such major magical sites are more often than not constructed on power spots. There are lesser and greater spots along the earth's energy matrix but those with significant sites, for example Avebury or Stonehenge in Wiltshire, England, are certainly aligned with major well-springs of inherent life force. The portals on the land create great vortexes of raw elemental dynamism that the ancients knew how to work with instinctively. Such power will simply be too much to handle if we are not fully conversant with a wildwitch's work.

One of the keys to wild witchcraft is to know our current levels of expertise and to act accordingly with neither overt modesty nor pride. Official sacred sites are best left to an occasional reverential visit (a pilgrimage in honour of our wise ancestors, perhaps) and doing a little protection before entering the sacred space is always prudent for the sensitive wildwitch.

Psychic and Mystic Fairs

These are events held in halls where people go to get clairvoyant readings to help them with their problems. Not all psychics have self-discipline and they may even contact unscrupulous spirits. Walking into a room full of such beings will be rather overwhelming and psychically confusing to say the least. The "psychic fair headache" is a common phenomena, the force of such energy being felt in the mind's third eye very quickly. With all the mediums and card readers vying for trade, some of the energetic overload can actually be caused by the great spate of low-flying egos present at such a competitive event. Plus, once again, we have many desperate folk seeking guidance and they carry all sorts of thoughtform baggage in one confined arena. Much protection is advised before going to such an event and much grounding afterward.

Confined Quarters

This includes underground trains, long flights, and large conferences. For example: a man suffering from mental illness may be dragging a very unsavoury thoughtform behind him in a train carriage; there may be much repressed fear on an airline flight; and much stress or competitive, unscrupulous thoughts may float around a conference room. It is the "highly peopled" and the contained nature of such situations that obviously brings a host of unpredictable energetic influences to the wildwitch.

Among Strangers

By this I do not mean you should do a quick protective fix when someone asks you for the time on the street! Rather, protection is of an issue when we are in a situation when we may be counselling, teaching one-on-one, healing in a hands-on fashion, or even working in a magical group such as a coven or Druid grove. As a personal example, when I first began tattooing, I was exhausted as I was assailed constantly by my client's energy. I put my hands on them to do the work and they opened up to me (and I to their needs) because of the situation, and this could go on for some hours. Since the situation was not deemed purely "spiritual" I hadn't considered I should be protected. Of course, when you have physical as well as mental (and sometimes emotional) connections with a client, you should be aware of that energy exchange (and often energy drain) that can occur. If clients are in pain, upset, or confused, as they may well be in any of the situations I have mentioned here, they may well "leach" valuable life force from you and end up feeling much better than when they made contact with you whilst you feel utterly exhausted. A circuit of two "opened" people (one needing help, one offering it) means that energy is inevitably exchanged. A simple protective gesture before meeting a client can save us a lot of personal discomfort afterward.

I am sure more of these types of situations can be thought of with these examples in mind. The most obvious situation that requires protection is when we are directly confronted by threatening spirit beings. Often we can see such beings in physical form, which in turn may create a more immediate response in us than a threatening, but unseen, energy. We must be familiar with safety procedures for both situations. Perhaps we now can better understand the importance of protection. And this is only the beginning. Please read on!

Sharks and Wasps

It is well to accept that not all beings who exist in their own right in the universe, independent from human influences, wish us well. Some indeed do mean us actual harm whilst others cannot help but affect us adversely by simply being who and what they are. The unseen realms reflect the same principles as the seen realms and therefore contain the energetic equivalent of icy inhospitable planets, spluttering volcanoes, and predatory sharks. None of these are hateful creations, each simply does something that humans find disturbing or unacceptable. They are quite different from the thought-forms or other entities that deliberately attack us in order to feed.

For example, it is well to understand that wasps sting. Therefore, we can respond to them appropriately. When we are stung painfully by a wasp, it is easy to feel that all wasps are a threat, that they are evil creatures. If we are stung again, it may seem as if these fiends are out to get us. Stinging is simply what wasps do naturally, no more evil than what a rose does naturally with its thorns. From our perspective, we find roses pleasant but wasps unpleasant. We should be wary of embroidering this into a stereotype such as "rose is good, wasp is evil," for we all have within us the capacity to act in similar opposing ways and such definitions are subjective. In spiritual terms, some spirit beings and energies are simply incompatible with our own but this does not make them wrong. Some will repel us by their very psychic emissions, others attract us, and still others will leave us dazed and energetically damaged if we recklessly interact with them.

As wildwitches, we have a deep understanding that there is inspiration to be found in the storm-tossed sea even though it has the power to overturn boats and dash them onto the rocks. Storms are just as much a natural part of life on Earth as the bluebell woods of spring, and decay and rot are as valid as fluffy yellow chicks. Nature needs shadows as well as light in order for either one to be appreciated. The natural food chain means the lion needs to bring the zebra down in a way that is not pretty. With this in mind, it may be easier to appreciate that rattlesnakes and tarantulas of an astral kind are just as much a part of universal creation as the familiar image of the benevolent spirit guide. They simply have such alien viewpoints and ways of being compared to our own that they appear callous or cold to contend with.

Without doubt we are energetically connected to all beings. We can never sever our spiritual connections because they spiral across all dimensional aspects of the universe. We are all linked to the source energy, whether we are a Fey-souled witch or a strange space traveller of a hue that we as humans do not have the capacity to imagine. And there is no hierarchy of worst or best. We just need to understand this and act accordingly. It is foolish to go swimming when we know there is a hungry shark in the bay. It is madness to build a home on the slopes of an active volcano. It is equally unwise to dive into energetic work without some safeguard against what may be encountered.

Currently, we understand that there are incredibly diverse energies floating in the ether, and they are not all present for our greater good. As the book progresses we will spend more time looking at exactly who and what we may encounter on our journeys, and we will learn how to ensure spirits are who they say they are by means of authenticity testing methods.

We will now begin to learn pre-emptive safeguarding strategies and we can employ them at any time for any reason. The following methods will get us started on the right safe path even though we cannot control what spirits may try to approach us unexpectedly. Our basic formulae is threefold like the clover and without it what we will have is a mishmash of illusion and reality with no means to differentiate which is which. It is part of the blood and bones of our craft.

The Threefold Unfolded

The following system can be expanded upon but shouldn't be shortened, even when confidence in the work is blooming. To say it "unfolds" is an accurate description. The simple, effective gestures we make to ensure we are safe in our endeavours can be carried out with seamless grace. It is vital to remember that through our wild witchcraft we are entering a world of symbol and gesture, focused intent and visualisation. What we do makes good sense and is tried and tested to work effectively, it also resonates deeply with our new greened perception. It is a way to help us understand our world as a place of enchantment as well as a solid form.

This threefold sequence can be performed indoors or out in the landscape, on a bus or in the bathroom. It does not necessarily require any outward gesture other than closing one's eyes, though such additions as sound and gesture are included for when there is time to practice more fully. It will be described both in its complete form and in the way it can be utilised on the spot for a quick response to an immediate situation.

Stage One: Placement

This stage involves the positioning and comfort of the body and pertains to the manifest aspect of what we are about to do. We want to find the best possible place to begin our wild work. If we are allowed the luxury of time for our work, then any extraneous sound should be filtered out as much as possible prior to an otherworldly journey. It is worth considering that the Otherworlds are "timeless" and do not tend to contain modern human attributes like loud hip-hop music, electric drills, the shrill of an alarm, electronic beepings of mobile phones, or revving engines. These sounds cannot be easily assimilated into our work, and it takes a very relaxed, or very versatile, person indeed to find an otherworldly equivalent to these sounds! Birds chirping or cows mooing are not too invasive by comparison and such natural sounds present no threat to our work. This said, if we work outside we do not need to filter out natural sounds. In fact, working outside can be very nourishing—all that lovely green Earth energy to draw on and work with—and natural sounds can even enhance the work when one feels comfortable enough to allow them to be part of the proceedings. It is easy to assimilate the barking of a dog or birdsong into a trance journey.

This "noise-free" environment may be an impossibility if the work has to be carried out in an impromptu fashion in a public or unfamiliar place. However, we try to avoid disruption whenever possible. We cannot expect to be entirely hermetically sealed before we begin all spiritual transactions, but we can be sensible about the level of distraction that is probable and minimalise this to the highest degree. Carrying a travel pack of foam earplugs can be a great way of shutting out extraneous noise as long as it does not compromise safety by having noise shut out in a public place.

The aim is to be as comfortable as possible whilst not presenting ourselves with an opportunity to fall asleep. In the early days of our practice we may find that we nod off, this is quite usual and not anything to worry about. However, it should not be the goal! If we fall asleep when going into a trance journey, then it is sensible to assume that either we are tired (and therefore the healing sleep, rather than a journey of work, was what we most required at that time) or that we are on some level afraid of engaging in the work and that this sleep mechanism is one way of gently opting out!

If sleep overcomes every attempt to trance journey, we must then position the body in a way that is appropriate to suggest connection. Remember, we are conduits in the great tradition of the trees and therefore the most appropriate positions are those that allow us to have a firm contact with our feet on the ground and our spines upright and erect. The aim is to let energy flow around the body while we connect to the energy and the ground. This means no tense areas and a broadbase connection to the earth (or the floor if you are indoors). Although standing seems like the logical position, it is perhaps not sustainable if we are to undertake a lengthy trance journey as any physical discomfort halfway through will be distracting. Being seated on the ground—preferably directly on earth—with a straight back and feet firmly planted on the floor is suitable.

Knees Bent

If we are able, we should sit with our spine as straight as possible and have our knees bent, feet resting squarely on the floor. We may, of course, lean back against a wall, chair, or even a tree to help us keep our back straight. First we ask the tree for permission to lean against it by using our ability to feel subtle shifts in energy, our seeing and knowing. Relating to the tree with respect for its individual being, instead of assuming it is just a part of the scenery, and asking the tree for permission is enough for the tree to grant our request. Either we have our hands on the floor, palms down, or have them resting on our knees similarly. This connects us further to terra firma, making a solid bond. Alternatively, we can have our feet squarely on the floor with palms resting on our knees and facing upward, symbolically open to the energies around us. If it feels natural, we may connect our index finger and thumb, making a mini-circuit. We may find the fingers have an urge of their own to form this shape!

Crossed Legs

There are two variations on how we may choose to sit for our meditational practice. If we feel that sitting with crossed legs, in the yoga "lotus" style, allows our energy to circulate without being able to escape through stretched limbs and feet, then sitting cross-legged with the palms either face up or down on the knees, or resting on the floor, is acceptable. This method is only recommended for those of us who are conversant with yoga techniques, for lotus is a seated position that requires much physical practice. If we find being cross-legged for a prolonged period is difficult and uncomfortable, we should try to avoid crossing limbs. Also, if we feel crossed legs is more like crossed wires, then we may prefer to create a smooth circuit between our flowing energy and the ground beneath our squarely-planted feet, as in the bent knees example above. Given any method, we will find several different views but the importance here is to keep thinking of our whole being as an uncluttered circuit. Keeping this in mind, we can use whichever variation makes most sense to us.

Frog Style

If we feel more confident about our ability to sit still, then we can place our hands in our lap, fingertips together as if we are in prayer; splay out our legs (frog-style); touch the soles of our feet together. Our legs will make a diamond shape. This allows the spine to act as a grounding rod, reaching into the earth via our bottom on the floor. Our hands and feet join our energy in a circuit that points outward. It is a symbol of connection while being open to external influence. The majority of what we do physically while in meditation is symbolic of our spiritual intentions. If we find our own comfortable variation on these themes, then we should consider the symbology of that position and allow our body to echo our spiritual intent.

Lying Down

It would be wrong to assume that all wildwitches are physically able to sit on the ground. If certain postures are uncomfortable for us, we should simply lie down, or sit with our body supported in a high-backed armchair. It is vital that the position we choose allows our body to firmly contact with the earth and allows our spine to act as the grounding rod (the trunk or channel). Hence lying down is acceptable but we may find the important tree visualisation to be discussed shortly hard to do while lying flat on the ground, because we associate the spine with the trunk and it is preferable, if physically possible, to echo this with an upright position. We must make sure that at all times we feel connected to earth—the solid manifest realms—while also feeling relaxed and comfortable.

Standing

Now, to a practical consideration. We will not always have time to do a formal protective act and there are a number of quick fixes that can be used when we need an instant way to attune to an energy or situation. Sometimes we will need to act with a moment's notice and there will be no time for sitting in silence. Such an instance may be when we enter an unknown building and are assailed by a rogue energetic presence. We would then apply the checking-out procedure we will discuss in chapter 4, but even before we do this we must be protected or we will risk being confused, hoodwinked, or even attacked on an energetic level. If a situation like this occurs, we simply affirm our connection to the earth beneath our feet and feel the power of our own energies running up and down our spine. We make the connection firmly in our mind and feel the strength that the connection gives to us, instantly. The more we practice this aspect of protection the more of a reflex reaction this connection will be. We will soon look at the complete quick-fix equation, but for now it is important to note that there will be times when we need to begin our protection while standing.

Stage Two: Breathing

This involves the relaxation of the body and the transition of our consciousness from an ordinary point of perception to a deeper level. First we close our eyes. We aim to have a clear mind, so we must let any extraneous thoughts drift across our awareness and evaporate clean away.

Next we take several (three minimum) slow, deep breaths. What constitutes a deep breath? The sort of breathing advocated in yoga is the one to apply here. We breathe in through the nose while inflating the abdomen. To practice, we can place our hands on our belly and feel the air physically inflate us like a balloon; or we can similarly visualise our belly expanding. Then we hold this air in our lungs for a few seconds, maintaining our physical comfort before we release, as long as we are able, the breath through the mouth. It helps to make a drawn out "pfhhh" sound and simultaneously let the belly deflate inward. Now we put our hands to our belly and feel it concave as it deflates completely. And again we imagine the balloon, only this time watching as it deflates slowly, pausing as long as is comfortable before taking another deep breath, and so on. This may feel opposing to normal breathing. It is common to associate the "in breath" with somehow pulling inward, and the convex, puffing out motion with exhaling. This said, breathing exercises can take a lot of practice. We should not feel downhearted if it takes a while to get into a rhythm.

The sound that our rhythmic breathing cycle makes is like the sea. We can imagine hearing the water coming in to the shore and being drawn back to the sea with each breath cycle. If we are able to tune in to this rushing, "whooshing" sound then it can be a great aid for relaxation and it can help our own body's drawing in and expelling of life-giving air. This breathing style can also be assimilated to a tree sucking up life-giving water through its roots. The lungs even physically resemble such a system in their complex inner branchings. Furthermore, the tree's vital connection to our life breath is obvious and should always be honoured.

Our breathing takes us deeper into a relaxed state and tunes us in to the inherent way our body takes in life-nourishing oxygen and releases waste in the form of carbon dioxide. We seldom breathe properly whilst engaged in human worldly pursuits, ending up with a shallow and unsatisfactory way of inhaling and exhaling. This breathing exercise will help us enormously. It centres us in the bodily processes while letting us experience the alchemical action of sucking in all that living energy, transmuting it and releasing it again. We can enjoy this sensation, and by keeping the mind clear we should not become tense. Our conscious human aspect will get impatient and want to distract us with all manner of mental trivia and will no doubt tell us that we have an itchy big toe, we need to feed the fish, and so on. To avoid such distractions we can let our thoughts waft away like smoke while focusing entirely on our rythmic breathing. The breathing is all that matters; we must become absorbed in it, slow it right down, and have a full awareness of it.

As well as slowing our heartrate and changing our brainwaves, we are aiming to let the body find a more restful pace; we are relaxing with the natural rhythm of our body's breath cycle in order to focus beyond daily human operations. The aim is to make it clear to mind, body, and spirit that something "not of this world" is happening. There shouldn't be any rush about the process. We can take as much time as we deem appropriate. If we find relaxation hard at first, as so many of us do, then we can connect to each area of the body, tensing it and letting the tension release until it is limp and slack. We can break to talk to a specific area, telling it what we are doing; informing our body that we are clenching that area to subsequently allow all tension to recede. We must remember to keep the deep, rhythmic breathing going at the same time! It is valuable in itself to connect with our temporary fleshy selves in such an intimate manner, for we are rarely so aware of how each bit of our valuable human "vehicle" feels to us. Being incarnate has many pleasurable facets that we never give ourselves time to appreciate and we can so easily slip into the mindset of "oh this old clumsy thing!" when we think of the body. Instead of such an attitude, we can think of our body as a sacred vessel. And we should spend ample preparation time for a spiritual journey in loving communion with our sacred vessel because it will transport our essential essence with incessant fortitude.

Stage Three: Visualisation

This involves seeing what we desire to become reality. Here, we wish to see ourselves protected in a suitable way.

Although we may feel that a suit of armour or a bearskin cloak may be very protective as symbols, it is vital that we remain within our energetic framework. The key to self-protection is organic substance—for we want to visualise a material that is flexible and will "give" in relation to our body. On a personal note, I was told initially by spiritual advisors that I could place myself inside a glass bubble for immediate psychic protection and this worked at a time when I was so bombarded with unwanted spiritual intrusions that I was desperate for some help. I can now see from experience that such glass barriers may not be terribly healthy. Placing the astral self inside a substance or structure that has an inability to respond or move with the astral form itself is restrictive. This can deaden any interaction and can also feel unpleasantly alien.

I would recommend the use of such an impervious and unyielding structure as glass only in cases of profound psychic attack—hopefully such instances will not crop up very often in the wildwitch's lifetime. I have only had to resort to the "when all else fails" measure once in latter years. No matter how skilled we are, we can sometimes find ourselves out of our own personal depth and in need of external help with a psychic situation. It is then that the hard and rigid bubble can come in very handy.

With the tree exercise that we will encounter shortly, we will visualise a beautiful auric field, rather like the gaseous cloak of the atmosphere that Earth herself wears as a protective layer. The golden cloak of energy moves with the tree, not acting as a casing but as a numinous garment that is tailored to fit, created of little material substance but still of profound vibrational relevance. As the tree breathes, so does the cloak swell and recede, echoing any movement with its energetic resonance. The colour, the consistency, and the sound (which we shall move on to in a moment) all help to make the secure nebulous cloak of energy around us.

With our understanding that the protective sphere (suit, bubble, or cloak) should be a material that breathes with us, like a natural fibre but more ethereal, we can move on to looking at examples. First it is good to know that our subtle energy field, which emanates from our living body and reflects our spiritual being, will not be damaged but it can certainly be muffled and made to feel distinctly "clammy" in an energetic sense. It is good for us to use different methods in different circumstances and the method we choose will also be dependent on our personal sense of safety.

The Cloak

We may adapt the golden auric field as an actual head to toe cloak to don, complete with a deep transparent hood that falls forward over our face. The hood or full face cap acts as a cover but is not too stiflingly. We can use our imagination but something like a balaclava may suffice. The cloak is a good option if we feel the need to cover as much of our astral selves as possible. We can imagine a suit made out of a light, bright, spangled airy substance. It may fit like a second layer of skin that we step into, rather like a one-piece stretchy romper or an astronaut's suit. The only difference between us visualising our garments and actually putting on physical cloth is that our protective cloak is made of light and energy and sound. It is not dense, choking fabric. It doesn't matter how delicate the fabric of our protective garment is, or even if we see it more as a cloud covering than a cloak. It is only important that it is shining and luminous.

The Bubble

The idea of a bubble is an excellent one as long as the bubble is flexible, not solid like glass, and covers us from head to toe in a bright protective glow. Think of a soap bubble blown by a child out of a hoop on a wand, and imagine it wobble delicately, reflecting the light beautifully. This bubble would be more egg-shaped, perhaps, due to the inherent energy field of the bodies that we currently wear. A "cosmic egg" shape is very resonant as it can remind us of our human origin as well as our spiritual hatching from the greater All. We can pop ourselves inside such a glowing bubble at any time when we are in a place that is crowded, "charged up" with an individual who creates a bad atmosphere, or in a place where we feel "out of our element," such as a city centre at rush hour, a badly designed building without adequate windows or ventilation, or a place where unpleasant events have occurred.

The Third Eye

A quick protective fix can also be achieved by placing a symbol over the third eye. Not slap-bang on it, but over it, at a distance that feels comfortable. If we place our hand some twelve inches away from the front of the third eye, slightly above but between the brows, and bring it in slowly, we will notice that there will come a point when we begin to feel discomfort, a kind of sick dizzy sensation, perhaps. This indicates how "open" we are, how much energy our psychically active region of the third eye is emitting. The closer our hand gets to the third eye, the less open we are. Consequently, this tells us how much life force may be leaking out from our third eye, which would make us less effective than we could be.

We must approach this sensitive area with great respect and delicacy. We do not want to cover this area too invasively when we wish to be pyschically open. As wildwitches we prefer to be open to spirit communication and surrounding energies as much as possible in order to gain insight and guidance. However, as a protective measure it is necessary to close down a little now and then. We will discuss "opening up" and "closing down" momentarily.

It is important to note here that in some traditions there is a physical symbol that is placed on the third eye to manifestly represent this mystic area. This nicely interrelates the physical and ethereal aspects of the third eye. The symbol is often a holy dot, or *bindi*, and it is believed to be a possible outlet for potent energy, which an experienced person may release into the world for different magical reasons. Also, it is believed that the bindi may be placed between the eyebrows to retain energy in the body. So it is in this belief that a physical symbol may represent an opened or closed third eye, whereas I am suggesting to only use a symbol in this area when you wish to close down completely. It is good to work with symbolic styles that resonate well with our personal feelings and this is why I have presented other opinions here.

The Star

I personally favour a shining star as a protective symbol, which I see as a spiritual sun that none with harmful intent can bear to see. I do not place this right on my forehead but I imagine it to be hovering a few inches in front of my third eye, beaming out a light that will blind any who approach me with a less-than-scrupulous motive. Sometimes I see this as a silver star, freshly forged and glowing white-hot. Others who come in peace, for my greater good, will find the light welcoming, not overpowering. Such symbols are entirely personal, just make sure that they are luminous and numinous. These may include silver pentacles, equal-armed crosses, a lucky clover, a horseshoe, or roses with petals opened. The symbol may be placed near the brow to reflect away all harmful thoughts and presences.

Placement

Such glowing symbols can cover any major energy portal on the body. For instance, if it was felt that some force or entity was attacking our ability to communicate, then placing our chosen shining symbol over the throat area would be appropriate. The seven main energy portals on the body are called *chakras* in some Eastern traditions; although, I like to think that these centres along the body's "spiritual leyline" are like the great places of power on the body of Mother Earth and I therefore think of them as power points by which we may access profound energies. These power points on the body connect to form the serpent/dragon energy that travels up and down our spine. It is the same energy we will be raising and allowing to travel downward in our tree visualisation, the very same energy that a tree has moving up and down its own "spine."

What is so important about these areas? Well, where there is power there is also vulnerability to attack. We have more to lose from our energy centres than from other areas of our bodies and this is why we may feel the need to give them an extra boost of symbolic protection.

The word "chakra" may not resonate with us as wildwitches. The overriding belief may be that the word restricts power points to only certain areas when, for us, it is well to refer to any point that we intuitively feel is important and energetically powerful on our spirit body. When we progress in our work we may well gain the ability to perceive the aura around all living beings and so we may have our own direct knowledge of how such energy centres relate to different people. There are many specialist books written on the subject of chakras already. For now, I will say that the body has the following major points, which the reader may like to refer to when performing a protective act. Eventually, it will be far more appropriate to get an individual sense of our points of power. The table below is best approached as a guide.

Region of Body	Energy Involved	Colour
Root/Base of Spine	Earthlink, life force, fight/flight	Red
Sacral/Lower Abdomen	Sexual vitality, emotions	Orange
Solar Plexus/Navel	Personal power, confidence	Yellow
Heart	Love, peace, compassion	Green
Throat	Communication, expression "in the world"	Blue
Third Eye/Brow	Psychic sight, intuition, inner vision	Indigo
Crown/Top of Head	Connection to spirit, thought, imagination	Violet

When considering these energy centres on the body it is also sometimes appropriate to "open" and "close" them. For this, the best exercise is to imagine petals on a flower opening and closing. We may simply wish to have the petals at our third-eye portal closed up, like a daisy at night, to stop any extraneous influence in a particularly difficult environment. Or we may like to deliberately open our third eye when in the safe space of a meditative journey. Once we are within a protective space, at the beginning of a trance journey, we can open each portal in turn. We can then close them at the end of our journey as we ground ourselves. This should be done before going about our daily business in the world. We will begin with the base (red flower) and work up to the crown for opening ourselves. And begin with the crown (violet flower) and work down to our base portal for closing ourselves. Such symbolic acts are potent reminders of our own connection to the earth on which we walk. Our bodies have places of power just like the ancestral sacred sites we observe in the landscape, and it is appropriate to seal them or allow them to flower open as the situation dictates.

Color

We may like to use the appropriate chakra colour for each protective symbol, as I have done in the above example. However, sticking to shining metallic shades or simply using a shade made of light will suffice. We may wish to study other traditional approaches before settling on a specific color. Using our own intuition is all important and having faith in that is vital.

While we are looking at the symbolic nature of colour in our work, we should acknowledge the bright and beautiful blue that is often associated with protection, spiritual strength, and great inner peace. This is the hue much like the blue that we are used to seeing in the paintings of the Madonna. The Virgin Mary's cloak symbolically represents all of the traits we desire for protection. The colours of a candle flame are important as well; the dazzlingly pure electric blue and bright shimmering gold are perfect for protective spheres. As long as the gold or blue is shining and possibly full of reflecting spangles of light, rather like glitter or tiny fragments of mirror, then our safety procedure has been done appropriately. Remember that energy dances, it is alive.

Sound

The power of a quick invocation or statement of intent should never be underestimated. It is possible to utilise sound for a quick burst of protective energy. We can use simple powerful statements and chants if we are in a hurry:

I stand within my sphere of golden light.
May only those who come for the purpose of
my greatest good speak with me here.
So may it be!

Or chant:

Let none enter this bright space
Let none look on my spiritual face,
'Less they come in love and shine with grace,
If not, may they go from this place!

Such affirmations will be of great help if we are in a situation where time is of the essence. To state that we are in our protective light, in whatever form it usually takes, will help the protective sphere take shape around us. The more we do the work, the clearer this protective milieu will come to us, instantly if needs be, and our confidence in the statement of intent will grow accordingly. This said, sound can also be utilised for the longer spiritual journey, in which a profound protection is needed. For both instances, a basic understanding of sound visualisation is needed.

To apply sound as a means of spiritual protection, we simply "tune into" (strongly visualise) the colour of our protective field. We can imagine we are searching for a signal amongst the static, as with a radio or television. Everything has its own frequency that we as wildwitches can learn to detect and one way that we can train ourselves is to envisage a shape or hue and then "hear" the noise it would make in our imagination. For example, when we picture a black triangle in our mind's eye we can probably perceive that it wouldn't emit the same pitch as a pale green circle.

One need not be an opera singer, nor an art therapist, to make the tone that a colour or shape suggests. For protection purposes we are obviously searching for a tone that suggests bright clarity, purity, and strength. It could be a sound like a metal instrument striking crystal glass, a kind of resonant "ting"; the chime of a brass bell, or it may be a long, high vowel sound kept at one pitch ("aaaaaaa"). We can either make this noise aloud, in our mind, or physically create it using an instrument like a tin whistle or chimes. We simply fit the colour and lightness of our protective sphere with a suitably bright, high tone.

At first this may feel a little embarrassing, especially if music is not on our list of talents, but we should play with the idea. Even if we cannot physically "hear" a colour, we can imagine a nice, clear, pure sound and then create a similar sound that feels most comfortable. This exercise is certainly not essential but it can really help. The tone can be used to such a degree as to create the effect of resonant ripples. Often when I make my own protective sound—just a long drawn-out "mmmmmm" at a reasonably high pitch—I can hear it echo and reverberate for quiet some time afterward, which gives me the sense that I have cleared the energies all around me and my intent has spread out far from me, like radio waves travelling into space, vibrating on and on with a clear and positive resonance.

Even if we cannot trust our human ear enough to hear our own sound, we should imagine sound emitting from our protective layer. If we can imagine it clearly and often, it will be so. We can also attempt to see the coloured ripples of clear sound spread out around us in concentric circles, getting ever wider apart and fainter, until they disappear from view. We may not hear a thing but we know that the colour and shape suggest the perfect tone and pitch for us and that, on some level, it is heard. Sounds can be the bridge we need between our physical aspect and our spiritual aspect. They let the ethereal intentions of our eternal self travel beyond us while originating from our human form.

The "Quick Fix" Equation

To be protected instantly, understand that focused visualisation plus a statement of intent equals change. If we state and actually see with our imagination, or "mind's eye," that something is so, then it is so astrally. We are protected "above and below." We have effected a change on this Earthly level, where the energies are pliable. Such is the basis of all our magic. We can be protected almost instantly if we truly focus on what we wish to achieve. The more we practice our protection during longer mediations, or in more suitable settings, then the more faith we will have and the quicker off the mark we will be. It will be our second nature, like putting on clothes before we leave the house.

The "quick fix" routine for the wildwitch in a hurry or on the move would be "rooting, breathing, cloaking." The rooting can be backed up with an invocation for connection, which can be a few lines stating our intent. We could refer to this also as a focus point. A piece of word magic can get us into the required frame of mind very quickly and remind us of our focus. Obviously we don't have to enunciate the words out loud, but repeating the verse up to three times can really set it firmly as reality. An example of what we may say at this juncture may be:

> *Like the tree I bond with soil,*
> *Beneath my feet the root is strong,*
> *And up my spine the power goes,*
> *And through the trunk the life force flows,*
> *Up through the heartwood to the crown,*
> *Up to the leaves and then back down.*

Next we take three measured, deep breaths and envision the protective sphere of light around us. If we are familiar with the use of symbols, then we can intuit where it is best to place one on our astral self. Sound is also very handy if we are now adept at hearing a tone inside our head, or if we feel confident enough to actually vocalise the sound as we take our breaths and visualise. The main thing is to state our intention, get ourselves protected, and then assert that we are protected by ending with a short affirmation of this fact. This can take a couple of minutes maximum and the more it is practised at leisure as part of our work, the more we will be ready to do it on the hop.

Since we are never alone on the wildwitch's path, asking spirits directly for assistance is another effective way to root and cloak ourselves. The spirits must be approached in a reverent and appropriately worded way. Even if, at this stage, we do not know who our companion (guiding) spirits are, we can still ask them for help by acknowledging their existence. Whether or not we perceive them, they exist. When we know their names and have a good working friendship established with them, all the better. For now, we could send out a prayer such as:

> *Spirits who come for my highest good, hear me,*
> *Companions who guide me, I ask you to shield me,*
> *Spirits who come for my greatest good, heed me,*
> *Protect me with love as I ask you to help me!*

Grounding

We must always ground ourselves after psychically opening up to external energies. We refer to this as "closing down." Although, as wildwitches, we are never fully closed down, we need to reconnect with the manifest levels, regaining a sense of place within our bodies and in our environs. Grounding is an act of bonding with the physical plane that we have all made a commitment to by being incarnate beings. It draws a line underneath the otherworldly interaction and states that we are once again fully present in our human role. In doing this, we can state: "The work is done."

We may find it especially hard to establish this if we have been off on a particularly long and involved or amazingly enjoyable trance journey. Even if we have only opened up briefly to check out an atmosphere in a disturbed area, we need to ground ourselves afterward.

The easiest and quickest way to do so is by physical activity, such as stamping the feet, clapping the hands, or eating and drinking a little. A cup of something hot and a biscuit is appropriate for grounding. Writing notes is also a good grounding activity. A very simple way to ground is by placing our hands flat and directly on the earth. As we do so, we can state something like:

> *She who sustains us welcomes me back,*
> *I touch her body, skin to skin,*
> *Back down to Earth with a stomp and a clap,*
> *I am returned and back within!*

At this time, if we have used the protective gesture of placing opened flowers (usually roses or lotuses) at each "power point" on our energetic bodies, we can now go through the process in reverse, closing the petals on each flower and sealing the energy centres securely against any further energetic interaction at this time. From a personal perspective, I used to see such protective flowers as being made of brightly painted wood, and when I closed the petals I saw that they interlocked like a child's wooden jigsaw puzzle, leaving no gaps. That felt secure and very grounding.

If we forget to do this simple concluding act we can feel nauseated, confused, light-headed, or dizzy and disoriented. We have left ourselves too open and have not "come back" to the current manifest reality fully. The aforementioned feelings occur because we are being buffeted by energies. It is like leaving the door open so that the wind comes in and knocks over our belongings and whips at our body, trying to carry us off our feet. We must "close the door" to some degree and specifically make that link with our body.

Not being "fully in one's body" can be a curious sensation and, if we are prone to escapist tendencies into otherworldly reveries, can become a way of life that leaves us strangely disconnected, our memories of reality vague for prolonged periods. A good way of curing this and encouraging our spirits to be fully present in the manifest human form we have taken, is to place the palm of our active hand on the forehead, fingers on the scalp, and gently massage the area. If we are diligent about grounding ourselves then we will never run the risk of becoming floaty and only semipresent in the world.

When we feel secure and confident about our protective "drill," we may want to move on to the next phase, which incorporates so much of what we have already discussed here eloquently. It is a perfect system for making ourselves ready for inner work. We can always choose to use the threefold system (placement, breathing, visualisation), as discussed above, for times when we need to immediatly interact with whatever is happening around us energetically. The tree visualisation described below allows for the process to unfold more slowly and can be highly satisfying if employed before a trance journey or preplanned spellwork. It is a beautiful and suitable tool for the wildwitch to employ.

The Tree Visualisation

The tree crops up again and again in the wildwitches work and it is the mainstay of our world in more ways than one. Not only is it the primary life-giver of oxygen and the representative of a balanced way of being, but it is analogous to how we make our connection between Earth and sky. More than this, the tree provides a symbolic way of moving between the worlds, which we can employ when we become familiar and comfortable with the concepts involved in this visualisation.

The visualisation has two purposes, the first is to root us, for protection, and the second is to avail us to external energies above and around us. Trees have chosen to be "the standing nation," although, perhaps this was not always the case! At any rate, we currently witness these wise healing beings as fixed and solid. Yet they are also more than a little mysterious, having immense power drawn up from the sustaining Earth and down from the heavens. Trees are special teachers, much beloved by our kind.

As a note at this juncture, it is well to remember that our work comes from an animistic perspective and so we will always engage with our teachers, be they in plant, mineral, or animal form, with respect for their own individual energies—they are living energies that are no greater or lesser than our own, only different. These are our relations on the Earthwalk and our allies in spiritual work. Ours is certainly not a humancentric work and at no time should we adhere to teachings advocating a hierarchy when it comes to a spiritual ascendancy of beings.

To begin our tree visualisation, we should be physically positioned correctly for a trance journey and be rhythmically breathing. Then we can concentrate on both connecting to the sustaining ground beneath us and linking in to spirit above. Spirit is, of course, not in one place, like a biblical heaven in the sky, but all around us and within us. Here we speak symbolically, referring to above and below, upper and lower, for the purpose of creating an effective dynamic. For the purpose of this exercise, we will express spirit as being in the "above" position for simplicity. We are acting as the conduit to transmit and transmute energy between two levels of existence—the manifest and the ethereal. As we can literally feel the manifest below us then we can easily relate to the spiritual realms as being above.

When we root ourselves into the Earth reality, that which holds us for the duration of an incarnation, we make certain that we are aware of that manifest connection; the wild craft is not an excuse to forget our bodily selves altogether. We have chosen to be here for the Earthwalk and we should not forget that present reality. This element is often missing from primary spiritual instruction resulting in spirituality and the development of our inherent awareness being open to both retreat from the world and ascension from it. As wildwitches, we acknowledge our chosen path and do not seek to flee from our responsibilities, but we wish to expand upon our resouces; we are also not attempting to rise above our daily manifest being so as to be better than any other people currently joining us on the Earthwalk.

The best way to do these three things at once—root manifestly, connect universally, breathe rhythmically—is to imagine that our human host body is a tree. As we have discussed, trees are the most perfect representatives of earthed spirituality, their trunks connecting the leafy boughs that stretch skyward, seeking the life-giving energy of the sun's light, while the roots dig deep, maintaining that essential grounding connection. Trees show us that it is possible to be solidly present in the world (as we have all chosen to be at this time) and yet spiritually open. We need not favour one or the other way of being.

Indeed, if a tree was in denial of its roots it would not be fed or kept upright for long, and if it ceased to find connection with the sunlight in the spiritual "above" position it would not have the energy it needed to maintain its healthy existence. Our body, like the fine example that trees share with us, is a channel for perfect balance between both states. And we should aspire, beyond all other ways of being, to be balanced.

In this instance, we will perceive our body as having the same capabilities as a tree. We can spend time in wonder as we consider our own complex inner systems working in harmony to house our spirit and to enable it to have Earth experiences. We relate our own spine to a tree's trunk; think of it carrying energy and information to the brain, which has many complex nerve endings branching out like a tree canopy. Similarly, we witness our spine continuing down, as if it has a prehensile tail, pushing into the earth like a great taproot. Now we see all the nerve endings coming from this central spine point and twisting and twining their way into the soil beneath us like subsidiary roots. Roots may also sprout from the soles of the feet. We can visualise them pushing the dark earth aside as they wriggle to find purchase and imagine the gentle scuffling sound they create as they stretch and find their place of security among small stones and carapaced creatures.

There is no need to worry if we haven't literally got the earth beneath us. On a personal note, I myself currently live in a first floor flat and have to imagine the soil, which is far below me, as if it were indeed pressing up against my body's base, supporting and energising me. Remember, our work here is all about visualisation, symbolism, and intent. Remember also that it is very beneficial to get out into the landscape and actually feel the soil directly beneath us as often as we can.

As we breathe in, we feel our sap (vital energy) rising up to our leafy boughs, out around our head, stretching up toward the light. Then we feel and see this light strongly above and all around us and feel the roots of our hair straining upward with the irresistible urge to reach the light. We are being pulled up toward it, growing closer to its warming, illuminating source, yet our position is firm and rooted. The light that enfolds us, nurtures us, and urges us to spread our great branches out and upward is clear, bright, and golden yellow. It shimmers, seeming to contain tiny reflective fragments like glitter or infinitesimal pieces of mirror caught in its glow. It is like sunlight but this is the brightest, purest light that we have ever witnessed. It is warm, strong, and, above all, protective. It is alive.

As we breathe out we feel the energy pull down into our taproot and push deep into the ground beneath us. We pull the golden light of protection down into us and all around us and then let it rise again as we breathe in. This golden sparkling light should keep spreading around our vast branch system above (around all that extends from us, travels away from us, and eventually connects us to the universal energies), and should surround our root system, which reflects the shape and size of our branches above. We become a mirror image of ourselves, above and below the Earth's surface, surrounded by this protective dancing light. This reflects the magical maxim "As above, so below." This means that whatever is in the seen world finds its refection in the unseen.

We may understand at this point why it is appropriate to sit upright, if possible, in order for that sense of above and below to be experienced fully. Once we slow our breathing we can imagine our glowing protective aura, which advances and recedes with every breath, as an organic cloak of shining light. The light is enveloping our trunk as it rains down from above. We feel our roots searching for water in the loam beneath us.

We are now completely surrounded, above and below, by glittering golden light. We are anchored into the Earth level and yet open to the spiritual realms. We may like to accompany this visualisation with an affirmation, something like:

> *I surround myself with protective golden light,*
> *Each time I breathe in, it swells,*
> *Each time I breathe out, it recedes.*
> *I am in the light, it is part of me,*
> *I am rooted like the greatest tree,*
> *I am protected, so may it be!*

It is worth noting here that the protective glow we "see" around our person, or know to be there, does not mean that we see the world through a golden mist. No, it means that it exists on a profound level as an energetic shield, not a literal cloak. We are in the realm of subtle energies. Our visualised (perceived) protective layer will fade away if it is not replenished. Of course, if we spent time making it strong and bright then it will not fade until long after we have completed the work.

The World Tree

As backup to our tree visualisation and as a confirmation of our intended relationship with these venerable beings, it is important to understand the concept of the World Tree. The World Tree is familiar to many indigenous cultures. It is sometimes referred to as the *axis mundi*, the pivotal point that the universe turns around, which links the Underworld via "middle" Earth and the heavens by means of roots, trunk, and branches, respectively. This axis mundi makes the all-important power circuit between Earth and sky possible. Not only this, it makes the vital connection between the spirits above, those from the sky with an airy quality; the physical creatures in the middle, including humanity dwelling on the surface, the area that consists of what is considered to be "real," as it is tangible; and the denizens of the hidden aspects of below Earth, those who are inside the Earth and that represent the mysterious Faery element.

With the World Tree, the heights and depths are bridged by living wood. We can relate these dimensions to aspects of ourselves, to our deep unconscious aspects, the roots of all things kept in the darkness of ourselves; the vulnerable yet strong core that keeps us together in the world; and up to the inspiring heights, to the spiritual light we aspire to reintegrate and rekindle in ourselves. We can seek to "bring up" the hidden from the depths of ourselves, and shed some light on these hidden truths in the manifest world by gaining spiritual guidance from "higher" external sources. Higher does not refer to the top of a hierarchy but rather to something that is removed from our own earthed perspective.

The World Tree is represented differently in many cultures. In the ancient northern European mythos, the ash was considered to be the World Tree, the evergreen Yggdrasil being the most famous of these. Perhaps this is because the ash has roots that grow particularly deep and spread for some distance around the tree itself, while its branches grow upward and touch the sky. Also, the ash can produce flowers of either gender on one tree, thus lending itself further to representing unity and harmony in the universe. However, the apple and oak have been similarly revered in the Celtic tradition, perhaps for their strength, protection, longevity, or ability to bear the fruits of love. This is the love that makes the world go round in all spiritual belief systems.

After having bonded with a tree out in the landscape or in a garden we can work with the World Tree concept in a way that feels real to us. We can experience the interconnectedness of all life within ourselves. Our tree visualisation aids this process. Finding our own living representative of the World Tree to give us a magical focus in our daily lives is very beneficial, and undertaking both a physical and trance journey to discover our manifest and otherworldly representatives of this tree is recommended. This should be done once we are able to undertake inner work safely and after we have positively opened ourselves to an energetic dialogue with an independent sylvan-spirited being who could join us on our journey.

Before we do so, it may well be appropriate to state that trees are individuals. Even within species that may have certain group attributes, each tree will have a different way of expressing itself in accordance with its distinct personality. For example, it would be rather racist to assume that all hazels are alike. They may all be fundamentally concerned with knowledge or healing, but they each have unique quirks. To make such assumptions is as outmoded as suggesting that all Asian or Caucasian peoples are the same. I myself know of two ash trees on opposite sides of a Faery hill who have quite diverse roles and very dissimilar personalities.

Some trees are wholly reticent, others gregarious and full of fun, others dour and menacing. For us, the real pleasure comes with being able to make that bond after the ages that humanity has spent considering trees as nothing but mute insensitive timber.

Sacred Landscape

With so much emphasis on trees in the wildwitch's work it makes perfect sense to not only consider but to positively seek out places to work out of doors as often as possible. In doing so we can bring greater depth, colour, and meaning to our work by becoming one with the land and her cycles, breathing that verdant energy into our very souls in order to be more effective, more alive. We end that terrible estrangement from the rest of nature that humanity feels by having a friendship, a kinship of profound poetic beauty, with a green place that is special to us.

Now that we know much more about our protection and what it entails, as well as how energy works, we are in a better position to decide intuitively and practically where it will be appropriate for us to practice our craft. And if it is appropriate with us, we want to make sure it is also appropriate for the land we choose. All our interactions are based on the consideration that we cannot simply force our will on another living being or energy and so it needs to be a two-way decision. Perhaps we already have a place that attracts us. If so, the next stage is to go beyond its aesthetic appeal and experience its energetic response to us, to hear it speak with its own distinct voice.

The place we are in search of will be our *nemeton*, which is a Gaelic term for "sanctuary." It is like a church, only it is not made with human hands. We hear a lot about natural sacred sites, yet a wildwitch knows that everything is sacred as it all derives from the one source and no exceptions occur in this. All things, places, and beings deserve some degree of reverence. However, we can make things "holy" in a human sense, interacting with a particular place to consecrate it further. Interaction is not to be confused with control. We would not bend a particular place to our will but we would merge with it for a shared end, a greater good. Although the whole of the natural world is blessed, we can help bless it anew with the permission of the genius loci of the place, the spiritual essence that governs and resonates with the land, and the site's ethereal guardian—its *nemetona*. We can work with this spirit to ensure that our sanctuary is kept free of both material and psychic human litter and clear of any unpleasant memories that the land may hold from a human event in its past. In honour of its real beauty, we make it a haven for ourselves and a safe place for spiritual guests and wildlife.

When we learn how to commune effectively with otherworldly beings, we can undertake specific journeys whilst sitting on the sacred land. For now, at this stage, it is well to find a spot that appeals to us and visit it frequently, observing its nature whilst unobtrusively practising our protection routine. It is particularly satisfying to practice the deep breathing exercise in our chosen area. We can take in the pure air, permeated by the special scents of each season that are unique to this place. It is wonderful to feel for the first time the thrill of doing the tree visualisation outside, truly experiencing the power surging up through us as the heartbeat of the Earth pounds beneath us and the buzzard cries overhead. There is nothing more satisfying to us as wildwitches than to have the evocative aroma of wet woodland in the nostrils whilst hearing the leaves whisper together, perhaps caressing our face occasionally as they fall. It is direct, potent, and effecting. It is the essence of our natural enchantment.

We should always walk lightly upon the site we choose to visit and leave only footprints. We should "make badger tracks" (make our intention to connect with the place known by going there repeatedly) in peace and with a sense of positive purpose, gently forging a link just as the badger does as he repeatedly flattens the grass on his nightly food runs. Our badger tracks build power, our intents to connect with the place on a deeper spiritual level become shining strands on the web of life to be seen by those who guard the site and dwell there. This visiting gives advance notice of our intentions and gives the residents a chance to show how they feel about us. We can sense the changes in atmosphere as we approach, perhaps, or feel a certain welcome or unease as we sit quietly on the ground.

Have we observed a crop of inhospitable thistles growing up where we like to sit? Do we trip over what we assume is an exposed tree root only to find that there was nothing in our path? Or, does a robin alight on a low branch to sing to us as we arrive? We can read the subtler signs in the atmosphere that tell us if we are desired as company. If we use our wildwitch's ability to observe whilst being fully sensate, we can interact practically with our surroundings. It is well to remember that they are not only "surroundings" (in the sense of scenery to our human endeavours) but energies that interact and experience life just as we do. The spirit of the place, and its attendant residents, can become our companions in a very real sense.

Once we have made contact spiritually we can begin to engage practically, leaving organic offerings suitable for the spirits and denizens, as they desire such acknowledgement. These are gifts for our new friends. We will cover gifts in chapter 5. For now, try to get out, practice what we have covered so far as much as you can, and remember to use an innate sensitivity to gauge the right place to frequent.

It is advisable to pick a place that is not considered to be a "sacred site" with a capital S, that is, a place that has been honoured in the past by humans who built shrines or monuments upon it. Such places include circles of stone, chambered cairns, and hillforts of our ancestors. As mentioned earlier, these locations are regularly visited by other magical folk as well as curious tourists, and therefore may have too much external energy put into them, energy that is not all beneficial. We need to know that in our sanctuary we aim to be largely undisturbed both in terms of energy and human interference and so prescribed sacred sites are largely unsuitable. Besides this, we do not know the original intents for some sites. Informed guesswork and psychic information aside, we may not know what the sites were used for nor whether the intent behind the site was positive or negative. This is yet another reason why it is not appropriate to work at such a place. We need to know that we are not going against the land, which may have long ago been consecrated for some entirely dissimilar purpose to our own. We should use our own discernment and pick a new place of power that inspires us personally. It is a good exercise to use our intuition rather than relying on someone else to designate a special site for us.

Sacred Safe Place

Here we are visualising our own Garden of Eden just as earlier we were seeking its manifest counterpart—our sanctuary in the world—and we will make it exist on an etheric level by our focused will, our clear intent, and our ability to visualise it in our imagination. It will be a place where we would feel totally safe doing the subsequent otherworldly (astral) work that we will undertake as wildwitches. This is a once-removed reality from the cluttered human astral, which buzzes around our very human aspects all day, every day. We are going deeper into the realms of the unseen, beyond the regions of temporary thought. We actively seek the place within us to access a more profound understanding. By reflection, we seek all that is without us, delving deep in the hidden weft and warp. In a protected state, we breathe deeply and we focus on reaching such a place. We actively intend to be there, even if we do not know its physical location.

We have our physical eyes shut but we must open our mind's eye in order to observe our sacred inner landscape. We must "see" by using our intuition as a guide and by envisioning all that we wish to engage with. Because this level of existence is made of the same pliable energetic material as the human astral plane, we are going to work with this environment, as the cocreator, to shape it to our own ends. Basically, we will use the blank canvas of our internal vision to imagine, creating an image that will become an astral reality. We will create a safe place in the universe that is uniquely ours.

Blocked Imagination

I will pause here for a moment to relate with those who find it difficult to visualise. Although it helps enormously to be able to perceive what we are creating in glorious technicolour, we can also witness it by feeling the feelings we want to invoke in our safe and sacred landscape, or by simply stating that certain things are so and knowing that they are. For example, while some of us are able to visualise each petal of a stunning blossom created on an apple tree in our safe space, others may remember what an apple blossom smells like or feels like to the touch. Still others may only be able to declare: "There is an apple tree here." I cannot honestly say that this latter approach would work indefinitely but certainly initially, to find our feet in the visualisation process, it can be helpful. Naming what we desire to see and feeling the beauty in our soul may eventually trigger an inner image.

The more we can connect with our imagined safe place, be this visually, emotionally, or in a more tactile sense, the more it becomes an astral reality. The more personal energy and focus we put into this place, the more it takes form, the more "real" it becomes. We must think of it as a tangible place even if we cannot see it all yet. Remember that in the etheric realms, what we think or state will become reality. The process is similar to that of making a clay pot and the outcome is just as much a visual statement. Our safe place in the astral plane is created from mysterious and flexible ether, which is an energetic equivalent of fine clay. We are the potters and if for now we have to work "blind," then we can feel our way, strengthening our ability to pick up the patterns and shapes of all we encounter. Likewise, if we cannot envision our safe place, then we can just describe our landscape, over and over, and it will begin to take form.

If we really do have a block on visualising, perhaps it is worth asking ourselves if we have ever been described as an unimaginative sort of person. If we have been told this, then it is a thought well worth banishing. Who has not pictured a loved one's face in their absence, or imagined what's for supper (replete with associated smells), or day-dreamed an ideal partner or a scenario in which personal success is achieved? To get back into this daydreaming mode, where the emphasis is on playful and relaxed visu-alisation, we can try thinking about hopes we have for ourselves. Or we can delve into our memories to remember past incidents we enjoyed. Is it possible to tap into such memories without seeing images?

If we truly cannot see any images when we daydream or reminisce on past experi-ences, we can try picturing simple and familiar objects; for example, toothbrushes or cups. We can look at the object and then remember it. Then, we close our eyes and use our memory to see the object. We'll soon find that we are visualising! Is the pear in our mind as real as the pear on the table? If not, this simple exercise can continue to improve our visualisation over time. We should try using different objects; as we do so, we can increase the amount of detail to remember.

Before we begin to become the landscape gardener and architect of our safe place in this fantastic inner realm, we must first know who we are and therefore what sort of place would suit us ideally. Do we want a predominantly watery landscape, maybe even a coastal spot? Perhaps we would prefer to begin at a high altitude, in a mountain range; or, maybe climate is equally important as design and tropical weather seems just right. We should focus on our essential wildwitch nature and reflect that aspect of ourselves in our list of attributes for an ideal place. We can think of this creation as nothing less than a reflection of ourselves. We should play with combinations of landscape features and see what appeals to us. Maybe we can even use some magazines to help us make a collage, a montage of images showing all the sorts of places we may like to spend time. Or, we can write a list. Then we want to work out how we could blend this seamlessly together to make a place that feels friendly, familiar, and real to us.

We can utilise actual Earthly places when we create our landscape; we simply adjust them slightly to be more personalised. This means that we put more of our own self and energies into the work, rather than simply replicating what we already know. We should be aware that when we use actual locations from "real life" in creating an astral safe place, the real place may be energetically affected. It is better to create an imaginary landscape that is inspired by, not lifted directly from, the manifest world. We should just use favourite places as a guide to trigger more personal responses.

Another point to address is the elements. We should try to include an aspect from each elemental way if we can. Even if, for instance, water is the element that makes us feel most at home, we can try to include an area in our sacred place that feels earthy (perhaps a cave), airy (such as a clifftop path), and fiery (something that has a warm, glowing feel, maybe a place where we can build a fire or perhaps something more symbolic, a bush with red blooms or a copper beech tree with fiery coloured leaves). We shouldn't be too bound by this but we should try to have a balance; a safe place that is all water and no land may be a pretty unbalancing sensation and certainly our land's visitors (spirits who we talk to, be they invited or not) may find it rather hard going if their own elemental way is not completely watery.

Here is a starter list to inspire us. These are features that I have incorporated into my own safe astral places at one time or another:

Waterfall	Sandy cove
Clearing in a copse of trees (grove)	Standing stone/dolmen
Hollow hill	Stream with stepping stones
River with canoe	Mystical greenwood
Hollow oak tree	Crystal cave
Rocky outcrop	Reed bed
Well	Field of corn
Lightning tree	Faery ring
Wildflower meadow	Dunes

We may notice a magical slant—not as in spellcasting and witchery but as in fantastic and enchanting—to some of these suggestions. I have been known to describe the otherworldly or astral safe place as *Alice in Wonderland* meets *National Geographic* magazine. I encourage potential wildwitches to similarly create a place that incorporates the fairytale element of existence. It may be inspirational to look at my *Waking the Wild Spirit Tarot* (Llewellyn 2002) as this is packed full of such imagery from mystical, mythical folk stories and it took its inspiration from my own otherworldly journeys and encounters. We are aiming to escape the mundane and to create a vibrant and wonderful reality when we sculpt our inner landscape. That is, of course, if we feel happy with such an idea. I cannot prevent anyone from making a safe place grim and forboding, or rough and inhospitable, for such a place may actually suit one's nature!

Most people feel happy with the idea that there is somewhere in the universe where the sun always shines, the unicorn still lives, and the water is crystal clear and drinkable; well, such is the flexibility of the "etheric" astral level. We can mould the flexible energy to bring the vision ever closer to reality. Bringing the magic back to human life by engaging in the creation of such enchanted inner landscapes can be an act of great service to the All. Our world, which is rapidly becoming removed from such a lush idealism, needs a little rebalancing. If we create an astral reality, a little of that energy gets reflected in this manifest realm. Thus, we act as the link between the two energetic planes of existence. We are crafting this place for our own pleasure, yet it cannot help but affect the universal energies. "As within, so without."

Can such a place of beauty exist if the universe is populated by unscrupulous energies as well as beneficent ones? All the more reason for it to! The thoughtforms and other intrusive and incompatible energies found in the universe are not welcome here, even though they may attempt to appear from time to time. Our system of protection should see them off adequately, especially if combined with the checking out technique revealed in the next chapter.

If we see the beautiful and informative film *What Dreams May Come*, starring Robin Williams, then we will have a feel for the nature of the astral levels closest to our own. In this movie, his character dies and ends up in the "transitional place" between human death and spiritual being. It is a place very similar to the otherworldly level we are describing here in that it moulds itself to suit whomever is there. It blends with one's energy to make that person feel welcome and it shows the person whatever he or she wishes to see. In this sense, the state that is immediately after human demise and our meditative reality have a lot in common; they are both coloured by our human and soul beliefs and experiences. In the case of the character played by Williams, this reality takes on the form of one of his wife's stunning oil paintings, complete with all the gloriously tactile qualities of wet paint!

Getting used to his new reality causes him consternation at first. Eventually he learns that this realm is his to control—he can stop the ground swallowing him up with its gloopy paint consistency. He also learns that when he gives his astral place enough energy and once he truly believes in its existence it takes on a life of its own. We shall come to this presently.

Our safe place is not a mundane place; it has no human structures in it, at least to begin with. We may find that within time we go further into the inner landscape around our astral home and as we branch out we encounter cottages, castles, and inhabited camps. For now, we must try to avoid placing manmade structures in our astral environs—in other words, we do not imagine houses of any kind. We will not need shelter here, it is a place that we control and therefore it does not need to be cold, damp, or uncomfortable in any way. It is not a human place at all, but a spirit place, and so it can remain free from human clutter and the essentials that make manifest life so bearable.

If we really invest wholehearted time and effort in this stage of the game we will be richly rewarded. It isn't frivolous but it is meant to be enjoyable. Once we feel like we can, we should make a map of our realm; or, if we can draw, we should sketch our realm. If we feel happy writing, we can use poetic or descriptive terms to describe all that is to be present in our safe place. We can make a model if we enjoy making crafts, or cross-stitch a design to represent our new realm. If we are musical, we can play a song that conjures up the feelings we have for our astral home, or sing a song that celebrates our realm's loveliness. Whatever we do, we must devote sincere time to creating manifest descriptions of our safe place. Also, having gone through all the relaxation, breathing, and protecting routines, we must continue to take time to visualise this place over and over, tweaking anything that doesn't work well and perhaps expanding our horizons a little every time. For instance, we may not have seen around the bend of that track but somehow we know there is a bluebell wood there. Remember that Rome was not built in a day and so this environment, this living reality, will only be ready to safely travel once we truly believe in its existence as a functioning astral home.

We can now reach out with all our senses—sculpt or paint them into reality. If you don't yet know what is beyond a ridge, then we can imagine what we would like to see. We can taste any water we create and smell each flower, touch the moss on trees, feel the bark, and smell the loam while plunging our hands into it. We can walk around rocks and get a sense of their three-dimensional reality; wiggle our toes in the warm sand; hear the sounds of small creatures in the undergrowth, of larks ascending over the moorland, or fish jumping in a lake. We can see reflections and shadows; feel the breeze on our face as we watch the grasses gently bend.

When we have understood that thought has the power to mould the ether, we will be well on the way to becoming effective wildwitches. Understanding the power of imagination and thought apply to so much that we do. Like riding a bike or driving a car, once we suddenly find that we are miraculously doing it, we can have faith in the process and in our ability to engage with its rules.

Review: *Safe Journeys*
I will recap what we have looked at so far in the form of a checklist so that all of our future journeys may be undertaken with confidence, in complete safety.

☐ Make sure we're not hungry or overly tired, and especially not ill. We do not engage in craftwork under the influence of any drug or alcohol. Also, we try to avoid any inner work for at least an hour after eating a full meal.

☐ We find a place that is comfortable, warm (we will expend energy during a trance journey and it is advisable to keep well wrapped up), and that is free of distractions. We want to make sure we're not going to be interrupted by extraneous sounds, especially those of a manmade nature. We can apply earplugs if needed.

☐ We have a notepad and pen at hand for recording our experiences.

☐ We sit or lie in one of the recommended positions, connecting to the earth.

☐ We close our eyes and try to empty our mind. If thoughts intrude, we acknowledge them and then let them float away or evaporate; they are not important.

☐ We begin the deep, slow, rhythmic breathing; expand and deflate the belly.

☐ We visualise our protective sphere of shimmering gold or blue light. Or, we follow the tree meditation to the same end.

☐ We state (aloud or in our mind) our protective invocation. We call on companion spirits to be with us. We state that we are protected, rooted, and supported by the spirits. Then we place a protective symbol over sensitive portals on our body, paying specific attention to the third-eye region. We relax and continue the deep breathing until we are one with our breath.

☐ Now, in this calm and centred state, we begin to see our safe place emerge from our inner vision, from the blank screen behind our eyes. We see it form, like a favourite memory in living colour, complete with sound, smell, and movement. We smell the ozone and allow the trees to shimmy and sway if it is windy or hear sea birds crying if we are in a coastal position.

☐ We now spend time wandering around our realm. We understand that we can change it just as easily as we mould it. We know that this place reflects our deepest, most intuitive self—the eternal part of us. We let the whole place resonate with our will and we permeate it with our essence. It is ours. We can then rejoice in our creation in a way that feels best to us. We can go skinny-dipping, run through the poppy fields, roll down a verdant hillside, or we can sit and reflect, taking it all in.

☐ When we have repeated this initial journey several times, we will feel secure enough to begin exploring a little or to invite guests. For now, we aim to establish our connection to this place and know that it will be here for us as long as we invest energy and love in it. It will only fade if we no longer dwell on it.

☐ Upon completing a journey, we bring our awareness back to the room, to our sitting body. We should not rush to open our eyes but take a moment to wiggle our fingers and toes, sense our body again. Chant an affirmation for returning. We may like to close up any portal we have protected by imagining it as an appropriate coloured flower, with its petals closing shut tightly. Then we can open our eyes. I suggest we make any notes, be they reflections of our feelings on the work or what we did on the journey, immediately. Writing is a manifest activity and will ground us well. We should also make sure we eat and drink a little afterward as this symbolically states: "I am back in the world, at a human level."

To conclude, here is an example of a trance journey to an established, safe astral place.

Trance Journey: Travelling to Our Safe Place

I enter my safe astral space by means of a gate into a meadow. By climbing over this simple wooden gate I have symbolically made the transition from my conscious human state into the spiritual realms of my trance journey. I pause for a moment, feeling my bare feet on the sun-warmed ground, the grass tickling my toes as it moves in the gentle summer breeze. Above me the sky is cornflower blue, flecked only with insubstantial whispy white clouds, and the sun is high.

I survey the land before me, to my left the meadow slopes down to meet fields that lead away as far as my eye can see. Some fields are golden with wheat, others green with tall sweetcorn plants, while still others reveal their rich dark soil. To my right, I am aware of hills that I have not yet explored and behind me lies the gateway that I came over. In front of me I follow the winding badger track through the grass with my eager inner vision. I know that I am ready to travel.

I walk on slowly, noting the wild scarlet poppies nodding their delicate heads at me, and hearing the plaintive cry of a buzzard as it circles way above me, nearly out of my sight. Tall buttercups and ox-eye daisies line the shallow track and all around are forget-me-nots and dandelions, some in flower, some as seed-clocks. The air is full of butterflies of all hues and bees laden with pollen. I follow the track to the woods, standing still at its edge in order to catch a glimpse of the deer that I know reside within its cool green shade. I see a fawn, its eyes wide with surprise, skip off after its disappearing mother. A hare hops out, its loping stride always making me smile. It accompanies me as I leave the bright sunlight and step into this dappled world, the greenwood of my heart.

The badger track leads me deep into the forest. I sense changes in my environment, hearing the "coo" of wood pigeons and the song of blackbirds filtering down to me from the dense leaf canopy above my head. Occasionally a squirrel bounds from tree to tree. The air is pleasantly cool and smells of secret places, verdant and damp, and my hands reach out instinctively to touch the smooth bark of beech trees. As the track peters out, my feet brush through ferns and my toes feel springy, damp moss between them. Late bluebells cluster around the base of tree trunks and I stoop to hold one in my hand briefly, admiring the shape and shade of this tiny flower. Sunlight shafts through into the glade, illuminating fallen tree limbs wreathed in ground ivy. My companion hare lopes away and I bid him farewell, for now.

I pause as I approach the hollow oak. I must pass through this tree in order to feel myself going deeper into my spiritual awareness. It is another symbol, like a bridge between the worlds, which means that I am leaving the manifest realms behind. I always ask the tree if I may pass through its dark interior. I wait for the response that, as with all voices in this realm, I will hear in my mind. Sometimes this tree, which I know is named Melerai, allows me only to pass around its girth, not through. Some days I am not allowed to pass at all and must turn back. Today however, I am granted safe passage through the heart of the oak. Once inside, I pause to appreciate the chill air, the scent of loam, and the feel of living bark surrounding me. I hear the tiny scurryings of bark creatures, insects feeding on the soft interior. I feel the sap travelling through the remaining bark-skin, keeping the tree strong even though the inner wood is beginning to die back.

Passing through, back into the green and gold world of the wood, I give my thanks to the tree and continue. I walk down a small bare slope of earth, lined with briars and brambles, and see that the trees are thinning now, letting in more light. I have reached an area of open ground, where the grass is glistening and luxuriant again, and I see one of the most beautiful of all sights on my journey, the bubbling stream. I hear its musical voice greet me as it rushes joyfully over the pebbles, its crystal clear water washing them smooth. I move forward and peer hopefully into this bright water, hoping to glimpse a tiny silver fish, or two. I scoop the deliciously cold, clear essence of the stream up in my cupped hands and bring it to my lips. I taste minerals, the collective distillation of all beings that live here. The taste refreshes my very soul. I ask that such clarity be granted to me to energise my own creative being. I then thank the stream for its gift and ask if I may cross it.

The stream is bridged by three broad, flat slate-grey stones that look slightly pink as the water passes over them. This stone crossing is yet another symbolic passage between manifest being and spiritual understanding. Granted permission, I step boldly onto the first stone, aware of its slipperiness and its unyielding but not unpleasant chill. I pause on the second, looking down at the tiny insects darting around the surface of the water, skating and skimming over it. Onto the third, which is a slightly irregular shape, and then I step onto the bank, with gratitude.

Before me there is a high hillock obscuring my view of whatever may be ahead. It is relatively steep and a good few heads taller than I. In order to reach whatever lies on the other side I must climb it with care, engaging fully in the activity, feeling my toes gain purchase in the soil and my fingers clutching at clumps of grass. This is my final barrier between the human manifest level and this place of spirit. I pull myself up to the top.

On the other side of this bank there is a plain. On this plain I may journey to wherever I wish, seeking meetings with spirit guides and mentors, or looking for adventures to broaden my horizons and understanding of the interconnectedness of the All. For today, I return down the bank and retrace my steps. The bonding with my safe place is done, for now. I am strengthening my link with it and thus strengthening its astral, or "etheric," reality. I go down the bank, across the stream, through the hollow tree, out of the wood, and across the meadow. When I climb over the gate I am ready to return to the manifest realm again.

And on returning to the present manifest reality we must proceed with the necessary grounding techniques. Again, one of the very best ways to do this is to immediately write down everything that we can recall from our journey. As mentioned earliar, it is good to regularly keep such notes in a magical journal. This can be anything from a sumptuous engraved "Book of Shadows and Light" to a simple spiral-bound notepad enhanced with lovingly drawn symbols or green-themed imagery. At this time, we could also have a cup of tea and a biscuit. If outside, we could stamp our feet or clap our hands.

*   *   *

In the next chapter we will explore the work we do when we have established our safe place. Hopefully we have begun to understand the nature of protection, astral reality, and etheric energy and will be ready to employ further techniques based on the principles we have already covered. We can then continue to engage more fully with other spiritual essences. We may soon expand our journeying techniques into pathworking. This is a trance journey undertaken for a specific purpose, a questing journey.

Chapter Four

OFF THE BEATEN TRACK

Wings beat time to the ghost-owl's drum,
Foxes bark as their night-blood hums,
Wild is the starlight that we become . . .

Before we can progress into the real wild realms of our own deep magic we must have an appreciation for who we are. That is to say, who we are beyond our current human personas—who we are in a more eternal sense. Once we have discovered this we can then take the steps to make contact with the spirits who walk with us on our path. If we know our own energies, and those of our close companion spirits, then we are in a much better position to detect any extraneous or unwanted energies that filter into our daily lives and magical work. We can also tune in to the prevalent energies of any time, situation, or place with much more ease as we know what is ours and what is coming from outside of our field of influence. This is important, for as wildwitches we need the skill of authentically sensing (feeling) what is going on inside of us, as well as around us. This response ability will aid us in our work. We constantly need to assess what we pick up intuitively and respond to it in a genuine manner. We must first consider the effects of a sensed energy and then reflect upon the many responses we could have to the particular situation rather than spuriously reacting to it without applying thought or skill.

We have already discussed how we are wildwitches, not simply as a career or hobby but as part of our nature; being wildwitches is our innate disposition. "Wildwitch" is therefore a soul label, describing who we really are. Yet we all have other magical names, personal to us at this time, that we can discover and work with. These names are formed from our very essence and give us that essential link between our human selves and the eternal. They are names filled with shimmering otherworldly potency.

As well as an Otherworld name, we all have a guise that we favour, an astral costume that we choose to wear on our trance journeys into the beyond. We will soon learn how to discover these attributes to our otherworldly self by embarking on a trance journey. By knowing these personal attributes we will better understand our individual roles as wildwitches in the greater scheme of things. We will know that we have a purpose and that our existence weaves through this temporary human life and on to all realms of possibility.

Having an otherworldly name and a guise helps us to grow as magical beings, enabling us to transcend the transient and all that is born of limiting or damaging human desires. Our aim is not to transcend our human forms and selves, but rather to move us to a new place of confidence born of profound inner knowing. The knowledge we gain has nothing to do with the ego. To know the spiritual self intimately does not mean that we wish to transcend Earth nor does it mean that we do not love Earth. On the contrary, it simply helps us feel a sense of continuity within ourselves, which gives us a greater sense of purpose and belonging. And if we feel more confident, surely we can open ourselves up more successfully to the eternal in every being, knowing that it too has purpose even if we do not understand it. Inner knowing gives us greater empathy and an enhanced ability to truly identify with our personal natures.

To clarify, we are talking here of further revealing to ourselves our own spiritual nature. We can call this our "vibration," the frequency at which we energetically express ourselves, or we can refer to it as our inherent "soul nature." An acceptance of this eternal energetic essence—the soul that resides within horse, hillside, and human alike—and, for that matter, the interconnectedness of all life, is essential to our enchantment. We must have a grasp of innate inner energy, the life force that animates even the inanimate, to give any degree of potency to the unseen part of our wild craft. Spirits aren't just disembodied things "out there," floating around churchyards at Halloween. Spirits are embodied things "in here," found within ourselves. We can't see our soul but we can feel it inside; we can't grab it to dissect it for meaning but we can observe how it affects our manifest roles. We can accept that if we have spirit inside us then so does the holly tree and the squirrel, all beings being equal and born of the same source. We can accept this by observing the mystery of resurgence in a purely poetic sense, allowing ourselves to feel the possibility of its truth through a lyrical interaction with life. Perhaps we can believe in it because we have already had direct personal experience with the presence of spirit energy or have felt our oneness with all creation when we acted as mediators between the spiritual and manifest realms. We can also accept it in a strictly scientific sense. For example, though we cannot always see electricity, we know that the power of electricity exists. The lyrical, the experiential, and the scientific approaches lead to the same point. We can appreciate that things do work without actually seeing or understanding exactly how.

To meet with ourselves in a spiritual sense, to begin to recognise ourselves at an energetic level, we can work in two ways. The first is to simply analyse and correlate what we know about ourselves already, the second is to employ a trance journey of the kind we looked at earlier, in the previous chapter. On this journey we can discover our personal magical name and our preferred spirit guise. Once we have done this, we can undertake the same journey to meet our companion spirits, the beings who assist us in all enchantments.

Know Thyself

The path toward knowing must always begin with the self. We must have an understanding of this self, the being that results from a blend of our eternal spirit energies (soul) and our human incarnate experience, before we can hope to work with the Otherworlds for the good of the All. By looking at our innate qualities, and the unique human expression of these, we will, by direct reflection, come to understand the ongoing processes of life much more closely.

Looking at the elements that make up our own selves will demonstrate where the balance lies between what we have learned or have been given in this incarnation—that is, skills, attributes, and ways of being that can be linked directly to specific events and familial circumstances in this lifetime—and the soul qualities that we have been born with. Here I do not refer to inherited genetic material but to our spiritual core. In the "nature versus nurture" debate we find that the soul's influence is not even considered. All possible innate features are attributed to the parental genetic inheritance (bloodline) rather than to spiritual sources. This is an extremely flawed theory. In fact, we will find that the soul is the missing component in many equations that consider only manifest factors.

Looking at these elements may be a challenging exercise as some aspects of our self may be currently quite ambiguous. For example, we may not be clear as to where our inherent ability to calculate mathematical problems in our head comes from, while we can directly attribute our quick temper and politeness to things we have inherited from our families via their genes (like red hair and freckles) or via behavioral influence.

As a rule of thumb, those things that we do not have an explanation for, qualities which cannot be traced back to a physical root, are soul traits. Using the example above, it may be impossible to explain how someone with no training in working with figures, and who was born into a household with a poor level of concentration and patience, has an exceptional ability to work with figures. The lightning-quick mental capacity to successfully work with figures was simply present in that individual.

How can mathematical skill be classed as a soul trait when the soul, without a body, does not need to do mathematics? Surely being good at mathematics is a very human trait? Well, it could be said that a person gifted at mental arithmetic or advanced mathematics is adept at interpreting symbols and at working with abstracts in a swift and uncluttered way. As a soul trait, this could be translated across to all sorts of other human activities in other life situations but the hypothetical soul we are discussing chooses to demonstrate this specific soul skill through mathematical means. The point being that working with figures would be only one expression for a soul who was inherently suited to deal with symbolic representations, concepts, and theories as well as hypothesis.

Such a person could be said to have an "airy" soul nature. This airy person may be happy in the realm of thought, and would have the ability to visualise, solve problems, and work with speed and precision. However, one would need to look at the whole person, including physical skills and other innate qualities, to build up a bigger picture of a possible soul type or way of being. We can further this ability to understand our soul type with the exercises in chapter 6 when we explore other lives, selves, and soul relationships. We will also look at the transference of our soul's natural skills into many bodily situations.

For now, as a further guide to discovering our eternal spiritual attributes, we will probably feel that our soul traits are deeply resonating parts of us. The key word here is "feel." The whole thing may seem irrational but we cannot deny our connection to that aspect of our self that resonates strongly, even if it has no root in our lifetime's experiences thus far. In some cases we may even have a recollection, like a distant dream, of where we have used these facets of our eternal self before, that is, in another existence, place, or time.

For example, these aspects may equate in manifest terms to a musical gift that has never been trained nor encouraged by one's tone-deaf family, or the ability to do fine needlepoint with no instruction, or to work with wood with no formal introduction to the specific tools required. Such gifts usually show themselves early in childhood, much to the bewilderment of the family members who observe them! The gifts reflect soul traits, it is the soul trait that prescribes the skill.

The thing that we love to do the most may well be our most profound expression of a soul trait and therefore part of our soul's purpose, the soul's purpose being the things that we do in the world that make a difference as well as what we have opted to learn in this life. Making a difference does not only mean being famous or single-handedly stopping war. As we are single notes in a huge energetic musical score, we all have our carefully orchestrated parts to play, parts that only we can play, be they solitary lines, flowing cadenzas, or frenetic bursts, to ensure the harmony of the whole. Making a difference means doing what we do, being who we are, expressing both the subtle and profound things in life that affect others, ourselves, and our environment in a positive life-enhancing manner. This concept is at the root of our wild craft.

A soul connection to a particular skill is usually revealed when we lose track of time and when whatever we are doing does not seem like work. Or we may just have an outstanding gift for something and so it becomes the driving and guiding motivation of our existence. However, we must recognise that the talent or expression of a soul trait is only a part of that soul's purpose. Finding this talent does not mean that we should exclusively focus on the talent, ignoring all other worldly activities.

The selfish indulgence of what we love must be balanced with active service in the world, we must engage with our wider communities or become jaded, uninspired, and ultimately purposeless. That would be like hoarding beautiful treasures or growing sumptuous flowers only to let them wilt in dark rooms. Sharing is the ultimate expression of our soul traits. "Service" and "balance" are key words in our work and are well worth remembering!

Finding Our Manifest Gifts

We are going to make a note of everything that we feel we have as a human strength. We can begin by stating something that we do well in the world. Perhaps this will be the way we are classified by others, such as "John is an excellent jeweller" or "Liz is a great mother." Maybe it is the thing we trained to do as a profession or the hobby we wish was our job. How would someone introduce us to a stranger at a party, would they use our career to sum us up or describe what we love to do most in our leisure time? Does our occupation bring us satisfaction and do we mind, if applicable, being defined by it? Our career or talent is not our self in entirety, it is but one aspect, one expression. However, our career gives us many clues as to the overall nature of our spirit within. In looking at how we express ourselves most regularly in the world, we can identify the attributing soul traits.

This exercise may not be as cut and dry as it seems. We may have many equal gifts or several roles of equal importance or we may seem to have no outstanding talent at all, rather several talents that seem inconsequential when compared to a musical genius or academic whiz. Just make a note of everything at this stage even if it seems fairly unexceptional. Remember, there are no "better" or "worse" ways of being and just because we explore certain examples here, some that may seem more worthwhile than our own role, we should refrain from thinking that we have nothing to declare in terms of who and what we are. We are looking at unique expressions and not making value judgements. The only reason that we may have to feel disappointed in ourselves is if we identify what we love and what we are good at and find that we have deliberately abandoned those means of self-expression for the sake of money or to impress another person.

To further enhance our understanding and bring our traits to the fore, we can simply list the subskills that brought us to our current level of being (or achievement). For instance, in our previous example John may be an excellent jeweller but what makes him so? How would the qualities he brings to his work be further defined? And how did he become such a fine jeweller, what was his process? Similarly, if Liz is a great mother then what aspects of herself does she bring to the fore, naturally, to be a nurturing and responsible parent? What else had she done either personally or professionally to enable her to be such a good mum and how else does she express these core qualities in her life?

Here is another example, written as if this person was analysing his own personal skills and traits. We may want to write out our own personal analysis in a similar way.

"In order to become a college lecturer I had to be able to memorise facts to pass my exams. I had to write stimulating, original essays that discussed the historical period we were studying. I had to become skilled at analysing key characters and looking at the overall effects that political decisions had on social change. Whilst doing my postgraduate teacher training I had to work hard on my communication skills as I had always been a bit quiet and happy in my own company. I had to begin looking beyond my own thoughts and needs and get inside the heads of those I was trying to assist in the classroom. My memory was useful again as I had so many new faces and levels of ability to learn. Organisation and preparation of my work became paramount. It was no longer just me but all these other people who were relying on me, so I became even more responsible."

This may seem a bit long-winded but it is natural to be detailed the first time we have considered all the steps we took to become what we consider ourselves to be in human terms. Here is a list relating to the above description:

- Ability to memorise facts
- Written and verbal communication skills
- Analysing information
- Empathy
- Ordering information
- Preparing information for others at their level
- Taking responsibility

We could observe that the overall soul nature of the person able to do these things may be predominantly (not exclusively) "of the mind," being concerned with thought and the translation of thought into effective communication—an airy soul. However, because the person is able to apply these more nebulous concepts into practical work for students, there is also an earthed element present. What else do we know about this soul from what it has revealed to us here? Well, this person is most likely a loner by nature, which is a withdrawn, watery aspect. This is revealed by the person's seemingly content feeling to be alone, thinking and stimulating thought by fresh learning and academic challenge. Still, there is an apparent willingness to try new things and apply onself, which takes courage. This presents a slightly more fiery element and is the dynamic that drives this soul to do work that involves active participation.

The overall aspect of this hypothetical soul is predominantly airy—intellectual, bright, direct, focused, and ruled predominantly by the mental sphere of human expression. We can break our own life patterns down similarly, in simple statements, such as: "I have an ability to see how machinery fits together, how it works and how it could be improved; I have the ability to be precise and steady-handed under pressure; or, I have the gift of fearlessness when faced with sudden change or adversity." These are all appropriate elements to note.

We are aiming for an overview of the self by bringing together every aspect of that self. Although it is not necessary to dwell on them, or overemphasise them, we should list the things that we are not so adept at, too, as every way of being (every energetic soul type) has a flipside. The reverse of our essential nature may be considered negative (as it represents things that we may view as failures) but it is essential to acknowledge and understand these aspects. Without this rounded approach, we cannot hope to witness our own bigger picture and balance the positive and negative aspects within ourselves. It can be quite a liberating experience if we can cast off what we may have been carrying as the "truth" of who and what we are when really it was all based on someone else's expectations of us. To be honest and really look at what we are not, with reference to how we feel inside, can free us up to express more of that innate soul energy that may have been wasted in maintaining a false front.

Having to interact in a fast-moving, hypercritical modern world does not always foster our being ourselves. In fact, we shouldn't be surprised if we find that going beyond our public facade is a little tricky at first. Indeed, the whole idea of our self may have become confused with our own worldly roles, false assumptions, and other external expectations. We may have lost direct contact with what the eternal self is all about as the concept of "ourselves" is usually applied to a very manifest and temporal sense. This is illustrated nicely in the way we ask children, "What would you like to be when you grow up?" The child is probably still close enough to his or her spiritual essence, having only recently come into the manifest world to wonder: "Why do I need to be anything other than myself?"

The spirit only assesses itself on its spiritual achievements. It does not strive for a universal perfection, only a personal best in terms of self-expression, and it certainly doesn't strive for a standardised human perfection! As we are following a path of nature magic, it is always valid to ask ourselves questions: What hare is preoccupied with social climbing? What salmon worries that it is not flawless? What daffodil dreams it were a snowdrop?

It is folly to try and hold ourselves up against anyone else's standard as it immediately negates our own unique way of being. When we are led by spirit, or expressing our truth with ease (as are the other beings of Earth), then we are quite oblivious to society's mores and can just get on doing what we do with simplicity and grace. This said, it is appropriate to acknowledge a most valuable maxim: "May I keep what is mine and may you keep what is yours." When we know what is ours we are much more adept at responding to external energies appropriately.

When looking at the soul traits that give us an idea of our soul nature, we are considering them in their broadest possible sense, bearing in mind that there are countless soul types and groups and permutations on any single theme. At least this way we have a place to begin, and a place that can help us understand ourselves a little more. We can add to this understanding as the work progresses and we become more confident. The more spiritwork we do the more we will know ourselves. Often what is revealed to us in our spiritual encounters is a direct reflection of what we most need to know at that time about our own eternal selves and our life paths. The more we understand this, the stronger our magic will be as it will come from a grounded place of authentic power and freedom.

Finding Our Element

To begin, we can apply the four elements to our own nature. When people are totally at ease with what they are doing or with their environs we say that they are "in their element" and here we look at these elements. We may find that we are a blend of several elemental ways or have one very dominant way of being. Regarding our innate soul nature in this way offers further dimension to our complex selves, but is by no means a complete definition, for nothing about the soul can be completely pinned down or defined in human terms. These ways of expressing our core self, or spirit, are symbolic but they have literal correspondences in the spirit world. Remember that all soul types are equally valuable and valid.

Water

Flowing and lyrical (a swelling ocean of emotion).

This energy relates to emotional, dreamy, psychic, imaginative, creative souls who have a tendency to get depressed, introspective, and to be a little too "fey" for the modern human world. They can find society too harsh for them and prefer escapism into gentler realms. Water-type souls may dwell primarily in the heart-centred sphere of human expression, being idealistic, romantic, and intuitive. The wild craft and this watery nature go well together, predominantly due to the fact that a water type has a natural openness to all things that are not seen but rather felt. Their ability to translate spirit communication into the world may be expressed through art, creative writing, fashion design, cooking, playing music, dancing, and drama—anything that moves, uplifts, affects, and inspires. Water souls are also adept at the nurturing roles such as motherhood or caring for and serving others. *Note:* This kind of watery caring, if it becomes unbalanced and overly sentimental, can sometimes lend itself to damaging martyrdom and bring with it a tide of guilt for those on the receiving end.

Water is an element that likes to express itself in poetic and profound terms. Its nature may be quiet, enigmatic, and mysterious, or oversensitive, melodramatic, and prone to moods. Watery traits also include being secretive, jealous, and passionately loyal. A flowing and lyrical spirit may feel drawn to live by the sea and may even find that being landlocked is too oppressive. As the moon is a poetic symbol of luminous inner vision, as well as the ruler of the tides and fates, the watery soul will find that their emotional mood will wax and wane just like the moon's phases.

If we have these aspects or soul traits, perhaps we have chosen to incarnate under the sun (star) sign of Pisces, Cancer, or Scorpio. This is certainly no hard and fast rule but it may be true to say that our spirits take the positioning of all astral bodies into consideration when choosing a birth time. Of course, positioning of other planets within our chart may also strongly suggest this theme—the water sign need not be our sun sign.

Air

Notion in motion (transmission of information).

We have looked at this elemental way of expressing one's soul nature already in our previous example, when we looked at the hypothetical lecturer's skills. An air type is defined by thought, communication, and analytical approaches.

Those who are predominantly airy in soul nature are usually disciplined but can be absent-minded in "the real world" as they are too caught up in detail and ideas to care if they have eaten or not! Air types readily accept change, challenge, and stimulation. They are brilliant at solving disputes, problems, and at understanding how things work. Yet they are not always as good at knowing how others tick emotionally and can also be distant, self-opinionated, and as unpredictable as the wind itself.

Composing music, lecturing, writing academic books, piloting, following complex instructions, dealing with several ideas at once, inventing and building machinery, diplomacy, law, scientific research, and design (including architecture) are all airy pursuits. Such a being may have chosen to be born under the signs of Aquarius, Libra, or Gemini, and may have chosen a very liberal-minded and stimulating family environment, or a loosely woven home structure. An air soul will find itself craving freedom in lifestyle choices, being hemmed in by people or places will not suit them at all and having nothing to discuss or think about would be a torment of boredom!

Fire

Bright flight (mission and ignition).

This essential elemental expression allows us to show great energy and outstanding bravery. In order for such an animated soul trait to find expression in the world a person will need to be actively engaged with others in a gregarious way. Direct action, positivity, decisiveness, and immense passion are revealed through this way of being. Although, the flipside of this expression may be anger, tactlessness, and physical "burnout" leading to illness. Fire types may be pioneering or overly impulsive, as their boundless energy leads them to act one way or the other. The idea of stagnation would be an anathema to a fiery sort. They desire to be effective in the world and this requires vim and verve by immediate interaction and challenge.

Being a professional athlete or actor would suit fire types well, as would any other career or pursuit that wasn't mundane but allowed for a challenge and expression of that vigorous, wilful, dramatic nature. Likewise, fire types will be intrigued by roles that involve leadership or direction or something such as a war reporter, in which risk played a part. The danger in these types of souls is that they need so much variation to keep them focused that they are adequate at best at many things but never accomplished at anything that is not instantly gratifying and stimulating to the body as well as the mind.

The fiery energy can be wild and dangerous or warming and attractive. Perhaps it is the natural way of being that makes fire types unable to tame their true impetuous, vivacious nature. Sometimes a blaze may be as adequate an expression of this way of being as an inferno; in fact, it may be preferable to burn steadily and brightly during an Earthwalk rather than incinerate everything in the way. The nature of fire may be more accurately observed by how others respond to it. The blaze may be too intense for other soul types who have not the same resonance, while its heat and light may make it overwhelmingly magnetic to others—the fiery sort may have a really polarised effect, far more so than other types. Perhaps a tempering with other soul aspects would be beneficial, whilst not negating the core way of being but perhaps damping it slightly so that it may be directed more effectively in the long term, for the good of everyone involved. A fire-type soul may likely incarnate in an Aries, Leo, or Sagittarius body.

Earth
Fixed and firm, solid and stolid (stable and able, rooted and muted).

This way of being relates to grounded practical works and application: pursuits like gardening, homemaking, interior designing, and cooking. The focus is on the comfort of the body and aesthetics. The earth is a solid and dependable energy to have as a dominant force in our nature. Although, earth types have a tendency toward slowness and being stuck in a rut with a reluctance to expand horizons and accept change. The caring professions, healthcare or working with children, may suit the need to be hands-on and practical; as may work like building or crafts.

Patience and reliability team with hard work and manual dexterity to bring a faithful, if not entirely dynamic, soul. These souls are best at simple, unremarkable gestures and methodical, responsible actions. The whole process of incarnation may seem like a responsibility to be undertaken methodically and while this is admirable on some levels there may be a benefit to tempering this way with other aspects as a wholly earthy person may find it hard to take on the risks and leaps of faith so often needed in terms of personal spiritual development.

A need for a secure environment and home is paramount for those with a very earthed nature. But this security must be combined with the good things in life, things must be beautiful as well as comfortable and functional. There is no real need to be flamboyant or different but there is an overriding sense of what is important in a purely manifest sense, which can ultimately render this elemental type as dull and uninspiring. Routine and restriction will not be as unpalatable to earth types as they are to air types, and as long as the surroundings are comfortable, it would not bother an earth type to be trapped in a very material world. They may find the overt emotion of the water sort or the unrestrained dynamism of the fire type too galling, preferring regulated order to their lives.

Not all earth types need to be plodding donkeys, as there are many means of expressing this genuine and staunch way of being, from the wild beauty of a snow-capped mountain to the charm of a leaping hare, from the strength of a bear emerging from a winter sleep to the fertility of the dark earth in the spring. Creatures of the earth need not express themselves as dull or slow! The earth soul may incarnate during the Taurean, Virgo, or Capricorn cycle of the year.

It is important to stress at this juncture that the elemental and astrological ways of assessing our nature are only a broad generalisation as there are no "compartments" in spirit, just one way of being that folds and flows seamlessly into another. Therefore do not set too much store by these classifications. Only treat them as a useful way of gaining access into our fascinating inner nature.

In order to better understand how our nature is formed, we could consider the "centre of the circle" (the internal point between all four elemental ways of being), as a melting pot or cauldron. In this cauldron a creative blend of each and every way is achieved. Imagine air blowing into the centre, water flowing, earth rolling, and fire shooting sparks until all merge in the wholeness of the vital, elemental brew in the middle. From this seething, bubbling pot, the source of all possibility, every soul was born, reflecting the subtle shades of all that is. We can see this vast vessel as the holder of creation, the great universal point of all beginnings, which lies at the heart of the matter yet encompasses all things. Think of us, consequently, as more of an organic artistic endeavour, a beautiful one-off piece forged lovingly from the essence of creation. Instead of thinking of our unique soul type in a cut and dry sense, as an already boxed and labelled entity, we can think of it more as a fluid poetic expression that cannot be quantified, only felt and experienced. Our eternal nature may be understood while remaining mysterious, like creation itself.

Finding What's Inside Our Vessel

If we see the Creator, or creation, as being a boundless brimming vessel from which we emerged then we can see our current human forms as reflections of this, our bodies act as containers for our raw spiritual nature, they hold the energy. When we have an idea of our basic, predominant, or blend of, soul energy (for example, earthy with a little air), we can make further attempts to understand who we are inside the vessel of our present host body. For example, would our liquid, the soul essence that fills us, be a deep crimson or mint green? Would it be bubbly or still and calm? Would it taste sweet or salty, tangy or bland? We can give the vessel a symbolic shape and form, just as it has a manifest one (our physical body) to match the liquid it holds, such as a fluted, cut-glass vessel or a funky orange plastic beaker. In much the same way as our soul prescribes our choice of body in life, so can we use our imagination, intuition, and the understanding we have gained of our elemental nature to describe what our soul may look like and what containers would be appropriate to hold that energy.

The choices we make should be informed by all of our essential qualities and so a "mostly watery with some air" nature may be described as a light, clear, fizzy, blue liquid in a tall, elegant, gently curved glass with lots of ice. If we are mostly earthy we may be like thick, warming vegetable broth packed with nourishing lentils in a stout earthenware mug, or we may feel more like a soft, burgundy-hued mulled wine in a hand-turned wooden cup. And, by direct contrast, fiery may be a wild cocktail full of spicy rum and exotic fruits in a great big neon pink jug! We are not attempting to find a be-all and end-all description of the spirit but more of an imaginative and symbolic statement that we may erase or further develop at any time. Play with the ideas encompassed here. Also, it may be fun to observe what qualities friends, family, or colleagues may have while within their own particular vessels. This is not to judge others but to better understand them. We may think to ourselves: Does their human vessel seem to suit the soul within?

Now let's move on to other ways of reflecting our primary soul selves. What time of day, season, landscape, smell, and creature describes us best? Obviously we have more than one favourite of each of these things but remember we are looking for our broadest essential expression. It is a summing of all the parts of our selves. This personal information may not come to us immediately and it may be that we need to begin the exercises in this book in order to ascertain the truest expression of who we are at our spiritual core. For now, approach this work with a light heart and a sense of being an internal explorer, it will give us a sound basis from which to approach the trance journey we are to undertake. Some sort of symbolic yardstick to measure our personal development is always useful and at a later stage we will be able to look back and see how our understanding has grown.

Now we can move on to actually meeting that self one-on-one and we can see how our human perceptions of our eternal essence compare to our spiritual expression. Our aim here is to find our magical name so that we may be fully in our own power and thus fulfil our worldly role as wildwitches with more fluency and eloquence. It is also to meet and meld with our Otherworld self so that the spiritual essence of who we are can be better expressed at a manifest level in the world, and "for the good of the All." Before we do this we should learn how to check out spirits for authenticity.

What Do We Do with the Stranger at Our Door?

Although we are attempting to contact our otherworldly self, other spirit beings may approach us first. Like wandering into a public shopping mall, we cannot guarantee who we will encounter once we open ourselves up energetically, and we will not know the innate nature of the strangers we see milling about. If one of these strangers followed us home would we invite him or her in? Shouldn't we have a safeguard that allows us to discern who we allow into our psychic threshold? We need to adopt a technique to protect ourselves that is a reflex action, second nature, as opposed to an unrelated chore.

Checking Out Spirits

Although there is kinship to be found in the Otherworlds, we should never accept what we hear and see at face value. No matter how glamorous and virtuous a spirit may appear to be, this may just be a facade. And beauty most certaintly does not equate to integrity. Such superficial judgements on appearance must be left behind in the human realms, they have no part in our wild craft.

It is very easy to want to react rather than respond when faced with some rogue manifestation that chooses to appear to us sporting a twelve-inch beak and a billowing black cape! Indeed, spiritual shock tactics may be employed deliberately to test our ability to remain calm and centred. That centre, an authentic acceptance and working knowledge of how we feel inside the shockable, flappable human shell, is as important as learning seasonal correspondences, herbal lore, and divination techniques. It will stand us in good stead for the rest of our wild life.

Note: Many people who seek answers from the spirits as part of their witchcraft may be tempted to use a Ouija board or séance. Both are renowned for dramatic results and both are extremely dangerous. Likewise, some people may engage in a trance journey through a course or workshop as part of a guided meditation for a specific purpose. Such journeys should not be participated in if they are unprotected and unregulated.

Testing Spirit

For a quick and accurate response we use "the pointing," a simple and effective means of ensuring the spirit reveals itself to us authentically. This can be backed up or replaced with "the mirroring." Both will be explained so we may always feel safe and confident in our ability to remain in control.

Pointing

For the pointing we can literally point any extention of the will at the subject, in other words, any instrument that acts like an extended part of our hand. This could be described as anything with the same qualities as a conducting baton or wand, a tool for directing energy. For example:

- a visualised beam of light emitting from our finger
- a polished wooden stick with a crystal tip
- a shining, slim gold dagger
- an ornate metal rod with a fiery glow on the tip

Note: Our will is the perceived cold, blue-gold fire that streams from the tip of our pointer. This is more important than the actual physical tool we choose. Our tool should be one that simply aids in our visualisation.

Mirroring

The mirroring is equally literal and symbolic. We can hold a physical mirror or visualise one before us. When we hold up the mirror to a spirit it will reflect that spirit's true essence, which cannot be concealed from us no matter what the spirit's outer countenance may be. The mirror acts as our tool for true sight.

The Test

Now, to test a spirit we point directly at it. A thin beam of luminous, blue-gold light, like the protective flame we use, travels from our fingertips. Again, the flame represents our directed will. As it is our sacred land spirits often come to, they must adhere to our rules. (We can, if we wish, also hold a mirror up to the spirit at this point instead of pointing with the flame.) We circle the spirit with the protective cold fire, blue-gold and dancing with elemental energy, and demand that it show itself truly to us. Now, speak with authority:

"Show yourself truly, spirit!"

We ask this three times while we point at it, the same blue-gold fire streaming from our fingers or pointing tool. The spirit must be revealed to us in its true form at this point. Any "impostor" spirit will vanish, not wishing to be unmasked. Any true spirit will stay and be revealed. If on the first try we somehow get an intruder, then the procedure should be calmly and carefully repeated until the true spirit appears before us.

Such procedures keep our gentle craft simple and uncluttered. We want to experience magic unadorned, as nature intended. We do not wish to put on an ornate display for the sake of high drama. Because we practice our craft on the hop and in the midst of life, we need to always be ready and never overburdened with complex routines. Like the magic found in fairytales our work has a childlike charm. Still, the work has its unpredictable side and we do well to be prepared when meeting spirits.

Trance Journey: Meeting Our Otherworld Self

We will begin by following the route we took in chapter 3, that is, undertake the journey to our safe place. The only difference will be that at a given point we will veer off our already beaten track and find an appropriate spot to do the work. In order to do this successfully it is suggested that the basic journey to the safe place is undertaken several times beforehand so that the process seems natural and the environment of our envisioning becomes more defined as an astral reality, something in which we can have faith. This is only an example of how it works. Our own journey to our own safe place will clearly differ from this example in many details.

So, go through the process as described. Ensure we are connected, positioned comfortably, breathing deeply, and well protected. Now follow the instructions (on page 127) for travelling to our safe place. Continue on our journey to the point where it reads: I have reached an area of open ground, where the grass is glistening and luxuriant again, and I see one of the most beautiful of all sights on my journey, the bubbling stream.

Instead of crossing the stream via the stepping stones, either turn to the right or to the left—here we use our instinct, we will be doing this a great deal in the future. Observe a bank of trees in front of us. Notice that they are in full leaf but perhaps just turning to autumn's gold. Can we hear the wind moving their branches? Are there birds in their boughs? What scent reaches us from their verdant place?

Now, we continue on our journey:

I walk toward the trees knowing that somewhere beyond them there is my glade, circled by an ancient grove of protective Wise Ones of the Bark. I step forward off the pathway, and hear the change as my feet touch the rich, loamy soil again, feeling my toes snag against gnarled roots poking up through the layer of mulch and leaf litter. I glance down and see a tiny iridescent beetle scuttle away as I disturb its lair. I reach the first trees, a host of silver birch with leaves that pour down around me like a soft green rain. I hear tinkling laughter like tiny silver bells. Perhaps I see pale and shining forms flitting hither and thither on gossamer wings. Then I reach out and touch the bark of a magnificent ash, a tree with a deep bowl formed in its divided trunk. This bowl has filled with rainwater. I reach into this cool, dark pool with the index finger of my right hand and touch the liquid to my forehead. By this gesture I pray for myself and the trees:

> *Spirit to shining spirit we are joined,*
> *Aware of the sylvan sanctity within,*
> *From the hallowed bowl I touch my soul,*
> *With teardrops of sky I bless my kin.*

I then step between the trees. At first there is much clear, golden light filtering downward as the leaf canopy above is not so dense. I am moving between bodies of living wood, beings of all shapes and sizes, their skin is warm brown flecked with the softest green. As I walk carefully I listen respectfully to their voices, to their lighthearted whisperings and stern old creakings. I hear the call of a jay and jump a little as I disturb a brace of well-camouflaged female pheasants, smiling as they rise, squawking indignantly. My feet take me down a dip, springy with bright fungi and slippery with lustrous fallen leaves, and as I rise up the other side of this shallow bank I notice that the trees crowd in on me more completely.

These trees are older, far older. A squirrel gazes down at me from the lower bough of an impressive oak, whose bark has a texture like old hide and is alive with wisened faces of fantastic proportions. Dryads and druids mingle in the ridged and wrinkled grain. I look into the squirrel's bright button eyes and it chides me for distracting its endeavours before bounding off with an endearing undulating motion. I move deeper into the protective shade, into a subterranean sylvan world of moving shadows the colour of ripe plums. These shadows dance deliberately, draw back, and reveal shining emerald leaves before enfolding all again in velvet mystery. There are no trails and tracks here, it is uncharted territory. Am I afraid? I do not know human fear but rather a deep awe, which would have me trembling if I would allow it to. Instead I focus on my destination, a place that only I know how to reach.

And suddenly I am through, the encroaching shadows whisked back like a May bride's veil to reveal the dazzling beauty of a small glade. I step onto fresh grass of such a vivid hue it makes me blink to check that this vision is real. Behind me the ring of trees imperceptibly closes and I am in a perfect circle, surrounded and embraced by ancient throbbing earth wisdom. In the centre of the glade there is a stone monument made of slabs of sparkling granite that lean in slightly. There is a capstone balanced on the top of them. They make a kind of flat mushroom shape, creating a stone table in the clearing. It is big enough for someone to hide in, if they chose to. Sunlight hits the fragments of quartz in the ancient rock and it dazzles me temporarily. I marvel at the construction, its simple jaunty elegance, the strength inherent in its pitted stone sides.

The glade seems empty of any other being. This place is only a few paces across from side to side, yet it is humming with power and the air almost crackles with expectant energy. I know that none shall come here unless it is for a special purpose, indeed.

I drop to my knees. Around myself I imagine a flickering circle of protective blue-gold flame on the ground. I do this using my will and wish. It is a magically protective fire—I deem it to be so—bright but cold. It cannot harm me, I am its creator. It is a flickering yet constant flame, like that of many fiercely burning candles.

I close my eyes. There is an expectant hush, they want to know why I have come here, to this most sacred secret place. What do I want?

I walked the way of the woodland elf,
I walked with care and with great stealth,
Betwixt the guardians of green wealth,
I walked that I may find my self.

And so with reverence I came,
To bow my head and state my aim,
For I wish to know my rightful name,
To find myself is why I came!

By every leaf on every tree,
If my aim is true, so may it be!

With my eyes still closed I knock my fist gently on the ground three times as I say:

Know myself, know myself, know myself!

I open my eyes and the brilliance of the day is almost overwhelming. Each blade of glossy grass stands out in sharp relief, each clump of moss or fern glows with health. The colours are so vibrant here, the pulse of life so strong. I feel the aching tenderness of creation, its promise of renewal.

I stand up and, sun-wise, circle the stone monument, spinning as I do so. It is a dizzying effect, the whole glade seems to be whirling and wheeling, and for a moment all becomes white light. I raise my arms and shout:

Show myself, show myself, show myself!

I stop my spinning and twirling and let the land settle under my feet. Before me, by the stone monument, is my Otherworld self.

I must check the spirit with appropriate tests (see page 146). When I am clear that it is my true Otherworld self that I am witnessing in the glade, I am free to observe it's (my) appearance. What a wonderful opportunity! This is the shape my soul takes to express itself perfectly to me. Is the shape humanoid? Do I find my shape surprising? Familiar? Confusing? It is for me to absorb the sight and decide how it makes me feel. I can take all the time I need for this.

I am at liberty to ask three questions before the meeting must end. I should choose these carefully in relation to my purpose, my true nature, and anything special that I should know at this time.

My Otherworld self may speak to me in riddles or rhymes, may show me symbols to interpret. We may just converse in a human fashion. Whatever the spirit's means of communication is, it speaks to me of who I am at the source of my being.

When this exchange is over, this self invites me to join it inside the stone monument, which is a place of transformation. I wonder if I may squeeze inside but my Otherworld self holds my hand and tells me to close my eyes. I do so and count to three. I find myself crouching within the stone, though I never try to enter it. It is dark, darker than it should be as no chinks of light seem to filter in from between the stone sides. I reach out with my hands and touch the worn walls, it is bigger than I expected. My Otherworld self crouches before me, we are forehead to forehead and I place my palms flat on the floor to steady myself. It seems to be as if the place at which our skin touches is so cold that we have fused together. Or is it so hot that we have melted into one? The spot on my forehead, just above and between my eyes, is almost numb but tingling.

I wait. Snatches of memory enter my conciousness and I feel as I do before I fall into a deep sleep. I don't know if my eyes are closed or open now, it is dark yet fragments of images come unbidden out of the darkness and swirl around my senses. It is unsettling yet deeply familiar. I breathe deeply and let the sensation pass.

Now my Otherworld self says:

> *Repeat with me, three by three: I am as I am and I am whole!*

And I feel myself embracing my Otherworld self, clasping its body, which becomes more ephemeral, growing more transparent and insubstantial by the second, and I take a deep breath, breathing the spirit in now like smoke. I am expanding as if I had swallowed the stars, filling up with the wisdom of eternal light. I breathe out and feel sated, whole, content. I thank my self for I am now fully *my self*, with knowledge of what that means.

And then I am alone inside the stone wondering how on earth I will get out. But I do not wonder long for as I stare ahead of me I realise that the gaps between the ancient stone supports are letting in a great deal of light. How did I not perceive this before? The gaps are quite large, so much so that it now seems easy to slip out between them. Before I do slip out I realise that there is one more thing to do. I must find my name. So I ask:

> *As I step into the world,*
> *Show me what I may be called!*

I realise that the first thing I see when I slide out of the stone room into the sunlight will be that which gives me my true name. It may come to me as a voice in my ear, a vision, a symbol carved on a rock, or something lying on my path. It may be an animal running or bird swooping, a leaf tossed by the wind, a cloud covering the sun, a tiny flower growing at my feet. It will be a green-spirited name suitable for a wild-witch and it will feel right.

I step out and take the time needed to claim my name. When this is done, I walk the perimeter of the glade three times, walking close to the venerable grove of trees that make up that mystical border. I say to them:

> *Witness me now for I am N*
> *Born of the stars, embraced by the Earth,*
> *Accept my thanks for I am N*
> *Be it so 'til my death as it was from my birth!*

Note: We replace N with our magical name.

At this point I may take my leave, with all due respect, and using instinct find my way back through the ancient woodland, to the thinner trees, out on to the path that leads me back to the present manifest reality. It will take me through the hollow tree, along the badger track, into the meadow, and so on until I cross through the gate. Then I will be back.

We must remember to ground ourselves after this exercise and make notes. This is very important. Perhaps we could draw the Otherworld self? Or make a collage? If not, we simply describe the self in words. We could write our magical name in our journal and decorate it appropriately, in celebration. Although it is impossible to say what a suitable name may be from an outside perspective, such names may be along the lines of:

Autumnus of the Copper Beach Hearth	Rides-the-Wind-Singing
Oak Apple	Running Red Fox of the Winding Trail
Sparkling Dew	Willow-Herb
Dancing Star-Fire of the Dusk	Rain Tree
Elraei of the White Flame	Bright Shadow
Night Bird Calls the Moon	Green Vision Keeper

It is pertinent to give these examples to express the simple lyrical charm of magical names. Perhaps if we are given a string of disconnected words or images in a trance journey this list will help us combine the words to form an appropriate name. Such acts of manifest concentration and application also help ground us upon our return.

We may feel, being given such a beautiful title, that to change our given Christian name to that of our magical one would be appropriate. But we shouldn't use our magical name directly in the world, that is, in our current physical reality. Instead, we let it be a source of personal power that shines from within. There is much to be said for keeping our peace in magical terms, as we will see when we come to spellcraft in the next chapter, and it is a healthy discipline to exercise here. When we allow the inherent energy and potency of our magical title to remain hidden within our wild heart, instead of allowing it to dissipate in manifest reality, we keep the key to our power guarded instead of letting all and sundry have access to it. After all, it is our own personal link with the beyond, which we all have if we take the time to look within.

From this point onward we will be fully integrated with that named magical self. Because of this full awareness and unity we may notice a strange thing occurring—we may feel the urge to look as spirit does. Perhaps we find the look of spirit to be physically appealing and would like to assimilate that look by similar clothing or hair styles. This is not necessary, though it can be tempting at first! There is no need to do this as it is spirit's energy, or rather our true energy, that will filter into our manifest life. Appearances don't matter, only the energies involved. It is that all-important vibrational expression that counts, not to mention that wonderful inner glow that comes from knowing who we truly are.

In future trance journeys we may notice that we have naturally taken on the guise of the Otherworld self and this is perfectly alright. When we look down at our hands and feet, or when we get a glimpse of our reflection in the stream, we may actually see our spirit appearance. If this does not happen spontaneously we can make sure that, on crossing from "ordinary" reality into our astral safe place, we put on our spirit mantle, willing ourselves to shapeshift into the guise of our Otherworld self. We can don spirit's clothes at this point as well. Perhaps we can store the clothes in a special place on the journey route, for instance in an old wooden chest under a bush.

When we are in that magical place, that otherworldly domain visited in the trance journey, then it is appropriate for us to be seen as we truly are, in our chosen spirit form. However, when we are in the world, we should honour the manifest human form we have been given and try not to obliterate its original features for the sake of an otherworldly ideal. If we truly wish to bring through the energies of the eternal Otherworld self into the physical plane, then wearing jewelry, which reflects our spiritual affiliations, or having a symbolic tattoo etched onto our physical bodies are more appropriate sacred ways. Such symbols of spirit can be empowering and transformative. Such acts achieve the balance we desire without our spirit rejecting our physical shell and its own unique attributes. After all, the body we currently "wear" was chosen by us for this Earthwalk and is also special.

It is well for us to understand that spirit does not wear a costume except when it undertakes a human interaction—that is, when it communicates with us. Our eternal spirit, our "self," simply chooses an appropriate guise to wear for us. It dresses up to show us the sort of energies that are relevant to us. It may have dressed up in a guise applicable to another life we have had, one that resonates with us positively. Although it may wear this costume for us, in truth, spirit is pure unadulterated energy. The vibration of our spirit influences how we, with our current human perception, see it. If we see a gnome or a willowy alien or a warrior, we simply see the frequency of our energy made into a tangible human shape. It's more fun than relating to our spirit self as a swirling pearlescent cloud or a greenish miasma!

The same goes for our spirit companions, they will simply choose a guise to wear for our interactions together, which we will find pleasing. Once we are in spirit we are no longer in human shape and so do not need human labels or clothes. However, in order to talk to us, our spirit selves need to make us feel at ease rather than swirling around us like the aforementioned mist. As most guiding spirits have at one time been human, they often pick a past (or other) life mantle when they appear before us. Perhaps we knew them in that life and so they will seem very familiar to us. Or perhaps they know we are just drawn, energetically, to images of Indians, monks, or beautiful faeries. Perhaps our current human bodies even share that bloodline and so the memory of the particular race is strong within us and feels good. It is that good feeling that spirit aims for, choosing a guise that gives us a sense of compatibility and innate rightness. We all have a particular style or mantle that, in manifest human terms, suits us best.

If we complete the trance journey to meet our spirit selves successfully (and this need not be on the first attempt) then we have something very precious indeed. We truly know who we are and that offers a great source of strength. But, more importantly perhaps, when we end the estrangement and separation, we feel as though we are helping to heal that rift we experience with nature and all creation. It is another step toward completion and communion. We can now meet our companion spirits and begin to work with them to bring nature and all of creation closer together.

Familiars

For the witch, the companion spirits we communicate with are often known as familiars. This may conjure up images of sinister vampiric animals and imps but it simply means that they are the spirits that are closest to us, the most familiar, and walk with us much like our closest manifest friends and companions do. They are unseen, that is the only difference in our relationship. They are once-removed beings, slightly removed from human affairs, and they can see our situations more clearly from a less physically dense and more spiritually connected perspective. They can see the webs of fate that link us all, incarnate or in spirit, and can have a much better idea how our well-intentioned green magic can affect others around us inadvertently.

They are also commonly known as spirit "guides" as they give guidance as opposed to laying down the law and controlling us. Guidance gives us the chance to weigh up the pros and cons of our magical work as well as to understand the energies involved more clearly. These spirits are still close enough to the Earth level for them to be able to communicate with us clearly and their energetic resonance can be felt strongly around us. This nearness means they are not so far removed from our daily lives as to be perfect and infallible, rather they are fully involved with our human endeavors whilst retaining the "bigger picture" afforded to those who are not limited by physical incarnation. So, our companions may help us talk through a proposed enchantment or life decision just as a true human friend would—with the added advantage of that far-sighted detachment of vision, which gives them a little more scope. They are those who have chosen, usually because of soul links or long-lasting spiritual kinship with us, to assist our incarnate learning process. As with all ways of the wildwitch, this kinship is not just for our own good but so that we have a better chance of walking here on Earth in a harmonious way, for the good of the All.

It must be said that not all of our companions are humanlike. Some may appear as animals, birds, or representatives of the Faery realms, including elves and pixies. Remember that it is the energies that are important, not the costume. It's just that it really is easier to relate to an incarnate being in full fancy dress rather than a flickering cloud of light. It is important to state that everyone has spiritual companions on their life journey and so, using a combination of psychic protection and meditative (trance) journeying, we can all contact and maintain a relationship with such familiars in a safe and effective way.

Trance Journey: Meeting Spirit Guides

Again, for this we employ the journey to a safe place that we adopted in the previous chapter (see page 127). It will form the basis to pathworking and exploration from now on. So, choose an appropriate spot to work in and then go through the process—connect, breathe, protect, invoke, and so on. Go through the tree visualisation and undertake the trance journey. When the bank in our safe place is reached, climb it.

As before, the other side of this bank is a plain. On this plain, we may journey to wherever we wish, seeking meetings with spirit guides and mentors, or looking for adventures to broaden our horizons and understanding. This is where the current journey picks up.

Today I stand and, using my will and wish, I visualise a circle of flickering blue-gold flame around my feet. It is a magically protective fire—I deem it to be so—bright but cold. It cannot harm me, for I am its creator. A comfortable distance in front of me I imagine a second circle of flickering yet constant flame, like that of many fiercely burning candles, on the ground. It is big enough for a figure to appear in when I am ready to bid them to do so.

I invoke for my true companion spirit, the one who walks with me at this present time, to appear in this circle. I know that I am addressing a friend, not a servant or a god, and so I could say something like:

> *You who are wise and generous,*
> *You who walk with me, ever faithful and gentle,*
> *Please join me now for my highest good!*
> *I have prepared a space for you and you alone,*
> *If it is your will as it is mine then come!*

Then I point a finger at the space and wait. As mentioned earlier, whoever appears, no matter how they look to me, must be "checked" for authenticity (see page 146).

When a spirit does appear to be who it says it is, then I spend time getting to know this new companion. The spirit's appearance may be dazzling or disconcerting. Although, if it is my true companion it will wish to blend with my inherent energies, not distract me totally! It will probably have chosen a guise pleasing to my soul type and interests. I will try not to dwell too heavily on apparel or physical appearance but more on how the spirit feels. I should sense an energetic resonance so that, in times when I call on this companion to be by my side, I will know its presence by emanation rather than visual cues.

I should not ask too many questions on the first meeting (three is adequate) as I will simply forget the answers by the time I return to manifest reality. I must remember to ask for spirit's name and if I may call on it when I weave magic. I should ask if there is anything that I should know at this time. I could ask if any planned enchantments are appropriate. I thank my companion for turning up and take my leave of it for now.

I return down the bank and retrace my steps. The bonding with my safe place is done, for now and I have met one of my spirit mentors and friends. I am strengthening my link with it and with my sacred place and thus strengthening the astral, or etheric, reality. I go down the bank, across the stream, through the hollow tree, out of the wood and across the meadow. When I climb over the gate I am ready to return to the manifest realm again.

Our Spirit Kin

Of course, we may have more than one familiar spirit. We can ask the first companion we meet about this matter on subsequent journeys. It is commonplace for a witch to have two such guiding spirits, not necessarily both in human form. Or even three, one of whom may come and go as necessary. There are no hard and fast rules except that everyone has at least one! We can ask our companion spirits to introduce us to any other beings we need to meet. To do this we just need to employ a third circle of fire and repeat the process we went through to meet our first spirit guide on the plain.

Guiding spirits do come and go on the wild journey. This depends on what we need to know at any one time and what the spirits themselves have committed to do with us (and elsewhere). We may find that the spirits who we bond with initially introduce us to other new communions as we progress naturally. As we are on a spiritual path that allows us to grow, it is not surprising that we may need to work with other compatible companions who can guide us in other ways as we journey as wildwitches.

Creatures

As this is a green-spirited way, it would be rather surprising, and a little disappointing, if some of the spirits we work with were not four-legged or winged beings. If our companions do not show themselves to us in animal, bird, or reptile form, then perhaps it is appropriate to undertake a special journey to meet our nonhuman helpers, those of feather, fur, and fin who lend us their wisdom, their qualities, and the benefit of their nonhuman perspective. We can undertake the trance journey to the plain and use the circle of fire to call on them. Or, perhaps now we feel confident enough to devise another way of making contact in the astral safe place. Now that we have the tools for safe practice we can begin to improvise and work intuitively. We can devise new routes, new ways of approaching a magical quest, or simply new ways to interact with our surroundings.

Now is a good time to note that we may even notice that the plain, that area of the astral safe place designated for meeting spirits, has taken on its own form. Perhaps it has become a grassy or sandy expanse, with pine trees or mountains in the distance. Since this is an organic process in which the elastic energies of the ether will mould themselves to whatever we personally wish to create, either unconsciously or deliberately, such details may even change over time.

A suggestion for making contact with our animal helpers may be for us to make the trance journey to the mystical place of power, the ancient grove, as we did for the meeting with our Otherworld self. We could sit in contemplation, with eyes closed, on top of the capstone of a stone monument in the glade, and with prayerful intent we can focus on our aim. An invocation, or request, could be made along the lines of:

> *As pollen to stamen, as sinew to bone,*
> *Which being cleaves to me, calls me its own?*
> *Descend from your heights or rise up from your lair,*
> *Or leap from the water and make me aware!*
> *You are my familiar, my bold spirit creature,*
> *I open the way for you, natural teacher.*
>
> *By tooth and by hoof, by the flick of a tail,*
> *So may I look at you, welcome and hail!*

When we open our eyes, the being appears. Use the circle of protective flame to then test its authenticity. The dialogue to ensue may be image-based, or symbolic, or entirely human. Or there may simply be a sensation of calm or comfort. Every being is individual, every situation unique, and therefore the method of communication will fit perfectly with our needs and the being's abilities. At a later stage, when we feel more confident (and if the being is willing), we could venture inside the stone monument and blend with the animal familiar's energies, taking its inherent qualities consciously inside us as we did with our Otherworld self. The purpose of this would be to assimilate its way with ours for the sake of positive transformation. For instance, it may be appropriate for us to have the physical vigour of the bull or the ability to spiritually soar like the eagle.

Again, these familiar spirits will be of an ilk that resonates with us at a deep level. This does not mean that they will be our favourite animals. On the contrary, they may be beings who we have never considered as being particularly attractive or special. However, once we get to work with them closely, and observe their energy in our lives, then we can gain an understanding of why their particular vibration was aligned with our own. And again, this may be a transient situation, with several creature teacher spirits moving through our lives at a particular time, only to be replaced by others as that life phase is over.

Meeting our familiar creature spirits is very important in that it gives us both extra support as we move through our magical lives and also greater insights into the non-human realm. We can then relate with more ease to nonhuman beings we encounter on our physical journey, perhaps giving them much more credence and significance, both symbolically and within the manifest matrix, than ever before. Our familiar creatures can broaden both our horizons and our compassion. They also teach us to read omens and to be aware when we see the physical representation of their form appear in our lives. They help us align the unseen with the seen as their form walks in both the Otherworld and in the manifest world and we can relate to both accordingly, with newfound respect and understanding. In wild witchcraft nothing is coincidental, everything has meaning. Familiar teachers enhance our ability to appreciate this.

Rogue Spirits

We briefly mentioned the possibility of encountering rogue spirits in our discussion on protection. We are aware of places that such rogue presences dwell, and we know that despite location we must always engage in a protective act before opening ourselves up to energies. We're also familiar with the checking out procedure, but what exactly is out there that we should be cautious around? As we have previously discussed the unintentional "shark" or "wasp" thoughtform, we understand that it is not possible to state that we are protecting ourselves from specifics in terms of "this single creature, that one entity, and half a dozen villains masquerading as our dead aunt, Buddha, or the Ascended Master Zylon." There are as many individual rogue spirits, thoughtforms, and lost souls as there are incarnate (or discarnate) humans. There is an ever-changing array of beings we should protect ourselves from, uncountable and unnameable—in fact, naming them is the very last thing we should want to do. Let me stress here, we are specifically not to engage with rogue spirits. We cannot be the one to save them by rational discussion nor can we change their nature. *Note:* We may encounter spirits we can help, as will be discussed shortly.

We strive to be the best we can be in accordance with our inherent soul nature, moving toward the ultimate expression of that unique essence. We can change our own personal spiritual environment, and our own attitude and understanding, but we cannot change the essential nature of spirit. This is an important point to acknowledge and it requires a clear differentiation between our spirit and human traits.

The essential spirit can be damaged or lead astray in an incarnation. Damage can occur from suffering torture or a sudden, shocking death, and a soul can be lead astray by manifest temptation such as wielding power, taking drugs, or stealing. The essential soul nature can suffer warping or trauma during an Earthwalk just as much as it can experience a flourishing through a life lived harmoniously, with love, and all experiences can leave an impression on the soul, to be carried over into another incarnation. However, such influences on our souls do not restrict us to similar reenactments in this life. For example, the soul cannot be an alcoholic but the body can. Alcoholism or murderous tendancies are human traits relating to human actions, they are not eternal soul traits. Still, the effects of such human behaviour should not be underestimated. Eventually, they damage the soul inside the shell by the experience. This would also be true when the human self works as a nurse in a war-torn region, acting with bravery and compassion. In this example, the spirit would be enhanced accordingly. This explains how the eternal essential essence cannot be be changed, but it can be enhanced or damaged.

A soul can be predisposed to expressing itself when incarnate in a creative or nurturing way or indeed in a nasty and ugly way. An incarnation gives us the opportunity to either encourage these soul traits or disregard them when faced with human trials and tests. We can therefore enhance the spirit by its incarnate experience, being in complete harmony with the positive aspects of its inherent nature, or we can go against our soul's positive inherent grain and choose temporary human pleasure, which can lead to harming that soul in some way. The aim of incarnation is for the soul to experience all aspects of itself in physical being and to grow accordingly. The soul itself is neither good nor bad but has the ability to express either energy when in human form. With this understanding, it is the human "us" not the eternal "us" that becomes an alcoholic, murderer, or thief. Souls that repetitively continue negative human behaviours in an incarnation can become hideously warped and may find themselves dispersed when back in spirit. That is, their energy is broken up and reassimilated by other souls willing to take on this corrupted essence to transmute it. Soul energy cannot cease to be but can be redistributed if it has become too distorted to continue in that form.

Not only do souls corrupt themselves, but rogue spirits can attach themselves to us when we are incarnate, becoming partly responsible for encouraging our addictions, depressions, etc. What we do when we encounter such a spirit is to encircle them in our protective blue-gold flame. Then ask for our companion spirits to help us. We then ask that they be sent to the place in the universe where they should be at this time and (if appropriate) where they can receive healing.

This "sending on" strategy will on occasion seem harsh, even cruel, and we will probably find ourselves getting upset at having to send some of the more pathetic specimens on their way, but we are not doing them any harm. In fact, we are doing a great deal of good; astral beings who are invasive, persuasive, plain disorientated, or down-right angry are not in the correct place. They are out of time. It is okay to send them to where they should be, even if it seems like a horrible place to us, it really is the right place for them. We need not engage with where they are going either, or who may come to collect them when we call for them to be moved on. Remember, as we have asked for it to be the best place for them, so will it be.

Astral interactions are simple, we state our intention and it is so. Our intent is the law. Remember that it is our space, we occupy it either manifestly or astrally. We make the rules and as long as the rules are consistent, firm, and are made in the right way—in a state of protection, with a grounded and calm manner, and a prayerful attitude—then our will truly will be done.

So, what we protect ourselves from is really none of our business! This is not callous disregard but a sensible precaution. Our role is only to act like the maligned landlord who may occasionally have disruptive, destructive, or dishonest tenants and we must give them a notice to leave (even get the equivalent of a police escort to take them to the place where they belong). Yet, what manner of entity or being may we encounter that makes us evict them? What, besides amenable teaching spirits who come to guide us, may we encounter regularly in our work? There are several broad categories that are more than useful for the wildwitch to beware of and to understand.

Unintentional Thoughtform

We briefly discussed the energy generated from thoughts in order to express the importance of protection earlier, but here we will look more closely at exactly what we are dealing with when we confront an unintentional thoughtform. The unintentional thoughtform is a common beast in that we are all creating these every day of our lives. They only grow and become a nuisance when they are constantly sustained and fed. If we wondered once in the last half hour, "What's for lunch?" then we have not created a thoughtform. Our thought about food would melt into the ether as it was, literally, a passing thought. However, if we became obsessed with food we may continue dwelling on our next meal, the huge size and luscious contents of it, and we would then be "feeding" the thought with emotion. At this juncture we could then possibly have given form to our thought by passionate wish and will, which shapes the ether on the other levels of existence closest to ours, the human astral planes. What would be such a thought's form, symbolically speaking? Perhaps a great greedy entity with many mouths, and highly unpleasant to encounter.

Thoughtforms are to be sent packing. They are not human spirits, nor are they elemental beings, angels, demons, or any other kind of independent spiritual essence that can be reasoned with or learned from. Given enough rope, a thoughtform can turn into a very troublesome collection of energy, indeed. Given an inflated sense of its own worth, as well as the equivalent of a fat belly (a gut full of fear), then it can be the sort of entity that goes on to claim it is Henry VIII or the goddess Sekhmet during a trance session. Very impressive to the novice and slap-dash wildwitch alike . . . and very troublesome.

We will notice that the thoughtform can hardly stop itself from picking out an easily recognisable, dominant, and superior figure from our psyches. That is because it is borne of thought and is therefore adept at reading them. I personally have met many, all who have the temerity to call themselves something grand, from the Devil himself to the aforementioned Henry, erstwhile monarch of Britain! Without adequate protection, and a system to check out the claimant, how would we ever know otherwise? And what may the form do once it gains our confidence? In answer to this question it is sufficient to say that we would become prey and it would feed in whatever way was appropriate to it . . . not to us. We can see why the wildwitch has no preoccupation with worldly glamour or prestige when, in spiritual terms, these can so often be the calling card for rogue entities.

Think of a thoughtform as a dirty snowball that should have melted. Instead, it was not party to a thaw but to more flurries of snow. And someone or some*other* just kept kicking it down a hill, allowing it to grow with every tumult. There was no collective intention of making it the biggest snowball ever but by passersby contributing, unwittingly, it grows and grows. No one would really be afraid of the tiny snowball it once was, but the big one has enough momentum to cause fear as it rolls down the hill, out of control, straight toward us.

As something to ponder, imagine a few million people all at once dwelling on war, injustice, and disaster and then worrying about it afterward. What sort of collective thoughtform would that create? That scenario may well be what happens every supper time when the evening news is on television. Perhaps as wildwitches it is something to be aware of as we cannot simply be attuned to the more appealing natural world and discount all the horrible human stuff, we must engage with both as all levels and beings are connected. A wildwitch asks what they can do to be of service to the All rather than aiming for an isolated ideal. The aim is to heal and help, to bring about a green resurgence of health and hope, after all. The Greening we pray for is for Earth and all of her children, whether we personally find them exasperating, contemptible, or just plain stupid!

Intentional Thoughtform

An intentionally created thoughtform is a rarer specimen altogether but one we may need to be adequately protected against. Here we enter different territory in that some people have the inclination and skill to actually consciously manufacture such beings. Why? Well, to intimidate or control others, to frighten them into capitulating with the creator's wishes, maybe. Or, in a less dangerous but equally manipulative way, to get them to carry out acts for us in our absence. Such beings can be known as "servitors" (because they serve us with no will of their own, at least initially, like astral robots) and could, for example, be used to collect energy from a particular place that is geographically far from our position and bring it to us while we remain in meditation.

Because the thoughtform levels of existence are not bound by manifest rules they can move quickly and with stealth where we, being body-bound humans, cannot. They can snoop for us, "shop" for us (in terms of energies), and act as messengers.

We can use thoughtforms to do our bidding, in much the same way as we use cars or work with tools, if we feel comfortable with this idea. However, if we are to exploit energies then there are ethical ways of doing this, which perhaps in our throw-away society we haven't quite grasped. Something that has been deliberately fashioned from the ether—using visualisation and focused intent as well as symbolic (magical) acts—that has been given a purpose and energetic resonance, cannot simply be discarded at the end of its use. Like an old-fashioned vacuum cleaner, we cannot simply chuck it into the road and forget about it once it has become obsolete in our eyes. What if everyone simply threw out their old vacuum cleaners, fridges, and food processors into the street? Such items would sit in situ, never rotting down, clogging up habitats, and causing hazards with everyone declaring: "Well, so and so threw theirs out first!" and "That's not my Hoover, what's it to do with me?"

We must be accountable for all we create, energetically, and be aware of what has been created outside of our field of influence. We cannot truly separate the two as we can no longer see ourselves as separate beings but as part of a functioning energetic whole. Therefore it is our duty to remain aware and act accordingly.

With the rarer breed, the intentional, manufactured entity, they must always be sent to the place in the universe where they should be. We can hope but not actively request that this thoughtform will be back with the person who created them!

Would it be right and proper to send a deliberate blast of intrusive energy back at the sender in retaliation? Such deliberately controlling intent as to create a servitor thoughtform will surely guarantee that the creator would have problems of his or her own sooner or later anyway; to willfully shape such energies would surely be to experience them directly in another form at another time. With all things being connected energetically it is not surprising that a boomerang effect can be experienced in such instances, so we need not actively send the thoughtform back to its master, only to where it should be. We can trust in the laws of exchange and return, whether we think of this as "whatever goes around comes around" or "what we put out energetically so do we get back, eventually." Whatever exists, or is made to exist, has an energetic reflection somewhere.

It is not all doom and gloom on the thoughtform front. Such servitors are also created for positive protective purposes. However, they can still be extremely scary with their dominating presence even if they are just doing their job, as it were. This may include intimidating anyone perceived as an intruder, if needs be, just as one would defend a home and loved ones if they were unreasonably threatened. Remember, these entities are preprogrammed and totally focused on their given task. They are easily identifiable from the servitors who have been created to do a one-off job because they remain in place, usually by old sites that we may deem sacred, and will not actively seek out individuals in their own homes. They will not show themselves at all, unless they are specifically contacted or if that which they guard is broached invasively (even if inadvertently).

We should never judge such guardian servitors as "evil" as they are just being what they be, inherently, just as a slug isn't evil or even deliberately nasty simply by eating our prize lettuces. Generally, such guardians have been in the landscape for hundreds if not thousands of years, created by the people who had more energetic know-how than we do at present—and who wholeheartedly believed in the power of the unseen— the same folk who lovingly crafted the earthworks, stone circles, settlements, and tombs. Hence the lasting effectiveness of their guardians today.

Such entities may also be found within churches where repeated positive prayers, perhaps to local saints, have created another kind of thoughtform, which acts in a protective capacity. Any such repeated focus in one place, combined with a request for protection, will manifest the equivalent energetic form. Sometimes this is done deliberately, othertimes it is simply a byproduct of an age where faith and focus on the otherworldly aspects were more prevalent.

As a personal example, which also refers back to the idea of a sacred place, discussed in chapter 3, I will mention a site guardian I encountered at the round barrows (burial mounds) opposite Stonehenge in Wiltshire, England. This formidable shining figure had obviously been created by people far more focused than the modern mind can ever hope to be as it was still probably as powerful as it had been when the (Neolithic?) creator had fashioned it from the ether. It stands approximately twenty feet tall.

It had the ability to physically throw me to the floor for daring to challenge its presence and purpose. On that occasion, I did not feel willing or indeed able to put it in a ring of fire to banish it! It was, after all, doing its job and was no doubt going to keep doing so. I'm sure my own fear gave it a nice new boost of energy, and no doubt, with all the visitors the Henge gets it can boost its power on a regular basis. It would have had no compunction, at all, siphoning off a little human energy. It was an energetic form that positively radiated a kind of cold power, rather akin to the bleak and not altogether hospitable energy of the land around the Henge itself.

We cannot give a thoughtform feelings yet we can attribute its behaviours to its creator's viewpoint. The guardian of the Henge barrows was not enamoured of the modern human race and bore all the pride and prejudice of a long dead and infinitely superior (in terms of uncluttered spiritual energy, focus, and wild power) race of humans. It had views programmed into it, which it bombarded me with, and although I wouldn't go so far as to say it had a personality, its original purpose had certainly imbued it with forthright opinions on how its domain should be kept—that is, free of any intruders who felt as if they understood the mysteries of a race able to build Henges. Its shining pride was awesome to behold.

I do not believe that it could have left its post to chase me over Salisbury Plain but it had the capacity to render myself and my companions nauseous and disorientated for a considerable while after the encounter. Its presence was more on the scale of a massive energetic charge, like being in an electrical storm, as opposed to anything one could deem human. It was raw power given a focus.

Unless a thoughtform guardian is harming us or others indiscriminately, then leave it well alone as it may be serving a clear and defined protective purpose. It is only our decision to intervene fully if we are up to the task and also if it would be truly helpful in the long run. Sometimes it is best to simply apologise profusely for causing offence and bid a hasty retreat with a lesson about deference learned.

Lost Human Soul

This is a completely different category than the previous two. We are now discussing spirits like our own, those that have been human and have become stuck between their human role and the realms of spirit. Why? How is it that some souls pass freely into the next state of existence, unencumbered by their bodily shell (or any attachment to it), while others remain locked into that very transient human identity and place in the world? Why can they not seem to grasp their new liberated state? I could write an entire chapter on this subject alone, but for now it is suffice to state that there are far more of these sad cases than we can imagine.

These human spirits are real ghosts. They are not simply energetic imprints left behind after death, which can cause us to witness "psychic replays" of significant or emotional events. For example, seeing an army marching along a stone wall, or someone walking through a stone cellar, is often only a replay. True lost human souls are more troublesome to us than a simple energetic replay. They affect us as they are distressed, confused, or even angry at their predicament.

As a personal example, I encountered a spirit who claimed to have been struck by lightning a few hundred years previous to our encounter. I tested him out and found him to be genuinely the lost soul of a human. Apparently I was the first person to "talk" to him in all that time, yet he was still standing in a field on the exact spot on which he was killed. From that spot he could see the (now demolished) group of dwellings used by peasant farm labourers where his family had been at one time. Even though they had long since died and the houses had been knocked down he was still stuck in that frame of reference.

He was aware he was dead and had even seen his own body being turned over, gingerly, by the foot of a fellow labourer. Yet, he couldn't accept that he wouldn't go home and be with his wife and children that evening. And so he had remained . . . and remained. Time seeming to pass quickly, a disorientating process. Eventually, by the time I spoke with him, he had no memory of how to be anywhere else but right where he was, the memory of "the light" (into which he should have passed to move on from this level of existence) having faded.

To cut a long story short, this man did not wish to be moved. He was completely rooted in his last human reality. There was nothing sinister or special about him except he had died suddenly and did not wish to be dead. His lack of acknowledgement of his abrupt loss of human life had kept him in situ. I thought that I would bide my time and gain his confidence, talking with him about the actuality of his situation gently and regularly. Yet one night he appeared as a presence in my house, away from his usual haunt, completely shaken and distressed. The farmer that now owned the land had begun to plough up his field, he told me, and it made him feel very odd indeed as it had never been done before.

I asked him if he was ready to move on and he agreed to let me help him. As he had given me the details of his family I was able to ask that they (or representatives of their spirits who could make this man feel better about his journey) appear to guide him onward to the place where his spirit should be. I visited the field the next day, for confirmation that the man's spirit had told me the truth, and found that the current farmer of the land had ploughed one great furrow right through the spot where the spirit man had stood in confusion for so many years. I never saw him again and I do believe he went on, willingly.

I assumed, somewhat naively, that there where few instances when a soul would feel the need to stick around the Earth level after death and that my meeting with the soul of this disorientated land-worker was a unique one. Yet when one considers the sheer volume of human beings that have existed, do exist now, and who have met their demise within the timeframe of humanity's existence on this planet, then it gives us a vast figure to work with. If one considers how many of these souls met sudden and completely unexpected deaths as in the case of a natural disaster, attack, or murder, then it is possible to begin to understand how many may have become lost. In such instances the humans may not even realise that they are dead at all due to the abrupt change between living and ceasing to live. This is not to mention the humans who were so completely absorbed by religious ideas or a simple fear of the unknown as to not want to leave their Earthly home after death for terror of what may await them in the afterlife.

Again, as a personal point, I have encountered souls who were stuck in the moment of their sudden human demise, eternally caught in that moment, just screaming. One vivid image was the lost spirit of a soldier who appeared in my living room one evening. The chap appeared behind the TV, screaming and with only his top half of his body intact—nothing was below his waist, his lower body having been blown away.

He was clutching his stomach and howling, not able to assimilate what had happened to him at all. His terror would have prevented his guiding spirits from moving in to assist. Spirits can only do so much, just as they never manipulate in life so do they never force anyone in the other realms of existence. They guide, not compel, hence the name "spirit guide." We always have free will. Yet what if we are too distressed and disorientated to exercise it? Well, once again this is where we as wildwitches can come in, to assist the process and intervene. Since we are midway between the realm of spirit and the realm of mortal being, we can act as go-betweens to reassure and redirect. In this particular case of the soldier, I had to call on his companion spirits, and mine. Then I had to allow them to intercede with the man and take him to the place where he should be, away from his traumatic death and into the spirit realms.

In such cases as violent incidents or environmental catastrophe one can perhaps see that anger as well as shock may have rooted the victim into their human role. A need for retribution may be prevalent alongside a feeling of unfairness, since they hadn't finished their human life yet. There needs to be a strong emotional reason why spirits feel reluctance to leave their human form and accept their physical death. Unless the desire to remain in situ on Earth is overwhelming—for example, a desperate need to stay with a young child or the need to avenge a crime or the inability to accept death due to a confusion or terror experienced at the moment of death—the usual motivation would be for the spirit to go into a realm where peace, love, and happiness radiate.

Our human belief system can limit us so badly as to make us terrified of making the transitional journey into the light. For instance, consider the period of the Middle Ages right up until the early part of the last century. As we have previously discussed, a particular breed of guilt-ridden and terror-laden Christianity had a stranglehold on most of Europe during this time. Indeed, Catholicism still confused and spiritually strangled some of its adherents until not so long ago. It is possible to meet those who still live in "mortal fear" of some concepts preached during their Catholic school days and have a complete confusion or block against any other sort of spiritual understanding. With this in mind it is easy to grasp an understanding of why, when people died in an age so completely immersed in such thinking as the medieval period, they believed wholeheartedly in their own sinful nature and also in the demonic presence that awaited them.

When we realise that we are talking about almost a thousand years of such bondage across most of Europe it is plain to see, in potential, that a lot of lost souls may have been kept Earth-bound by religious fears. However, religious indoctrination and fear are not the only things that confuse the departing soul. Addiction can keep a soul in situ by making them crave physical sensations. The loss of the body isn't liberating, it is terrifyingly disorientating, as the soul has become used to existing in a deadened and controlled state with certain artificial stimuli. To spiritually fly away from the body that provided such sensations is a scary and unwelcome experience. Souls who think that they keep craving (even though it was their body that craved, not the soul) will look for a way of maintaining that norm.

Other souls can keep us held in place by their terror and need for us to stay with them. An example situation is in a plane crash or war situation where there is a sudden explosion and a great number of people end their lives at one instant. Although there would be ample "spiritual rescue teams" at hand, human spirits would be so disorientated by a sudden removal of their human body as to refuse to leave the space where they had so recently been solid. With these mass destruction scenarios, there would be so many distraught souls all together that they could easily bind each other to remaining ("Don't leave me!") and convince each other that they were still alive. Such souls could be so disorientated that they may well refuse any help and cling to, as examples, the nearest familiar thing to their so-recently departed human selves, another spirit, a place, the scene of the disaster, or a piece of recognisable building. I believe that many witches and spiritwalkers went to assist the lost souls who were trapped at the site of the World Trade Centre in New York after their untimely and traumatic death en masse on September the eleventh.

As an aside, general spirit guidance is unequivocal in its view of humanity's folly of putting so many people into one confined area—witness cities as well as plane travel—because it makes the spirits involved incredibly vulnerable should something go wrong. Perhaps we cannot avoid travelling on jumbo jets or living in highrise blocks in the centre of a large conurbation but we can be aware of the pitfalls in spiritual terms.

Wildwitches have such a vital part to play in the modern world, bringing comfort and understanding to those we encounter. As we remember our true nature, putting all parts of ourselves back together again to form a whole being, then we understand the nature of temporary human experience and have no fear of death. How can we fear death when we see it as another phase in the never-ending cycle of life, of renewal and dying back? We understand the process and have no need to resist a new stage in its unfolding. We have faith in ourselves as eternal spiritual essences.

Unnameable Being

There are spiritual presences in the universe that we may find distasteful, draining, maybe even downright terrifying in their emanations. When there is a chance that we may encounter such predatory beings in our physical life we simply take precautionary measures and be aware of their presence. Some beings may indeed mean us harm while others cannot help but harm us just by their being in existence. The former is more than likely going to be something that was preprogrammed to be cruel or destructive as few beings will go seeking trouble deliberately. Yet, if the lion is out hunting and catches us unawares it will surely pounce. It is for the chance encounters that we should be prepared with our protective routine.

Why call the equivalent of an astral shark "unnameable?" Well, there would be little purpose in connecting with these often primal and difficult energies, so there is no need to allocate them human names. Also, there are no formally defined types; trying to name each individual specimen would be impossible. These beings are beyond humanity and in the same way that we would not categorise spirit beings from a realm way beyond the Earth level, those beings that are almost unknowable from our earthed human perspective, we would not give these beings names that limit them. It would be like calling the higher astral entities, the powerful beings of light we may be aware of yet cannot contact, "Bob" and "Julie." This reduces the being to a conceptual level that is on one hand manageable but on the other hand dangerous, for personal names make us feel perhaps a little too secure.

We do not need to contact these beings, nor relate to them, nor reduce them with our labels. They are "other" to us, as other as a vast cold planet is to a tiny ant. We both have the same original creator but we cannot possibly relate. If we push ourselves to think of colours or shapes that do not exist on our Earth level then we come close to confounding ourselves totally, yet this is the sort of concept we may have to deal with when we're away from this familiar manifest realm. Unnameable beings are alien to us in this very way, yet they share our Earthly space. Unseen, unnameable astral beings are from mysterious realms like the astral equivalent of the deep sea and deep space, places that we, as disciplined spirit travellers, most likely will not explore. Yet, these beings can touch our lives and our journeys if we inadvertently stray into their territory or if they willfully stray into our astral territory. This would most likely happen if they stretch out their sensors in search of the energetic "food" we have for them. This sounds alarming but they do it with no malice, they are simply being themselves, unfathomable primal beings.

What can we do if we cannot interact with these creatures whilst knowing they are in existence? We must simply be aware and never fall into the trap of assuming that the universe is a place of nothing but light and love. Remember, different and opposite expressions of the full spectrum of energetic being exist and although unnameables may not be hateful and dark they are not operating by our principles; they cannot be worked with and are essentially unknowable. The good news is, the major-league unnameables are rare. Like dinosaurs, they belong to a different age, perhaps when the world, or worlds, where made. In this sense, they are primeval, but not evil.

These beings are not the result of incautious human thoughts but are living energies in their own right. We may find them to be the astral equivalent of wasps but we have no real right to wipe out all wasps from our human levels—we just try not to let them sting us. If they cause havoc when we cross into their path or if they meddle with our affairs when we try to coexist with them, then they are being as quirky and irascible as a dog who refuses to be trained to our orderly will. Such beings will never psychically consume us but they can psychically invade us.

I have a disturbing example of this, and it illustrates my point that unnameable creatures are in the world, whether we can see them or not. All we can do is be aware, protect ourselves as well as we can, and steer clear. This particular unnameable coexists with a family in a Victorian house, a house I would hasten to add was built on a place once known as Standing Stone Hill, renown for its "haunted" air and suspicious creatures such as goblins and the like. While the family lives there in relative peace, the unnameable has taken up a portion of the house for itself, an area which could be said to be unlived in, where human activity is kept to a minimum. It is a rather dark and unsettling area to visit as the unnameable may not make itself known immediately but will send out its "feelers" to test what is approaching while not encouraging us to stay in its zone.

For a wildwitch, the temptation when visiting such a place is to "take on" the unnameable, especially if no one has ever been able to shift the being, as was this case. There is a combination of the human ego and a genuine need to help at work when confronted with something that makes a place basically uninhabitable. The urge is just to be the one who can make it all okay again. Yet apparently the family was used to living with this unpleasant presence. This was surprising to me as they were convinced that it interfered with their lives even if they left it alone to haunt its domain. It loved them to argue, creeping into their awareness when they became tired or stressed and making their anger flare up outrageously in a manner totally out of proportion. They had to be very careful about letting it creep in at such vulnerable times. As the family members were themselves spiritually inclined and possessed of at least one natural psychic, it seemed odd to me that they had not asked for a psychic clearing to be achieved in their own home. Living with such an unpleasant and tangible presence seemed rather unnecessary to me, at least at first. Surely they had all the information needed to go in and clear whatever was "out of place and time" in that area of the house, so I thought.

Whilst visiting there (still with the attitude that the thing needed to be sorted out) I was subjected to what I deem as my final warning—a warning to leave things well alone. Since initially going to that house I had suffered recurrent, virulent dreams involving parts of the property. I had also been trying to work out what to do about the problems associated with the property. It was only after a pleasant evening watching a video, talking and laughing, that I was suddenly sucked out of my normal conscious state and into what can only be described as a tunnel, or windpipe. It had the feeling of a vast rippling throat dragging me down toward a great gaping chasm. This awful feeling was accompanied by the most profound feeling of depression and despair. I had felt as if at any moment I may lose my mind completely and never return from such a state of hopelessness.

I reached out to my friend as if I were drowning, asking for help. Fortunately he was used to the machinations of his family home and knew what to do, gripping my hand and calling for spiritual protection, remaining an anchoring force as I struggled to come back from the dark place I was being pulled into. The terror of such a spontaneous attack was overwhelming to me and my first instinct was to get the hell out. I knew that there was no way I could deal with such a being and fully understood why the family had learned to accommodate it on its terms.

As I pulled away and made for the door we heard a click and a whooshing or rushing sound as the energy of the being entered the room next to ours. This was followed by a terrific bang as the energetic being slammed into the next door, the one nearest to us. It seemed, in a psychic sense, to bounce off the door, and there was a profound silence. It was then, if I needed such an illustration, that I realised the infinite importance of working protection, astrally, when in a vulnerable position or on dangerous ground. Or, for that matter, as part of any work with energies. The protection that my friend had invoked for me was enough to stop the invading entity, which had crept in when I was happily chatting and had made its intentions known in no uncertain terms. Still, I figured the message was either I should leave or abandon any hope of making it leave! Of course, I accepted the "request" of this unnameable and have never tried to engage with it, or even really discuss it, again.

It was also made very clear to me that every energy has its opposite. The family may have lived with a nasty piece of work, in spirit terms, yet their protective companion guides were just as strong, only in a positive and loving way.

One can spend a whole life as a wildwitch, engaging in daily spiritwalking as part of our craft, meeting only profoundly wise and caring guides. Yet we still co-inhabit a universe with energetic beings who are not of our kind, not at all. As matter of caution, not being the harbinger of panic, I consider it pertinent to pass this information on. Moving on from this, we still have one more type of spirit who we should be positively encouraged to contact on our journeys.

Green-Spirited Avatars

We have already encountered this concept when we met Jack, the Moon Mother, and of course Mother Earth and her consort the All-Father who are both revealed in the beauty and power of the land and in the seasonal dance. Avatars are not to be confused as our companions, yet we may respectfully work with them to enhance our craft. To clarify, we are not discussing deity, but profound energetic principles embodied in the form of wise shining beings. They are not our familiar spirits and so they will not be with us in the same capacity. They are independent spiritual forces who we have the honour of working with when the time is right. We may ask for their help, invoke their presence, or perhaps they will come to us spontaneously if they feel it is appropriate. Avatars resonate with their own energy, be that of love, prosperity, or creativity. They are patrons of these qualities, they emanate them. They are archetypal beings, representatives of particular primal forces, and they are our spiritual benefactors.

As wildwitches, we will clearly relate to those beings whose aspect is green, that is to say those who simply and eloquently embody nature's own qualities. For example, in England we have Herne the Hunter, who protects and guides us. Leader of the Wild Hunt, he shares his archetypal energies with the Norse Woden. With his pack of spectral dogs, Herne also shares qualities with the Welsh Arawn, Lord of the Underworld, also known as Gwyn-Ap-Nudd, whose subterranean dominion is said to be accessed under Glastonbury Tor. As a representative of the sovereignty of the land, he shares energies with Arthur the Pendragon. He is a virile horned man—an image he shares with Cernunnos—who can be seen as either a terrifying huntsman with his ghostly hounds or as a guardian of the Faery Forest, a champion of the Greening, an aspect he shares with Robin-in-the-Hood.

There are many such beings and often, as with our example of Herne, there is one energy that is known by many names. For example, Jack-in-the-Green is amongst a host of other evocative names for the same being. Jack is also known as the Green Man, Robin Hood, Robin-o'-the-Wood, or Robin Goodfellow (a Faery Hob or wild goblin), the Fool, the Trickster (or Lord) of Misrule, and the Wildwood King. All have his essential "wild man" qualities. If we invoke an energetic being by any one of their familiar names we will meet with the appropriate universal aspect. When they appear they may be coloured by our human perceptions and needs. As we stated before, such spiritual essences are not ruled by ego or a need to be adored. They will not ask for worship. Their desire is only to work with us for the sake of nurturing and enabling the Greening.

Seeing as they echo human principles and have human names, are the avatars man-made beings? By no means. Sensitive humans throughout the ages have simply tuned into these energetic principles and felt them worthy of homage and acknowledgement. The names were created, or given, through this interaction; they reflect different belief systems and different regional needs. Sometimes a figure in history may have embodied these qualities perfectly and become mythologised as such a being—witness Arthur and Robin Hood. It matters not that they were once men in flesh and blood, only that now they serve as the spirit behind the men.

These beings are independent forces to be reckoned with, not figments of our imagination craving to be recognised as gods. How we relate to them is up to us but they do not require, or expect, grovelling supplication and certainly not sacrifice, the latter being abhorrent to any balanced being. We are all born of the same source, as are the avatars, even if they are a little closer to the knowledge of that source than we are at this time. Therefore, how can we offer back a part of creation to that which is of creation? It is nonsensical at best and a criminal waste of life at worst to dwell on such a concern.

We may call on these wise and wonderful beings when we need help with a particular spellweaving or with a phase of our magical life, in which we need a singular resonance to help heal or move on. We can honour them by dedicating an appropriate piece of work to them. We can celebrate their principles in our lives. There are more beings than I could ever begin to list here but as a very limited example of what we are discussing I will mention a few reasons we may wish to work with green avatars.

Romantic Love

For help with romantic love we can work with the young maiden or Jack energy. For example: Marian and Robin, Queen of the May/Young Lord of the Trees, Grainne and Diarmuid, Tristan and Isolde, or Niamh and Oisin, Blodeuwedd, Arianrhod, Freya, Aphrodite, Venus, Aengus, Eros, or Guinevere.

Psychic Sight

For help with pyschic sight we can work with the enchanter or enchantress, the energy of the wise woman or cunning man. For example: Morgan le Fay, Merlin, Cerridwen, Bel, Selene, Luna, Hecate, Badb, Vivianne, or Nimue.

Protection

For protection or strong guardianship we can work with the energy of the warrior or wild man or woman. For example: the Morrigan, the Dagda, Diana, Jupiter, Thor, Arthur Pendragon, Herne, Robin, Boudicca, Dornoll, Cuchulain, Lugh, Lamhfadha, or Artemis.

Fertility

For fertility of land or self we can work with the energy of the mother or green man. For example: Gaia, Ana/Anu/Dana/Aine, Nair, the Woodwose or Woodwife, Sheila-Na-Gig, the Dagda, Elen, Modron, Brighid, Green Man, Jack, Corn King, Faunas, or Pan.

Although this list includes beings from "around the globe" it is always appropriate for a wildwitch to invoke a being with the name that relates to his or her place of dwelling or origin. It adds a grounded dimension and honours the ancestral traditions of that land. However, when we acknowledge ourselves to be spiritual beings in transient human bodies, beings who have feasibly had more than one human incarnation on Earth, then it can also be appropriate to honour our soul heritage. By doing this we can tune into an avatar using a name that comes from a place with which we have a spirit link. To know why we do something is important, but to feel its resonance deeply is paramount, to have that sense of continuity and purpose mixed with an intuitive sense of what is truly fitting.

We can meet an avatar by using the trance journey technique we employed for meeting our guides (page 155). Or we can create a specific questing journey to ensure that we meet the avatar we seek. I will give two examples of the latter. They are examples for inspirational purposes and are not intended to be followed to the letter, rather used as a guiding framework for our own journeying. As before, they are written in the first person so that we can identify with the experience on a personal level.

Note: It is expected that by now it will be second nature to employ the usual protective and connecting techniques before beginning any trancework, including asking those who come for our highest good, the companion spirits, to be present.

Trance Journey: Meeting Jack

We introduced Jack in chapter 1 but here we can meet him for ouselves. Here we are pathworking to meet Green Jack as a cunning wise man.

> I am walking along a quiet lane, in daylight. To my left and right there are banks of trees in the process of shedding their crimson and saffron mantles. There are also bushes bearing the last bright gifts of their fruit, small succulent blackberries and shining scarlet rosehips that attract both my admiring gaze and the approval of small brown birds. The birds call their warnings to one another as I approach, reluctant to leave their feast. I walk on, observing a few hanging elderberries that are trembling in the afternoon breeze and a scattering of soft-sheened sloes that are bobbing and dancing on branches.
>
> I am in love with the autumn, captivated by the dazzling confetti of whispering leaves as they tumble in profusion around me. They are of a red hue like spices from a souk, cinnamon, cayenne, and chili pepper, while their fallen counterparts are already turning to dull brown under my boots. For a moment, as the wind picks up, I am totally surrounded by leaves, spinning, twirling, and I am dizzied, disorientated, and drunk on leaves of rich claret and deep burgundy. I seek something steady, something that isn't whirling, and look above me to where I know the solid branches of the trees are clearly defined. Yet their tangled skein of branches suddenly seems unfeasibly stark and black against a sky slowly turning from cerulean blue to the colour of blanched almonds.
>
> Without warning I am enveloped in mist and the bright day is gone. Something is happening, that much is clear, even if I cannot see the hand in front of my face. The sound of my boots on the track, calling birds, and whispering leaves are all dulled to a heavy hissing silence. I stand and breathe steadily but I cannot feel my feet, nor do I get a sense of standing on a path any longer. Instead it is as if I am suspended in a cold, white world that billows and shifts around me. I feel the weight of damp air pressing at me, seeping into my pores, and I cannot help but shiver. This is strange and unnerving yet there is nothing to fear. He is testing me, I realise. Of course he is! I have come to meet the wise man of this wood, the cunning man, and I feel his

slightly mocking, deeply discerning, disconcerting presence within this silent, white realm I am plunged into. From somewhere in all of this rolling, roiling mist he watches and waits. What will I do?

I breathe slowly, deeply. I am at peace, even in this unexpected situation. I will wait. And with this thought the wind rises again, whipping that oppressive cloak of cloud away from me as abruptly as it was wrapped around me, releasing all the woodland sounds it had muffled. The sky above me is deep blue again, perhaps a little darker as the day has worn on, and the trees are clad in their brown bark mantles once more. The air of strangeness has past.

I look around, noticing that on my left there is a raised bank of earth where before there were only trees. A single track is barely discernible on its leaf-littered swell. Am I to follow such a faint track? I cannot, will not, turn back, even though he has disconcerted me with his tricks. There is nothing to do but follow the path, even though the wind now rails at my decision and plucks at me with unseasonably icy fingers.

The track leads me up and down, up and down, over endless earth banks and slopes, each with a steeper incline than the last until my pounding heart matches the steady plodding of my boots. Here and there the leaves make a slippery carpet and I slide back, struggling to find purchase. Sometimes the wind stirs up a whirling mass of damp, rotting leaves to blind me and make me stagger. I plod on with my head down. I am losing daylight and must get to see him before dark. Just as I am thinking this I walk straight into a large flat rock, which suddenly looms up at waist height from the undergrowth.

I fall backward but my fall is cushioned by leaves. I hear his laughter before I see him. But there he is stepping out from between a duo of slender rowan trees, the cunning man revealed. I regain my composure as quickly as I can and envisage this figure surrounded in a circle of protective blue-gold flame. I say: "Show yourself truly spirit!" I point at the figure, directing my will, and make my demand.

The man in the circle of flame does not waver, his image stays true, his face stern but impassive. Another bubble of laughter escapes his thin lips before his features arrange themselves back into a state of craggy imperviousness.

His attire is as grey and featureless as the rock that made me stumble, he is well camouflaged in this, his own realm. He is not an intimidating figure, instead rather birdlike with quick economic movements, slender to the point of being reed thin and with a slight stoop. Yet his demeanour is imposing even if his bearing seems perhaps to verge on the weedy. His face is weather-worn, lean and lined, the nose a sharp beak that seems to stretch the thin skin that covers it. He leans heavily on a forked staff; long, bony fingers drumming a tattoo on the wood. He lifts his chin, eyes steely as they meet mine for a long moment. I realise he can read every judgemental thought I have had about him and I blush to the roots of my hair and bow my head. There is a silence and eventually I am compelled to look up again. His eyes meet mine again, softer now perhaps, and then skim over me, doing a little appraising of his own. Then those silvery-grey eyes dart away from me, seeming to notice each fresh leaf that falls around us. I feel inclined to drop my gaze again but he speaks and his voice cracks like dry twigs and bristles like a hog's back.

He says: "The place is here and the time is now! So it is!"

I look at him expecting more but he only gestures at me, a curt nod and a flick of his hand, and I know he wants me to follow him deeper into his realm, into this place of tricks and illusions, and of wisdoms beyond my own current understanding.

I follow. I have a job to keep up with him, elderly man or not. I notice now that his shoulders are broad even though he is wiry. Straggles of whispy, whitish hair stand up around his head in a corona and snake down his back. His plain garb is held together with frayed hemp rope and as he strides onward I see, or I think I see, tiny toadstools and acorns sprout from it, turn brittle, and fall away to dust. His boots make no sound, appearing to be made of felt or some soft grey material. He is like a whisper, and is a whip-smart man. As I trail in his wake I feel infinitely humbled; my guts churn with anticipation. A hawk alights on his shoulder and eyes me dispassionately as I struggle to keep up. Where are we going and how will I ever find my way back?

"Please?" I say breathlessly, willing him to slow down, to stop, to explain himself a little. The man does not turn or falter, instead he suddenly ducks under a low branch and disappears.

I stand and stare ahead of me into the gathering gloom. Why is it going so dark, so quickly? Before the thought is properly formed I am surrounded in darkness as effectively as I had been cloaked in mist. Shrouded in it. Concealed. An impenetrable inky gloom covers me like a heavy woollen blanket and all falls eerily silent.

This time I do not feel so calm. I reach out ahead of me, waving my hands, trying to make contact with something solid. I take one tiny step, then another. I find the low branch and duck slowly, carefully. Then my hands strike stone. Stones. I feel them, roughly piled one on the other, making a wall of sorts. And as I reach higher my hands find a smooth yet pitted surface, a cross beam of timber . . . a door lintel. My breath releases in a long ragged gasp and I realise I have been holding it. I must remember to keep calm, to breathe. After all, I have invoked for my familiar spirits to be with me, I have protected myself. I have a focus for my journey. All is well, even if all is pitch black and silent. I wait.

He says: "Well, come in, come in, don't stand on ceremony!"

I see a tiny flicker in the darkness, a dancing light suggesting warmth and hope . . .

a candle! And bearing it in a simple wooden holder is the cunning man, his face partially illuminated, a map of hollows and crags. He peers out of his doorway at me, an entrance almost hidden by the trees ahead, and the clarity floods back into my world. I hear the birds flying home to roost above me, see the tiny flying insects hunting and being hunted. I smell woodsmoke and see the dried herbs above his lintel. The sigils on the heavy wood of the door that he has flung open for me stand out in sharp and beautiful relief. I step inside his home.

There is a fire burning in the hearth already and I am struck by how low the ceiling is, from which a myriad of treasures hang. There are amulets of fur and feather, carved bones, dried plants that give off scents both spicy and sweet, woven bags tied tightly with wool, and even tiny clay and glass bottles nestling in the densely interwoven branches that make up his rafters. There is an underlying smell, slightly musty, almost animal, yet familiar to me in a way and certainly not unpleasant. The walls seem to be a mixture of packed earth and grey, rough-hewn stone, and here and there a tiny green plant pushes its sinuous, tenacious way through. The floor is the woodland's own earth, swept clear and dry, with rushes strewn liberally across it.

Suddenly I feel incredibly tired and totally overwhelmed. As I realise this, a stool, the only one in the tiny dwelling that I can see, is pushed toward me to catch me as I sway on my feet and droop downward. A wooden bowl, stunning in its simplicity, is pressed into my hands and I am about to drink, when I remember to point my finger at the contents of the bowl, a thin, honey-coloured liquid, to test its safety. I will not drink that which I have not checked out. I say: "Reveal to me your true nature!"

The liquid glows, warm and tempting. It is as it is, a safe and healing brew. I drink and am filled with warmth. It's like good whiskey but sweeter, it does not burn but makes me feel infused with something that sings of the last of summer sunlight; the glow that filters through a glade at twilight, a mellow poignancy, full of the promise of returns. I thank my host and feel a little more at ease. I shift on the rough stool, even though it is topped with a skinny cushion of worn green velvet it is harder than the chairs I am used to. The man hunkers down by my side and smiles. He says: "You can ask the stool to be more comfortable for you, if it pleases!"

"How?" I look at this strange old-young man, genuinely curious.

"Wish and will, you only have to ask for what you need. To ask for it to be more comfortable, to be what you need now that you are tired, that is reasonable. Now, if you asked for a stool to become an ornate golden throne then the spirit of the wood would find that a little excessive and drop you clean onto the floor. But if you ask for it to mould to you to ease your bones, which is what you need after that unaccustomed hike back there, then it will oblige you!"

I ask, trusting this man. Knowing the rightness of what he says. This is a magical realm and I am a magical being. So I ask, with all due respect, for a chair to ease my aches and my wish is granted. The stool shifts and I am sitting in a pleasant rocking chair with a soft cushion on the seat, which fits to my shape just perfectly.

More at ease than ever, and beginning to enjoy myself, I look at the man again. He has reached behind himself into the shadowy cluttered gloom and presents me with a huge and heavy leather-bound book with a tooled cover depicting a woodland scene in intricate detail. As I stare at the image the squirrel I see etched into the branch of an oak bounds up the trunk. I stare in amazement but the cunning man only shrugs in what seems like impatience. He says: "The lives of all lie within. What will you see there?"

The book falls open and releases a little puff of dust as it does so. I catch the fragrance of a thousand lost nights, of wind-lashed, rain-soaked moors and hidden places where the stalactites form over centuries. I see glimpses of many faces, some burned dark by the desert sun or glowing paler than the moon with huge black eyes that speak of the spaces between the stars. I sigh.

"Ask! Ask!" he blurts. "For the time is now and the place is here!"

The cunning man moves the candle closer to me so that the pages are illuminated more. Images that I cannot yet quite discern leap and unfold on the living page. Words mutter and melt back into the vellum. I know that I have no question yet the question forms . . .

Now, I ask any question of the cunning man and my answer is given through the book I hold, the book of life that he has opened for me. I can ask about him and his role, or my own purpose in this life, or for insights into other lives. I can ask for magical understanding, for knowledge about divination or journeying, or for a deeper understanding of the meaning of existence. I can ask for anything that a wise man may reveal through word and picture. I give myself time to witness this.

The images dance one last time and then fade. The words blur.

He says: "That which you have seen will stay with you. Its message unfolding, its mystery weaving into your waking hours, into your future visioning. Keep it secret, for this knowledge is yours alone, hug it close to you like a dream-lover who may vanish if you speak its name aloud. The book of life stands ever open, all pages are as one page and yet still they turn. So it is and so shall it be, for the time is always now and the moment is always here!"

I thank the cunning man for his knowledge, for his testing me, for his care and custodianship of that which is forever sacred. I know my time with him has ended, for this meeting at least. I make a gesture of heartfelt soul gratitude, touching my brow, lips, and chest before bowing in the manner of the old green ones, one hand sweeping back, head bent low. He almost cracks a smile but inside inclines his head slightly to know my acknowledgement is accepted. Then he gestures to the door. But, how will I find my own way back?

As if he hears my thoughts, he says: "You are tired, child. Stand on my threshold a while. Now, close your eyes and think of the place in the universe where you have safety, where you have a spirit home."

I do as he suggests and stand with my eyes closed, imagining my astral safe place, with its hollow tree, magical brook, and grassy plain. And slowly I become aware that I am in my safe place after all, with the sound of birdsong filtering through the canopy of trees and the gentle babbling of the stream reaching my ears. I open my eyes and take a moment to become accustomed to this new and familiar reality. Was my journey into the wildwoods all a dream?

I begin to make the walk back to the everyday realm. I go through the hollow tree, up the badger track, and into the meadow. Before I come back to the waking world, I realise that my hand has been clenched tightly around something. For how long? I cannot remember. Opening my hand I see a gift from the cunning man. . . .

This gift may be a soft-skin pouch to wear on all journeys, to fill with spirit treasure garnered on the way, or it may be a sprig of rosemary for protection, or a carved ogham stick or rune. It is a unique symbol of the interaction between myself and the cunning man and cannot be described here. I give myself time to appreciate this. And whatever the gift, I decide where it will be kept in the astral safe place: perhaps with my otherworldly clothes, under a tree root, or in a box stored in a hole. Then I think of a similar symbol that I might carry with me in the "ordinary" world I inhabit as a human.

I make the rest of my journey back to manifest reality. After this deep meditation on Green Jack as the wise man, I write my experience in my notebook or journal. I also eat and drink a little to further ground myself.

Trance Journey: Meeting Moon Mother

As with Jack, we previously were introduced to the Moon Mother but here we have the opportunity to personally meet her and interact with her. Here we are pathworking to meet the Moon Mother as wise woman.

I am walking along a clifftop path. It is a day with a sky the colour of cold pewter and the wind is whipping my clothes and hair into my face, making it difficult to see where I am going at times. I could question the validity of making such a journey on such an elemental day and yet I realise deep within myself that to be exhilarated and perhaps a little frightened by what I am doing is part of this journey.

The rocks lie beneath me, the sea crashing mercilessly against the jagged, slate-coloured beasts. White foam gushes and spills over their backs, concealing and revealing these savage, grey stone beings. There is a curious music to the crashing of the waves, which makes the blood in my veins course a little stronger. It is a primal music, compelling, never comforting, cruel and dispassionate yet all encompassing, and terribly alive. I feel a strong connection to that powerful tide, simultaneously drawn to it and repelled by its fierce beauty. I walk to its rhythm, I dance to its tune, but I will never surrender myself to its hunger totally.

The path begins to curve downward a little and as my course changes I see an outcrop of rock where cormorants huddle, one occasionally stretching its wings against the cold spray of an angry sea. Gulls swoop and try to hold their own course as the wind snatches at their white bodies. Everything around me seems to be sketched in hard graphite, scudding clouds and bitten coastline are rendered in shades of cobalt and lead, all except the pale diving gulls and surging spray that leaps to meet them.

The salt air clings to me, the wind driving me on and then pushing me back, the choppy sea empty of boats, no seal or dolphin breaks the surface. I am seemingly alone with the wheeling, shrieking birds and my own thoughts—in actuality, I am surrounded by elemental power. I become aware of the manic cackling of the sea sprite and wind rider, their howling, screaming pleasure. I scream along with them and my scream is flung from me to be smashed on the rocks and taken by the sucking tide. I laugh and the sound flies free from my cold lips, dipping and soaring on a current of chilled air, plummeting to the sea. And beneath it all I hear the drumming thrum of the sea sprites and the wind riders; their howling, steadily beating even as it is pummelled, lapped, torn at, and eroded. All life is change, and here, for me, is part of this eternal process being acted out, a great ritual drama that cares not for an audience. A perpetual performance for its own sake, the interplay of earth and sky, the frenzied caress of the jealous sea, the fiery passion in each living molecule that urges them on. Creation and negation, new shorelines and lost horizons, death and rebirth . . . the dance of life.

And me, up here—small, helpless and vulnerable? No, I am part of it all. A tiny vital part. I see through the continual drizzle of spray that reaches me even up here, on this clifftop. The path now winds down to a deserted circle of dry beach, a cove. The sand, in this stormy, half light, seems to be a shade of steely grey yet it invites me to move toward it. The path, I notice, spirals down and I have to concentrate hard so as not to lose my footing. The motion is almost dizzying in itself. Back and forth, round and down, I move with care and focused intent. The wind mocks me and almost takes my own breath from me but I move onward as steadily as I can. I walk until my feet touch the sand, hard-packed by water but still softer than the stone path, and I release my breath in gratitude. I am here now.

And so, it seems, is the person I seek for a fire is burning at the mouth of the cave at the back of this cosy cove. I would love to warm myself by the blaze, fatigued by my travails against the wind, dampened by mist and chilled by spray, but I know that I must be invited to her fire. Where is she? A movement catches my eye where before there was none. Could it be a giant cormorant, a scraggily sea bird? No, instead it is a hooded figure moving with its back to me by the water's edge. A figure seemingly unperturbed by the cold sea rising over bare feet. A small scrawny hunched figure in a dark cloak is gathering pebbles, driftwood, and broken seashells. It pockets the treasures and cradles them lovingly in its arms. Can I scent madness on the wind?

It jumps around suddenly, startling me and dropping a few of its precious sea-begotten things as it does so, and I move forward to offer to pick them up. Before I can, the figure cries like a crow. "Caaaaa!" And rushes at me, half hopping, half flying, wet old cloak flapping. Pale feet moving too rapidly over the sand, leaving prints like a bird's. Before I can even register how it happened, the figure (a woman) is up to my face and dancing before me, leering, pecking at me, cackling, and whooping. She drops her treasure at my feet for inspection, stepping back and observing me with head cocked, still hopping from one bony old foot to another. The toenails are yellowed and cracked, more like tiny curled horns.

"Show yourself truly, spirit!" I demand of the figure, circling her in blue-gold flame immediately. I point at her, more flame shooting from my finger.

She chatters and snickers incomprehensibly. Her image wavers. I see her sprout great, shining moon-white wings, then her figure shifts so that she is an obsidian-eyed skeleton wrapped in dark rags just before the vision again falters, energy flickering, revealing a tall austere woman with hair the colour of winter waves and eyes like weathered granite in the moonlight. Then she is back, this hopping mad crone in her shabby garb. She is genuine. But genuinely what? Is this the wise woman?

I nod my acceptance of her, bowing in the old way, and stoop to look at the bounty she has gathered. As I gaze downward, a chalice, an amazing silver goblet, is thrust under my nose.

My hands clasp this beautiful artefact lest it fall and dent. Such a vessel from such a poor figure! I take it and look up from my crouched position to thank her but she is gone. Turning carefully, so as not to spill the contents of the chalice or disturb the treasures strewn about me, I see she has retreated into the cave mouth, behind her fire.

I look into the silver cup, and say: "Show yourself truly to me, before I drink!" I shout the instruction at the contents, to be heard over the sibilant hiss of the sea and the hollering of the wind.

I see in the finely wrought cup a strange cloudy mixture that is the constancy of egg white. The liquid shimmers and swirls. It is made of milky moonlight and full-bodied magic. It is wholesome and good.

I drink, tasting a hint of the sea, a coldness which fills my belly with something far more nurturing than the simple warmth gained from a hot brew. It bubbles and boils in the cavernous depths of me, licking my insides into a crescendo of wild pleasure, then soothing me, lulling me, rocking all my senses. I hold the chalice away from me, amazed. Can I taste mugwort or yarrow, bitterness and dried bones? Can I taste the tang of tears, the spun sweetness of spider silk? Do I sense the essence of my own heart's blood on my tongue?

With new eyes I look down and see the treasure of the old woman afresh, the colours subtle and shifting. After the monochrome of this day the colours shock and delight me. The brew has awakened my senses, given my poetic soul wings with which to fly beyond the mundane. I put the chalice down and admire the bounty, the stones of mint green and palest violet, pebbles streaked with ochre and henna, and the spiral of a shell outlined in duck-egg blue, its tender inner curves in rose madder. Wonderful! And I see more, fossils of forgotten creatures peeping from pitted lime-stone shards, driftwood shaped into gnarls and whorls like ancestral faces, and each filled with their own specific wisdoms. And best of all, I spot a large conch shell, smooth and creamy.

I pick it up and gaze inside its smooth pearly depths, the colour of secret, woman flesh. And in doing so I enter not the shell's pale hidden labyrinth but the dark cave of the wise woman. I am within her tunnel. But where is she? Someone takes my hand in the shining darkness and leads me in. I am in a passage, a curving spiral into the depths. Disorientated, I reach out and find that I am hemmed in on either side. The walls feel slippery to my trailing fingers; my nose is filled with the scent of all life, of the fertile void, sharply salty and damp. The figure that pulls me has a bony hand like ice and yet I cannot let go, it pulls me and its urgency to reach some unspoken final destination becomes my own. We hurry on, surrounded by rippling folds of living rock, which presses close to us, breathing out its own essence of tide and time.

And suddenly we stop. A candle flickers to life, gutters and flares in the dripping darkness of this subterranean place. We, the slight-cloaked figure and I, are before a door—a slimy arch of green-brown wood, studded with limpets, shrouded in sea-weed, but still recognisable as an entrance. My guide hands me the key from her rope belt, a huge, black unwieldy thing. My hands are so cold from her grasp that I doubt I can lift this key let alone handle it into a lock, yet I do.

There is a creak and a moan as the old one pushes her ancient doorway open for me. I give the key back to her and she ushers me wordlessly inside. And what is inside this cave is amazing to me. A fire blazes impossibly brightly in a hearth that should not be feasible here, so far underground. There is a wooden table, which is lined with many candles singing with welcoming, pale golden light, and two chairs, rough-hewn and simple. The figure gestures to my place at her table and I accept her offer. I see more torches in sconces set into the cave walls. The place is aglow, alive with flame. A regular little warm womb in the depths of the cold earth.

My host, this woman, throws back her hood and unties the belt that holds her cloak closed. It falls away from her in a sodden heap, her keys falling soundlessly among its wet layers. She stands revealed before me, naked and unashamed, yet so terribly old. In my life I have never seen one so revealed, for age is concealed, not celebrated in the reality I walk from day to day. Should I feel revulsion, fear, amusement? All basic human reactions that I wish to move beyond. What is my response?

She smiles, like ice cracking in the thaw and throws back her head as I gaze on her in wonder and awe. Eyes of palest chambray are set in shadowed depths like the moon's own hollows. Hair spun of silver silk is almost lilac and floats like a miasma around her. Her body, ropy with blue veins meandering like rivers set on well-worn courses, has delicate skin falling away from her frail bones. She stands tall and straight, her flesh has almost forsaken her and is now becoming luminous. As I watch she becomes as mesmerising as the moon, she commands my attention and reverence as if she were the most beautiful of them all in our human eyes; or the richest, robed in sumptuous velvet and bedecked in jewels. I gasp aloud. Has she transformed, or am I simply seeing what is truly there, behind the physical facade?

Her nobility is an aura that no amount of age can strip from her, her presence an intoxicating blend of energy that no gown nor adornment could better. She is a vixen in her earth, her legs the potent roots of healing elecampagne, her arms the boughs of flowering hawthorn spilling blossom, her hair the web caught in hoarfrost, glittering. Her eyes speak of the first and very last days, they are cool pools and the deepest wells. I drink deeply of them.

Smiling still, the tattooed crescent of blue at her temple shining, she reaches beneath her table and pulls from the darkness three bright cloths, three silken squares in red, green, and yellow. She says: "The red for love, the green to be healed, the yellow for that which will be revealed."

I do not understand. I look at her, bewildered. She takes my hand and lays the first square, the red, down next to me on the table. She places my hand upon it, palm down. She chants:

Oh, what of love that you would ask?
To vision this is now your task,
To ask and see and place it here,
To place it here and hold it dear!

I say: "I would like to know about love and put my envisioned question here?" I point to the centre of the square of cloth.

She nods and smiles and jigs a little, rising and falling like the tide on her skinny legs, with one long bird-foot lifting.

Then wrap it up inside the red,
As in your vision saw it,
And pop it then into the fire,
And let the flames adore it!

I think of a question about love in my life that I would like the answer to, a truth about love I would like to be revealed to me at this time. I picture the question and image in my mind and then I put it in the centre of the red silken square of cloth. Then I fold the cloth around it and tie a knot in it, to keep my vision in. The woman, hopping in glee now, gestures to the roaring fire. I stand and take it to the flames and, counting to three, I cast it in. There is a whoosh and then the flames gut as if I have cast water upon them. When they rise again, I see a picture in the flickering fire. I stand and watch as the answer to my question about love is revealed. I see images relating to love in my life (or in the life of another I envisioned for).

"Ha!" the wise woman cries, slapping her hands together. "You see?"

I nod. I sit back down at her table and she places the green square down. This one is for placing a vision of healing. As I cast it into the flame I get an insight into how the ailment or problem may be healed, or how soon this event may occur.

Finally, in the yellow I place my vision for revealing a truth. This could be a universal truth or simply to see the facts behind a situation in my life, to cast some light on it, to have clarity and deep insight. This is what the spell we are engaging in is all about.

I turn and the woman is more sombre now, her cackling countenance replaced by a sober and staid yet infinitely caring look, rather like an old-fashioned school marm. She has somehow donned a woven robe of greyed lavender, plain and loosely belted over her wrinkled form, and her hair is now apparently pulled back away from her strong face into a plait. What a myriad of guises this wise woman has to show me! From her almost insane vision of the delinquent harpy to the queenly priestess figure to the mysterious half-hidden witch by her fire to now almost grandmotherly, and all shades inbetween.

My attention is caught for a moment by a small movement to our right. I notice for the first time that there is a second door there and that it is opening slowly into the gloom beyond. I ask: "Must I leave, lady?"

She replies: "Your time with me is done for this day, but not for all time. What will you take with you to remind you?"

I think about everything she has shown me, from the place that we are in to her appearance and aura. I think of the magic we have made in her cave. I answer her question. Perhaps I choose to take with me the knowledge of the true nature of age and beauty or the ability to see what is truly there, or real strength and wisdom. Or maybe I share a personal revelation. It is between myself and the wise woman at this juncture what passes between us. I give this interchange ample time.

Then she says: "And what will you leave for me, what bright promise in the darkness?"

Here I must decide, before I can walk through her door into my otherworldly reality, what I can pledge to her as a gift of thanks. I can offer her something like my devotion to spellcraft or herbal lore, I can vow to volunteer for age-concerned charities, perhaps, or to clear up a local beach. I can promise to come to her, at the time between full and dark moon (especially the latter), and share in her wise ways, for the good of the All. I can offer her my allegiance in a human world that has little respect for that which is old.

Whatever I offer, she takes time to accept. She then grasps my hand and again I gasp to see how strong she is, her hold is as taut as a wire and thrumming with energy. Then the door swings open fully as I say my goodbyes, for now. Next I step on through.

Where am I? Do I have to find my own way back through the winding labyrinth of cave passages? I blink in the darkness, but is it really that dark? Am I at the cave mouth? I sniff and smell damp earth, mildew, and loam. I reach out and touch familiar bark-skin. I am no longer in her realm but in mine, inside the hollow tree!

Stepping out of the tree, onto the side that takes me back to "ordinary" reality, I thank my friend, the hollow oak, and step onto the badger track that leads me to the meadow. This journey is done.

But what is this that swings around my neck as I step from the tree? I reach up and find a stone tied around my neck on a waxed thong. Water has made a hole straight through this irregular shaped pebble, with its relentless ebbing and flowing, by its wild power. It is my talisman, thrice blessed. I can keep it safe by hanging it from the lowest branch of the tree to await my return. None can remove it as this is my safe place.

Smiling I return and begin to ground myself fully. I take up my notebook to write my experiences of meeting she who is the waning mother, dark queen, ruler of tides, and spinner of fate, the wise woman.

Review: Reasons We Trance Journey

Trance journeys both clarify what enchantments should be undertaken—for it is in the Otherworld that we are able to ask our guides for help—and also they back up the magic in an unseen way. For example, we can go to a manifest destination and plant a seed for certain magical purposes and we can plant a seed in our astral safe place also. "As above, so below." . . . "As within so without."

As we have already covered many reasons to trance journey, including specific path-working (a journey taken for a specific purpose) here is a list of reasons that will be used over and over again. This list is not exhaustive, but gives a broad flavour.

Supportive Magic

To back up any worldly magic by replicating the gesture in an otherworldly sense.

Rogue Cleansing

To meet with a spirit who may be causing trouble or consternation in the manifest world. To move on lost souls (known as "spirit rescue"), or to banish thoughtforms.

Finding Soul Purpose

To quest for our soul purpose, magical meaning, symbols, and signs that help our life path/understanding and that of others. This could help us gain clarity about our direction and help us make decisions.

Seeking Advice

For advice and guidance pertaining to casting spells. Getting a spiritual overview on whether a spell would be appropriate, understanding the resonance and repercussions of what we do.

Soul Retrieval

To find lost parts of our own being, which may have fragmented from us in times of trauma. This is part of the work known as "soul retrieval" and can be undertaken when we have an excellent working relationship with the Otherworld self and know our own energies intimately. Without this we will never know what is ours to keep and what is missing. This is a more advanced technique and will not be covered here, although it is good to mention that when we are confident and proficient in working with energies we can engage in this sort of work. We can also undertake it on behalf of others.

Personal Development

To quest for aspects of the self as yet undeveloped. A quest for confidence or resource-fulness may follow a fairytale path, we could be the ones to rescue the Sleeping Beauty, for instance. The Sleeping Beauty is an analogy for the wild spirit of the land, therefore this would be a quest to wake up the land and bring about the Greening against the odds wrought by modern society.

Healing

For the sake of healing by calling up the Otherworld self of the person who needs help (with his or her permission).

Meeting Other Beings

For the purpose of meeting with other beings to better understand them, such as gnomes, unicorns, warrior men, or bears.

Other-Life Discovery

To find out who we, or others, were in past (or other) lives, but only for the sake of answering pertinent questions in the current life and resolving deep-seated issues. This is not a technique for the curious day-tripper. Details will be discussed in chapter 6.

Greater Consciousness

The World Tree allows us to journey toward greater consciousness by travelling up or down the "trunk" of the tree, which connects the upper and lower worlds of spirit and consciousness. We may envision ourselves entering a tree, for example, the hollow tree in our astral safe place, and move up or down the trunk, either in a beam of light or by using physical means such as ropes or steps (these may appear in the tree if it seems appropriate). The lower and upper levels are the roots and the branches we discussed when we first looked at the tree visualisation. We understand the glorious heights that allow us to contact bright truths and the depths that draw us down into the dark heart of wild being, which is at the core of ourselves and all existence. It is the trunk, or ourselves as wildwitches, that makes the connection, acts as the conduit and becomes the living wood.

The upperworld is a place above our mundane concerns and the lowerworld (also referred to as the "Underworld," as discussed in chapter 3) is the place that reveals what lies beneath daily human reality. The upperworld journey allows us to obtain starlight insight, connecting us with beings for inspiration and guidance, and to gain the bigger picture in terms of universal energies. The lowerworld journey allows for profound transformation, to find the root of things, to reveal that which is concealed, to connect with ancestral wisdom and our own ancient power. Both are places concerned with fate, one on a deep personal level, one with a wider perspective—one weaves from roots and shoots, one from sun and moon beams. In the World Tree concept discussed in chapter 3 we also mentioned middle Earth, which is also known as the "middle world." This is where we walk with spirit on a daily basis, the realm of our Otherworld self, the safe astral place. It is that place that is closest to, and which echoes, the physical world. This is the place we will be most used to, the place of our familiar spirits.

All we need to know can be imparted to us in our astral safe place if we work well with our companions and pay attention to the symbology of our journeys. We may ask our companion spirits if we need to travel up or down the World Tree for any reason, but we should not feel as if we should be doing this as a matter of course. All aspects of spiritwalking can be experienced for specific purposes in time. When we feel that we have the confidence, experience, and working knowledge, then perhaps our companions will suggest that our time has come to purposefully venture outside of the middle realm.

*   *   *

In the next chapter we will look at how our companions can help us create sparkling, positive, green-spirited spells by utilising all that we have learned so far in an active service to the All.

Chapter Five

WILD ENCHANTMENTS, GREEN WILFUL WISHES

Poppy petals fall on swaying corn,
Antlers rise to meet rosy dawn,
As a velvet secret on a breeze is born . . .

We are now becoming aquainted with the key concepts and the wild essence of our craft. We know it to be a blend of sensuous spirituality, intrepid yet sensitive interaction, and inner exploration. We understand that at the heart of our wild craft there is balance and harmony, which depends on our consistent approach to the unseen and our behaviours in daily life. We may have experienced a profound familiar resonance within us and have felt the deep roots of the land. We accept it to be a way that requires both inspiration and perspiration on our part. It is an exquisite and intimate way that we may walk whilst walking it for all our relations, for all beings.

So, what else do we need to know before we begin to really bring the green-spirited way to bear in our own lives? How do we go about integrating wild enchantment into our daily existence? What sort of magic may we practice and why?

Firstly, let's just reaffirm our purpose. Wild witchcraft is about making a positive contribution to the All by enhancing it through enchantment. Wild enchantment is about recognising and celebrating the eternal animating force that enlivens all creation. We tap into this force creatively and we weave it into the mundane, namely human existence. To live magically is to be fully sensate and willing to work with shimmering, free-flowing universal energy. To practice wild magic is to know that we can best do this by having one foot in the human manifest world (whilst not being of it) and one foot in the spiritual Otherworlds (while being grounded), to effectively blend the corporeal/temporary and the ethereal/eternal. As wildwitches, we are bridge-builders, the living wood that spans the distance between levels of existence, and we are the ones who try to close that gap a little—bringing the magic of the Otherworlds back to human life.

How may we be effective bridge-builders and therefore be confident and accomplished practitioners of meaningful enchantment? By means of a simple but enduring enchantment. In order to create this enchantment we must follow a time-tested equation. It is:

Protection + Guidance + Tides + Focus = Magical Change

This is a necessary formula for our progression. Without any one factor in it we will be ineffectual bridge-builders. We then risk our enchantments being as structurally unsound as a real bridge without supports, our living wood will not be strong or flexible enough to span the distance. The equation makes for rounded results as it encompasses all aspects of our craft. Take any aspect away and we will be making empty gestures, our magic vague and formless, our energies dissipated.

The first two aspects of this equation, protection and guidance, refer to the "unseen" or spiritual aspects of our work. The third aspect, tides, refers to the energies involved, be they seasonal (solar), elemental, or lunar. The fourth aspect, focus, refers to the practical manifest things we can do to support the unseen aspects. Our interactions with spirit, with the essence of nature, and with the waxing and waning energies of existence are woven into our daily reality with the specific intention of bringing about a particular resonant result. This result is a shift in the energies that connect, and indeed constitute, both levels of existence, thus making our desired difference in the world (our magical result). Our aim, as we have previously ascertained, is to do this for the greatest good.

We have already begun to transform our lives by walking the wild way and have certainly started to realise that we are beings of enchantment. Now we are ready to take on the responsibility of having a truly charmed life. To live a charmed life does not mean that good fortune is entirely ours, nor will every single thing go our way. If this was the case then what would we learn? Where would our challenges be and without them how would we grow? To live a charmed life signifies that our lives are alive with magical energy, we are enraptured and spellbound by our part in the dance of life. We are ready to plan, cast, and assess more formal, but no less joyous, spell-weavings. Throughout this chapter the equation helps us to do this.

Protection

One brief note on protection. The first aspect of our equation is protection and we have covered this in-depth elsewhere. As we know, protection is vital and the more we practice the more we need to rigorously apply our own particular protective process. This is because we will hopefully be going further and deeper on each trance journey, making greater explorations into inner space each time. Also, the more proficient we get the more we need our protective routines. We should never be tempted to get blasé. Protection isn't only for journeying, it is to be used every time we open up energetically. When we weave our enchantments it is essential to protect ourselves.

Guidance

We have briefly looked at guidance, this being the advice and inspiration we gain from a healthy interaction with our companion spirits but here we will look more closely at this. The relevance of working with these trusted companions should never be overlooked, so we will look at ways of obtaining and noting their observations. In order to practice any enchantment our relations with the companions must be close; only they can give us the overview of a situation that allows us to make informed decisions. Basically, guidance is anything that shows us how the webs of fate we seek to weave link us in to those around us. Guidance can be philosophical and impersonal, relating to external energies and the nature of existence, or it can relate to deeply personal matters of the soul. Either way it helps us more fully understand the unseen dimensions of being, which enables us to be more ethical spellcrafters.

We may have the best intentions possible and create a simply beautiful spell to be worked for what we perceive to be in the best interest of the All, yet without guidance, we could inadvertently be going against the flow and so unwittingly cause great harm. Knowledge is power. To seek out any consequence to our actions is to be wise and considerate. Regret is a terrible thing when it could have been avoided by simply asking: "What will happen if I do this spell at this time? When would be a feasible or fortuitous time for me to ask for its fruition to come?" Sometimes we aren't meant to ask for certain things as life has other things in store for us on our path. It is good to know this, too. The spirits will tell us such information if we ask them directly.

Our companion friends are invaluable. It would be folly not to consult with them on such potentially far-reaching matters. It is interesting and advisable to converse with guiding spirits on the matters of ill wishing and making negative magical requests even if we have no intention of ever weaving such spells. We should do this as soon as they are willing to discuss it with us. They can adequately advise us of the payback we may receive if we dabble in such tempting fare as curses and hexes. If we truly believe in "As above, so below" and "As within, so without," and if we understand our energies to be connected to all other energies on the web of life, then how can we intentionally do harm when we understand it will be felt by us on some level, sometime, somewhere? If we are practising wild enchantment then the well-being of Earth and all her children is paramount. When we harm one on the web of life we harm all by connection. The energy of harm is sent into the world, it is that simple. We must let our familiar spirits give us further insights of their own. We are, of course, free to take the risks if we know the consequences.

Techniques to Remember Spirit Communication

It is often difficult to recall the answers to the questions that we ask of our companions on a trance journey and this is why it is sensible to keep such requests to a minimum. It is only courteous to limit ourselves to three questions—the spirits may be our guides but they are not here to give us the answer to every single matter bothering us at one time. We need to prioritise our needs with respect for their selfless service to us. We are not just referring to quotable spoken guidance. Often from our journeys we can bring back more in the way of visual impressions. While this is valid in itself there are occasions when it pays to have a direct transcript of the advice given so that we may be sure that any actions based on it may be truly engaged in for the greatest good.

Spiritual guidance is notoriously subtle and symbolic and if we remember even the slightest turn of phrase incorrectly by the time we get back to "ordinary" human reality then we could alter the whole meaning of a discourse. It is especially pertinent for us to have an accurate record of what has been given to us as spiritual advice when we are asking about spellwork as here we are actively wielding our power and affecting our energetic environs and therefore we need to act with the utmost care and consideration. This is where written guidance comes in. It is a new skill for us to learn but once it is mastered it is invaluable as a way of maintaining a journal of magical progress. The directly dictated words of our companion guides, even if they seem impenetrable or irrelevant at the time, can be referred back to in months or even years to come as ways of both uplifting our spirits and cross-referencing current understandings or subsequently prophesied events.

It is vital that we become familiar with this technique before we intend to cast any potent, long-lasting, highly effective spells. It is one thing for us to have invoked so far for a plant to grow, for the health of a close friend to improve, or for inspiration in our own creativity, but as soon as we are considering spellweaving to enable us to move house, or for a new partner or colleague, or for the end of property development on a local site, which is home to many wild creatures, then we are entering an arena where our energetic input will affect many. We will never even see some of the effects from our spells but the energy will spread nonetheless. For instance, how are we to know the rolling chain of events that occur after one house move or a sudden job loss? And how are we to know if, energetically, a new home is actually right for us if we do not ask those who have the overview of the situation, our companions? We could save ourselves and others much inconvenience and even heartache by consulting with our guides and then recording their thoughts upon our spells. They can bring to light any potential pitfalls that we will want to avoid and we can always refer back to this guidance once we have it written down.

Example: Chain Reaction

Here is an example, taken from the *Stories of the Wild Spirit* book that accompanied my *Waking the Wild Spirit* tarot deck (Llewellyn, 2002). It shows just how our energies travel onward without us knowing. This illustrates a positive chain reaction of energy (although think what a similar negative pattern could do if the person began by frowning rather than smiling).

> . . . You may smile warmly at a stranger in the street, even though you are late for work and the day is damp and miserable. That one smile lifts the spirits of the stranger who has just had some bad news, which has made them feel suspicious and mistrusting. They then find a wallet in the gutter. Before your smile they may have kept it, along with its contents, thinking that humanity wasn't up to much and the owner deserved to be robbed if they couldn't keep an eye on their own property. Instead the wallet is handed in to the police where the owner, frantic, then claims it later. They are then able to take their elderly mother out for a birthday meal with the cash they had saved in the wallet.

While they are out, the mother makes eye contact with a gentlemen at the next table and soon they are all sharing coffee and conversation. The mother, who is terminally ill, gets to know the man who becomes a great comfort to her in her last days. The man himself then goes on to donate a great part of his wealth to a hospice, which gives care to those with the same illness that she had. That hospice is then able to open another wing, enabling your own mother to be cared for instead of remaining at home alone.

With this example in mind we certainly need to be mindful of what we "put out," energetically speaking! Written guidance helps us to weigh the energetic resonance and potential outcomes of our actions over a period of time. We can ponder on the written words without fear of forgetting them. In order to become conversant with the method, practice is needed. It is essential to be fluent before we think of "heavy-duty" spellweaving in the community. So, initially we should practice our written guidance technique when we have questions of less pressing importance to ask. Sample questions may be something like:

- "Tell me, trusted guide, why do humans feel the need to go to war?"

- "Companion spirit, please share with me the energetic implications of cosmetic surgery for its own sake?"

- "Familiar one, will you give me some spiritual advice on the matter of genetically modified food?"

Channelled Written Guidance

To obtain a reliable written dialogue we can use a straightforward approach that requires us only to be protected, connected, in contact with our companions, and deeply relaxed enough to be open as a channel for their words. To start, we should have a pad of blank paper in front of us, one with large sheets that turn easily, and at least one full ballpoint pen. Familiarity with our tools is paramount. Pencils can break their leads until we know the speed and pressure at which we will be writing so they are best avoided, at least at first.

To begin we must go through our regular journey process—grounding, relaxing, breathing deeply, and visualising protection. At the protective stage it is important, whilst envisioning the bubble or cloak of light, to see ourselves sitting with straight back, and connected in a circle of cold, blue-gold flame. This requires concentration on the circle as it arcs behind us, ensuring that the whole ring of fire is complete and burning with an equal intensity.

Once we are sitting in a circle of flame we should employ the extra protective symbols over each of our bodily portals or energy points. We either place a shining symbol over each in turn, beginning at the base or lower region and working upward, or imagine a flower opening at each centre. Why do we need this? Well, as our guidance will be channelled, we need to have a very cautious approach to our own safety, ensuring that only those who truly approach for our highest good come through. State your situation and intention clearly but poetically:

> *I am linked to the loam whilst my spirit does roam,*
> *I'm sky-touching like the tree while my spirit walks free,*
> *I'm protected by the fire while my spirit soars higher,*
> *And I'm walking deep inside to talk with my guide!*

We can now make our journey to our astral safe place and through to the plain where we may meet our companion spirits. Perhaps by now our sacred place has evolved and shifted to fit us more comfortably and when I say "the plain" please do assume I mean any place in the safe place where we customarily meet with our familiars.

Use the circle of fire to call up the guiding spirit and test them out as per usual (refer to page 155 and 146). We will only have a dialogue with one of our guides but if we wish for the presence of all of our guides then we can call them up and they may act as "watchers" to the proceedings. If we have more than one companion currently then we will probably find that one is more happy to enter into this form of transcript with us than the rest. We must inform them of our intention. Are they willing to assist? We ask for their patience as it is our first time. Then we give them a philosophical question to work on, as per the examples previously given.

Limit the guides to a certain amount of time. Spirit dwells, as we know, in Faery time and companions can often quite happily chat to us for a solid hour at a stretch unless we first put a definite boundary on our time. An hour of channelling spirit using a pen can lead to a cramped hand, numb legs, and an aching head! Five or ten minutes would suit a beginner to the technique and fifteen to twenty minutes is fine for an experienced worker. We must also be specific with the desired timeframe in which our spell will come to fruition. We can do this in a lyrical energetic sense, stating that we would like to see the spell come to being when the next frost is on the ground or when the next apples are on the tree. Such requests must, of course, be checked with the companion spirits to see if our designated timeframe is appropriate.

Now, we open our eyes. We pick up the pad of paper and open it to a double page so we have lots of room. We pick up the pen in front of us and ensure that it is held flexibly in the active hand, but we don't grip on to it for dear life! We should ensure that the pen is at the top of the left-hand page. We can choose to keep our eyes open or we may shut them again. It is all trial and error at first. We shouldn't be afraid of the process, it is an experiment to begin with and will take us several tries to perfect our own techniques. If we choose to work with our eyes closed all the time, then we may like to be ready at the very beginning of the journey. If so, we would have pen and paper in our hands before we even enter our otherworldly safe place in trance.

Now we breathe deeply and free our minds again of any extraneous thoughts. We aim to just be at peace while we focus on the link between our spiritual self and that of the companion we are to meet. If we have our eyes closed then we must visualise the companion before us, holding their image, focusing on them, feeling their energy. If we have our eyes open we can let our surroundings blur just so we remain aware of the pad and the pen and our link to spirit. We may then hear their words in our own mind or see them speak to us and simultaneously hear them. They may send us an image to begin with or a string of images. Whatever or however they begin to address us, we write down what is being given to us. If we see a house then we write down "house" followed by a visual description. If the guide has begun to dictate information to us then we simply note what we hear.

If we have our eyes open, we do not try to read what we are writing as we write it. If we have them closed, we should try not to get too caught up in worrying where the edges of the paper are, but just let the words flow. At first we may come out with several illegible pages but in time we will have much more of a sense of trust, which will allow us to step back and act as nothing but a hand that channels the information as it comes through us. When this happens we will find that we have an innate sense of the boundaries of the page.

At this stage, we try to be aware of when our own conscious mind intervenes. When the information is personal to us this will happen much more and we will probably find we are blocking the companion guide's own voice by anticipating what we think will be said next. This is why it is much easier to step back from the proceedings when the subject matter is general and broadly philosophical.

After the allotted time prescribed at the beginning, the trusted companion should round up and sign off. This signature will be another calling card for you to recognise. They may say: "Be at peace, child" or "Go well!"

We now thank our companion for their insights. If we have our eyes open then we can close them and see ourselves standing back on the grounds of our sacred place with them. If we have had our eyes closed all the time, then we focus on our wider surroundings again. Then we simply follow our tracks—using our sample journey we would walk back through the hollow tree, into the meadow, through the gate—back to "ordinary reality." As we are not necessarily following the sample journey, rather following ones we ouselves have created based on its framework, we simply reverse the process we followed as we were on the outward leg of the journey, moving back from the Otherworld into our physical existence. We must then ground ourselves. It is advisable to make a hot drink and eat a biscuit or cracker before looking at what we have written down.

We should not feel disheartened if at first we cannot read our transcript, it will come! We will find advantages and disadvantages to having our eyes both open and closed for the proceedings so we can try either method on different occasions. With our eyes open we have the advantage of being aware of the empty page, where to stop writing, and when to turn the pages, but we lose that deep focus on the companion spirit. With our eyes shut we maintain that focus but may lose track of our page. We can ask one of our watcher companions to help us remain on the page and write more clearly. In time this will happen anyway, as our intuitive abilities will flourish.

Another problem may be that we find the dictation to be too speedy and we end up writing too fast. This will result in an uncomfortable experience and an illegible transcription. The same problem as with Faery time applies. As the companions have no physical body right now, they can easily forget our limitations. We must simply remind them of our specific limitations and tell them to be more measured in their delivery!

Automatic Writing

There is another method of transcribing spiritual guidance straight from the source. Whereas our first method works by us taking dictation down, the second method is more like "automatic" writing—writing that is channelled directly to the page without us having to hear (or see) what is being said. This is achieved by means of us using our active hand to write down questions to our companions on paper. The inactive hand then writes the answers we receive from our companions. In this method we channel our guide's answer through us by means of our inactive hand.

By our "active" hand we simply mean the hand we most favour, for the majority this is the right hand. If we are right-handed then the left hand is our inactive hand and our guidance will flow through the left hand. Since the inactive hand is not as controlled by us, the likelihood of information being able to flow through us is increased.

Clearly all the usual sacred precautions and pre-journey measures are put in place before we begin to channel any spiritual information. By "channel" we simply mean that we become conduits as we have discussed before, it certainly doesn't mean we lose conciousness or control but that we allow other energies to flow through us whilst remaining vigilant and relaxed. We do not need to go on a full trance journey to channel in this fashion, rather we may invoke our companion spirits, those who come for our highest good, while we sit in our envisioned circle of protective fire, calm and accessible.

We need to have in front of us a large paper pad, open to a double page, and two different coloured pens, say red for the active questioning and black for the inactive response. It will, of course, be obvious which is a question and which is an answer but, initially, our inactive hand's writing may be rather illegible or may run off the page. It is good to have some sense of differentiating what is going on. Having two distinct coloured pens also helps us to get into that ritualistic space of entering into a specific spiritual exchange. By taking up different coloured pens we get into the mood of receiving and asking for information from the spirits. It is like having different coloured wires in a plug.

To begin, we take up the red pen in the active hand. We take several, measured deep breaths and reaffirm our position and purpose:

> *I sit alone in my magical ring,*
> *Alone but never truly so,*
> *And I ask that those who wish me well,*
> *Draw close and speak of what they know.*
> *Come now companions of ultimate truth,*
> *Come now and guide, sayers of sooth!*

Now we write down our request formally in red at the top of the left-hand page. This is a request that our own true familiar spirits will answer for us to the best of their knowledge, sincerity, and ability. We call them by name if possible and then ask the question we first wish to address.

When asking questions in this fashion remember that three is a sensible number as this can be an intense way of gaining insights. Keep the questions to either (a) philosophical or magical issues that relate to universal themes and topics or (b) to any personally pressing issue or current problem. Do not try to engage in a discourse about the future. This method is not about divination or "far seeing" but rather a channelled discourse. If matters of future importance crop up in the course of our exchange with spirit then this is one thing, but to court answers into the more distant future can be confusing because, as we have already come to appreciate, the webs of fate can change and be rewoven over time. We have free will, as do all beings, and can choose to veer off our life paths (to some degree) at any given moment. Major life themes and patterns always remain, but the issues that thread through the broad band of our lives can fluctuate greatly. Multiply this by an unfeasibly large figure to see how world or even universal patterns can shift!

Divination certainly is valid and has its place in our craft but even then it is best, perhaps for the previous reason, to avoid specific global prophesy. It is easy to think of people who have prophesied major global catastrophe at a given time only to find their guidance was incorrect. Although, this could also be due to the fact that they did not rigorously check out the spirits who divulged this information and rogue elements got through. Saying this, it has also been known for genuine and trustworthy spirits to totally flounder when asked to predict world or definite far-flung personal events. The spirit companions only have the overview pertaining to that moment, snapshots in spirit time. To push them on future predictions may result in us then losing our trust in them when predictions fail—and failure is inevitable since futures change in a blink of an eye; one choice can alter an entire web of future outcomes.

To get an answer to a question, we first pick up the black pen, lightly and flexibly, in the inactive hand. We breathe deeply and wait with it poised over the paper. We must not transmit a sense of panic or pressure, both of which may distort the communication. As we have said, what comes forth for the first few sessions may be nothing more than us and spirit trying to work out a way of writing that feels comfortable. This may just show itself as a lot of dashes and squiggles. We must bear with this, as for coherent words to form we must "bed in" with our guiding spirit. Our companions have no bodies at present and so we need to get used to the whole process of working with a physical body again, and this time someone else's—ours. If we have the patience, this method can be very fulfilling indeed as we have the satisfaction of knowing that we have little or no control over our inactive hand writing in "ordinary" life and yet with spirit's help we can express valid and interesting concepts through the very same hand.

When waiting to ask another question we can try to get a sense of when the answer has concluded. We may not be able to read what we have written to ascertain the true end of an answer but we can allow a few moments after the writing has apparently ceased before taking up the red pen again to ask another question. When we become au fait with this method we will know what we have written and can gear the next question to the last reply. This sort of fluid and immediate exchange is one of the many benefits of sticking with this channelled technique. We can have a written conversation and can respond to the flow of what has been said just as we would when directly talking to the companion. At the end of the session, we close by giving thanks and asking for the companions' continued support and care. We then bid them farewell.

If, after half a dozen attempts, no progress is being made at all, or if we feel really uncomfortable with the whole process, then we should not feel obliged to stick with it. Confidence can be undermined if we are skeptical or afraid. Please understand that by channelling we are not being taken over. We are well protected, we have invoked for the highest guidance, and we are not in the sort of deep trance that some mediums use when they are temporarily "taken over" by a spirit. We also checked out the spirit when it first appeared (or upon our initial sensing its presence) so we know the spirit communicating with us is genuinly guiding us with care.

However, if this active/inactive method really doesn't seem to be working for us, simply revert to the first suggestion of the technique, where we enter into a dictation with our companion. Not all methods suit us as individuals. On a personal note, I myself can take down wonderfully accurate dictation from companion spirits but I am hopeless at using a pendulum for divination. No matter how long I work at it, the pendulum always hangs slack and inert. I have tried many types of pendulums, from a pebble on a cord to a shop-bought crystal device to a gold ring on a piece of string, and the result is always the same . . . nothing! Yet I have seen people with no other magical skills use a pendulum with ease. There is no set rule for which skill we should have and, indeed, we could come up with our very own method for taking down notes on spiritual guidance. This would be truly of the wild nature and to be encouraged as long as the practice remains safe and within our usual perimeters of care, courtesy, and caution.

So, we should stick with our chosen written guidance technique. It is eventually very satisfying and infinitely useful even if initially it yields only frustratingly scrappy fragments. We should employ it to gain true insights into the validity and appropriateness of any wild enchantments we have in mind for the near future. Through this written guidance we can gain so much about our craft, specifically how magic works and how we should approach the weaving of it into the world. It is an invaluable aid and helps our magic to be truly unique, divinely inspired, and unfailingly ethical.

Magic Guides

Who or what can help us and guide us when we work our magical spellcraft? Here we will take a look at our companions in magic, including the Fey, elemental, and nature spirits, as well as means of communicating with these friends. We will find great respect for the advice and inspiration they can offer.

Fey

To discuss our craft is most certainly to discuss that which is Fey but what do we really mean by "Fey" and what kind of beings are we really speaking about?

One view is to call effeminate males "fey," being that they are comfortable with expressing a more intuitive, creative, and sometimes flamboyant energy in the world than their more overtly masculine counterparts. It is no coincidence that such men are also called "faeries," although usually in a way that degrades the individual concerned and disregards the true meaning of this most beautiful of epithets. It should be regarded as a high compliment!

To be called "fey" can also suggest a certain ungrounded, vague quality; perhaps referring to one who is possessed of an artistic or poetic nature. It may be used to describe the sort of visionary or romantic soul that is considered "away with the faeries." Fey energy is essentially watery, that is, dreamy and lyrical. It could also be said to be airy in that it is suggestive of gossamer and gauzy wings, drifting and wafting thoughts, and all that has a mutable and ephemeral essence. Fey energy connects us to the bright blaze of a distant star on which we may hang our aspirations, one that brings us down into the deepest pools of inspiration. It flies us to the heights and lets us dive to the depths in order that we may gain both insight and sublime creative impetus. It is of the Faerytide, of both freedom flight and ebb and flow.

The word "fey" also alludes to fate and is therefore concerned with magical seeing and knowing, spiritweaving, and spellcraft. It embodies the intuitive side of the element of water and the mercurial communicative side of air. This is why the wonderful mythical enchantress Morgan le Fey is actually Morgan the Fate, or Morgan of the Faeries. The true Faery beings who still dwell alongside humanity are fashioned directly of Fey energy. Fate, Fey, and Faery energies are all inextricably linked.

When we are fey we have starlight vision, the clarity of being guided by whatever lies beyond, we have one foot in the Otherworlds and one in the manifest Earth, maintaining the balance of ethereal magic and physical matter. The Faery races themselves exist in this glorious state and although we may not have their nebulous quality, being bound in mortal skin as we currently are, we may share their natural desire to bring balance. So, by choice and by the bidding of our own wild spirit, to be a wildwitch in the world is to be a Fey worker—literally, a fate crafter. The darkly shining energy of Morgan (also known as Morgen, Morgana, and Morgaine) is more than appropriate for a wildwitch to work with, she is a patron of our art.

If we talk of the Fey (or the Faery) then we are discussing those who are fashioned directly from this energy, the Faery kin or fair ones ("fair" here meaning beautiful and shining). The Fey are the personification of enchantment as their whole existence is bound free by the spirit of the wild, they are disembodied but embody all the qualities we have discussed. They are of the Earth but never of the Western human society, which is made up of inorganic structure and meaningless ritual and law. They are of nature but not the elemental nature spirits who we will come to discuss briefly.

The Faerytide is that which touches us when we look beyond, into the green. We can perceive (or psychically see) the Faery kin as cool, calm elves, grumbling goblins, or pert, pesky pixies, but they are never truly static or classifiable by their assumed appearances. Just as our companion spirits dress themselves in a guise so that we may recognise them and resonate positively with them, so do the Fey appear to us in whatever guise they think we will find most pleasing—or unpleasant, depending on their ever-changing moods. We may also discern their purely energetic forms in a way that is filtered by our own personal level of understanding, coloured by our expectations, and tempered by the attitudes of our current sex, race, society, and so on.

The Fey are pure vibration and only dress up to reveal themselves to us. Their true nature still shines through the guise they assume for us. Several people could observe the same Faery as looking quite different, perhaps with a longer nose, more slanted eyes, or a contrary-coloured hat. Or perhaps one would see a classically lovely woman with defined breasts, flowing hair, and wings, whilst another would see a sexless willowy dancer with no hair at all. The point is that the Fey are close to spirit and to that untamed expression of elemental force and therefore have no one stable rigid form, rather they are fluid and shifting.

The Fey *are* mystery. In our work as wildwitches we are primarily concerned with aligning the mysteries with the mundane, whispering subtle secrets and profound wisdoms into the world with humour, compassion, creativity, and joy—all Faery traits. By "mystery" we mean that the Fey are unknowable yet they become accessible to us through our relationship with the wild. They are our link into the hidden realms and at the same time lead us into untamed nature. They are the ones that can help us understand both our own deep essence and that of the land.

But do the Fey really want to help us humans, even if their nature is magical? Here lies the paradox of Faery. Just as they may choose deliberately to charm or frighten us by their appearance they can either court human affection or despise what humanity does in social terms. They hold us responsible for the destruction of the Faery way and of the very environments they seek to protect and merge with, yet they want us to help them re-establish their link with the physical plane in order to harmonise the material with the magical.

Where are the Fey to be found today? They hide in the last vestiges of the remote places and can be felt on the moors and in the depths of any unfarmed forest. They live off the beaten track, flitting with the exotic wings of a butterfly or wearing an acorn cap and an oak-leaf jerkin. We are most likely to find them within such places as the west coast of Ireland, the Scottish islands, the West Penwith area of Cornwall, Dartmoor in Devon, England, or in the southwest or wild rugged north of Wales, and in countless other lonely windswept places or regions of untouched splendour across the world and no doubt in countless isolated hollow hills, Tors, Faeryforts, streams, remote woodlands, wells, and caves into which they come and go, disappearing back into the less manifest levels of existence and making themselves known to us at will. A manmade site would certainly not appeal to the Fey, unless it was placed on a particularly resonant natural spot.

Their energy is not compatible with our homogenised nature trails and parks, they are at odds with our sanitising of nature and have sought refuge in the places man finds inhospitable and unworthy of too much attention and conversion. And yet they do seek us out when it suits them because, although they want the human realm to shrink back and, perhaps, be gone, they want us to help them bring back their own way into the world. Their dilemma is that when we find them, or rather, when they choose to reveal themselves to us in these wild places, they want to say, "Leave us alone!" At the same time, they know the world needs what they possess, that glorious enchantment, and they accept that we are their hope of transmitting it.

But how may we relate to them at all, if they are so fickle? A relationship with a Faery being can lead to much confusion and disillusion at first as we can find that one day they welcome us and share their ways with us and the next they tell us to go away, that they are tired of all two-legged beasts bent on destruction! One day they charm us with wit and wile, asking for sweet treats to be left for them, wanting our sparkling jewelry; the next day they spurn any suggestion that human contact is anything but an anathema to them. We will find that it is common to find ourselves welcome in a Fey place for a day, only to be chased out on the subsequent visit. And even when we are welcome, they can very quickly tire of our slow and relatively dense way of relating, consequently banishing us after only a short interaction.

If this is the case, why bother? Is having any sort of relationship with the Fey worth it? Well, if we can stick with the contact and make the required offerings, displaying the very nonhuman traits (in their eyes) of patience, courtesy, and sensitivity, then we will have made a link, which can indeed help filter that shimmering starlit grace back into the world. Then we may find ourselves speaking in a subtler way, in gentler voices that lilt, with words that have new depth and meaning. We can be the ones to carry that playful, mercurial but infinitely insightful way back into the world. And the best way to establish and maintain this link is by a blend of otherworldly journeying to meet Fey contacts and actual pilgrimage to the remaining Fey places so that we may reveal our intentions and blend with their energies in a physical sense.

Until we accept that the Fey are not human and have a very different way of relating than we do, we will remain frustrated. If we accept their nature, we will gain an ability to respond in the moment, as the Fey live very much in the now and have none of the limiting human preoccupation with past and future. This is their greatest gift to us, along with the ability to laugh more at ourselves and our rigid constructs and expectations.

Example: Faery Tale

Here is a Faery tale, a lyrical description of the possible nature and origins of the Fey, which may help us to understand their relevance in our lives and work. It may resonate with us at a soul level and tell us something of our own wild nature and, indeed, of our own source. In this respect it is worth meditating on. Our interaction with the Fey is precious and here the aim is to experience their nature and to see our potential relationship with them. The tale is called "The Children of the Greening" and is told by spirits who remember the elder days of Faery. The story was shared with me through channelled spirit writing.

Once upon a tide of time, before we lost the shining forms we wore so well and became dusty memory, before we lost sight of the starlight and became a frosty parody, before we hid the truth in the silent stones, in the deep pools, in the land herself, and withdrew into her welcoming womb to that place between realms . . .

Yes, there was a before.

Before there was fear there was love. Love was natural and free and love was the way of things. At the heart of all creation there was love and transformation. Out of this pure love, the Way birthed the web of existence and fashioned from these sacred shining strands the citizens of Itself. For the Way wished to make love with Itself, over and onward and eternally, a great sensual spiritual unfolding, lapping and entwining with Itself in the bliss of reunion and the pain of separation. In the desire to experience its own great love reflecting back, It gave birth.

Fountains of love fuelled the process, a process of illumination, a great light that was only given meaning by its opposite, the velvet dark of dreaming depths. The dark was not greedy, it willingly gave up the gems of glittering, sparkling life that tumbled from the womb of Itself. It was a nurturing darkness, the polar opposite of the brightness, but not its lesser partner, and from the black well of its ever-spiralling tunnel of love burst the stars, gleaming with newness. And the stars in turn birthed the citizens of themselves, the Shining Ones. The dark bore the Children of Light.

These Star Children were miraculous beings of pure energy and raw power, fired by sacred intent, sustained on the pure harmonious tones of a cosmos in tune with Itself. There was a universal shimmering and shuddering rippling throughout the All during the first time the passionate throws of creating were experienced. As It created, these glowing Star Children danced the dream of being to the undulating rhythm of the beginning. They were the original soul singers, singers of the untamed song, the beloved ones of All-that-Was. In this bliss of white light, in the heat of the eternal moment, they sang the strands of starlight into swirling, wheeling arias. Spun them round and round in a dervish dance of pure delight, creating celestial webs that spanned the universe. Each gossamer thread of gold, each opalescent strand vibrating to its own true note, singing.

For aeons they worked magic, self-seeding, glorious and giving, the precious, nebulous Children of Light. Of that tide of time, there is no abiding memory for all was One, all was created by a flight of communal fancy, a melding. These primeval beings shone in the darkness, expressing themselves freely and with infinite love. Their thoughts and feelings rose up on the heavenly fountain of becoming and made worlds. Their dreams of all possibility brought colour and sound and texture. They were the artists and the architects, the visionaries and poets, working with the essential essence of everything for the sheer unbridled pleasure of just being a part of it all.

It was an age of beauty and freedom without boundary or limitation. But that age, like all ages, had to pass. Let us not lament that passing but instead remember its being. It was right and it was good that these original seeds of change spread their fiery wings and headed out into the infinitely expanding oceans of space and place, the seas of swirling constellations and galaxies full of promise. Their original stars grew hot then cold, their light winking out and their time and tide moving into another phase. From the embers of their original homes, the Star Children moved to other levels and dimensions, forming new and fantastic dwelling places in an infinite, unfolding universe. Blessed by their loving Creator, their kisses rained down on astral winds and where they fell the Children followed, filled with the spirit of adventure.

And so it was that some of the Children came to Earth.

The sacred marriage between the heavens and Earth was made, the snaking serpentine flow of energy grounded by the Children as they walked with wonder on this new and verdant planet. Their cosmic energy seeped into Earth Mother's soil, touching her molten core, only to pour forth from places upon her, rising up at natural centres of energy on her lush and beautiful body. She had been resting after her own birthing process and now she was fully awake. She called the Children to her and there were vows made, in love, for her protection and care. This was the eternal promise, which can still be heard and honoured by those who walk lightly, in green truth; and remember in their wild spirits. And the resonance of the vow spread out in rippling rings across the land, translating into the many languages of the creatures there.

This was a living planet, one amongst the millions that seethed and boiled in their own processes of death and rebirth, a place of unlimited possibility and breathtaking beauty. A planet uniquely washed by the seas, which themselves followed the tide of the universal flow, guided by the enigmatic Moon Mother, Lady of Mystery, inspired by her haunting, fluctuating face. It was blessed by the warm embrace of Brother Sun who kept his benevolent distance in Father Sky. It was a good place to call home.

All of the inhabitants of the small, blue-green planet named Earth were spiritually awoken by the presence of the Star Children, the Shining Ones, and they flourished. The furred, finned, and feathered ones, the land dwellers, high flyers and deep swimmers, the stone-people and the green indigenous plant-folk, they all embraced the Children's gifts knowingly, willingly. All except the two-legged humankind.

The native humankind of planet Earth were worthy in that they were still fresh from the Creator's own awakening touch and so they had reverence for their own manifest being. However, they were simple people whose love only extended as far as what they could physically experience. Their five senses were honed and sharp, their wits worked well for them, yet they were dense, grounded in matter and the reality of existence. If they could hit something with a stone mallet then it pleased them, if they could not, it phased them. They were not opened to their own spark of spirit, their sixth sense remained asleep.

They were brown and red skinned, these humans, burned dark or left pale, as the climate dictated, as nature intended. They had simple eloquence and a grace and harmony with their surroundings. They were of the soil and waters, hardened by a foraging existence, accustomed to looking no further than their next meal. In their nomadic lives, across continents that shifted, through climates that fluctuated, across terrain that could be harsh or nurturing, among creatures both deadly and charming, the inhabitants of Earth had a stolid acceptance of whatever they had to endure. They did not give thanks, nor did they celebrate, they just accepted. Oh yes, and these first humans with their uncomplicated souls, they had respect. For without respect for the land there was no next meal and where the next meal came from was of ultimate importance. They did not deplete the land or her resources because that meant individual human depletion. They moved on from place to place and took only what they needed without awareness of anything save shelter and the seemingly constant rumble of hunger in their gut.

Bare, essential survival was their only motivation. And yet they had understanding of Earth's ways, of their fellow creatures, of the seasonal cycles. They even spoke of the moon and sun and stars around their fires at night, but only in terms of the observation of their movements, never in glorious inspiring tales based on the sacred energy involved. These people, they knew only what they could experience by direct bodily contact, they were motivated by the body alone. These humans were no myth-makers, no seers. Their lives had no joy, they were dreamless sleep-walkers, survivors.

Without intuition they could not sense the presence of the Shining Ones on their planet. Without the gifts of the Star Children their existence as lacking in passion and romance, pleasure and purpose. They did not know that life could be beautiful and not just a struggle.

When the Children of the Stars first came among the humankind there was confusion and blind awe. They, the solid and hirsute Children of Earth, saw radiant beings, made seemingly of some less dense source of inner luminosity. They could see no expression on the strange faces that seemed to shapeshift and remain beyond description. They were not in the human range of categorisation and for a time there was complete bewilderment. Surely such beings were their superiors? Or their masters? Or their enemies? Surely not their enemies, these gossamer beings who floated on the wind and gave so much. The Shining Ones did not reach the humans with their visual impact so much as with their emanation, something so pure and affecting that it made the people weep for the first time in human memory.

And so the first human tears were not tears of grief, for when a loved one died it was as nature intended and hunting and eating and sheltering went on just the same in their passing. Endings were inevitable and to be avoided if possible, but they were always final, were they not? Yet the Shining Ones, these fair folk, had offered by their very presence the possibility that there was something beyond that terrible nothingness. And so the first human tears were tears of joy and utter unbridled wonder, shed because there was hope.

There was a period of confusion as the two species met but there was no killing. The common, natural sense and rational way of the humankind came back to the fore. How dangerous were these beings if the animals and birds did not shy from them, rather they came to them and played around them in a way they did not with people? How dominant could these beings be if they did not command or demand, but simply stretched out their long limbs to reach out with the utmost gentleness?

There was no way that a human would attempt to kill such a being, for killing was for food and these light creatures were not food. Nor did they appear to have a useful hide or pelt, like the creatures of Earth. There was no sign of where they came from but they walked in peace. For the first time the humans saw something beyond themselves and were touched by another being, which could not be used. They experienced connection for the sake of connection, love apart from physical gratification. It was a pleasure.

Moreover, the fair ones brought new benefits to the physical side of being on Earth. They healed the Earth's children who did not thrive. They saved the mothers who laboured long and painfully. They showed the way to work with the wise green plant people so that they yielded their secrets. Likewise, the Children of Starlight knew which animals dwelled where and how best to work with their individual spirits to ensure a honourable, clean death. How could anyone find it in their hearts to despise or ostentatiously revere any being so extraordinarily virtuous yet totally simple?

Instead of impassive acceptance, the humans began to develop an attitude of gratitude. And as the life-enhancing gifts of the Shining Ones opened their eyes to new meaning and beauty in life, and as they helped all creatures to blossom and bloom, there was celebration as well as plain thanksgiving.

So it was that the inhabitants of planet Earth came to know these new and beautiful shining beings as the Children of the Greening, the name refering to their energy of resurgence. The Children of the Greening aided the wild blessings of the land as they sang new life into all that was and would be; they inspired every living being to be the best, most bountiful version of themselves. They brought new elements to existence and made it more like living, these were the gifts of dream, magic, and imagination.

This was their biggest blessing to a diligent, practical species such as humans. The gift of imagination, the belief that one could picture what wasn't and make it so, for the sake of the joy of creation, was amazing. A being could share in the ultimate experience of being a part of their Creator, at the heart of existence, by bringing something to bear from nothing. In this way, the Shining Ones could connect with the Source. It was extraordinary, they were extraordinary, these intermediaries between the Creator and creation. To experience the Creator was to create!

And so on a cave wall, in daubs made from the Earth's own pigments, there could be a prancing heard of beasts where before there was only bare rock. Adornment was made for the human self from shells and bells, cones and stones, strung together in visually stimulating ways. There could be vessels fashioned from the body of the Earth which looked beautiful and enhanced the experience of drinking. There could be music plucked from the air by the creation of a simple gut-strung instrument or reedpipe. A story could be woven from fragments of fact about a man who never was, for the sake of hearing another's laughter. With all these new creative pursuits, and with a newfound fascination with aesthetically pleasing attributes, the humankind learned about the quality of life. And about the possibilities it had to offer.

For the first time, humankind had fun while remaining fed and watered.

There were demonstrations of song and dance daily. It was hard not to dance when you heard the rhythm of being. The Children saw much beauty in their origins and wished to enhance life with the retelling of the Mystery they had experienced, so the stories of the stars were woven into the fabric of daily life over countless seasons. There would be no forgetting of connection, for the forgetting would bring confusion and with it, fear of the unknown. It was understood that without the root, the route back to Source, there was no connection. It was the knowing of truth, the belief in connection, that linked all to All and so their tales were continually woven into every aspect of this fecund landscape, bringing harmony, balance, and growth to the land.

The desire of the Children, unique of all creations, was to entertain for the sake of bringing joy. Joy and the enhancement of life was their purpose. In so much as a bird sings simply as part of being, so did the Children sing, to celebrate Being. They were like liquid starlight fashioned into slender two-legged forms. Willowy and sensual yet sexless, for they had no limit of gender, of structure. Fluid and perpetually in motion, yet filled with calm serenity. They were terribly beautiful. Frighteningly radiant. Alien and yet so hauntingly familiar.

Within the family of the Children there were many races, as there were within the human, bird, and fish families. The longer they dwelled on Earth, the more variations of themselves they dreamed into being. They did not need to mate or breed, although union could be enjoyed for its own sake. They simply became from the fabric of existence, mingling with the Earth, birthing themselves from a blend of starlight and soil. They asked the question, "What if?" They became expressions of their surroundings, acting in perfect empathy, in a creative sculpting of fluid form from the environment. There was no selfish desire to replicate themselves, for their essence was eternal and unique, there was simply a joy in finding new ways of expressing who they were, by blending with the fibre of the living Earth that gave them a home.

And with the humankind who loved them.

The dreams on Earth were peaceful for a boundless time, for it was a time of no time save the marking of the seasons within and without. Life was as life is. Life was good. And peace . . . peace just was. The season of abundance, sometimes yellow-gold, other times green and glistening, had simply been for a seemingly endless age. Humans passed away, to be reborn into other lives, other selves. Their spirits returned, as did all creatures, into new bodies to gain new experiences. This was accepted, welcomed. The Children were not mortal but immortal. They simply evolved without shedding their nebulous forms. They did not remain static, they grew while adapting and changing. Like the seasons.

Like seasons, all things must pass, even those energetic beings who are deemed immortal must eventually pass on and be reborn as some other energetic form. Un-peace came with the transmutation of Fey energy, their death signified a new beginning. At this point in our story, un-peace is about to be birthed.

As the patterns of life formed and reformed there was no warning of the universal shifting. There was no conception of un-peace so it was not imagined how a shift may occur. How could this be if it were unimaginable? So it was that bears still hunted, the insects still darted, and so did the Children play. They felt the pulse in their hearts' blood and knew they were a part of the Dance. The healing and regeneration amongst all things continued with no heed of impending change. And the Lady of Love poured down her light upon them and the Lord of the Trees spun around and around with them under the growing, glowing firmament, through the spiralling maze of the ancient Ones of the Bark.

But everything is change and flux in the cycles of life and some dances have to end for others to begin. Stars turn cold. Everything has a season. The citizens of the Way began to feel the unimaginable shift, like a cold, bitter wind that blew relentlessly for no purpose other than to chill. One day it simply was. The rhythmic, unfolding pattern was overridden by another foreign vibration. It was not born of love and its harmony was nothing more than a discord. The children had become used to aeons of bliss and were unprepared for this intrusion. This . . .

What?

A lack of peace.

The Creator was birthing something that did not come to pass gladly and with joy. The All was shaking with the birth of a reluctant creation, one that trembled and spat, kicked and screamed. One that did not See. And as the Children were such a part of the All they felt it deeply, at their very core. It was not their way to feel sorrow, yet an unsettling ache began inside them. The Creator had to birth the opposite in order to give choices, so that all beings may exercise their free will. In order to choose, one must have something to contrast peace with. All-That-Was had to experience every possible expression of Itself. That was the way of creation. It was a hard way indeed yet one with ultimate meaning.

A vision came to the Children of the Greening of a terrible blight, a dark cloud upon their horizon. It did not rain and pass on its way as was the way of the cloud people. This cloud was filled with rage and noise and strange shapes fell from its broiling centre. Things of dull colours, hard and angular and heavy. Things that the Children could not recognise. Things with points and brutal edges, wrought of dark metal with no shine. The Way was of curves and spirals, the Dance of Life was round like the belly of a mother. These sharp planes were the harbingers of another era.

The Children were born of truth and honour and natural justice, of hope and free-will. They did not really know how to be afraid, or how to judge, or how to be bound to another's will. They did not know how not to hope. They were open-hearted, not defensive, nor reactionary. But when the Makers of this hard rain came to the forest they had but a short time in which to understand these new rules.

Oh, the Makers. Who were they? The Makers were your earthly forefathers, the Makers were human. They were not a race apart. Oh no. They did not descend pure and shining as the Children once did, born of starlight, a different kind of entity. The Makers were humans turned wrong by a spirit of disharmony, which some say is ignorance, others evil. A spirit like a virus, infecting the simple souls of humanity as they slept. A spirit that brought the forgetting.

This spirit manifested on Earth and slowly infested, slipping into the dreams of the weakest humans, ensnaring them with tempting images, filling them with insidious greed and an overwhelming desire to behave in a way that was not beneficial to anyone or anything but themselves. It stole into the consciousness of a species and seized it. Through dream-sleep, it corrupted adn twisted the gift of imagination. It showed a way not borne of bare survival as in the old times, nor of joy and pleasure as in the good times, but a third way.

These poor humans who fell prey to the offer of power and the choice to be either passive or dominant, for they had the free will to choose, were your human ancestors. They may be your spiritual gaolers even now, or your closest kin, and how I hope that you may know the end of their reign. Can you believe the Makers make for the sake of making? Why of course you can, for theirs is the era into which you, dear friend, have been born.

And oh yes, they make. Not for beauty, not for pleasure, not for giving joy. No, only for power, for pressure, for prestige, for owning something earthly that they were not born with, which they could not take with them when they died, and oftentimes what they desire, they do not even need. To have the most things—possessions—is to have the most worth in their eyes. To have most things made barriers and delineations that never before existed.

They speak of separation and ownership—"this is mine, that is not yours" and "I have and you have not"—as if those born to the planet Earth had a hierarchy, or some right to preside over another! As if one being could stake a claim on the free and bountiful Earth herself and divide her up for the sake of setting themselves apart or above. What folly, what tragedy! They began the separation of above and below, light and dark, as if one were better than the other! They placed human values on an equal level and judged according to human law, not universal law. They called their own values and opinions, measured in wealth and based on status, the Way. Where there had never been judgements, and hence no injustice, now there was. And still is.

As you were born to them, of them, into their era, I feel love for you, for that is what you need now to break the bonds the Makers have placed upon you. Remember yourself, child. Recall the spirit within you, that which was not manmade and is not owned by any but your own self. Acknowledge the gift of spirit, bestowed by the Creator, a gift never to be retracted, bought up in a market place, or apportioned to another; never to be forgotten.

And who am I, or who are we, to advise you? We were born of the first starlight on the Faerytide and we have been burned, broken, beaten, boxed in by the humankind. And I speak from experience, not bitterness. I know something of the pain of times past, maybe the pain of your present. Bear with me, for I have been through the re-membering. Believe!

Believe me when I say that the Makers were forgetful of their true selves and their spiritual origins at the heart of creation, they instead actively sought disconnection and separation. How difficult it is to comprehend that a spirit born into a body, born free, born connected to the Source, actually wished to be so bound, tied, and alone. They wished to build walls, doors, fences, and defences. They wished to manufacture, to fracture, cause disharmony, rape, reap, ruin—all for the sake of forgetting. For to remember was to recall connection and harmony. To forget was to believe that they could be all-powerful, maybe even above the Creator. That they could rule and govern and own, above creation's plan of unity.

The Makers hated anything that would not submit, serve, or satisfy the immediate needs, based on their forgetfulness that they had a soul that craved balance with the harmony of the universal Way. They despised free-thinkers, creative spirits, the weak, the mild, the unusual. These things had no rhyme or reason in a world devoid of charm. They desired order, rank, file. They liked a bottom so that they could stay on top. They craved authority and dominion. They used the sacred gift of imagination not to bring pleasure but to dream up weapons of destruction, to envision new ways to kill, new methods to make a mess.

They turned the gift of imagination that the Children had once bestowed on Earth beings against the very Children who they perceived as the worst, most useless, and somehow most irritating of all Earth-dwellers. For the Children did not know how to submit or to subdue themselves, to cease to be just as they always had been seemed an insult to the Creator. Moreover, the Makers were more deeply afraid of the Children than of any other living thing. They were terrified of the alien forms, the enormous slanted eyes that seemed to look within them, making them feel uncomfortably naked. They hated their differences, the Children's seemingly insubstantial bodies, the way they could change shape at will.

The Children did not know why their natural way should be such an anathema to these folk. The more upset the Children became the more they changed shape in order to try and regain a sense of something pleasing, calming. The more they shimmered and became insubstantial, elemental, intangible, the more the Children intimidated the Makers. Physically they posed no threat but on every other level the Makers sensed their power and sought to exterminate these seemingly passive, yet deeply potent, lifeforms.

They wanted to eradicate all they feared for it belittled them but mostly they wanted to do it because they could. They imagined many new ways to torture and tease out death from their supposed enemies. And the Children and those loyal to them suffered most of all.

The Makers met their opposites in the Children and the Children saw all they did not wish to imagine in the Makers. One chose to annihilate the other while the other, the Children, chose to learn how not to respond. There was both unbridled horror and great sorrow on planet Earth. There still is.

And so it was that the Old Lord of the Trees was redundant to them for they did not require the services of a Lord of joy and strength. The Lord of the Dance was turned into an enemy for their convenience, an enemy of their newly invented, rigid, unbending Lord of Sorrows. And so the Dance became a pale memory, forgotten at best, outlawed at worst. The majesty and might of the Old Lord were reduced to a moonlit shadow, a mist-cloaked form leaping alone at twilight, fading.

The Lady of the Tides, Sister Moon, wept bitter tears alone. She wrung her hands and gave a mother's lament, knowing that her Children were temporarily lost to her. The Children must learn the lessons of this cruel season, which would pass—and it would pass, as everything must. Like a good mother she knew when to let go, she accepted that the seeing and she bestowed would grow dim and the knowing would become vague for a time. For a time . . . and time passes.

It was a time of rending and tearing and of undoing, of old ways slipping into seeming obscurity for the sake of survival. A sterile, two-dimensional Lord and Lady were placed by the Makers in dominion over all Earth beings. This Lord and Lady were fashioned in the image of humans and so were as deaf and as blind as the fools they served. This enforced regime held sway over all wisdoms, coveting them and seeking to bind them, thus the Makers tied truths in knots, and tied them tightly, distorting them as they did so. Bound freedom and integrity in hairy twine, obliterating them effectively while controlling them completely.

Ah yes, it was an unholy time.

The Makers had no respect for the life force. They massacred the tree people, the sacred wise guardians of root and bough, to build their barricades against nature. They dammed and drained and poisoned the waters. They filled the air with foul smoke and fouler words. It was heartbreaking. It still is.

I remember when a tear, the first tear of grief ever shed, ran down a pale cheek and another of our kin licked it away, tasting the precious salty pearl and the pain within. The Children learned to weep bitterly. But never openly. They learned to keep secrets. To hide. And some of them did physically hide. In the hillsides and caves, within the rocks and in the wild places, they ceased to walk the Earth but walked in it. They became a part of the Earth Mother, watching in pain and sorrow as their bright kin were slaughtered for sport. Watching through the leaves of an ancient forest, emerging and disappearing into a stone, becoming part of the rolling mist on the moor. The Children integrated themselves in another way. They slipped into the Otherworld, another layer of the Mother, one with less density, less form, one step away from the realm of killing and fear, behind the sun, shining in shadow, half hidden. But alive.

Oh the strength it took for the Children to abandon their kin in order to preserve their Way and the courage it took to wait. . . . And keep waiting.

Breathing steadily with the heartbeat of the Mother Earth they learned to distrust and to be cunning, learning to frighten these blunt idiotic human travesties as they lurched stupidly drunk off their beaten tracks. Terrorising the Makers as they strayed alone into the territory of the wild became a means of release for some of their own grief. They would not hurt these humans but they could frighten them, they became those who haunted the land, the Shining Ones in the darkness. The Pixies, Elves, Faery folk, Knockers, Hobgoblins, the Tuatha, the Sidhe—a thousand local variations on the theme of the Children in hiding. They were the Fair Ones who could bewitch with beauty and lead a man astray to his doom, the creatures of Fate who could charm you if they chose, laughing all the while at the Maker's expense, then hiding again in the mists. The Children became those who chose to step out from the Otherworld to cause dread and superstitious panic when they were all supposed to be long dead and part of the forgetting. But what sadness even so, for they were becoming the stuff of folklore and legend instead of a living, breathing part of manifest reality.

And yet nothing is ever forgotten, not even a sigh or a caress on the wind. Much less a song, a dance of life. The Fey are still among us and not only in hiding in the wild places, half seen, half remembered. Their dancing blood is in the veins of those whose kin, long ago, once lay with the Children in waving fields of barley at sundown, loving them, skin to skin—it is blood that sings as it awakens. And the spirits of the Children of the Greening who had fled from this mortal plane have today chosen to come back to Earth in human bodies, making the ultimate sacrifice for the good of the All—to bring the magic back to life while wearing the body of a potential Maker, the skin of an old enemy. Yes, the green spirit dwells in human form today and the ancient Fey blood sings softly in human veins. We live!

Aye, we speak to you now as a Child of the Greening and say to you that which you already know. We can keep our spirits strong and all who are of our spirit will see the green flame in our eyes and recognise us as kin. And we will shine together until the Maker's ways are passed and the wild way of things returns. Old becomes new becomes old again, so it is and so it must be. It will never be quite like before. Although, with our new knowledge of how not to be, there will be changes for the better. There has to be hate and hard times for us to know how not to be. Time may seem to pass slowly, there may seem no end to the terrible season of the Makers, but with faith we know there are always returns. Energy cannot die and your energy is the magical healing power of creative joy.

Keep the Fey faith, dance the enchanted dream, and remember the wildwood vow!

Elemental Spirits

As we have just seen, the Fey are not strictly nature spirits in the sense that they are not purely elemental—fashioned directly of air, earth, fire, and water. They are individual essences we find in wild nature, certainly, but they do not exclusively embody elemental qualities or remain connected to one particular place necessarily. Elemental spirits do indeed represent natural forces and, although they are all unique, they are bound by the laws of their element and the particular area they inhabit.

A fire elemental can appear in a hearth or a water elemental can manifest at a river or waterfall. An earth elemental could form directly from a rock whilst an air elemental rushes out, for example, of a west wind. The fire elementals are sometimes known as salamanders or gnomes, the beings of air are sylphs, the water elementals are undines, and the energetic creatures born of earth are dryads. Of course, these are human labels that may unnecessarily limit our perception and interaction with the true nature of the elementals. Our human need to personify everything can be a restrictive practice as well as a useful one! It is most beneficial to experience elementals; they animate their particular element, the conciousness or awareness that gives it life, character, charm, and raw power. We work with them, for this reason, with infinite respect.

Nature Spirits

The term "nature spirit" can also refer to the spirit of a place directly. For example, an earth elemental can live as part of a particular tree, guarding it. Such a being may be clad in the same bark and share the very same energy as the tree. In this case the name given to a tree spirit is "dryad." They are not completely independent but belong particularly to that which generated them. It is possible to gain much personal experience of this symbiotic relationship in our own safe and sacred place outdoors. There we will no doubt meet with the nature spirits of the plants and trees, rocks and shells, and pools and marshes of that place.

We can meet the nature spirits of apple trees and heather, the elemental beings of a local stream, or the nature sprites who inhabit a grassy knoll. Through our own direct experience, and that alone, will we come to differentiate the essential elemental or natural spirit of a place from Fey spirits, those who are of the Faery races and not bound directly to one type of region, plant being, or elemental realm. The Fey are bound instead into fate. They are weavers of destiny in a way that the elemental or nature beings are not. Although elementals are powerful, marvellous, and inspiring, they haven't the same enchanted aspect as the otherworldly Fey, who are from beyond Earth's earthliness. It is their starlight vision that differentiates them and something subtle that we can only experience for ourselves in firsthand encounters.

The elementals and nature spirits are no less wonderful, only different to engage with. They can still share with us invaluable insights into their particular resonance. Through them we have the unforgettable experience of finding out how it feels to be water, or we may come to understand more fully the true nature of wind. We can relate to clouds and mist, raging blazes and cool breezes, and boulders and fragments of flint alike. The elemental and nature beings act as our intermediaries between our level and the realm of the stone people, the plant folk, and the four elemental essences.

Trance Journey: Meeting Fey for Magical Purposes

In this journey we are going to truly travel off the beaten track of our usual trance journey haunts. This journey's aim is to meet a Fey helper for the specific purpose of our spellworking. The Fey helper is not our guiding spirit and may choose to work with us on a one-off basis only. If it suits the Fey, they may extend their contact with us but we will not be able to call on them ad infinitum (as we can our companion spirits) as they have not opted to dedicate themselves to us in that way. However, they may agree to stay with us for the duration of a particular group of spells if they share a similar energy. Or if they feel that, from their further involvement, there is a benefit to the Faery realms.

The Fey can help us enormously as their energy is obviously magical and they are used to living wholly integrated and successful lives of wild enchantment. Although we ourselves aim to lead such enchanted lives on a daily basis, incorporating simple spellwork into the mundane aspects of living, we also choose to work prepared magic (spells that we craft to fit in specially with the seasonal, lunar, or energetic tides). We can ask the Fey to help us with these spells. Fey help can bring even the most highly planned piece of fateweaving a fresh spontaneity and joyful lyricism that we alone could never achieve. They can make magic sparkle with vitality, linking us in to the All with ease.

Remember that before we plan any such spellwork we must also consider the tides. The energetic tides are the third aspect of our equation for magical change. If we have no idea of the moon's phase or how far we may be from a solstice or equinox then we have little chance of flowing effectively with the potent tides of life. By now we should have gained a much deeper understanding of our own interaction with daily, seasonal, lunar, and personal tides, and how we as individuals and how nature as a whole, experience them. We should be ready to include such information in any act of wild enchantment. If we do not consider the tides, then all the Fey assistance we can muster will not carry our spellwoven strands onward and into the glittering webs of fate. We need the energetic current to be with us, not against us. Without this, our magical equation cannot deliver the desired result.

Our own dear companion spirits are more than willing and able to assist and advise us on our everyday magical living, yet the Fey are especially skilled at really ensuring that our more ritualised or specific fateweaving is full of wild power and utterly pertinent. Being poetic by their very nature they are the ones that can advise us on appropriately animated chants. They will also suggest any tools we may need to enhance the manifest side of what we do along with suitable locations and any ingredients such as herbs or oils. They can help to broaden our understanding of what enchantment really is and open our eyes to its place in our human existence.

Depending on the nature of our spellwork, we may want to meet upper- or lower-world Fey contacts (also referred to as Upper- and Underworld helpers). Remember, working with the World Tree as a reference, the upper level of the tree is for wider insights, high aspirations and universal ideals and the lower level is for fateweaving, more personal revelation, and deep emotional/psychic connection. As the living wood and bridge builders between both levels, it is for us to discern which energy applies to any of our magical acts whilst fully appreciating that all we do echoes energetically both above and below. We may want to have an Upperworld Fey helper for our spell if it is concerned with the birth of new ideas, fresh inspirations, cosmic understanding, or illumination on a philosophical issue. An Underworld helper would be more appropriate if we want to reveal something that is hidden or if we want to explore feelings (the roots) of a profound personal issue.

An Upperworld helper may take on the guise of a high elf or Shining One, an ariel creature, or "picture-book" Faery. The lowerworld contact could be connected with water, such as a mer-creature of some kind, or may appear as a creature suited to subterranean living, like a troll. Fey helpers will only ever show us a guise so it is not necessary for us to get too caught up in their apparel. We know by now that in all spirit-walking we should aim to feel the resonance of our companions and helpers, not rely on purely visual cues.

Don't forget that with both levels, upper and lower (and, indeed, middle), we are referring to otherworldly realms of existence. The Otherworlds encompass all such aspects and planes, just as our own physical plane encompasses both sky and mountain top, cave systems and ocean floors. The middle level of otherworldly existence is something like ours as we have already seen, or at least it appears to be the closest to our current bodily experience. This is why this book concentrates on the middle world aspects to start us off. In the magical middle level of otherworldly interaction we are working with that highly malleable realm closest to human wish and will.

As has been suggested previously, to travel to other realms we may work in our safe astral place with the hollow tree (acting as the World Tree) and travel upward or downward in whichever way that presents itself—perhaps a special staircase will appear inside the bark or maybe we will be able to simply fly upward or sink downward through the earth. We must choose (or intuit) whether up or down (or middle) is the best place to be for the work involved and allow the environment to mould itself to our desires. It is best only to approach such work when one is completely at ease with the whole journeying process and confident about testing out spirits to check authenticity. It could be a complex and challenging journey and so we need to have all our resources at hand.

Although the journey to meet an Upper- or Underworld Fey helper is certainly worthwhile (and should be undertaken as part of our own personal growth process and training experience) there is certainly no need to hurry into it. A middle world contact is more than adequate at first as such spirits balance both aspects within themselves, as should we.

It would be impossible to prescribe an upper- or lowerworld journey as we would be totally out of our safe territory (our sacred journey space becoming as familiar to us as our companion spirits are). The individual must experience this or her own landscape when visiting each realm. For now, a journey into the middle realm will be described as an example of how to meet a Fey helper from this level. The middle realm has been chosen as it leads away from the safe landscape we already know from our previous trance journeys, but doesn't require us to change our journey procedures too much; therefore, it is an excellent starting place. It may have elements of both the upper- and lowerworld within it; depending on what manner or helper we wish to find, we may wish to focus on elements of this journey that enhance our chances of finding an appropriate helper.

By this stage we should feel confident enough to adapt the given journey to our own purpose. That is, follow the standard precautions and directions, but once we have read through the following prescribed journey, we can embellish it, take diversions, and seek other regions. For example, if there are opportunities to go to a more subterranean (lowerworld) level—looking perhaps into deep water, a cave, a tunnel—then we should take the opportunity to do so. Or if an Upperworld helper would be more fitting then we should go for options that lead in an upward direction, to treetops or up hills, where an elevated perspective may be reached.

The middle world journey about to be described will give us the chance to ask for the most appropriate helper to come to us, whereas on subsequent journeys we may want to put ourselves in the active role and find the helper ourselves by choosing the level that is most attuned to our needs. In the middle world we may meet all the creatures familiar to our own manifest human realm along with wood-elves, pixies, goblins, and other creatures not of our manifest realm. We must remember that this realm is closest astrally to ours and it also attracts human psychic debris so we must always be vigilant!

It is now assumed that we have made all the usual protective preparations and are suitably equipped to make a trance journey. There is also a need for us to identify some manner of prospective spellwork or enchantment we have in mind so that we may attract an appropriate helper and be able to discuss the matter with them. State this intention poetically in a small chant. If a prospective spell was about healing then the chant could be something like:

> *Oh fair ones help me weave my strands!*
> *My call goes out to the wildest lands,*
> *I've a need of healing in my hands,*
> *Who'll help me heal one of my friends?*
>
> *By wisdom held in the rings of trees,*
> *May you catch my scent on the Faery breeze,*
> *And offer me your expertise,*
> *By the will of the green ones, may it please!*

Also, we should invoke for our companion spirits to be fully present, if not visible, on this endeavour. We can spend a few moments in meditation, that is to say, in contemplative prayer, for the work ahead.

Now we proceed with the trance journey to our safe place. We go as far as passing through the hollow tree and then wait. We should have the hollow tree at our back and face forward, awaiting instructions, which are as follows:

I am standing facing the familiar landscape of my safe place. It is twilight here and the realm looks very beautiful. I rarely see it in this light, it seems softer somehow, the hues shifting and shimmering as the land seems to sigh and stretch, readying itself for slumber. Looking down I see the now well-worn dirt track that will lead me to the now familiar stepping stones and eventually toward the stream. Yet there seems to be another fainter path today, which leads abruptly off to the left, swinging sharply off through what appears to be a group of low scrubby bushes.

Do I go straight on, as I always do? No, this time I must follow this new and surprising pathway and knowing that I should go this way I begin to walk. As I approach the darkly bristling shrubbery, I sense that my passage will not be easy. A surreptitious shuffling seems to have taken place and what appeared at first glance to be a group of bushes, now has turned into an effective barrier. My way is barred by spiky spines and prickly leaves that gleam, glossy and sharp, even in the half-lit atmosphere. Thorn clusters cruelly close to holly, and perhaps some kind of gorse joins them . . . even though I doubt it normally grows in such a place. A formidable obstacle indeed! I frown, perplexed, the feeling growing inside me that I have to be on the other side of this wall of bushes, somehow. The track definitely leads through it. Or it did . . .

I ask for a spirit sign, some idea of how to get through this seemingly impenetrable thicket. As the light fades further into dusky memory, muting the tones of the land and making me squint slightly, the area grows in its menace. Is it deliberately intimidating me with its energy? I feel as if I am being tested so I simply do what I have always done. I remain calm, take a few deep, slow breaths, and ask my companions to give me some help: "Spirits who come for my highest good, advise me now!"

Their voices come to me: "Ask, and it will be given!"

So I ask the bushes politely for safe passage through them but to no avail. Do I hear sniggering? I look from left to right. I know that my friend, the hollow oak, lies some way behind me but it is getting harder and harder to make out what lies on either side of me. Shall I try to walk around the bushes? I take a few paces to my right but stumble. I try to my left but feel dizzy and disorientated. The feeling is that I should follow the path, the track through the scrub. But how? I've asked once and nothing happened. This time I state my aim as part of a chant:

I've come for healing, not for harm,
I've come for help with a simple charm,
Yet you wish to cause me some alarm,
Pray let me pass, return my calm!

I speak my piece but realise I have said it with little conviction. It is as if I am missing something valuable about what has happened. I close my eyes and ask for further guidance, needing an insight but all the words that come to me are as before.

"Ask!" the companions whisper in my ear.

I look at the bushes, wondering what else I can ask for, and am presented with two alternatives, either I travel under them or over them. How? Certainly I am to pass through this region by a lower or upper route but I have no tools by which to address the problem, no rope, no digging tool. I sigh and scratch my head, sinking down to my haunches and staring through the densely packed spiny bushes in front of me as if I can will them to part. Maybe I can? I notice the odd glint within the bushes, which now are starkly silhouetted, black against the last roseate glow left by the setting sun on the fringes of the wood. Are these glints eyes watching me, full of mocking glee? There is more than suggestion of a scornful presence, certainly.

I won't become angry and I won't be intimidated. If I will something to happen in my otherworldly safe place then I need focused intent and belief that it will be so. Here off my own beaten track, I can have the same belief in my ability to focus and change things. And I can imagine that I have the tools I need and truly it will be so!

Would I like to travel over or beneath the bushes? I consider this. It is for me to manifest what I need, and to then ask for it! And I will need either the means to swing over the top of the thicket, perhaps by hooking a rope over the nearest tree branch, or I will need the equipment to tunnel my way beneath it. Again I hear snide laughter and decide how I would like to approach this task. I can then manifest what it is that I need. I visualise the tools I have decided on with my eyes closed and recite a prayerful request. When I open my eyes I have what I need at my feet and I go about preparing and executing my way over or under the problem.

If I wish to go over, I could have asked for a bird to carry me on its back across the obstacle. If I need to go under I could ask for a mole to dig me a tunnel. Everything I do in this realm has symbolic relevance and an energetic impact. Although the result is the same in either case, and I will be on the other side of the obstacle, it is for me to decide the symbolic energy of travelling over or under.

Once on the other side I take a moment to relax and let my eyes accustom to the gloom of approaching darkness in this unfamiliar territory. I am on level ground and in an open space, a clearing. Suddenly I see a host of tiny winking lights and I shield my eyes as the brightness is unexpected. This time the accompanying laughter is warm and welcoming. Blinking, I see now that the lights are flickering candles . . . in lanterns hung from bushes, in high branches, and at the base of tree trunks. All around this place there are lanterns of all shapes, sizes, and colours. And the path at my feet is illuminated again, enough for me to see that it swings away again into the trees. Trees, which I now see, have doors cut into them.

I follow the path. Some of the doors are ajar, others fully open but I have not yet managed to see any of their inhabitants. Now and again a snatch of gay song reaches my ears, along with more furtive but well meaning giggles. I get the sense that moth-like insects, or tiny winged beings, which buzz and flit around me, are trying to distract me from the path, behaving in a playfully irritating way, a high-pitched buzzing noise and a barely perceptible whirring sound occasionally making me shake my head and reel slightly.

There is a warmth given by the lanterns and almost a sense of a party that has not yet begun. It's a festive mood but no one is around to celebrate. An occasional squirrel on its way home knocks a bit of tree debris onto my head and the chattering of a bird fighting for a prime place in the roost occasionally makes me jump, but besides that no being is visible. But they are certainly present.

Without warning, the path forks into three. The central path leads to a particularly fine specimen of a beech tree with a vast knotted system of roots. It seems to rise out of the earth, elevating itself to an even more impressive status. At its base there is a small door, but large enough for me, perhaps. To its left and right the paths lead off in unexpected ways. The left-hand path vanishes into a cavelike entrance, formed from a region beneath a storm-felled tree. The roots hang down like gnarled bars, trailing ribbons of ivy, obscured by creepers, but there is still a way through into the suggestion of a dark cavern beneath. I would have to crawl on my hands and knees if I chose that route, perhaps even snaking on my belly. It looks tempting through, cool and greenly dark, even darker than the surrounding night, an arboreal entrance into the moist soft earth. There is a tiny lantern placed near it so that it could be carried within if I chose to enter. Someone here is looking after me, that's for sure.

The right-hand path simply leads to steps that ascend, uneven yet smoothly carved, from the body of a tree so old and dead looking as to be petrified into stone or bone. A plain set of curved steps wind up and up to what appears to be a platform, or some manner of suspended bridge. This leads to a place that is difficult to see clearly for its elevated position makes it unknowable and I peer into the advancing night, hoping for a clue. I then realise that I can take one of the lamps from the central beech tree and raise it up as to see the platform better. I discern that behind the petrified tree's steps is a sort of rocky incline, which ends in a flat plateau just before the steps. As I strain to see, several more lanterns are lit around me as if they, these invisible folk, have taken advantage of my looking elsewhere. I try desperately to see who is doing the lighting, I even call out a greeting, but am simply rewarded with more soft sniggering. It is an annoying sound because it has no apparent source, but it is not cruel laughter.

I know that for today I must advance through the door in the bark of the central beech tree, travelling through this formidable being to whatever lies on the other side. Or to whatever simply lies within its trunk. It is not for me to know until I have opened the door. So holding my acquired lantern aloft I raise my hand to knock. The door itself is barely discernible from the greying bark of the beech, it is merely a suggestion of an arch, slightly more scratched and lined than the rest of the trunk. A round iron ring serves as the handle and there is a quaint bell-pull to one side, that I may ring. Do I address the tree or the tree dweller? I decide to do both and stepping back, gazing with reverence at the truly stunning tree that stands at least six full-grown men high, I ask:

> *My journey leads me to your door and though I find you grand,*
> *I humbly ask for a passage through to your enchanted land.*
> *So, mighty one of bark and bough, whose sylvan spirit guides,*
> *I ask for your admission and that of who'er resides!*
> *I'll knock and ring both three times three,*
> *For the power of magic in every tree!*

And I proceed to knock and ring, three times three, contemplating my task ahead, to find a Fey helper for my enchantments. I know when the door opens there may be a figure there so I ready myself to psychically check out whomever emerges.

When the door opens I am still taken by surprise.

Instead of a figure at eye level I am greeted by one who has rolled himself into a ball and bowls himself at my knees. Jolted and disconcerted I still managed to put my protective ring of flame around the hunched rolling form immediately.

"Show yourself truly spirit!" I say, pointing at the ball, my finger emitting a stream of the same cold, blue-gold flame that now surrounds the being at my feet.

As I watch, the being turns, with an audible "pop" into a hazelnut. The nut then appears to be wobbling around in the circle of flame, muttering to itself as it does so. Just as I bend down to peer at this extraordinary nut more closely there is another "pop" and I am face to face with a skinny nut-brown man, a bark-man, his limbs of wiry sticks and his face wrought from wrinkled wood. Yellow eyes widen and he pushes his face close to mine.

"You test me, eh?" He cackles and hops from foot to foot within the circle. "Who tests a skillern? A swindling and a swagling both, and a vimmish roguer besides, no doubt! I am a widderwadder, the boggling kind, and I am your friend!"

He bows, mock graciously, then sticks out his curious woody tongue, thumbs his generous nose, and flips over to show me his backside.

"And you are he who will help me with my proposed enchantments?" I ask, perplexed but amused. I must remember that the Fey come in all shapes, sizes, and temperaments. I know never to judge a spirit by its appearance and feel instinctively that this one has checked out well.

"Of course!" He looks at me and raises his mossy brow, as if I am the mad one. Then he hops again. "Look, look stupid human! Time's running for you, and I've better things to do than this so come now . . . come!"

My funny guiding Faery gestures with his elongated twigling fingers at the door and I follow him inside the tree. He closes the door behind us and immediately pushes me through another door at the rear so that I have absolutely no time to discern what the inside of the tree either looks or feels like.

On the other side I am stunned to find that it is broad daylight. When will Faery time cease to amaze me! We are standing besides a large stone well, a circular edifice of ancient construction. The stones are bound together not only with mortar but with the roots of a twisted crack willow, its silvered leaves weeping down around us as it crouches over the pool it guards. I hear it whisper and sigh, its fabulous old body one great mass of twists and turns, carbuncles of bark and great gashes. I reach out to place my hands on the grooved and pitted skin, to explore the caverns and crevices of its trunk, yet my Fey helper slaps my hand away at once.

"Don't touch!" he rasps, yellow eyes flashing. "How'd you like it when I prod you, eh?" And to emphasise his point one long finger shoots out and stabs me in the belly with all the subtlety of a sharpened stick.

I touch my finger to my forehead and bow low in the old way as an acknowledgement and apology to the tree and the little man I have offended. My gaze returns to the deep well. This is an incredibly serene place, birdsong fills the air, which is itself lilac hued, melting into glimmering opalescence at the edges. I am aware we are surrounded by other old stone walls, and I get the sense we are in the garden of a Faery castle, a romantic place of great enchantment. My eyes are drawn down deep into the water, which appears to be black, but not black at all. Instead it holds reflections and refractions, shimmering sky, my own wavering otherworldly face, now still as if shown in a clear polished mirror. A toad, bloated and blackish-brown, hops in and vanishes under the surface, making the whole mirrored world break apart and reform in ripples and rings.

I know that all I need to know at the present time about my spellcraft lies in the well. I enter a dreamy state, just gazing, and images form and melt in that circle of shining water. I take heed of these personal image messages.

Then I am rudely poked in my side again.

"Bucket!" says my woodling helper, this testy Fey being who I cannot help but like enormously. He rolls his amber eyes upward and I see, suspended from what appears to be a low cloud of pearly brilliance, hovering above us, a rope with a bucket on the end.

"Name your enchantment, give it life, and tell the well! Then lower the bucket, lower it and ask, ask for what you need to work with for your magics! Three times three, mind—only three things! And when you lower the bucket into the waters what you need will be placed in. And when you pull it up again they'll be there for you to see! Easy! Easy even for a human kind! Ha!"

And with that my Fey companion rolls up into a ball and then flips himself over. He's a skinny acrobat with a lithe bark body and waving branch limbs. So, I take a deep breath and I gaze into the waters of the well, trying not to become too hypno- tised by its visionary magnetism. And three times I name the enchantment I wish to work with at this present time. Then I take the rope, which hangs from the strange cloud above us, and lower the battered, old tin bucket into the depths. How can such a lovely old well have such a battered old bucket, I wonder? I lean on the stone periphery of the well and ask for that which I need for the named enchantment, three by three, to be placed in the vessel. And as I hear the bucket break the water's sur- face, I hold the rope steady as to not let it drop too far.

"No, no! Have faith! Let go!" the little Fey man at my side tugs at my arm and I let go of the rope, allowing the bucket to slide deeper into the water. I wonder how long the rope is and if the bucket will ever stop falling down. But eventually it seems as if it stops.

We wait in silence, charmed by the sound of sweet birdsong and the gentle inter- mittent sighing of the old willow as it creaks and shifts. Someone has tied tinkling sil- ver bells into its slender branches and they give a tiny ringing sound as the light breeze lifts and stirs them occasionally. It is easy to become entranced here, I notice. Even the woodling Fey man is quiet for a moment, just staring into the distance of our serene environment, as am I.

Then the rope jiggles before my eyes and I hear the bucket moving in the water as if it has a life of its own, which, no doubt, it has.

The Fey man huffs in frustrated derision, "Well, pull it up then!"

"Give me half a chance!" I say and take the rope in my hands, easing it up. The bucket is full now and the effort is greater. Water sloshes out as I pull it further and further up the ferny stone cavern of the well. The action keeps me from slipping into that reverie of Faery, this place is so gently absorbing, mesmerising!

At last the bucket is on the side of the well and I am able to fish out what has been placed there. I put each object on the stone side of the well and observe any meaning, symbolic or obvious. I am now able to discuss my magic, and the given objects with my Fey helper. And he, for all of his belligerent attitude, is more than willing to offer insights and suggestions. Magic is his life's work, after all.

I could go on asking him things all day and night and beyond but abruptly he shakes my hand and says, "No time now, no time at all!" and I find that I am holding not a hand but a single hazelnut . . . he has gone. I turn and behind me the door in the beech has opened again. Time, apparently, to return!

I thank the willow for its guardianship, reluctant to leave without touching its marvellous bark, but I do restrain myself. I go to put the three objects back in the well bucket but they too have vanished, leaving only wet traces on the well's stone edge. And the rope, bucket, and cloud have also melted back into the beyond, leaving only the well and the willow. And even they are wavering, fading a little. There is something achingly lovely about this place but I know my welcome has run out. But what am I to do with the hazelnut, that which was once my Fey helper? Smiling I take him with me back into the beech tree sanctuary and place him down on the floor.

"I thank you, woodling!" I say, touching forehead, lips, and heart in gratitude. As I do so I am pushed by what seems to be a slender foot, right on my own behind, and I fall through the other door back into the woodland on the other side. The door slams unceremoniously behind me and I turn to face my path home . . . only to find it festooned in yet more lanterns, gold, shiny blue, bright red, all sizes and shapes! The trees are laced with tiny pastel coloured lights—Faery lights!—and I finally see those naughty folk who have been playing with me on my journey. Small folk, some heavily bearded, others smooth-skinned and whip-thin, others flickering like lights themselves, all jauntily dressed in marvellous hues and rich fabrics. Some puff on pipes and wave amiably, others run wildly in circles, laughing, still more dart up trees, running vertically, only to jump off into space and fly. I clap and laugh with them, delighted to have such a welcome back and totally forgiving of their earlier jokes.

I know I must continue moving. As I set out along my path through the trees, heading back for the bush barrier of holly and thorn, the Faery party thins and their chattering and giggling grows fainter, their physical presence becomes more sparse. I see a last pixie leap into a rabbit hole, clad in scarlet and gold, as I end up by the thorn bushes. I wonder if I can get through this time?

What sort of creature could get through such small gaps I wonder? I put my lantern down and the candle goes out. I realise how dark it is. Nighttime. Which tiny creature comes out at night?

And as I wonder I focus on being small, smaller, smallest. This is my realm and I can mould it, I know that now. I have the power of the wild, a witch's fey power, and I can shift and shape and change things, magically. So I do. And tiny I become, tiny I am.

As a brown mouse, I run between bramble and prickly branch as fast as I can. I am vulnerable, being so small, but I am quick and neat. My little heart beats fast and my legs take me swiftly through. As I run I see all the insect life that scuttles as I do at this low level and I see each diminutive shoot pushing up from the densely packed soil. I am safe in the thicket but I must not be seen in open country as a mouse! I am wary of the owl that hunts me, of those on longer legs than mine who stalk and skulk with sharpened teeth. So going at my top speed I push myself through the final gap and out into the clearing chanting:

> *Size of a mouse has served me well,*
> *Back to my own size may I swell!*

And I see myself as my usual otherworldly size. I stand up straight brushing off dirt and dry leaves from my torso and legs, taking a moment to get used to my new perspective. Thanking the essence of mouse, I walk onward, back to my own familiar friend, the hollow tree.

I ask for passage through the hollow tree and then, after passing through his domain, I take the well worn route from my safe place, through the meadow, and back to ordinary reality. There I write down my adventure and make notes on my enchantments, as per the information given at the well.

Tides

Once again, tides refers to the energies involved with our magic, be they seasonal, elemental, or lunar. To highlight the importance and differing views of influential energetic power, we will now specifically look at the elemental energies. When we undertake trance journeys we do not need to invoke the elements to protect, guide, and bless us. Although, it can certainly do no harm, and will surely enhance our practice and understanding of the interconnectedness of all things. On the other hand, we always work with the elemental powers when we cast a more formal circle for a piece of planned spellcraft.

At the beginning of this book we mentioned having representatives of the four elements present at our magical rites. For example, a candle flame or fiery red leaf; some burning incense (for smoke) or a feather; a bowl of soil, a plant, or a stone; and a vessel of fresh water or water from the sea placed around us in a way that feels right to us. Here we simply look at how to enhance the physical presence of these elemental representatives by actually calling on (invoking) their essential spirit. We ask for the living elemental most appropriate to our work to embody the respective physical representation we've chosen, for example, a candle flame or the smoke from our incense.

How do we do this? Well, as wildwitches we would obviously work with a chant to focus our request. Before we can do this though we need to compare two prominent traditions already established in both contemporary Western shamanic work and in Wiccan witchery. Both deal with the direction that each element occupies. It is up to us to decide if we feel aligned with a particular traditional way and, if not, we must work out a new way to call the elemental powers. We can do this by directly consulting with the companion spirits, Fey helpers, and elemental essences in nature. We should choose a way that feels comfortable to us and our companions. We already know the deep significance of the sacred round of existence and that everything has a place on the sacred circle of life. We are all made up of, and linked by, the elemental forces of nature and it is truly up to us where we feel they fit on this circle within our own personal experience, or which direction they belong in.

In the Wiccan craft, it is stated that the power that dwells in the north is earth. In the east lies air, to the south is fire, and in the west we have water. This means that each direction is imbued by the qualities associated with these elements. For example, north is all about the material level and practical issues, while east is about thought and communication. In a Native American shamanic sense, it is believed that the elements are aligned in a circular fashion and together they create the circle of life. When we "cast" (or invoke, envision, or imagine) this circle it is known as the medicine wheel. "Medicine" is a difficult word to give a definitive description but it can be translated as essential energy; therefore, a medicine wheel contains all elemental energies, all life contained within and around, above and below, its loving boundaries. In this tradition, north is air, east is fire, south is water, and west is earth.

We will use, for the sake of this example, the Wiccan way of invoking the four elements and assume they occupy the four quarters as previously stated. If this is how we feel happiest, we can then call on the elemental powers of the four directions in this manner. We may also like to take into consideration the land we are working on and the traditional magical approaches used in that area. Start by facing northward and say:

> *I face the north with open arms,*
> *I ask for earth to share its charms,*
> *Spirit of soil, of sand, and stone,*
> *In my circle, take the place that is your own,*
> *As I call, so may it be,*
> *By cave and grave and shady tree!*

Turning clockwise to the east:

> *I face the east with open mind,*
> *I ask for air my space to find,*
> *Spirit of breeze, of gale, and gust,*
> *You'll join my circle, in this I trust,*
> *As I ask, let it be so,*
> *Of hurricane and tornado!*

And then turning again to face the south quarter:

> *I face the south with open look,*
> *May fiery power fill every nook,*
> *Spirit of passion, cleansing flame,*
> *I welcome you by your true name,*
> *I ask of you, "Be present fire!"*
> *By flowing lava and raging pyre!*

Finally facing the west:

> *I face the west with an open heart,*
> *I ask water to play its part,*
> *Spirit that trickles, falls and runs,*
> *Make rainbows in our circle's sun,*
> *Oh lyrical and generous essence*
> *Bless us with your flowing presence!*

While we invoke (or call in) by the way that most suits us, with reference to the tradition we work with, we should focus entirely on the representative of the power that we have placed in that quarter. For example, when calling in wild power of the element water we should imbue the bowl of water with its essential qualities—envisioning waterfalls, torrential rain, babbling brooks—and feel them too, if possible. A few moments of contemplation should be given after each invocation to really ensure we have channelled the elemental energy into our physical manifestation. When we say we welcome an elemental spirit into our circle we should truly embrace them. Therefore, when we want their nearness we should experience their powerful attributes, seeing images, hearing, tasting, and smelling them as appropriate.

As a personal aside, I recall being part of a guided group mediation on the elements. We were encouraged to connect with the element water via the workshop leader running her hands through water in a wash-up bowl. This was only conducive to my visualising someone washing up and certainly didn't invoke in me the untamed lyricism of water! As wildwitches we need to get out of doors as much as possible so that we are able to tune in to the elements effectively once back home. Perhaps using sound recordings or photographs can aid us if we have not physically been able to get out for some time. Our wild craft certainly doesn't assume peak health in everyone.

And what of the more mysterious fifth element, ether, which occupies the centre of the circle? The ether, as we know, is the malleable etheric essence, it is all-encompassing yet essentially nothing at all, beyond our human knowing yet inherently present. It resonates a powerful energy. It is the Creator's representative, the instrument by which all energetic impulses come to existence, and as such it is the animating force of creation as well as the medium from which it is shaped. The ether can be imprinted upon or we can feel vibrations within it. The other four elements are everything, the building blocks of our lives, both in symbolic and in manifest terms, but how they blend and flow to fashion the All of creation is part of the enigma of ether. Ether is not so quantifiable as fire or water but its energy is essentially of mystery and therefore its presence is felt strongly in us as Fey practitioners.

When working with powerful energies it is good to have an appropriate symbol to remind us of the energetic influences we are working with, to keep us focused. Sticking with our example of the elemental energies we will look at the fifth element of ether again. To symbolically represent this element, we may wish to use a small black pot, a cauldron-type vessel, which stands as the melting pot of all creation, the fertile void. There is a Welsh myth that Cerridwen, a powerful and wild Creatrix, had a cauldron from which the Awen (creative force of life) flowed. This Awen could be said to be the ether. The cauldron is a symbol of wisdom, inspiration, and transformation; as such it is appropriate to use to call upon the element water, but in consideration of time and cultural evolution, perhaps we can find a more personal symbol of this mystery to place at the centre of our sacred circle. It is up to us to either keep to tradition or improvise, but it is important for us to understand why we do as we do.

Experiencing the element of ether can make us feel the balance at the centre of all being, reminding us of the hub of the wheel of life, and so is a useful means of bringing a feeling of harmony, balance, and purpose to our proceedings. In order for the ether to be a part of our truth, a part of the dance of our lives, we must be able to feel it, or when we honour the ether in our workings we will be making a gesture with no resonance.

We can, with the proper reverence and intent, call upon all positive energetic influences we work with for protection and inspiration during circle work, for the purpose of gaining understanding on our path or as a boost for specific enchantment. For example, we may wish to call on the elemental power of fire to help us burn away doubt and see the truth in our lives as we light a bonfire of deadwood from our garden. Or we may ask for the element of water to be fully present in the spring water we use in our jar for painting, for the purpose of bringing fresh inspiration and clarity to our artwork. In whatever way we work with the powerful elements, and with the elemental spirits associated with them, at the conclusion of our work we must always remember to bid them: "Hail and farewell, with thanks."

Of course, this level of decency and respect goes for any spirit we have worked with who has given us their time and attention. Yet with the elementals it may be a particularly valuable way to behave. If we deny them this courtesy then we deny their very real presence in our lives and take them very much for granted in that slovenly way so typical of humanity. And if we fail to give them our gratitude and "shut the gates" behind them, then we are asking for elemental overload in our lives. If they haven't been asked to leave then why indeed should they feel obliged to go; hence their energy builds up. It has been known for those forgetting to close down the quarters in a magical circle to have floods or fires in their homes. Not allowing the elemental beings to retire gracefully can bring symbolic as well as physical problems including arguments, emotional turmoil, and physical illness. This is just another reminder of the immense power to their energies.

Is it worth risking elemental damage because we were feeling tired or a bit bored at the end of a particular interaction with spirit? More importantly perhaps, is it worth us losing respect (both theirs and our own self-respect) by appearing as yet another human being who has no sense of appreciation beyond their own limited demands and limiting viewpoint? All we need to do is close down our sacred circle in the same way that we opened it, by addressing each element in turn, bidding them your leave, and showing them your gratitude for their attentive presence. Again, although we are discussing elementals here, it is important to treat all energies in a similar respectful maner. Here is an example of this addressed to the spirit of water:

> *Now my weaving here is over,*
> *Oh spirit with the silver tongue,*
> *Essence of water, creation's daughter,*
> *I thank you for your sweetest song.*
> *May you process with endless grace,*
> *Return now to your own bright space!*

Focus

There are many ways to focus our intent behind a magical enchantment. First we can set up a sacred place in both astral and physical realms to work our craft. We want to feel safe and relaxed while on our journeys. Then we can use physical tools to represent our intent and to remind us of our goals. To further focus our intent on a tool we can chant life into the object, making it alive with symbolism. In all our actions we combine the seen—communion space and tools/objects—and the unseen—astral space and chanting—to create a balanced enchantment that reflects our balanced lives and magical intent for the good of the All.

Communion Space

In the last section we looked at ritual space, that which we set up when we draw a circle between the worlds in order to walk with spirit and create magic. Yet when we think of ritual perhaps we think of more organised religious practices and wonder what it has to do with our wild craft. Do not forget that ritual can also refer to regular activity, like taking the dog for a walk morning and evening or clinking glasses with the friend we meet after work each Friday. A walk with our dog has purpose and beauty, the clinking of glasses can be accompanied by a blessing, and so we see again that there is ritual magic in the midst of life if only we acknowledge it as such!

By ritual here we simply mean a beautiful ceremony that follows a flowing but set pattern, a lyrical and meaningful rite rather than an ordained service full of sober or overblown dogma. We have already established that wild witchery is not a religious practice or rigid endeavour and we don't necessarily need the regalia that we associate with formal spiritual regimes. So does that mean that we don't need, for example, an altar for our practice or any specially consecrated magical tools?

The answer to these questions is that such things are up to us but certainly not essential. It all depends, as ever, on our intent and what we ourselves feel we need in order to enhance our practice in our lives. If we can make an altar that generates an appropriate focus for our vibrant verdant craft, then this is all well and good as long as it does not become something that we feel we should have, or an excuse to stockpile spiritual trinkets of little real worth. Likewise, we do not need to feel as though we have to buy exquisitely wrought tools before we commune with spirits.

It is valuable to reassert here that we live integrated magical lives and so every object we touch has the potential to be a tool, from a wooden spoon to a knitting needle to a fountain pen. We need not segregate our lives into witch time and ordinary human time. Our enchantment flows through each act, each moment becomes enlivened with wild possibility. Yet sometimes we may like to set up a special sacred space to perform our magic. Perhaps at times we would like to take out special tools, kept for a ceremonial purpose. Maybe we would like to keep these on a small table, box, or chest that acts as a centrepiece for all our enchanted endeavours, a shrine to all we hold dear, an altar.

The word "altar" has unfortunate connotations that are simply not applicable in wild witchery. Mainly, the altar raises images of an austere place far away from the rest of creation, which has a sombre atmosphere, a priestly resonance. It suggests that only certain ordained places are holy when actually, as we know from our own practice and experience as wildwitches, everything is sacred. So to break the link with such disconnected thinking, let us instead call this shrine a "communion space," to suggest familiarity, closeness, and connectedness. Our own particular kind of communion is essentially green and so we can think of this communion space as an indoor grove, carrying the spirit of the wildwood into the home, working with plant people to give it life. Along with our wish and will that it becomes so, lush coloured fabrics and evocative carvings, lovingly rendered imagery and photographs, growing herbs and flowers can all aid the process of turning a space into a living environment with a burgeoning bucolic energy.

We may feel that we need such a communion space in our home or garden or even in our workplace where we may feel the need to spend quiet time, establishing our link to the All. We can further do this by displaying our personal sacred objects in our communion space, as they give us the impetus to break away from other mundane demands and attune us deliberately with all that we hold dear. We can ask those around us to not touch nor lay anything too close to our space, including coffee cups, magazines, or bills. The communion space is important to us and requesting their cooperation is both necessary and reasonable. When we enter this area of communion we can make it clear to family or others who share our space that we will be working in Otherworld time; it is a special time for us, and we prefer to not be disturbed. Thus the communion space gives us the chance to have something that is truly, deeply ours in the midst of an impersonal modern life.

The other benefit of setting up a formal place where we can actively connect with the spiritual essence is power. Repeated use of a thing builds up power as does repeated chanting and many return visits to one special place in the landscape. An energy or atmosphere is created. A bond is made, etherically and physically. We may notice this if we try to use someone else's drum or divination tools. The etheric imprint of the regular user is oftentimes too strong upon the objects for us to work with them. So it is with space. One can only imagine what a place that experienced violent arguements every day would feel like. Repetition, and the strong emotional charge made when we connect deeply with something, creates a dynamic. Thus our communion space is a powerful one to work in. Even a simple morning and evening prayer, invocation, or chant, along with the lighting of a candle can be enough to establish this resonance. When lighting a candle we can chant for peace in our lives, or pray in remembrance of all the animals that suffer at the hand of man, or we can invoke for renewed clarity during the day ahead. To build up even more personal power we can cast our magical circles in this space and journey within its sphere of influence. Of course, with the right protective precautions and intent we can journey or make magic anywhere, in a cafe or on a bus, on the moors or by the sea. With a communion space we are simply acknowledging the fact that we choose to also have a particular place where we practice.

The most appropriate way for us, being wildwitches, to approach our communion space is by placing both found and made objects there: these can be anything of particular resonance or relevance to the present time and to our individual preferences. We can have our special medicine items laid out there—our medicine being simply that which is of our spirit, our special unique vibration. As we know, everything has its own resonant medicine, that which keeps it in balance and harmony with the rest of creation, and here we refer to the items that resonate with our own green essence. We should ask permission of these items before placing them there, acknowledging the inherent wise medicine of all beings.

It is pertinent to mention here that it is a beautiful thing to return any found medicine object to the wild once our time with it has ended. Perhaps we may have gained insights through trance journey or spirit guidance on where our object (say a fossil, pretty pebble, or piece of wood) would like to be now that its time with us is over. We do not need to hoard each and every shell, bone, and feather we come across. Sharing space with such energy and beauty and then letting it go is much more in harmony with our path and it rejects the standard human way of thinking about ownership and acknowledges the spirit inherent in all things. Making such active statements of green-spirited respect in our lives is a vital part of our sylvan path.

Our communion space should be created with our intent to the fore and we should focus on its meaning and purpose in our lives regularly, giving thanks for the items that have come to rest there. We may like to keep permanent representatives of the elemental essences in this space. Or perhaps a drawing or cross-stitch embroidery of our sacred outdoor place. An applicable divination card may stand there, reminding us of a recent message. We can keep our magical journals there along with any books or photographs we find profoundly moving.

In the main, our communion space should be aesthetically pleasing to us and spiritually affecting. Yet it may need, for practical reasons, to be portable and have a lid or cover. It can be as understated as we wish but should be more than just a place to drop off all the things we collected on a walk in the woods. It is a reflection of who we are inside and a remembrance of how we wish to be in the world. It is a place of connection and reflection, a meeting of the ethereal and the corporeal, a life-enhancing idea made manifest.

Focus Tools

As for our tools, it should always be remembered that it is the effort and the focus of our will that makes something what it is. The symbolism we place upon each item and the personal interaction we have with these is paramount. In a ceremonial sense, we can wave our arms in sweeping gestures and use clouds of pungent incense smoke but without the defining energy of our directed will we have nothing but an interesting display. Similarly, a knife bought from an esoteric market may look very impressive and arcane but without our energy running though it as we point with it or carve with it, it is an attractive knife, not a magical tool.

We know that we can use a stick, a finger, or a wooden spoon handle if we have the correct amount of intention and focus on what we do and how we use it. Our tools can be the most basic items we have in our lives and still work with us fluently if our intent is honourable and our will is focused and strong. Or they can indeed be beautiful things, after all we are not living a dry monk's life! The point is only that we don't need glamour and glitz to be magical. Yet it is worth acknowledging the fact that it can be fun and fulfilling to work with stunningly-crafted items, relishing the feel of beautifully rendered cloth, metal, and wood. So, if we would enjoy having a special set of magical equipment we may have some of the following in our witch's tool bag or box:

Knife—often known as an "athame" by Wiccan witches. We can use a knife to direct our cold, blue-gold protective fire. We can see the fire stream from the blade's tip as we draw a circle or check out a spirit.

Wand—perhaps with a crystal tip. With a wand we can channel and direct our energy similarly to the knife. In these first two examples we have a correspondence to the swords and wands suits of the tarot and consequently we can see an energetic correspondence of swords being tools of fire and wands of air. However, we are working with them as directors of our will, and as we visually perceive our will as cold fire, then such a delineated correspondence may not sit well with us. As ever, we can reap the benefits of having a spirit companion to talk such issues over with and ask their advice on the matter. There is no prescription that can be given beyond the guidance of this trusted ally and our own intuition and experience

Communion chalice—perhaps of wood and a meaningful personal symbol either carved or pyrographed into it. From this chalice we can drink brews and blends that we concoct, toasting the spirit of a season with homemade nonalcoholic wines or cordials. *Note:* as we have already discussed we should not drink alcohol (or take any other mood-altering drug that lowers inhibitions) whilst engaging in spiritwork or in a sacred communion that requires us to be psychically open. To do so would mean we were impaired and not able to respond efficiently to any energy that was not appropriate to us at that time. Our vigilance would not be up to standard and this is potentially dangerous to the sensitive Fey-spirited wildwitch.

Traditionally, the chalice honours the feminine aspect of creation while the knife or wand is seen as male. Again, it is up to us how we respond to these sacred items. What do they say to us?

Staff—perhaps carved or marked with appropriate meaningful glyphs, and made of sturdy enough material to upstand outdoor work. A staff is a good way of directing our will when testing out a spirit. Pointing a staff may seem impractical because of its size but we can use it as a protective symbol of our strength and unity, with the land or the tree that it came from, by knocking three times on the ground with it. We can ask:

> *Three by three with wood I knock,*
> *On holy earth's good skin,*
> *For you to show me your true self,*
> *So that I may let you in!*

Magical clothes—the clothes we may don when we venture to our sacred place on trance journeys. We can adopt the same ploy manifestly and dress up (or down) to suit our own magical style and mood, perhaps reflecting (whilst not trying to re-create entirely) the guise of our Otherworld self. We know who we are inside and we can show this in an external way during our time at the communion place. Thus we may feel comfortable in a simple shift of cotton, or in brightly coloured leggings and a tunic, or in a full velvet gown. Only we know what will suit our inner essential self at any particular moment. Handmade or specially commissioned clothes taken from our own designs would work best in this respect, giving the items an immediate connection to our own energies. Once we have ascertained what we will wear then it is good to stick with the same clothes for as long as possible, building up that ritualistic element of putting on familiar garb so that we may enter another way of being and seeing.

We do not need to be wholly static in our appearance, rather we can go with the flow, observing the cycles of life in our ornamentations. We can embellish our costume with decorations pertinent to a particular personal or seasonal resonance; for example, we could pin may blossom (cut with permission and respect) on to a shirt at the beginning of May; we could wear a red scarf at the summer solstice and a white one for winter; or we could wear an ornate silver necklace at full moon and a black shawl at dark moon. We can use facepaints, headdresses, and temporary henna tattoos to embellish hands and feet, or we can dress our hair with ribbons or circlets of seasonal greenery. It is all about meaningful fun but it also offers that all-important connection to a mood or resonance that makes us feel comfortable. We have the freedom to experiment within the bounds of our own self-knowledge and our understanding of natural processes.

Medicine bag—a form of carrying our magic with us. It contains the magical items we consider to be "indispensable," those that we need outdoors as well as inside. It is a sort of doctor's bag containing the source of a quick energetic pick-me-up or a feeling of comfort and joy. The contents elevate us as they are a reflection of that deep inner being, the eternal spiritual or Otherworld self; then sing to our souls of our connection to all creation. We need to tune into that self as we know it from our meditative trance journeys, in order to make a medicine bag for ourselves. First we think of our spirit name, our elemental nature, the things we have learned so far, and the essence of our own path. How can we symbolise these qualities in a few items that will bring us reassurance as well an uplift us when we open the bag?

Some ideas for the items would be things like found animal fur, bones, teeth, or claws; found stones, fossils, or crystal formations; symbolic handmade jewelry or talismans made of respectfully cut herbs or other dried plant matter. An item should only be included if it captures that essence, the spirit quality that is our true and unique medicine. It is no good if we are just attracted to its visual impact. It is possible to undertake a special medicine walk (either in the physical realm or in the Otherworld) whilst asking to be shown, or to be given, a powerful piece for our bag.

Magical pouch—a smaller pouch can be worn all the time. It can contain items pertaining to a particular spell or season or it can affirm a dedication to the green way. It can also be a spell bag, sealed up but containing the essence of an enchantment. This doesn't even have to be objects as such, the spell can be spoken, breathed, or sung into the bag and closed or sewn shut with an appropriate tie. Depending on the overall energetic gist of the working, these bags can be carried, buried, placed in running water, thrown out to sea, burned, or given away. Each act symbolises the nature of the enchantment, for example, in burying it, the spell may be about growth; a chant could weave words into the act about how, when the bag rots down and the spell is released into the earth, so will the magic grow into the world, putting forth shoots like a seed in springtime.

Here is an example of a pouch that contains items dedicated to the Dark Moon Mother, the bringer of psychic sight. It can be carried and serves as a reminder or a commitment to such power. The bag is made by hand of recycled black velvet. On one side, a waning moon is painted in silver, on the other, a personal transformative symbol relating to the spider has been etched, again in silver. Inside there can be:

- A pinch of mugwort, beneficial to psychic sight, specifically opening the third eye
- A small pewter representation of a crow skull, the bird that is related to darkness and the transformation of carrion into flight, representing the cycle of death and rebirth
- A moonstone set in silver, representing the full moon waning, the moon bringing vision and psychic clarity, and the dark of the moon enhancing the ability to see what is hidden with pyschic vision
- A small mammal bone found on a walk to connect in with the energy of the dying year at the start of winter representing death as well as what lies beyond our fleshy disguises, again that which is hidden becomes revealed
- A few drops of the essential oil yarrow, which is resonant of the dark aspect and a beneficial herb for the pyschic sight in trance vision

It should be noted here that whilst herbs and other green beings have their own healing properties that cannot be disputed we may find that their essential oils resonate with us in ways that are not traditionally associated with them. For instance, vanilla is a "warm" smelling oil that we may then think is solar and so about passions, while it could also be said to have a richly romantic scent and so be more associated with the emotions and the moon. On a personal note, a friend of mine recently said that, to her, vertivert was evocative of the dark moon energy we have been discussing, reminding her of the waning moon or crone vibration. To others, vertivert is more reminiscent of the green man at his most primal and powerful (hence the *ver* part of the name in "verdant"); still others relate this oil to distinctly bright solar magical energies about wealth and prosperity. Again, the only true guide is our own spirit guidance from whatever trusted source and, of course, our developing intuition. It is well worth incorporating gloriously evocative scents into our crafts as we want them to arouse compatible feelings and spark certain energies. To choose these herbs we use our personal feelings combined with information obtained from books. I recommend the works of both Scott Cunningham and Anna Franklin as valuable primers for anyone who would like to have a solid written guide, based in tradition and modern research, on herbs and herbal scents/oils. Again, we can blend traditional wisdom with personal experience.

I will also note that both medicine bags and magical pouches should be handcrafted. Think of using natural fibres or recycled cloth that has been washed specially for the purpose. Juniper, rosemary, and pine essential oils make a good mix to drop into the water of any such "psychic cleansing" wash and does allow any previous vibration to be removed from the fabric. The simplest way to craft a bag or pouch is to lay two squares of cloth on top of each other and simply sew three of the sides together. Then turn this inside out and bind the top with a suitable tie made of wool, cord, plaited grasses, or a hank of hair. The bag can then be embroidered or drawn on using fabric pens or paint. The method isn't as important as the act itself and the attention we invest in the embellishment. Personal symbols, astrological glyphs, rune sigils, and simple images can be used. For example, an eloquent yet basic interpretation of a piece of prehistoric cave art depicting a bison or hunter could be painted or stitched on a medicine pouch used for "hunting for what we want." Think symbolically and poetically, as ever.

Cleansing

There are two more points to make about magical tools. The first is that each piece should be cleansed of its previous vibration—especially if it had been used by another human. This cleansing is appropriate, for example, for beads, which have been handled by other customers in a shop, before you bought them. However, if a piece is direct from an animal, bird, or plant, we do not need to cleanse because we will wish to retain that quality in essence—the spirit of rabbit, for example.

The cleansing can be done by either passing it through smoke made by burning cedar and juniper on a charcoal block (in a fire-proof bowl) or through the steam from burning juniper or pine essential oil in an oil burner over a small flame. Cleansing can also be done by placing the item under fresh running (preferably spring) water or set in a bowl filled with water and rock salt. If you are working with fabric, then wash it with a few drops of the essential oils previously suggested.

The process of cleansing is a magical act and should be focused on as such. A transformative rite with a suitable chant is necessary or else it too becomes an empty gesture. Although the herbs, oil, water, and salt do have innate cleansing properties, it is we who ask them to help us in our task of cleaning the previous vibrations of our tools.

Inherent Spirit

The second point we should be aware of is that there is a spirit inherent in each tool. We should ask the spirit for permission to work with the tool. We should never ask to simply use it because as wildwitches we do not *use*, we work *with* everything around us. Ours is a balanced relationship, not a master and servant scenario. Nor is it about our wielding power over something, or seeing it as compliant because, fundamentally, it is a dead thing. Our tools should be alive to us and treated as such.

Unseen Tools of Chant

Now that we understand our work and our poetic relationship with our guides, we may also come to a further understanding of the importance of enchantment in our magical work. A chant is a powerful means of helping us focus our intent. When we have crafted something by hand, such as woodworking, sewing, or handicrafts, and thus given it life, then it is easier to tune into that craft's energy when we sing the spirit to life. This is because we can infuse our craft with our intent during the entire process of creating the craft. Crooning or articulating someone else's words is never as effective. When we repeat our chant over and over, and when we relish the language used (and the imagery employed), we automatically become attuned to its purpose, captivated by its spell. We become enchanted. So far we have been using rhymes and curious, childlike incantations to evoke and invoke. We now know why the resonance of sound is so important to us but why must our chants consist of repetitive rhymes and verses?

To build up a rhythm is hypnotic, again not in the sense that it makes us lose control, rather it helps us slip deeper into an otherworldly, "nonordinary," reality. Like a lullaby repeated over and over to a child it lulls us and takes us beyond—beyond the mundane and into the dreaming. Here is an example. We can imagine our cares beings washed away by gently repeating the refrain:

Drift like a twig from a hazel that's fallen,
Into the river, the river that's calling,
Out to the ocean the water is swirling,
So may my worries be gone by the morning.

Our repetition can rock us more vigorously if we desire. We can create a beat that is felt more deeply and strongly, taking us into a dreamlike state as we tune into something akin to the primal heartbeat. Something like:

Into the Underworld we are stalking,
Like fox in the darkness we're night-walking,
Like wolf in the undergrowth we're all-knowing,
Like seed in the black loam we are growing,
Stalking . . . walking . . . knowing . . . GROWING!

Such verses can be repeated or the speed, volume, and level of involvement and emphasis can be increased in order to raise power by the continued focus of our intent and the physical act of vocalising. If we rock our bodies along with the chant we further raise power. Likewise, we can drum or clap along with the beat. All are basic shamanic techniques; they are applicable for those of us who seek to increase the power we are putting into the work. As we know, all our enchantment relies on that balance of the ethereal and the corporeal. It makes sense to become physically involved when we are chanting, thus expressing spiritual and material energies at once, one energy aiding the other.

An evocative chant, full of alliteration or onomatopoeia, rich with imagery and lush with allegory, can help get us in to the mood that we wish to create. Even the often understated pastoral imagery can be effective. We do not always need to shout or thump out a magical piece of poetry in order to raise energy. Sometimes just creating the right mood can enhance our connection with the work sufficiently for us to be more effective. Likewise, to gently sway, rather than rock or drum maniacally, can be just as hypnotic if it suits the atmosphere of the chant. To get a shiver up and down the spine is the effect we are aiming for in our more subtle and seductively lyrical chants. This shiver denotes that we have found the work thrilling at a deep soul level and have tuned in to its vibration. If we have managed this, then we have certainly generated the appropriate energy. An example of such an understated yet inspiring piece may be something like:

Silent the snowfall and muffled the footfall,
Bright is the hearthfire that crackles tonight,
Icicle quivers and spirit's a-shiver,
In the mid of the winter I call on new light!

Or:

With a woodsmoke smile of ancient guile,
In the voice of gently dreaming pyres,
Spit and spark and darkling dart,
I call on the shimmering spirit of fire!

The above is a rather picturesque rhyme and it is made clear by its eloquently graphic quality, which matches the sort of mood it would enhance. However, we do not have to be so subdued on other occasions, we can also use an element of nonsense in our verse if it may help us attain a more lighthearted mood. Such a playful mood would be suitable for an interaction with Green Jack as the young and infinitely jolly japester or for contacting the child aspect within our selves if we are feeling jaded. For example, this chant could be sung while we merrily jig about, invoking for more fun in our daily lives:

Skip like a lamb that's all springy and sprung,
Bop like a hoppedy hare that's a-lopping,
Pop like a pea from its poddington flung,
May this frolicy spiritedness never be stopping!

Or a Fey-spirited whimsical chant to sing while stirring an enlivening brew made from the fruit of a wild-rose tree could be something like:

Buckle-berry, hedge-pedge, fruit of wilder roses,
Brimble-broom, bramble-boon, hedge speaks of pixie's noses,
Cat-whin on the hip-tree, you haws with bright red lips,
Heddy-grinnel, nippernail, be sweet my pixie pips!

Note: All the above are colloquial/local English terms for the rosehip!

This spell-rhyme about getting a friend a new residence in his or her chosen area could be repeated in a repetitive way, over and over, to build up energy and focus:

By hank of wool from sheep who roam,
In the place that he would call his own,
May my friend go rolling home!
Yes, may my friend go rolling home!
By strand of hair pulled from his comb,
And wrapped around this local stone,
May my friend go rolling home!
Yes, may my friend go rolling home!

In the above chant we would have literally done what it suggests—gathered the relevant wool, found the local stone, and taken a few strands of our friend's hair from a comb (with his or her full consent). Our focus is not only the enchanted energy we invest but also the manifest symbology we connect with it. For every resonant gesture we make spiritually and energetically there must be a physical echo. So when we sing, chant, or recite our requests and prayers in this magical way, it is always appropriate to have a physical item or prop that reflects this. We can hold it as we chant, or simply look at it, imbuing it with our words, imagery, desires, and devotions.

Often our chants may have more than a little of the childlike about them and may even resemble nursery rhymes. This is for two reasons, firstly, we all remember our nursery rhymes, even though they were learned many years ago. The simplicity and wit contained in their short verses enable us to recall them over and over. Often the basic yet appealing tunes to which they were set help us tremendously, too. We shouldn't be afraid to put any, or all, of our chants to a tune as well as a rhythm. On a personal note, I find it hard to write any chant or poetic invocation without singing it in my head, they all have a tune that fits them perfectly. This tune then fixes the message (lyrics) in my mind. The trouble with sharing chants on paper here is that readers cannot hear my tune! And there is the real importance of crafting our own verses, not using prescribed ones, as everything has its own unique song to sing to us, and us alone.

As we aim to practice an unsophisticated and fluent kind of wild craft we should be willing to learn from musical nursery rhymes. How marvellous it would be for us to recall a protective chant or an invocation for guidance at any given moment in the same way we can spontaneously recall our childhood songs. We could use something like:

> *One's for connection, my roots going deeper,*
> *And two's invocation to my wisdom keeper,*
> *Three's for protection, the gold and the blue,*
> *And the fourth is my own intent, honest and true!*

Or:

> *Oh spirits who bother me against my desire,*
> *You'll find that you're bound by my circle of fire!*
> *And there you'll remain, of that have no doubt,*
> *Until those who protect me will escort you out!*

The second point in favour of chants or nursery rhymes is that they are very animated and imaginatively stimulating, conjuring up all manner of curious yet resonant representations in our minds. For example, in classic nursery rhymes we have the dish running away with the spoon, Jack falling down and breaking his crown, Miss Muffet sitting on a tuffet. We can utilise this same technique in our chants, ensuring that we have the same amount of evocation in our invocation. Here is another example:

> *A witch skips into a greenwood glade,*
> *And she spins in wide circles, three times three,*
> *Then she waves to the alder and bows to the ash,*
> *And she whispers "Which witch tree . . . which witch tree?"*
> *She salutes to the rowan and nods to the oak,*
> *She drops down for the hawthorn on one knee,*
> *And she puts the bright berries in the hood of her cloak,*
> *And she honours the witch tree . . . the witch tree.*

Here is another example, which gives a pledge to the moon:

> *Slender dancer, moving moon, oh take me as your partner!*
> *If you'll dance with me I'll bring you gifts and love you ever after!*
> *I'll bring you shells smoothed by the sea and kissed by little fishes,*
> *I'll bring you snowdrops in the spring and a thousand good will wishes!*
> *Oh shining sister sailing by, please be my life long muse,*
> *And I'll be your lover and your kin and I'll wear my dancing shoes,*

And I'll move with you across the sky and I'll seek you when your hidden,
Oh silvered one, from your sylvan one, I'm widdershins, moon-bidden!

Remember that such chants are just examples. We should not be intimidated by their length or rhyming quality. It is not expected that we would come up with something like this straight away. The purpose of giving examples is just to show how combining our purpose and our own green-spirited magical creativity can be immediately fashioned into a verse that flies our intent to the stars. A chant is just the means we use to take our intent onward and upward. If it does this, then it can be as short or as basic as we choose so long as it is pertinent and heartfelt, the meaning remaining inherent. We will quickly find our own wild way of working with words, sounds, and tunes. Indeed, the more we craft our own unique soulful song-rhymes, the more it becomes second nature to enhance our lives with en-chant-ment.

It is just as important to have fun with chants, as with this last example, as it is to create intense moods and dreamy invocations. And our wild craft allows us to be just as spontaneous and delightfully childlike when we choose our objects of magical focus. This is important to remember here since our chants often are accompanied by focus tools. This does not mean we are acting in a highly dramatic play, we are engaging with magic as part of our lives. This said, it is appropriate to work with everyday or found objects such as shiny bottle tops, wool, house plants, pine cones, empty jars, animal bones, feathers, beads, seeds, or modelling clay. And handcrafted items such as homemade dolls, cakes, biscuits, wine, cordial, cloaks, bags, and pouches are all perfect for imbuing the item with our intent as we create it—this is truly enchantment in the midst of life! The same goes for painting a picture, stringing a necklace, or weaving a rug. And if we imbue our item with power through word magic, enchanting it by chanting as we craft it, then all the better.

Review: Creating a Chant

To recap, here is a checklist of some things to consider when creating a chant:

☐ A repetitive beat can aid relaxation and encourage a trancelike state (entrance)

☐ A catchy tune and rhythm is easy to remember, while repetition raises energy

☐ Carefully chosen words allow the living language to awaken the intent (enchant)

☐ Simple yet affecting imagery stirs our souls and empowers our enchantment

☐ Tempo, sound, or linguistic/poetic skill creates an appropriate mood

☐ Dancing, spinning, marching, stamping, rocking, or swaying adds a physical momentum to the energies we invoke and aids the repetitive trancelike state

Ceremony

We may now use our knowledge of magical tools and communion space in ceremony. Our ceremonies are not meant to be pompous, complicated, nor dramatic. They are green-spirited celebrations that relate to the tides of life. A ceremony simply and eloquently brings together each and every aspect of wild witchery we have discussed for the sake of expressing a commitment or commemorating a particular time, act, or essence.

To create a ceremony we must have the appropriate enthusiasm, for it needs to be alive and not a performance or parody. We can plan a ceremony in which we incorporate appropriate painted stones, homebrewed, nonalcoholic drinks, or chants ready to hand, but we need not think of it as a rigid structure. If it is to be alive then we must be flexible, working as ever in our safe boundaries that give us the confidence to fly with any impromptu idea or piece of inspiring guidance. All ceremonies, prayers, and spells should be discussed beforehand with our companion spirits (as well as with a Fey helper if necessary) to ascertain their feasibility and suitability.

Do remember that if we choose to work a ceremony out of doors in our special site, we need to ask its permission first, we cannot just impose our will on it even for such a well-meaning and sacred rite! A ceremony takes place within the scared circle of blue-gold flame and can consist of a blend of any of the following:

• A specific trance journey taken to echo the ceremonial purpose—for example, to journey to a special otherworldly destination in order to meet a particular spirit, and to gain insight or information about a certain matter

• The blessing or dedication of an object, tool, or endeavour through chant, music, movement, and focus

• The creation of a special item, such as a piece of craftwork to be used in a healing spell, or the execution of a painting that expresses the Fey essence of the Greening

- Praying and envisioning for a compassionate desire, such as hope for the world
- Connecting with a specific spirit energy; aligning with a seasonal or lunar vibration
- Calling up a particular spirit who may need to be "sent on" if it is being troublesome or welcomed if its presence is needed
- The drinking and eating of seasonal fare, healing brews, etc., to celebrate or "fix" an energy; a communion between the spirit and the manifest levels

An excellent idea for a ceremony is to elaborate on our promise to the wild way (as described at the start of the book). Now we know ourselves that much better, and have more profound insights into the commitment it requires to be a true wildwitch. Maybe, for ourselves, we can begin to fashion a ceremony of rededication to the wild way. We have all the skills we need to create a vibrant and meaningful, as well as safe and secure, ritual. For this personal rite there can be no prescription. Let this be the first time we really fly alone while crafting a wild rite, which in itself is enough reason for us to celebrate!

Review: Magical Ceremony

☐ State the intention

☐ Root into manifest reality while you breathe deeply and relax on all levels

☐ Apply protection from energetic intrusion

☐ Connect above and below as energy begins to travel through the body

☐ Consult with companion spirits on the appropriateness of the proposed magic

☐ Think of a reasonable gift to give in return for the spell being a success

☐ Consider the symbology of the enchantment—its inherent energy or theme

☐ Observe the seasonal tides, lunar cycle, and consider the right time of day

☐ Respectfully acknowledge all elemental forces that will be called on for assistance

☐ Ask permission of any being, place, or object that will hopefully be present

☐ Gather any symbolic objects for further focus

☐ Choose a place to work and make the space sacred in an appropriate way

☐ Chant and sing to focus on the intent

☐ Do practical work: light candles, sew symbols on cloth, focus spiritual intent on tools

☐ Ground into the manifest reality after the magic is undertaken (write notes)

☐ Speak to no one about what has been undertaken until the spell bears fruit in the world. This last point reminds us again of our formula: "We say our piece, we represent our piece, and we send yet keep our piece . . . then we keep our peace!"

It is important to reiterate here that while power is released in chanting, power grows when held in silence. Discussing what we have done allows the energy to leak away and, as our work is primarily about energies and energy transference, we would be wise to keep our own counsel. To acknowledge and welcome meaningful silence into our lives as wildwitches is in itself an act of transformation, going against the grain of modern society, which is itself uncomfortable with mute quiet.

As witches, as we discussed in chapter 1, we are nonconformists willing to champion nature in a world that can value economic progress above the land that sustains us. Making a positive green-spirited stand for the things we hold dear is simply keeping up a long tradition of nonconformism. Giving silence credence and space in our lives is such an act.

Gifts

Finally in this section it is appropriate for us to consider that if we work our ceremonies out of doors—it is sincerely hoped that we will, as often as we can—then how may we "repay" the spirits of the place? Or, more appropriately, how will we physically interact with the spirits in an appreciative way? We, as wildwitches, endeavour to live life with an ongoing, ever-growing attitude of gratitude and therefore it should be second nature for us to ask the spirits we work with what they would like of us. Often this may be a spiritual offering, the making of a promise or vow, the sending out of prayers or healing energies, but it can also be a manifest gifting, a present from the physical world we inhabit.

It goes without saying that we should always ask if our gifts are wanted and appropriate. We can do this as part of our contemplative interaction with the essence of the place, during a trance journey, or when we are talking with our companion guides and Fey helpers. In the latter case, the companions and the Fey can act as our intermediaries and tell us what it is that the land, or the nature spirits of that land, may want at any one time. We will eventually be able to aquire this information for ourselves but at first we may need another, more familiar, spirit to intercede as it can be hard to accurately hear, (feel or see) what it is that a more distant essence may desire of us. For us as humans, the resonance of elements, or of the land, may initially be harder to contact or relate to with any certainty.

The Faery beings that we may encounter, if we are thus blessed, in a wild landscape will make demands on our giftings like no other spirits! To sum up the essence of what generally appeals to them here is a Fey-spirited rhyme:

> *A glimmer, a glamour, not a dismal dim-dimmer,*
> *Oh bring us your sparklies, we want things that shimmer!*

Personally I have been asked for gemstones, fizzy cordial, honey cakes, good quality chocolate, and pure apple juice. I have had offerings of silver and zirconium jewellery accepted gleefully by the Faery! On other occasions I have been asked for more staid gifts, for example when dealing with an elemental being who guards a stone I have been asked for local cheese and ale! The spirits that we encounter in the land are just as varied in their tastes and desires as any physical being and we cannot assume that, just because they are discarnate, any one spirit will want the same as a certain other elemental wanted.

Traditional offerings of giftings include strands of hair, blood, fruit, coins, seeds, and scraps of biodegradable fabric. A libation of juice is appropriate and nourishing. In the Romani tradition it is common to offer whiskey, of which oak trees are often fond (it is highly appropriate to take gifts to oak trees who share their wisdom with us). In the Native American traditions such gifts are known as "give-aways" and include cornmeal and tobacco.

People also offer flowers as spirit gifts; although, we would be obliged to ask if we feel able to take such offerings from their source as they are living beings in their own right. A wildwitch does not usually endorse the cutting of flowers, preferring instead to appreciate their natural beauty in situ so that they may live out their normal cycle in peace. This is a matter of personal conscience and inner guidance for each of us to consider.

Sometimes offerings can seem more rude than reverent. I personally have witnessed mounds of burned potatoes and a whole bottle of apple juice left at a standing stone (obviously someone's ruined supper). It is becoming more common to see inappropriate inorganic offerings left, especially at popular sacred sites. I have seen mobile phone cases, air fresheners, hair ornaments, and bus passes hung from a hawthorn tree like "clouties" (the traditional way of tying a cloutie of cotton rag to a faery tree in an act of sympathetic magic; as the rag biodegrades so does the healing spell get released). Similarly, crystal fragments bought from stores are often jammed into the earth at many sacred sites, which is highly inappropriate for the living energy of the place and the sensitive crystal itself.

Suitable gifts are always organic and indeed often symbolic and only left with the permission of a site and its guardian spirits. Sharing any food or drink consumed at a place is a kind act of spiritual communion is encouraged as long as the energy of both site and food are compatible. Impromptu prayerful gifts can be offered up rather than a physical item and these could include a pledge to regularly tidy up litter or a plea for the energies of the site to be felt strongly by those who visit it, engendering a desire to become more environmentally friendly or to plant a garden.

In special cases where we have an ongoing bond to a site we can craft individual gifts, bake cakes, weave small (vegetable-dyed cotton) prayer squares, or leave an appropriate carving. Whatever we do, our work is an interaction between the manifest and the unseen so we should always consult with the associated spirits.

Spell Examples

Now that we have covered protection, guidance, tides, and focus in this chapter and previous ones, we are ready to look at actual spells. But the wild craft is not prescriptive as we know, rather it is based on an individual daily relationship with nature and the unseen. Therefore to offer prepackaged spells is not appropriate but to state when magic may be used, and to give symbolic ideas for how to approach magic, is to provide a starting point. What follows are some suggestions of how enchantment may fit into daily life. As with all ideas in this book, we learn from these suggestions but we must add our own energy into the equation:

Protection + guidance + tides + focus = magical change.

Once we have a suitable need to weave enchantment into our lives then we must live enchanted lives on a daily basis. We can do this by incorporating simple spellwork into even the most mundane aspects of living. We must remember to choose prepared magic spells and craft them to fit in specially with the seasonal, lunar, or energetic tides. What follows is not a prescription, only a working example to inspire and guide. Our craft will not be remotely wild if it has none of our own untamed natural power in it. Our input and effort and our personal interactions both seen and unseen are everything! "Our energies are everything as everything is energy!"

Therefore, we learn from these ideas but we do not follow them as they are written, which is in a very basic form. Instead, we go our own ways as valuable, unique parts of the All, adding in all the poetic expression, spiritual guidance, and worldly experience that is exclusively ours. If we dance to someone else's tune then our own marvellous part in the harmonious symphony of life will be missing, and the overall symphony the poorer for it. And our magic won't fly as it should, for what bird shares its wings with another for a fear of travelling solo? At the same time, remember that these are the spells that we can ask the Fey to help us with. Fey help can bring to even the most highly planned piece of fateweaving, a spontaneity and joyful lyricism that we alone could never achieve. They can make magic sparkle with vitality, linking us in to the All with ease.

Seeking a New Home

Here we begin at a new moon, preferably in the waxing of the year, for both are affiliated with new beginnings. We consider the element of earth, explore what it means to feel secure, protected, and connected. Then we work with symbology appropriate to putting down roots or seeking shelter. For example, we could plant a tree seed in an area we wish to live. Or we could bond with a tree already there, taking it a suitably nurturing organic gift and asking for its roots to be as ours. We could make a snail-shell talisman to wear, symbolic of a home, by breathing our wish into it and sealing it up we weave our intent into it. We could undertake a walk with the sacred intent of "going home," to where we wish to be; carry a token from our current home and leave it at our intended destination; or paint a picture, weave a rug, or make something that we envision being with us in our new home. We should consider the fact that every being has its natural place—badger to set, bird to nest—and so have we.

Seeking Better Health

Here we tune into fire, for both vitality and burning away all that is not beneficial, and earth for physical strength. We work with the waxing moon to build up energy and with the waning moon to banish illness or infirmity. We focus with symbology of rejuvenation, thinking of dandelions pushing up through concrete paving, of shoots pushing up through frosted ground, of the sun returning at dawn. To banish ill health we link in with the dying back and breaking down of natural things, like leaves turning skeletal and acorns turning brittle until they turn to dust in the frost of winter.

For the growth of vitality, we can nurture a seed as if it was the sick person and plant it outdoors at midsummer. We work with the connection between the sun and the "atomic suns" that fuel our own bodies, strongly and repeatedly visualising the strength of our inner sun and aligning it to the outer sun's waxing. We can steep a round shiny pebble (to represent our cells and our wholeness) in an infusion of marigolds or sunflowers, and then remove it and paint a vibrant symbol on it. We can keep it close to us at all times. Of course, we can make a healing soup to be eaten over the three days of a waxing full moon so that the condition improves daily. To banish ill health we can ask that as the sun grows weaker in the day (or year) so may the illness fade away. We can also bury a cold, black candle that has been burned down, or a piece of rotten bark into the ground after pouring all the sensation of ill health into the object at the dark moon.

*   *   *

Remember this, that we have not taken on the greenmantle of a wildwitch in order to have a perfect human existence! We incarnate not to be paragons of virtue, living in supreme abundance with all our needs met. Rather, we engage in the Earthwalk to act out scenarios in our current guise in order to re-address old patterns, put right mistakes, and witness other ways of being. In short, we are alive in order that we may attend the school of life and learn. Anyone who levels accusations at us—like, "You're a witch, why can't you sort out your money troubles? Why can't you find a suitable partner? Why can't you just live wherever you wish?"—has missed the point and needs to be gently reminded that by being who we are, wildwitches living lives of enchantment, by no means entitles us to perfection in all areas of our lives, that is something exclusively experienced in the Otherworlds after human death! We are here to enhance life situations, and to bring healing and understanding, harmony and acceptance to the world.

Because magic is brightly and gently woven, and is not yet part of the "instant" society we live in, it works in Faery, not human, time. So when we ask that a spell works "soon" it could well mean within the next decade! We do need to be specific with our requests and know the result will follow, either by a drip-drip effect into our lives or by a sudden stunning response. Indeed, we are dealing with wild energy and part of its beauty is that we always get what we need, when we need it. It just may not present itself in the most obvious or immediate ways! It integrates itself into the web of life as is appropriate depending on, among many other reasons, the seasonal tide, the amount of energy put into it, and our receiving accurate guidance on the rightness of the request. If we understand the process of this equation then we can have faith that results will follow.

So, we now have a recipe for wild enchantment and the basis for creating our own meaningful green-spirited spells. We understand that communicating with the Fey is essential for this. Being poetic by their very nature the Fey are the ones that can advise us on appropriately animated chants, suggest any symbolic tools we may need and suitable locations, and they can assist us with choosing any ingredients that will enhance our spells, such as herbs or oils. They can broaden our understanding of what enchantment really is and open our eyes to its place in the world.

If we take responsibility, following the threads we ourselves weave as they spin outward from our being, and work with a heart full of rhyme and a good dose of balancing reason, then we can bring back that which is considered departed; we can bring the magic back to life.

Chapter Six

INTO THE WILD GREEN BEYOND

We have gone to the time that was once upon,
To a verdant place under spiritual sun,
For we are all that has ever shone . . .
And we find ourselves like stars.

To conclude, we will enhance our understanding of the wonderful and fundamental maxim "As within, so without." We will do this by studying three more green-spirited topics, divided into two sections for "within" and "without."

The first section is concerned with the "within" aspect, the deep inner work that allows for realisations and profound personal insights. It covers "pathworking" (a trance journey with a predefined route taken to achieve a specific aim) that we may use in order to know our eternal self better. It is an adaptable spiritual journey that gives us safe and effective access to other guises that we may have worn for our Earthwalk. Although such pathworking may, on initial assessment, seem self-indulgent and unnecessary, it will actually help us to develop our understanding of the bigger spiritual picture, enabling us to perceive the patterns inherent in life with more clarity. It will help us to feel more secure and confident of our own place in the scheme of things and will free up more of our personal energy that may have been devoted to deep-seated anger or prejudice. Therefore our own effectiveness in the world is enhanced, not only for our sake but for all our relations in creation.

The process of looking at our other manifest lives is often referred to as "reincarnation" but this title is a bit of a misnomer as it alludes to a linear progression concerned with *past* lives. As wildwitches, we are dealing with time, as with all aspects of the natural world, as cyclical and not linear. Therefore we will be certainly looking at other incarnations but not at past lives. We may wish to think of this as a soul resurgence. When we engage in the process of soul resurgence we will discover that we all have the opportunity to be anyone. With this understanding, we soon foster those traits essential to a true exponent of the gentle wild way: compassion and altruism.

The second section of this chapter is more concerned with the "without" aspect of being a fey witch, that is, with the more manifest side of our practice, the part that shares our skills with others. This section will give guidance on both simple herbal healing and uncomplicated divination techniques that are suitable for the green-spirited craft. You may wonder if there is a need for such a section when there are many excellent specialist books on herbalism and divination already available for any witch to dip into for reference. Well, here we see not potted version of such works but rather an inspirational guide, which can allow us to form our own relationships with the plant people and likewise create our own personal way of divining. As wild witchery is like a colourful folk art, a comfortable homespun craft, we would expect perhaps to be given the basic technique and ingredients and then invited to experiment with our own concoctions. Thus this section asks us to stand with one foot in tradition whilst being aware of our own unique sylvan vision and all the magical possibilities inherent in the present moment. As with all we have learned thus far it allows us to walk our own wonderfully unique way in a disciplined and grounded fashion.

Both herbalism and divination help us to work more closely with the rest of the natural world and to gain assistance and advice from the omnipresent but sadly often overlooked spirits of nature. This section really enables us to bring wild magic into every aspect of our lives with confidence and encourages us to balance inner work with enjoyable craftings. It will reiterate themes we have come across throughout this book; it will reaffirm the importance of infusing our otherworldly knowledge with daily routines, activities, and creations.

Please do treat this chapter as a way of voyaging further into the beyond by means of enhancing the inner self that maintains an awareness of the Source of life. By feeding our own roots we nourish the branches too. What we do at a profound level, at the heart of our spiritual selves, touches the far reaches of creation. And what we do for others at a physical, local level nourishes that which dwells at our core, our eternal essence. What we do matters. Our energies are everything and everything is energy, reflected, connected, there is no separation. . . . "As within, so without."

Section One: Going Within

Other Lives: Understanding the Spirit's Ongoing Song

As wildwitches, we strive to understand the maxim "As within, so without" because it gives us a sense of our magical ability to effect change internally, locally, globally, and beyond. As we appreciate this far-reaching, deep-seated effect, we aim to live magical lives and weave enchantments "for the good of the All." However, there is another guideline of equal importance to us and that is: "Know thyself."

Previously we have undertaken some work in order to know this self. We have met and melded with our Otherworld self, and have understood ourselves to be more than temporal flesh and bone. We have aquainted ourselves with the spirit that is currently housed in our temporary human body and we know it to be a shimmering independent energy, indestructible and inspirational. Moreover, we know our true self, above and beyond the body it has incarnated into, exists independently of any temporary persona we wear as humans. This true spirit self has simply incarnated into a suitable shell and will move on again at some point into another physical form. We know that flesh passes away to be transformed by the action of decay yet the soul experiences a resurgence, it carries on growing through new life in another body.

As wildwitches, this may present us with a bit of an ethical dilemma as we do not feel the need to distance ourselves from our bodies (which would be akin to elevating ourselves above nature). We know our part in Earth's dance is precious and we know creation, in a manifest sense, to be sacred and so we do not wish to transcend our flesh and bone or to become separate from it. We see our bodies as beautiful and respect them as much as we respect the soil and worms that will one day reclaim our bodies. Indeed, we understand that disconnecting ourselves from our human forms is potentially dangerous. How else has humanity made such a hideous mess of the planet if it isn't by considering themselves somehow separate from nature and all her fecund motions? However, we seek union with our temporary but no less special bodies as a holy communion based in our promise to walk with love upon Earth Mother, respecting all our relations on the planet for who and what they are.

We have vowed to be custodians of Earth's garden whilst incarnate and to enhance our lives, and that of others, with the magic of this green guardianship. Without our bodies we could not engage in such rewarding work and without our respect for our own physicality how can we hope to respect that which is physical? So yes, we can accept the spirit that dwells within us as a free-flying essence. And no, we cannot consign our bodies to being little more than a transient encumbrance. Like Earth herself, our bodies are part of the Creator's boundless and beautiful expression. With this reverence for the physical in mind, the next statement may sound harsh and unnatural.

Our current body is an overcoat that we will shrug off at some point on this Earth-walk experience. We will "drop our robes" as the Native Americans poetically put it. Our bodily overcoat is discarded, recycled back into the ground, of no more consequence to us than any worn-out or restrictive piece of clothing in our lifetime. It has served its purpose and its purpose was to allow the spirit to have new experiences and fresh perspectives on its Earthwalk. So here indeed is a paradox for the wildwitch; the body is both highly sacred to us while we wear it and yet we know it to be disposable, a biodegradable garment that we have used and will cast off without a care. Is seeing it as disposable akin to the old Christian way of viewing it as somehow a dirty and lowly thing? Are we consigning our flesh to the same pit that had people flagellating themselves in hair shirts?

By no means! What we are saying is this: the eternal balance that we seek to maintain between the corporeal and the ethereal can be maintained if we can see the body as part of a sacred process. We must remember that we are not the only beings part of this process. The corn husks, pea pods, and nut shells are all part of the sacred process, too. They contain something vital and when that essence leaves, the skin (shell or pod) completes its part in the sacred round and is consumed by the land to feed its denizens. Our bodies are unique and they serve a perfect part in the dance of creation, yet they are not eternal like the spirit. It is right and good that they are discarded without a backward glance after the spirit leaves, for it reveals our faith in that endless cycle of renewal and transformation and that we do not need to hang on to the past or anything that has passed away. Which nut clings to its shell? Do we see the nut as callous or superior for seeking freedom? So the body is a lovely shell, a wonderful overcoat, and we thank it for that.

We truly blend these two seemingly opposing views of revering yet dismissing the physical by actively experiencing our own ongoing sacred process of being born, growing, dying back, and being born again—our soul resurgence. Just as we can accept the cycles of regeneration and disintegration on the land, with our fellow creatures—from egg to fledgling to free-flyer to parent to sick bird to bare bones picked clean to feed another who then gives birth—so can we come to accept the soul dance that leads us on from body to body, a continuum that rises and falls, wilts and flourishes. The soul is not apart from the natural patterns that we accept and appreciate. It may be "unseen" but it has seasons too.

To engage in the soul's, or spirit's, sacred process of growth, we must first ask: "Why do we incarnate? What is the process all about?" We incarnate, as we shall witness for ourselves, to experience different aspects of being in order that we may learn and grow from having a fresh perspective on existence. Incarnation is like a schooling process for souls, a true education, which encourages learning by mistakes. Just as the ultimate Creator fashioned all manner of different expressions of Itself from the ether in order to experience life in all its myriad facets, so can we experience creation from many different angles and viewpoints to become more rounded in our selves.

Incarnation is about seeking balance by experiencing the dance of life from both oppressive or extreme vistas and scenic viewpoints. It is about literally walking in another's shoes, for example, taking on the challenges of being a spirit in a physically impaired body, being born in an impoverished war-torn land, or born in an abusive household. Equally, it can be about being born with a natural talent for music in a wealthy family or having good health in an age of disease. How will we work with what we have been given, how will our soul respond to the physical? It is about living with cruelty and prejudice so that we may discover how not to be, about experiencing the love and acceptance of others so that we can understand how it is most beneficial to behave. Incarnation is about learning lessons in many classrooms with a variety of teachers.

Incarnation is also about facing patterns, which we as souls manifest throughout lifetimes; it is about interacting with behaviours we find abhorrent, which in historical times we may have even found unbearable. It is about looking at everything we wish to avoid, dealing with old fears, breaking damaging soul habits. Yet it is not about suffering. We do not incarnate to be punished for past wrongs. Instead, we may choose to incarnate to witness life from another angle in order that we will not make the same mistakes again. We are our own judges and our own witnesses. When we know our spiritual or Otherworld self we know what we need, and we always incarnate in a way that allows us to experience just that, tough as it may seem.

And life can seem tough if we forget our soul purpose, and especially tough if we forget we have a soul at all. It is the inherent free will of the soul that allows us to forget the Source and to make choices based purely on destructive human desires. By this we may observe that no one soul is evil, nor is any one soul the spiritual enemy, rather we can all choose to react in a way that is ignorant of our true essence and fall foul to emotive sensations, which give us only temporary thrills. Humans are prone to self-gratification if they forget their own spiritual source inside. Each one of us can forget this to a greater or lesser degree every day. So the real challenge of an incarnation is recalling our spiritual source in the midst of physical life, knowing our true self when that self can be effectively buried by human demands, human foibles. It is about connecting to that eternal source and acting accordingly, in peace, wisdom, and with clarity, when the manifest realms seek to test us beyond endurance.

Although the self, our eternal spirit, is unique, we come to incarnate into a body so that we may understand another paradox: we are individual but we are also one another. That is, we have the potential to be one another in other lives, in another time or place, if our eternal self thinks that we need that particular experience. Our spirit can incarnate in any one of countless numbers of bodies, in an endless variation of circumstances, for the sake of growth through understanding. We can all opt for an incarnation that pushes us to our limits or that allows us to be privileged. We can incarnate into bodies of any race, creed, or state of health.

We can truly be anyone that we choose to be. Sometimes we are offered choices within a lifetime, tests to gauge the strength of our soul connection. A twist of circumstance, an unfortunate combination of events, a momentary lapse in concentration—all of these things can lead to us becoming a killer or a victim, a persecutor or the persecuted. We can all choose to be liars, murderers, dictators, or paedophiles in as much as we can opt to be dedicated carers, tireless campaigners for good causes, or wonderful parents. If we forget who we are inside our physical shells, then it is far easier to slip into the role of the cruel aggressor than it is to remain on the soul's suggested life path.

If we have lost touch with our eternal essence it may be hard for us to feel the empathy we need to feel with our worldly adversaries, those who grind us down or cause us pain. When we forget that we are potentially one another, we lose our ability to communicate, spirit to spirit, from a place of genuine empathic equality, regardless of the physical shells involved. This is why our study of the self through other lives can bring us renewed compassion, because we begin to experience life as the beggar or the fool in as much as the priestess or noble man. By looking at other (or past) lives, we can observe mistakes and choices we have made in other incarnations, and we can then note any personal courses of action that were based on human greed, envy, or lust rather than rooted in spirit. By having this view we can perhaps be kinder to the current mistakes of others. As wildwitches such compassion is essential.

When we begin to trace our own lifelines or incarnations, following the strands that weave them together, the destined events and choices that establish patterns within our way of relating to the world, then we begin to appreciate the webs of fate far more. Therefore the study of other lives is not separate from the rest of our craft, rather a deeply inherent part of it, for it gives us the chance to really witness the overview, the bigger spiritual picture, through our own experience. We can see the webs working in our lives and so can further appreciate the value of gaining an overview of the situation when we come to create spells and weave fate. Through our journeys into other lives we will see how it is easy to affect people we have never met by our actions, even by our thoughts. And we will understand the spirit within all things much more as we will have a far deeper knowledge of our own sacred soul spark.

Before we move onto the practical aspect of this section, let us consider this: wildwitches understand that we are all connected. Spirit to spirit we stand with the essence of mice, of grass, of mountains; we are all born of the same Source, fashioned from the same energy by the same Creator. The web links us, there are no exceptions. So how can we live our lives purely for our own soul's learning and growth? Surely we must affect other souls and their own need for experiential learning must affect our progress. Indeed, yes. We do not incarnate solely as an exercise to improve the self, rather we can opt for being involved in scenarios that engage us with the growth process of other spirits.

We can choose to incarnate to help a soul with whom we feel a kinship, aiding them in their process in as much as we aid our own by assisting them. We bounce and feed off one another, the purpose of life is not to be in isolation, rather to grow by interchange, by comparing energies and experiences, by deciding what we admire, what moves us, what makes us fearful. We are all teachers and all pupils in this respect. There is no hierarchy.

Saying this, there are those who have left, whether permanently or temporarily, the cycle of incarnation. They are of course our companion spirits. Their work has moved onto a different level, one that liberates them from having the "forgetting" of a physical shell and gives them a spiritual access to the webs of fate that link all creatures. However, their primary concern is for the manifest Earth level and they do not have a frame of reference that includes all cosmic existence. They can see more than we can in order that they may both guide and remind us of our connection to the source of ourselves.

Yet they are not ascended beings of supreme knowledge. They are spirits like us doing a valuable job for the good of us all. There may well be such superbeings in the universe but they are not close enough to our current level of being for us to be able to communicate with them or to relate to them in a trance journey, and I would be infinitely suspicious of those who claimed to be so superior if I met them on a journey.

Which truly enlightened being would claim to be more evolved than us or would suggest that they were a deity? True spirits of each cycle, realm of existence, or level of being know that everything has its own rightful place in the universe and just as we need not look down with condescension or disgust at a slug on our path, so they do not look at the beings currently on Earth in that fashion. Who can say which is the better expression of the Creator's energy, a slug or a human being, if both are successfully experiencing life from their own sacred point of view?

It would, with this in mind, be similarly outrageous and ludicrous to suggest that other beings like snails, fish, bears, or barn owls have no soul, or at least not one as we do. Our creature teachers are much more adept at remembering their true selves when incarnate than we are! They simply *be*, with no concern for pettiness or artifice. They live harmoniously as our fellow beings on Earth, not seeking to destroy their environs but to blend with them, and so who then may say our fellow Earth beings are soulless when it is we, the ensouled humans, who act as if our spirits have fled? Certainly a leaf may not have the same spirit as a woodpecker but it is an enspirited being nonetheless.

Each part of creation is animated, given energetic resonance, by the Source from which it was created. For a wildwitch it is unthinkable to suggest that our four-legged counterparts or feathered and finned kin do not reincarnate as we do. Why should they not if they so choose? A sentient being has a soul as we do and as part of the dance why should they not also return to Earthly experience?

It is probable that there are soul groupings that link the spirits of certain fish or birds together once they are discarnate. Similarly, there are affiliation groups to which we all belong as spirits. We can see these as classes that reconvene after a cluster of incarnations to discuss the team's efforts. We can also see them as reassuring collectives, our support network both on Earth and before and after Earthly incarnation. Those in our soul group may agree to help us grow by pushing our boundaries in a lifetime, giving us conflict to enable us to learn by trial and error. Or, they could agree to be a supportive lover or a close family member who helps us through such a soul test. Creation is all about connection and these soul connections link us at the most fundamental level. Our connections from these soul kin groupings spread out into the universe, linking us in with all energetic life to one degree or another.

Soul groups may be based on the same soul traits as we discussed previously in this book when analysing our own internal soul essence. We may belong to a primarily airy soul collective, or be linked by a watery creative energy. We can recognise our soul kin on Earth by soul vibration, almost always perceived in eye contact. It is from the windows of the eyes that the eternal spirit views the world and through the eyes we catch glimpses of this true essence. When our eyes meet with a soul kin we may not remember why we know them, or why we feel close to them, but we know that we do—regardless of the current body they wear. We may feel passion, longing, platonic love, or even jealousy and hatred but we will feel something strong that moves us on a level so deep and instinctive that we cannot analyse it.

When the emotions involved are destructive, is it always a soul kin connection? More likely when the emotions are profoundly negative we have met with a spirit who is elementally opposite to our own type. They can be the very ones who help us grow by sparking with us, repelling us but attracting us to work out why, and thus deal with pertinent soul issues. Our opposites can be very good for us, even if the connection is stormy and dynamic, for they enable us to regain balance within ourselves.

Sometimes soulmate scenarios with our close kin can be damaging and limiting, they can make us feel too complacent or can lock us into unhealthy codependant patterns. This is because the powerful pull of this link reminds us of the safety of our spiritual home beyond Earthly worry, it makes us want to give up all the fuss of being alive and just float in otherworldly bliss again. It would be possible to write a whole chapter on this alone. I can only refer any interested reader to my first four books, which cover the soulmate relationship in more depth.

As individual players in the symphony orchestra of existence, we have a responsibility both to our eternal sacred selves and the All to endeavour to reach our own most succinct expression of ourselves as balanced beings. There is no one universal perfection, only the most harmonious expression of our spirit. When we begin to look at our own lives we will see how we work at this process in our own way, time after time, time before time, in a cycle of beginnings and endings that segue seamlessly to provide us with the most appropriate scenarios to learn by.

Pathworking Into an Other Life

To begin to gain an overview of our own incarnate patterns we must have a starting point, an immediate focus. It is vital that we do not just go skipping blithely off into the cycles of existence held within the memories of our soul. We could get confused as we may simply step into another time when nothing of apparent import happened. Just as when we go on a trance journey, we need a purpose and focus when we walk into the spiral of our own existence so we do not become distracted by our own soul story or bludgeoned by something that would be too emotional for us to cope with on the first sitting. After all, this is our soul material, our own ongoing story, and will undoubtedly move us in the way a simple historical tale could never do.

So, we need to have a focus and begin with a lifetime that holds a key to how we experience life today, something we can work with, something that will give us a deeper understanding of our own process and the purpose of incarnation. This is not a daytrip into a more entertaining world rather it is a visit to ourselves and therefore it is only that self that we will harm if we are flippant or unfocussed.

To gain focus and ascertain the best place to begin this work, simply enter into a trance dialogue session (of automatic writing or channelled written guidance) with the companion spirits. It is courtesy to inform them of our intentions and to ask them something like:

> *Dear companion spirits,*
> *I wish to undergo a journey to another life,*
> *there to observe my self in another human guise.*
> *Where may I look to discover what I need to know*
> *about myself most at this time?*
> *Guide me to the place on my own wheel of being*
> *that will give me a focus.*
> *I ask this respectfully, with my heartfelt thanks, as ever.*

If we already have an idea of where we should look, such as a clue from a recurring dream, a current overwhelming fascination or phobia, or a memory from a spontaneous other-life recall, then we have our focus. Perhaps as wildwitches we will want to look at any life spent in the pursuit of natural magic in order for us to understand why we have been drawn to it today. If we already have a point to focus on then we can phrase our request differently:

Familiar spirits, loyal companions,
I ask that you accompany me on a journey
into my deep self to understand the source of (name the issue).
I believe that the issue is relevant to another life I have experienced.
Please guide me to the life in question
so that I may explore that which haunts me from it.
I ask this with love and commend myself to your care.
So may it be!

Of course, our companion guides already have a sense of what we have as intentions but they cannot act or advise unless we invite them to do so. They will not give unsolicited guidance nor will they control us by reading our minds. They will pick up an energetic feeling from us but will not approach us about it until we approach them. This is their role, not to actively intervene in our own Earthly processes, but to simply be there when we seek their words of wisdom and their guiding light. It must be quite a frustrating job for them!

When our companion spirits have allowed us to write down a dictation on the matter we should have a clearer idea of where to begin. What we need is a reference point. The companions may be very blunt:

- "You need to look at the root cause of your fear of fire as it is holding you back. Travel to the life in medieval France."

- "Focus on your life in Africa last century, it will help you understand your reluctance to marry."

- "Travel to the life you experienced in the wilderness of Canada and see how you may be in danger of repeating the pattern today."

- "Go to the birth of your son in the Scottish incarnation; this will help you work through a current worry."

- "There is a life as a warrior on the Russian steppes, it will shed some light on your relationship with your husband."

If we already had a focus the response may be more like:

- "Yes, your fascination for World War I is overwhelming; there is something you should remember from that time. Focus on the day you first left for the air base."

- "Your love of the wild craft comes from lifetimes of study. To understand the root then you will need to visit the lifetime in Neolithic Cornwall."

- "You have been dreaming of being chased as your last life ended in such a fashion. To cease running in this life you must re-experience what it was like to be pursued as a young Polish Jew."

If we feel confident enough in our ability to interpret more symbolic information or to remember chunks of conversation, then we can engage in a trance journey to meet the familiar guiding spirits and talk with them on the matter of our focus in our safe astral space. It will be important that we bring back accurate information; so we must make sure we can be relaxed enough to be receptive and alert enough to absorb all that is shown or told to us.

If we feel tense, as if this exercise is too personal and a little daunting, then we may well block any channelled information or even see nothing when we journey for clarity. This fear is natural if it is associated with finding out more about ourselves. What if we find out we were cruel or abused? How will we cope? It is also related to stepping into the unknown and engaging in something new, something that may well irrevocably alter our perception of ourselves and the world. Change like this can make us lose all sight of tl.e calm and balanced way we have approached our trancework with previously. If this is the case, then until we are familiar with the safe and effective method of visiting other lives, we can simply send up a prayer, something like:

Companions, beloved ones who guide with such loving clarity,
please cover me as I voyage into the heart of myself.
Lead me to the level of my existence that would be most beneficial for me to go to.
Draw my awareness to that which is pertinent to me today,

And let me walk into the life that reveals the most vital truth of me today.
Please help me banish my fear of the unknown, and of my deepest most hidden aspects,
so that I may be more fully present and aware of myself as a rounded being.
Bless me with your calm presence and infuse my sacred space with your peace.

I ask this with perfect trust in your kindness and constancy.
So may it be!

Next we may like to light a candle that represents our eternal spirit and dedicate it to the quest. Here is an example chant to infuse a candle with our intent:

Flame you dance as does my soul,
To know my soul is my truest goal,
I see your glow and I feel my own,
As I venture into my own unknown,

Oh spirit of all illumination,
Won't you show me my own part in creation?

When we feel happy that our pathworking will have a calm and genuine focus, be the intent known or as yet unknown, then we may prepare for a trance journey in our sacred circle. Now we have two choices here and the first option is the best, if you can manage it. We can either have a magical partner read us the journey's directions or we can tape them on to a cassette and play them back to ourselves. If we can get a friend or fellow magical practitioner to accompany us on at least this initial occasion then all the better. However the taped method will also work, though it does require us to change the approach slightly.

Here's the difference—and it is a very important one so please do adhere to what is suggested. In a journey with the friend reading out the directions we may experience the other-life memories in the first person directly, for they are indeed personal soul memories, belonging deep within us. We may even feel as if we are acting in our own film or have indeed gone directly back into that role, in that life. It is very immediate. In the solo taped version we will not be actively participating but watching a film of our life. So, we will not be directly there, but simply viewing our memories as we would at a cinema. It is too much to ask of ourselves to go alone into a life memory without suffering some sense of merging with the life situation of a character we once identified with totally. Therefore, when working alone, and for the sake of being able to come and go from the memory easily, we should be kept at arms length from the experience. If we do not, we may find it impossible to disentangle ourselves sufficiently in order to leave the memory and it may continue to haunt us, preventing us from living in the sacred now, for some time afterward.

When we are guided by a partner it is safe to become more enmeshed in the thoughts and feelings we once had in a different body, as our friend can ensure that we follow their voice and never lose track of where we really are, physically speaking. Also, we can feel comfortable that we are being watched over and guided at all times by a caring figure. A voice taped on to a cassette is not able to maintain this link. Our partner can lead us through a particularly affecting scene in our life play, responding to the situation as it happens. And who knows what we may see in such scenes? We should be prepared in case the life issue we have asked to resolve may not have originated in a mundane scenario—it has had lasting significance to us, after all, and so it could be eventful and maybe disturbing. We need not be physically afraid as we are experiencing it spiritually, not bodily, yet we will probably be emotionally moved.

In order to make ourselves as relaxed as possible we will need to have a pillow and a blanket within the space of our sacred circle as we are going to lie down on this occasion. Our grounding can take place in the usual seated upright position and we can lie down under the blanket once we have followed the regular trance journey procedures (refer to chapter 3).

When we are warm and at ease, either our partner or the taped instructions can begin to lead us into a deep relaxation. Again this is not hypnosis, we will not lose control, but we will benefit from being in a deep trance state. If we experience any uncomfortable sensations, we can leave the experience at any time. This is our life replay, we can shout "Cut!" and have the film halted whenever we wish. Or we can tell our partner that we feel unhappy and want to turn back. Any partner who is guiding the journey should be entirely focused on us as we proceed through the memory. They can lead us back to the present reality at any time they sense the memory is overwhelming us or distressing us too greatly. We are in control, these are our memories. Our partner should respect why we are undertaking the venture and see that we are able to do so safely and with ease. If not, then the proceedings should be brought to a close and a good deal of time spent grounding, and reconnecting with the current physical self afterward. We can then discuss the events with our companion spirits to find out what may have gone wrong and decide what we can do next.

If a partner is reading the following piece, then substitute each "I am" for "you are." If the partner is guiding us he or she will lead us straight into our memory for a first-hand experience (or re-experience). If we are recording the journey for ourselves, then we should follow the instructions below as they are printed, which lead us into a cinematic scenario and enable us to watch the experience.

Trance Journey: Travelling to a Past Life

I am standing barefoot on a lush green bank beside a river, which moves swiftly. The springy grass feels pleasantly damp with dew beneath my feet and the air on my face is fresh but not cold. I take three deep breaths, enjoying the brisk spring day. There is a small wooden boat in the water; it bobs with the current, urging me to make a journey in it. I release it from its mooring and quickly step down into it as it moves away, down stream. I pick up the single oar but there is no need to paddle, I am being carried to my destination willingly by the jaunty little craft. I notice the peeling blue paint around its gunnel and my free hand caresses the wood's grain.

I reach my hand over the side and feel the water as it rushes by, its cold caress washing over me. I raise the cupped hand to my lips and drink of the river's blessing, tasting the crystal clear liquid. Then I sit back and enjoy the journey as I move swiftly on through open country, watching the spring lambs frisk in distant fields, seeing the low hedges bursting into gleaming green, spying the pale suns of flowering coltsfoot in the grass. I am relaxed and happy, all is well.

The boat travels on and I see a copse ahead, on a raised mound. As it grows closer I hear the starlings chattering and the rooks cackling in the trees. A rabbit hops away from the bank as the boat draws alongside the copse, skittering sideways in its hurry to be away. I know that this is the place and to emphasise the point my little craft bumps the bank and stops. I notice a second wooden stake ready for me to tether the boat to and so, replacing the oar in the bottom of the hull, I stand and leave the vessel, with a word of thanks for its carrying me to this place.

Once on the bank I turn and face the copse. There are more trees than I first thought because they are densely clustered around a central point. It is that hidden point I am aiming to reach so I begin to walk up the slope that will lead me to the house I seek. I relish the feeling of my feet in the moist grass but keep my eyes on the trees, some mature with impressive roots showing through the shallower soil on the copse's edge, others young and willowy, but all in the lustrous green mantle of spring. I approach the edge, noticing wild daffodils nodding their welcome to me.

There are many aspen trees here and their new leaves tremble in the spring breeze, making them whisper conspiratorially at my approach. The air is resin scented and shimmering with expectation. A shiver runs through me as I step into the circle of the tree's tender embrace, asking:

I have come seeking what is mine,
To know myself as I step through time,
I have come to wear a guiser's face,
And find myself in another place,

Wind-catchers, watchers, will you direct me?
By the leaf's fine blade I ask, protect me!

The trees take each other's council, murmuring and hissing, and the sun dips suddenly behind a large cloud overhead and I am pushed from behind by an unexpectedly brisk rush of wind. I put my hands up as I stumble, wanting to break my fall, but instead keep my balance and find that I am walking through the inner sanctum of this coolly verdant grove. I pick my way between the shining celandines, weaving between trunks both ghostly grey and rusty brown and dancing with the dapples that flit across the green ground as the sun re-emerges once more, brighter than before. I keep walking with my head down as the trees thin. I only look up when I sense that the house is before me.

The house is large. It looks far too large to be contained, and indeed hidden, by this stand of trees. It is a silent sentinel, its curtainless windows reflecting scudding clouds or flourishing foliage. It could have been built in any age for it has a timeless quality, it is classic in its elegant simplicity. A graceful house but not a home. No one dwells here, only memory is its resident. Past and future coexist within its walls. It is the house of all-knowing and so I know it, it feels as if I have stood in front of it many many times before and yet this is my first journey. I approach and see that the heavy, wood-panelled door has been left ajar for me, it hardly moves in the considerable breeze.

I touch the walls on either side of the door, feeling their weathered stone, and then lay both hands on the door to push it wide open. I pause on the threshold and invoke:

Spirits who come for my highest good,
And those who guard this place,
Be with me as I venture in
To seek my own lost face.

Stepping inside I am struck by the change in atmosphere. There is a deep stillness in the hallway, a peace that is almost palpable. There is a large grandfather clock whose slow, steady tick is the only sound. The door sweeps closed behind me and I am aware how dusky dim the house is, a twilight place. I cannot make out the faces in the portraits that line the walls and the only brightness comes from the white floor tiles that alternate with black ones, like a chess board. The tiles are chilly under my bare feet and my toes curl a little in response. I stand and take in all the doorways and stairwells that seem to branch off this one place. I know that there is only one way for me to go today, however, and that is down. I must descend the stairwell and go to the lowest floor.

I reach the top of the stairs and grasp the gilt-painted handrail. The stairs are carpeted in a red pile that has been worn thin in the centre by many such visitors as myself, each seeking their own lost face. I find this comforting and begin to descend, one step at a time, a measured pace. I count myself down:

Ten, deeper and deeper,
Nine, deeper and deeper,
Eight, deeper and deeper . . .
I keep going, building up a rhythm;
Seven, deeper and deeper,
Six, deeper and deeper,
Five, deeper and deeper . . .
I continue, breathing steadily;
Four, deeper and deeper,
Three, deeper and deeper,
Two, deeper and deeper . . .
The last stair:
One, deeper and deepest.

I am in a corridor, it is dim but I can see that there are low-burning lights running the length of the wall. The corridor seems inordinately long, even for such a large house, and I ponder the many doors that are set into its length. Which one should I go to? Without thinking too hard I instinctively turn and go toward the direction that draws me. As I walk I breathe, keeping that steady pace:

Breathe, deeper and deeper,
Breathe, deeper and deeper.

I reach the door that I need to open. It calls to me even though it looks just like all the others, a plain brown door with a brass handle. When I open it and step through it I will be where I am meant to be, seeing another face of myself, witnessing another life.

Here I must state my aim once more, asking that the life I have chosen to focus on (I name the life and, if possible, the relevant incident) be revealed to me as I open the door.

Note: If we are being guided by a partner the door will open and we will step directly into that life. However, if we are working solo with the tape recorder we will open the door and step into a cinema. The screen will be showing a film clip of the life we seek. We can watch it with detachment. We are free to leave at any time or can watch the whole film if we wish.

If we are working with a partner then they will wait until we have stepped through the door before asking us several leading questions to help ease us into the other-life experience. They will ask us to look down and focus on our feet. What are we wearing on our feet, if anything? Are they male or female? Is the skin dark or light? Similarly, they will ask questions about our hands. What else are we wearing? How do we feel about ourselves? Are we in pain, sad, joyful, confused? Do we have a name? Where are we? What can we see in front of us? Is anyone talking to us? We should let the guiding voice of our partner bring us fully into the experience and keep listening to their voice and their instructions. They will keep in touch with us as we experience the other life by getting us to refer back to them, constantly questioning us: "Where are you now? What is happening now?" We should endeavour to talk them though what we see. Try to note as many clues as we can about costume, housing, and so on, but focus mainly on how it feels.

When our partner thinks that we have seen enough of this life, enough to give us some answers or insights, then they will gently ask us to see the brown door again and then ask us to open it. The door may appear to us wherever we are and during whatever we are doing. It could be incongruously placed, say in a battlefield, yet it will be there for us to go back though. If we wish to depart from the experience sooner, we can ask to see the door.

When the experience is over, or if we wish to terminate it, then open the door and step back through, to the corridor. Once we are there, then we can look down at our feet and hands and see that they are back to normal, that we are wearing our usual otherworldly guise and not the guise of the other manifest self in the recent vision).

I stand back in the corridor and know that I must go back up the stairs. As I climb them I count upward:

One, higher and higher,
Two, higher and higher,
Three, higher and higher . . .
I keep going, building up a rhythm;
Four, higher and higher,

Five, higher and higher,
Six, higher and higher . . .
I continue, breathing steadily;
Seven, higher and higher,
Eight, higher and higher,
Nine, higher and higher . . .
The top stair:
Ten, higher and highest.

I stand back in the hallway with the black-and-white tiled floor, hearing the reassuring tick of the old clock in the corner. As I walk toward the front door it swings open
slightly, silently, a bright shard of sunlight entering the cool gloom of the building. I
stand on the threshold again, this time looking out toward the trees. The rooks are
circling, making a racket. A rabbit, startled from its washing by my unexpected presence, lopes off at an angle across the grass, white tail shining in the spring light. I say:

> *Time has passed but I am here,*
> *My self is centred, strong and clear,*
> *And who I was I'll leave behind,*
> *And take only peace of mind.*

With that I walk free of the building. I give a bow, in the old way, one arm sweeping
back, to show my gratitude. Then I am walking into the green of this day, into the
sweeping arc of the aspens, flanked by the poplars and the hazels. I have a bounce in
my stride and cover the ground quickly, moving through the trees with ease, as if I
know every curve and every root that starts from the ground, every dip in the earth
and every unexpected thrust of a low branch. I hum a song of gratitude for the trees
that allowed me to pass through. I offer a prayer that they will let me pass this way
again if I so choose. I ask for their continued health and bid the trees a good day.
Then I am out of the trees and onto the slope that overlooks the river, standing in
long grass with the blue eyes of speedwells winking at me. I run down the bank
toward the spot where my boat is moored up for my return journey.

I feel incredibly free with the freedom that comes from knowledge. New energy has
been released in me through my personal discovery. My understanding has revitalised
me, I am like the spring day, full of bright hope, and as buoyant as my little boat.

I untie my boat and get in. Magically, the current has changed direction, it will
now carry me gently back to the place where I belong. I place my hands on the sun-
warmed wood and take in the fresh air. It is a good day to be alive, in this body, in
this time. And so I return.

When we return from this journey it is even more important to make notes and ground ourselves fully as we have been further, or deeper, than ever before. When we write up our journal on this experience we could focus on answering the following questions (if the cinema method is used change the questions accordingly):

1. Was there a sense of surprise to be in another body or did it feel familiar and comfortable immediately?

2. Was it a natural experience or did it feel forced or false in some way?

3. Did the level of emotion in the experience surprise me?

4. Did I feel as if I were "home" on some level?

5. Did the experience clarify the initial question I asked or did it leave me more mystified or confused? Will I need a second visit to that life? If so, why?

It helps to clarify how we feel initially and it is essential to write it all down straight away while the sensations remain fresh. Obviously we can discuss all of these points with our companion spirits afterward as well.

And what if nothing happened on our journey, did we fail? By no means, as this is a difficult exercise and if we don't get anywhere much on the first few attempts, it is quite usual. In fact, if we do succeed totally the first time we try this journey then we are doing very well indeed. Perhaps we get stuck when we open the door and cannot see things properly? Maybe the pressure to see something interesting is too great and instead we see blankness or blackness? There may seem to be an unusual amount of pressure on us to have a truly wonderful insight into our other lives and because of this pressure we may not be able to see anything with the clarity of our usual relaxed trance vision. If this is the case, we can simply have another go on another day. It does take a lot of energy to make this journey so if we are at all fatigued then it can tell on us. We can make several attempts when we feel more fresh or at ease with the process. Indeed, it may take us several goes before we feel fluent enough with it to actually make it work for us. Do bear with it over a period of time, it is certainly worth the effort as are all the things we seek in our wild craft.

On future journeys we are quite at liberty to visit at the same time and the same place and change the memory or vision if we feel it would be helpful. As a personal example, during a trance journey I had a very vivid other-life recall of being burned at the stake in Avignon, France, in the early fourteenth century. On a follow-up journey I went back to the same life and took a more active part whilst remaining in the same character as I had been in that life. I dismantled the stake, yelled at the priest and soldiers, and generally broke down the whole "victim" scenario. This is soul play as well as role play and it was extremely liberating; it is a way of healing our eternal self by saying: "I could do something." This is opposed to saying: "I can't do anything about it now."

It was not retribution that I sought when I returned to that life but more of a re-addressing of the balance. On some level, in some reality, my stake-smashing spree was the actual outcome. With our cyclical, nonlinear notions of time and space we can effect change. In this vein, if we are acting in our own film we can change the script. If we are watching it we can redirect it too.

When we get the hang of making these journeys we can seek answers to more advanced soul questions pertinent to our own wild path: "Have I ever had a Fey connection? Has my spirit any Faery link? Have I ever had a nonhuman incarnation?" We can then look at the intrinsic patterns in our lives, the patterns that reveal our soul's purpose, and see the core issues we are repeating on our current Earthwalk experience. With this overview of our selves we can see our soul habits, both positive and negative. Our wild craft will continue to benefit from this honest form of soul-searching, which enables us to feel empowered as eternal beings and therefore more confident in our current life choices. And as we see more of the other guises we have worn, we will surely feel more care and concern for those who wear similar guises in this current incarnation.

But what if, at the end of the day, our having other lives is a load of daydream drivel, a fantasy, something our subconscious has cooked up out of films we may have seen or books we may have read? What if there is only one life and then we die and no such thing as reincarnation? What if, indeed, there is no spirit and we are all just ruled by the body and brain after all?

We should, as wildwitches, be good at asking "What if?" by now! As questing souls we are open enough to consider this suggestion. And the answer to this may be "So what!" or even "It doesn't matter!" Whatever comes up for us as a result of our inner work means something to us on a deep personal level in the here and now. Whatever we experience on our journeys, be it pure fiction or spiritual truth, needs to find a meaning and expression in our lives today. So whatever comes up for us in this path-working or on a trance journey is relevant to the now, if nothing else. It reveals in symbolic terms what we hold dear or find repellent, what we need to work on in terms of tolerance or embrace in ourselves as great strengths. Whatever comes up for us has a message to our mundane self.

It may seem a little odd to end a section about other lives on this note but there is a reason for it. If wild witchery isn't about thinking, challenging, and understanding our own sacred points of view, and those of others, then it is not a living, growing way, it is not wild but as tame and boxed up as any other religion. We are bound to be challenged like this at least once in our magical lives and this may be a good occasion to test ourselves out in this way, to ensure that everything we have invested into our belief is still working for us.

And if it works for us we don't need to explain it away to the letter, qualifying every little thing we choose to do to a minute degree. We can feel its rightness in our blood and bones, and beyond that in our spirit, and can therefore feel it when something we do no longer sits well with us. At this point we need to quest for a new way.

Section Two: Moving Without

This section is about the aspects of our craft that are practised in a very external sense, working with manifest tools as well as our own intuition and spirit-filled focus. It is the more physical side of an equation that always blends the corporeal with the ethereal.

Firstly, we will begin to understand how we may work with the indigenous green people of the land we live in for the purpose of bringing magical change. This is not a potted guide to becoming a medical herbalist, rather it shares the essential wisdoms about wild plants and herbs passed on by professionals, wisdoms that anyone can use safely in their daily lives. The difference is, for us as wildwitches, that we cannot only accept these wisdoms and work appropriately with these wild-spirited plant helpers but we can also work our charms on them, adding in our starlight vision to bring about an enchanted blend. By this an herbal concoction for a cold can be infused with a bright envisioning of health, blessed by the spirits, and chanted into full vibrant life. It can be enhanced by the light of a full moon or enlivened by the midsummer sun. Our remedies fuse the natural attributes of the herbal helpers with our own will and wish. By the tides of life we bring that magical collaboration to fruition.

Before we enter into suggestions for herbal brews we need to be able to communicate with the essence of the herb or plant so that we feel confident that we can ascertain the information intuitively as well as by referencing it from books. That personal relationship with our helpers is essential to ensure that the pulse of our craft is felt strongly, our own interactions and intimate understandings will enable our magic to be truly alive.

Speaking with a Plant Person

To get ourselves aquainted with the energetic life of our fellow green beings, the people of root, shoot, and stem, we can attune ourselves to their mood on a daily basis. Their language is subtle but we can learn to hear what they tell us if we spend regular time with them, acknowledging the fact that they are communicating with us as well as with each other. We can practically initiate a relationship that will tell us as much about green beings and their friendship as fellow humans potentially could. This can be fulfilling, but like developing any relationship worth having, it can cost us effort. With this in mind we may think it would be easier to just ask our companion spirits to be intermediaries, allowing them to translate the plant ways to us. Indeed we can take the image of a plant with us in trance journey to our sacred astral place and ask questions of our companion spirits but what we are aiming for here is an immediate, rounded one-on-one connection.

Our houseplants, including herbs or flowers we grown in pots, are an excellent starting place to establish this link as we already have a shared history. We are joined by the familiarity of our environment, and, presumably, by the fact that we have them in our lives because we enjoy their presence. Their resonance must have called to us at some point for us to want to take them home with us. Any plant person who chose not to reciprocate and who found us, or our home, disharmonious would have long ago wilted away. So we can assume that there is already an energetic bond there.

Although the energies of the green ones are gentle it does not mean that they are not strong and clear. To start connecting with them we can get used to seeing their energetic bodies, their etheric aura, so that we can establish this fact for ourselves. To see the energetic imprint around any living being we do not need a Kirlian camera. We can see the auric field around our own hands if we hold them up against a plain darkish background. If we do not stare at them directly in a physical sense, but rather stare through them in a more unfocussed but unblinking way (much as we used to view the "magic eye" pictures so popular in the late twentieth century), we can begin to discern fleeting impressions of a fuzzy glow around our fingers. With repeated practice and a relaxed approach the glow becomes more distinguishable. The more playful we can be the better the results, the more serious or desperate we become the less likely it is that we will be able to attune to the subtlety of what we seek. We may perceive it as a luminous flame ringed closely around all lifeforms—a glowing life-force field.

We can also practice this by looking at the head of a friend against a plain wall. In fact, we may find this easier than looking at our own body. A luminous whitish yellow (or pale gold) effect, like a halo, will become apparent around the head and shoulders. Once we have seen such an energy, or tuned in to its existence, we will find that we see it at various times quite spontaneously. This is not the brightly coloured aura that is reportedly seen by psychics and mystics, rather the close etheric body that a healer can work with and see. It surrounds every living being without exception. We can continue to become aquainted with it in a personal human sense before approaching the plant people in the same way.

When we stare at the bright energy around an organism we can often see it flare or recede. It can be seen as a broad dense band or a flatter line following the physical shape. It is not to be confused with the "opposite colours" effect that we can get when staring at one image for a period of time. For example, if we stare at a wall painted turquoise for a few minutes solidly and then close our eyes we will see an image of the opposite colour of orange. If we look at a green piece of paper and then a blank page immediately afterward we will see the image as red. With blue we will later see yellow, and so on. This etheric energetic glow is not based on an optical effect, rather it is an actual energy that is omnipresent and not dependent on our surroundings. The plain background we seek initially helps us to isolate what we are looking for from the chaos of life, we do not really need it in order to see the life force.

Once we have become aquainted with the etheric imprint of a plant then we may be able to tune into that in order to discern the plant's current mood or state of health. With repeated study we can see when the energy flares and when it is low. We may also begin to intuit other hues around the plant leaves and stem, which could suggest to us vitality or poor health. Dull or dirty shades or bruiselike clumps of colour suggest the latter while clear and vibrant flashes or ripples of colour suggest the plant feels comfortable and well. From the point in which we are in tune with these emotional signals, receiving the plants energetic communication, it is only a small step to actually opening a dialogue and seeing an energetic response. Simple "mind questions," directed with love and respect to the plant, can be along the lines of: "I see that you are feeling a little down today. If I moved you closer to the window would it help?" Also try: "I see you enjoyed the food I gave you. Do you need any more?"

These sort of questions can be answered in a simple yes/no sort of way using flashes for a positive response. From this our green allies get much more of a sense that we will listen to them and support their own feelings and so it becomes much more worthwhile for them to talk to us. By this they may begin to send us "mind pictures," symbols, and words as we tune into their energy. We may start to hear their particular frequency, the sound that their own personal vibration makes. When we hear a plant's usual vibration we can then begin to tell if it is sick or if it is particularly happy by the manner in which we hear it "sing." For the way plants express their spiritual frequency may well be a melody and not just a pitch or tone. All such means of combination will assist our relationship with plants and help us to broaden our range of communication, enabling us to speak with plants from outside of our own home and garden. We will now look at a short example of wildflowers and hedgerow herbs as well as shrubs and trees.

Our awareness of the spirit of the plant beings can be expanded by our greeting a few local plant people that we pass every day as we follow our familiar routes. We can actually send out a mental greeting whilst observing their condition in the same way we may look at colleagues or companions throughout our day. Thus we can attune to their mood and their particular season or growth or dying back. Do they look in good health? What is their attitude, are they busily pushing up through a pavement crack full of determination or are they lazily lounging against a sunny wall? Are they in full bloom or showing no shoots? Are there any brown patches or lesions? Do they prefer a collective position or do they shun groups and grow in isolation? Do they like shade or strive to reach the sunniest vantage point?

Such attributes can be picked up and worked with in our magical chants. For instance, if we see a glossy ivy plant, which has managed to completely cover a low wall, we could add it into a chant about our own tenacity. If we see a delicate daisy standing alone in the middle of a manicured lawn we could liken its own wild face seeking the sun to our own at summer solstice. If we observe a hoary old nettle with its roughly spiked leaves blocking a path we could align ourselves with its stubborn need for self-protection. Or we can liken ourselves to the wilted flower or trapped plant through song, invoking for both the green being and ourselves to be uplifted or released from anything that confines us.

When we have aquainted ourselves with the plant people we encounter along our way, observing generalities about their mode, we can then get closer by observing the tiny hairs on their stems, the way the veins branch within a leaf, or the particular shade of green that it favours. Which insects dwell on or near it? Does it have a scent and, if so, what does that scent evoke in us? Finally, we can begin to observe its energetic glow and pick up its general ambience, how it feels, and how it in turn affects us. We may never actually work with it magically but we are getting used to seeing our green helpers with more clarity and acknowledging their individuality and their profound resonance on our own well-being or mood.

We are also getting used to seeing the world as being alive, breaking out of that crippling human condition of seeing our environs as a backdrop for our very human activities. As we observe the living plant beings who share our route home we begin to break down the walls of separation that stop us from living a fully integrated magical life.

When we grow our own organic herbs we have a chance to establish this bond and strengthen our communicative link from the very early seedling stages. Then when we need an herb for our healing or for a particular brew to celebrate a season, we can ask the plant if its suitable to work directly with us. We should then be able to understand what the plant says to us in response. We will truly appreciate that theirs is a language like any other. In fact, we will understand their own resonance, mood, and general outlook so well that we will have a much better idea of whether or not to approach it for help.

When we do need to cut a leaf or trim back a whole section of an herb for drying, we must first ask the plant person. We can allow them to respond to our request rather than letting them react to us inflicting our will on them. By doing this we give them time to assent or decline, which we must accept. If they do communicate assent to us then they will simply withdraw their awareness from that particular part of themselves that we wish to cut so that we can snip the desired section without causing them trauma. It is our lack of respect and sudden movements or interventions that cause plant beings disturbance and pain. They are more than capable of moving their living energy back for whichever part of them we seek if we only give them the opportunity to do so. If they know that this cutting would be against their own well-being at that particular time they will deny us the opportunity on that occasion but perhaps alert us to another part of them that could be considered.

Trance Journey: Speaking with Herb Spirits

If we wish to get to know one particular type of plant more intimately for the course of a magical working, or indeed a lifetime, then we can trance journey to meet its essence. We are going to attune to the overall essence, or collective spirit, of a herb in the same way that we contact the spirit of wolf or salmon. We are not speaking of an individual plant we may grow at home (we can talk to them directly after all) but the connecting spirit behind all herbs of that kind, the "oversoul," which is common as an energetic quality to all of its kind.

So, here is a short sample journey for meeting the spirit of sage, which perhaps could be done in its presence or at least outdoors, near to an area where the herb grows. Beforehand we could drink some tea made of responsibly picked sage or burn some sage on a charcoal block; to be near some of the living being would be most conducive, to smell its actual scent as it grows is very evocative. As always, all usual trance journey procedures must be completed before we travel (refer to chapter 3). When we have asked our companion spirits to be present we can state our purpose in a chant, something like:

> *By fuzzy leaf and pungent scent,*
> *By healing and by growing,*
> *By softest green and bitter taste,*
> *I now seek sage's knowing.*

I am walking down a country lane at first light, with hedgerows waking to full bloom to my left and right. As I walk with a spring in my step I am uplifted by the song of a female blackbird, whose trills and warbles speak of the resurgence of energy at the start of a new day. I see her bobbing on an elder branch and then she takes flight, I watch her rise and find that my own spirit is soaring along with her. I walk on with the whole world thrilling to the rising of the sap, glowing with newness, dew-kissed and sparkling as the pale rays bring illumination to the land. I then see a gap in the hedgerows on my left, revealing an old, metal five-bar gate, tied with twine to a wooden post. I approach and lean on it. Shall I climb over or undo the twine? I decide to climb over, relishing the strength in my own limbs as I swing my leg across the top rung.

I am now in a field in which two horses graze. One is sturdy and dappled grey, seemingly oblivious to my arrival as he keeps cropping the lush grass. His companion, a sleeker brown beast, eyes me with bright curiosity but he too keeps on eating. The field is full of waving fronds, meadow buttercups opening next to ragged robin and saxifrage; the temptation is to skip through it and let the long stalks and shining green blades tickle and tease my knees. The bees are out and the swallows are catching flies on the wing above me; all is activity, although, back in the direction I have travelled, from the town, the majority of people will still be asleep. I am glad to be seeing the start of a day, experiencing the joyful bustle of my natural kin in the fields. It is then that a voice greets me: "Mornin' m' dear, care for a brew? There's still a nip in the air and what I've got in this 'ere pot'll chase the remainin' chills from yer bones!"

I spin round and see, half hidden in the overgrown hedge, a wagon. A Romani-style caravan, its blue and gold paint peeling and chipped in places but still a cheerful sight. On the steps sits a man in a flat yellow cap with a red and white spotted kerchief at his throat. A single small hooped earring catches the sunlight and winks at me. He wears a big black overcoat and has grey fingerless mittens on his hands, hands that stir the contents of his black kettle over a small fire. A cat, ginger and white, weaves around his feet, which rest in their big boots on either side of the makeshift hearth. I approach with caution and point my fingers to reach them. A circle of cold, blue-gold fire surrounds both man and cat. I say: "Show yourself truly, spirits!"

For a moment nothing happens. Then this stranger and his cat glow eerily bright, almost as brightly as the flames in which they are placed. Then the image returns as normal. The man sits smiling expectantly at me. He is genuine. The cat miaows impatiently.

I walk closer and he stands, offering me his hand to shake. His grip is firm and surprisingly warm. I look into his face and see that under his cap he is not such an old man, yet his face is covered with tiny lines, intricately woven like the roots or branches on an ancient sprawling tree. The lines are deeply etched, like a birthmark or some arcane tattoo. I imagine green leaves sprouting on these twined boughs and his dark eyes crinkle as he smiles broadly. He is obviously used to being stared at.

"Welcome, stranger, welcome from Treeface himself! Aye, that's me! Won't you be seated?"

He makes room for me on the red painted steps of his wagon and I step up. His cat sniffs at me and rubs itself against my leg in greeting.

"I hear you've come to meet the spirit of the green one known as Sage?"

I nod my assent. He stirs vigorously his simmering kettle pot, which steams and hisses merrily over the flames. A familiar aromatic scent wafts up; it is a sage tea he is brewing for me. With one hand he reaches inside his coat and plucks out a handful of long oval leaves, downy and a pale shade of greyish green, and throws them deftly into the fire. Immediately a cloud of smoke, almost acrid but with that essentially savoury scent, wafts up. We are bathing in the essence of sage, surrounded in its green, peppery smoke.

When the cloud clears I see that Treeface is offering me a chipped, white enamel mug, half full of a verdant liquid. My first response is to check out that which he offers me and so I point at it, with my finger emitting a beam of blue-gold flame, asking that it may reveal itself to me truly. The mug shines with its own special light and I know that the liquid within is safe; it is what it is. I accept the mug and blow on it to cool the brew. The day around us is turning warmer and clearer, I notice a kestrel hovering some distance away, searching for its first meal of the day. The funny little man is sitting comfortably close to me on the steps of his jaunty wagon: "Close your eyes, drink the brew, and enter the realm!"

I breathe the scented steam and sip, wanting to know the herb that has given this woodily fragrant drink its qualities, wanting to experience the spirit of sage. I sip and breathe deeply, sip and breathe deeply. I ask for the essence of sage to be known to me.

When I open my eyes I am not sitting on the wagon steps but rather with Treeface before a wild tangled hedge, through which an archway has been cut. Gleaming leaves crowd in from each side, making the passage in the centre quite small. He smiles and nods at me and we both duck through this archway. I am aware of the leafy presence all around me, the pulse of life strong beneath our feet, and the corn-flower-blue sky spinning overhead. Before I know it, we are standing in a garden, a walled herb garden with a scent that overwhelms me—it's like the most beautiful balm, both sonorous and stimulating. The place is a feast for the eyes as well as for the nose, a riot of tiny flowers, white and pink and blue, and all the hues of green that there could ever be. I smile and sigh. Treeface leads me though the beds and I see that I have not had any experience with these sorts of herbs. They are as tall as we are and they are tended by ethereal beings who fly and flit, waft and weave. The deeper we walk into the maze of plants the larger the herbs become, some towering over us.

We stop and I find that we are standing before a huge sage being, its leaves bigger than my hands, each soft hair on them clearly delineated. The stem of the plant is as thick as a thigh. A delicious savoury scent fills the air around it. And then a willowy person appears from its midst, shining pale green eyes fixed on mine.

"You seek, now you find. Sage I am, asking-person you are. Here to tell you, so be asking."

Treeface takes a step back, leaving me and the sage spirit to talk. I am allowed to ask three questions of this wonderful essence. My time with it is wisely spent as, of course, I have thought of these questions before I travelled here.

When the last question is answered the being melts back into the silvered foliage. I wonder what I can offer as a thank-you and realise I am still holding my mug. I let the remnants of my brew tip out and filter down onto the soil around the plant. As I do so I give my sincere thanks and a blessing for the continued good health of the plant.

Treeface nods to the direction we should be travelling to go back and I follow him as he walks briskly though the many green beings who grow in this herb garden. As we walk the herbs become more reasonably sized again, shrinking back until they are knee high. With one quick economical movement Treeface is back though the arch and I follow, trying not to snag myself on the many limbs of the brambly hedge.

Back in the field once more I see the two grazing horses. They both look up and whinny a greeting to Treeface who lifts his hand in a greeting to his friends. The marmalade cat is stalking somewhere in the grasses. I know that I should leave this kind man to his own business and I bid my leave to him, with my gratitude for his help. Looking into his face I see wisdom beyond his years for he is not an old man at all, simply a young travelling soul with a green spirit, a spirit so green in fact that its mark has imprinted itself on his lean, sun-browned face. He is a green man indeed! He cracks into another beaming smile and raises his floppy flat hat to me. A spill of nut-brown hair falls loose, giving him a roguish look as it covers one eye. I know that I will return to this happy gypsy, if he allows me to.

I turn and make my way back across the meadow pasture and back over the gate to the lane. It is time for me to return to the world of people, a world just waking from its slumber, to write down all I have learned of sage this day.

We can meet and work with the green-spirited guide, Treeface, in this way again if we wish, visiting his wagon and allowing him to show us his herb garden, in any future journey of this kind. Or, of course, we can devise our own journey along these lines.

Simples and Samples

Rather than giving a list of herbs and their medicinal or healing associations here are a few suggestions for holistic spells involving herbs, all of which work with the energies involved and work a symbolic sympathetic magic. It is basic herbal wisdom for the wise wild one. Any other information on the attributes of our herbal helpers we can obtain from specialist books or study courses.

All the actual information about herbs that follows came from teachings given by a respected local medical herbalist. One of her primary pieces of advice was for us to know how each herb makes us feel while also looking at its own essential nature. Is it a warming herb? Has it got a drying quality to it? This should be done whilst considering the seasonal tides (is an herb in bloom or dying back at the time we chose to work with it?). Therefore her equation for successful work with helpful herb beings is:

Intuition + Essential Energies + Tides = Herbal Healing.

When we engage in this or in any other wild kitchen magic in the midst of life, we must remember to protect ourselves, for we are opening up to external energies. We should also invoke for the companion guides and a Fey helper, especially if we currently are working closely with one.

Note: Any spell that denotes "I" or "my" can be changed to suit our specific needs, for example, if the spell is for another person we may want to use "she," "he," or "their." These are only suggestions, included for inspirational purposes.

Hot Spell for a Cold

Make at or before noon with the waxing power of the day and then serve three times as the day wanes. Choose any of the following hot combinations, herbs, fruits, and spices. All have the fresh fire we require. Recipe options:

Garlic, honey, lemon juice, ginger

Echinacea, elderflower, horseradish root

Thyme, cayenne, honey, lemon juice

Apple juice, cinnamon, a small amount of cloves and nutmeg

Horseradish, black pepper, cardamom

Ginger, cinnamon, coriander, lemon juice

Peppermint, elderflower, yarrow

Ask for the sun's blessings upon the chosen ingredients:

Oh revered keeper of the flame,
Oh mighty sun of warmth untamed,
As you helped these grow, now help them be
Part of a vibrant remedy!

On the stove, heat enough water to make three cups of tea, allowing for evaporation. If using juice then allow one cup of juice to replace the water. Add a pinch, clove, or table-spoon of each herb to the water, using discretion to taste as these are strong herbs! My own tastes run to the strong so do feel free to use less. Perhaps start with a small pinch; at least more can be added at a later stage. Stir clockwise whilst focusing on the swirling liquid. Envision the sun in the centre of the swirl, infusing its nurturing warmth, its healing vibration into the brew. Continue doing this until the rhythm of the stirring combines with personal visioning to reveal the pan being full of strong clear sunlight. It is almost too bright to bear! Continue stirring and chant three times, with verve:

Roots and leaves and seeds go round,
As the sun in all its power,
The power to burn away all germs,
By seed and shoot and flower.
By flowering magic, hot and bright,
Burn the cold away this night!

And with that put the lid on the saucepan and let its contents gently simmer for ten minutes. Then strain and decant herbal water into a flask for storage, while chanting:

Liquid sunshine I am pouring,
By this my healing power I'm storing!

Drink one cup at a time, to total three cups a day; drink the first cup in the afternoon and save the last cup for the evening. Store the remainder. Every time this tea is used envision that it is a flowing liquid of fiery intensity and chant:

By grace of all within that grew,
I drink the fire of this healing brew!

If this tea is for someone else to drink, they can imagine this fiery intensity and recite the accompanying chant themselves, if they would like.

Soothing Spell to Aid Sleep

This brew and its accompanying slumber pouch should be made at twilight, invoking all the Fey spirits of the dreaming time. Call on them to bless the ingredients chosen by singing something like:

> *Oh wanderers in the melting mists,*
> *You Fey-souled sweet somnambulists,*
> *Oh gentlest of lyricists,*
> *You drifters in our very midst . . .*
> *Bless these green gifts with your kiss,*
> *Bestow on them a drowsy bliss.*

Choose a generous pinch or small handful each of any of the following combinations to make a mild and mellow tea of relaxation and rest:

Valerian and skullcap
Linden blossom and marshmallow
Passiflora and hops
Liquorice and golden rod
Camomile and lemon balm

And consider a combination of the following for the medicine pouch:

Lavender flowers or oil
Rose buds or oil
Linden blossoms or oil
Poppy petals
Hops
Camomile flowers or oil

For the tea, place the herbs in a teapot and pour boiling water over them. Use personal discretion on the amount of water to use. Now, chant:

> *Into the depths I gently place you,*
> *Let soothing waters now embrace you,*
> *Become a draught of lullabies,*
> *So that I may sleep when I close my eyes.*

Then, with eyes closed, breathe the words "Steep deeply, sleep deeply" into the pot three times and put on the lid. Steep for ten minutes.

While the tea is steeping, we can make our slumber pouch. Place the herbal ingredients for the slumber pouch in the centre of a soft, pastel-coloured cloth. Allow three drops of rose, lavender, linden, or camomile essential oil to soak into them. Then add the chosen herbs. Holding the pouch in hand, chant:

> *Become infused with sandman's stars,*
> *My little bag of charms,*
> *May your scent sing me to sleep*
> *And keep me in slumber's arms*

Draw the corners to the centre and tie them together with a silver thread. On the fabric, stitch a star in white, silver, or pale-blue cotton. As each stitch is wrought, repeat:

> *A stitch in time takes me deeper,*
> *For this is my slumber's keeper.*

Take the charmed slumber pouch and place it under the pillow used while sleeping.

Now as the evening wears on, gradually drink the tea, adding honey to sweeten. Close the eyes while sipping the warm brew, thinking of restful imagery, or anything soft, drifting, and floating. Focus on good night's sleep. Reflect on good dreams. Ask:

> *Of nodding poppy in golden hay,*
> *As I drink may I drift away!*

Herbal Spell to Aiding Digestion

This is a suitable tea for the abdominal cramps associated with irritable bowel syndrome but can help any discomfort after eating. Early in the morning prepare a brew that can be drunk after each meal throughout the day. It is to be both calming and warming and so will work with the waxing energy of the sun as it is prepared. Herb combinations with these qualities are:

Cinnamon and cardamom
Cumin and ginger
Cloves and fenugreek
Fennel and dill

Take care when measuring out these herbs for they are potent! A small pinch, small slice, or level teaspoon of each is sufficient. Make a tea from a blend of these herbs and two cups of water, allowing for evaporation. In a saucepan, simmer over low heat for ten minutes. Gently stir it in a clockwise direction and sing softly to it, or whisper:

> *There's a fire in the sky and it fuels me,*
> *There's a sun inside and it soothes me,*
> *As I stir sunwise so may there be*
> *A wise sun at the core of me,*
> *Bringing me blessed relief,*
> *As the sun kisses the earth beneath.*

While stirring the brew, imagine that there is a wonderful warmth and serenity present all around. It is akin to lying on a beach in pleasant sunshine with all cares on the horizon. Align deep breathing with the stirring, taking care to inhale the fragrant steam as the brew boils. Imagine this aroma seeping into the body like sunlight, bringing a deep inner calm and sense of well-being. After simmering the potion for ten minutes, strain it and transfer the liquid to a flask. Chant quiety:

> *Soothe and smooth, my calming brew,*
> *Bring into me what I've wished in you!*

After a meal, drink one cup. The lower abdomen should be gently massaged in the same direction that the food is travelling. This is a clockwise motion centred over the small and larger intestines. Envisage the warming sun's journey as it brings peace and healing. Rock gently with the rhythm of the massaging motion and sing softly:

> *Sun's passage is as smooth as glass,*
> *In the same way shall my own food pass.*

After drinking a final cup of the brew, pour a little onto the earth outside and say:

> *Sun is set and day is done,*
> *Pain has fled, discomfort gone,*
> *Earth has turned and sun moved on,*
> *Hurt no more, set like the sun.*

Likewise, bury the herbal remnants from the teapot in the ground.

Charm to Remove a Sore Throat

At night when the energies are waning, and preferably in the dark of the moon, make a tincture consisting of sage, thyme, and myrrh. To do this, chop the fresh herbs and place them in a clean dry jar. Fill the jar with up to two-thirds of the herb. Cover the herbs with a good quality vodka, brandy, or gin of 100 percent proof (this means that it has a ratio of 50 percent alcohol and 50 percent water in it and therefore is suitable, for water is needed in the blend), leaving a little air space for agitation. Place the jar in a warm, dark place, like an airing cupboard, for a whole moon cycle. Agitate the jar once a day, preferably again at night as it is to be a banishing tincture. While shaking the jar, sing something like:

> *Rasp and croak will all be soothed,*
> *By this brew sore throats improve!*

On the next dark moon, or the one after if there is no hurry for the brew, decant the tincture by separating the herbs and liquid through a tea strainer or muslin bag (a pair of fine mesh tights can do just as well as muslin). The brew should now be in a dark glass bottle. This bottle can be marked with a suitable personal banishing symbol. Such a symbol can be found on a specific trance journey.

When the tincture is needed for a sore throat then take five drops of it (or approximately one-quarter teaspoon) on the tongue or in a cup of boiling water (this removes the alcohol content). This is to be done three times a day: morning, noon, and night. At the same instance, take a small piece of rough wood and a piece of sand paper. Focusing on the pain and roughness in the throat, rub the piece of wood smooth. Every time the tincture is consumed, smooth the wood a little more, chanting:

> *Sand is rough and throat be rougher,*
> *Throat we soothe as wood be smoother!*

When the sore throat has gone, burn the remaining piece of wood while repeating the following rhyme:

> *Smooth's my throat without the germs,*
> *Germs that die with wood that burns!*
> *Throat be no more irritated,*
> *Smooth wood now be immolated!*

Brews (or teas) and tinctures are two of the many ways our versatile herb helpers can be worked with. There are also balms and ointments for the skin, and essential oils to add evocative fragrances to use for aromatherapy. We can also make soothing syrups with sugar or honey. Here we have seen just a few ideas to get us started on the life-long magical quest of working with herbs for health as well as for their uplifting, gently supportive qualities. We must remember that all herbs can be composted after we have finished working with them. We can empty out our strainers and teapots with a final thank-you as we return them to the earth:

> *From your beginnings in the soil,*
> *I bade you aid me with my toil,*
> *And now I place you down with care,*
> *And thank you for the gift you shared.*

Using Our Wild Gifts for Divination

By this stage in our work we will have no problem accepting, perceiving, and even working with the unseen wild spirit inherent in all beings. Such activities as communicating with plants, as well as sensing their energies, help us further develop the seeing and knowing—our intuitive faculty. All our trancework and envisioning (or wishful visualising) during our spellweaving should really be allowing us to look beyond with more clarity and certainty. Here we look at another way of developing insights by crafting a special divination that speaks to us and us alone. These we will call the stones and bones.

Stones and Bones

Crafting a wildwitch's divination tools requires us to undertake two journeys, one manifest and the other inner, in trance. The manifest journey is to actually find the initial items (or representatives) that will make up our divination set. This will be a selection of thirteen individual pieces; thirteen reflects the number of moons in a lunar year, the moon being our vision's guide, bringing illumination to the dazzlingly dark realm of psychic sight and divination. To augment the original thirteen representatives we can find subsidiary pieces later, but our initial foray should be to find these core items.

The best place to undertake this search is on a beach, preferably out of season, at the waning of the day, at the waning of the year, and at the full to waning of the moon (and at low tide). The energy of divination is of that magical crone tide, the wise woman being the patron of all that is hidden and that we wish to be revealed to us, and so the associated energy is waning to dark. Remember the trance journey that we previously undertook to meet the wise grandmother, spirit of the waning moon? Well, this physical journey will reflect all that we came to understand when we met her on that strange shining shore between that glowering sea and the cruel rocks. The seashore, where the sea meets the sand, is a place of mystery, a borderland between two elemental worlds; caves and rock pools, those secret subterranean realms, are her haunts.

Here on the shore we can find curious shells, shaped driftwood, and old bones and stones smoothed to a glassy finish by the sea. Each strange item we find will be highly unique and will call to us singularly from a place littered with such objects. We must search for them with a scavenger's eye, with our wild vision that helps us to instinctively know what we need. We are not looking for pretty treasure, although some of what we find may well be beautiful; we are looking for a stone, shell, or a piece of bone or wood that speaks to us of a certain quality. Each piece must symbolically represent an attribute. Therefore we must invoke for each symbolic piece to show itself before we begin, making it clear what we are looking for, and why.

List of Representatives for Spirit

Each item we find will have its own wild spirit. We need to go spirit to spirit with them to find if they are compatible with the energies we seek. Here are the core qualities for our initial divination set, each core quality reflects several other aspects as shown. We need to find representatives for:

1. Spirit—unseen influences, spiritual guidance or presences. The within.

2. The garden—manifest influences, physical presences. The without.

3. The wild child—innocence, new beginnings, enthusiasm, hope. Representing birth to puberty.

4. The wild man—waxing sun to midsummer, sexuality, protection, warrior energy, green issues. Representing youth to early middle age.

5. The wild woman—waxing moon to full, fertility, inspiration, creativity. Representing youth to early, middle age.

6. The cunning man—waning sun to midwinter, magic, storytelling, mythmaking, healing. Representing late, middle age to death.

7. The wise woman—waning moon to dark, divination, psychic sight, herbalism. Representing late, middle age to death.

8. The journey—moving in new directions, energetic shifting. Within or without.

9. The rogue—random events, the trickster energy, unexpected influences.

10. Fate—predestined issues of life-changing importance. Fey and spellweaving.

11. Love—romantic partners, family, compassion for others.

12. Integrity—honesty, discerning the truth in a situation or person, moral dilemmas, walking our talk. All aspects of the true self, all we are, within and without.

13. Oroboros—death and rebirth represented by the snake devouring its own tail, endings and beginnings, profound change.

Before we can find representatives for the above qualities we need to do two things. Firstly, we should know intimately the stretch of beach or coastline we intend to comb to find our representatives, before we go there to find our representative items. We should visit it three times and really spend time absorbing its energies and observing its physicality. We should know the colour of its sands, every curve of its coves, every crag of its cliffs, and the tang of its tides in our nostrils.

Secondly, we should be completely at ease with what each symbol's energy means to us. We should work in our magical journals, focusing on each of the qualities mentioned in our list, and draw any imagery or write any words that come up when we consider each concept. We can use the wonderful technique of making a collage from magazine cuttings to express how each resonant idea inspires us. We can discuss any tricky concepts with our companion spirits, spending a few moments meditating, allowing ourselves to explore each energy. We cannot hope to find the manifest representatives for our divination set until we are completely at home with the energy and meaning of each prospective piece.

When we have done these two things we should then work within the sacred protective circle of our trancework and visualise the chosen stretch of coast, conjuring up its likeness while meditating on it. We should invoke the atmosphere of the shore into our inner realms and walk there. To have any hope of physically finding these representatives we must first focus on them as we walk in trance, calling to them astrally, sending out an etheric (or otherworldly) invitation to the beings who will work with us. We need not actually search for each item during the journey, the point is not to find them but to alert their spirit that our spirit is seeking them. This is "the calling" and we can employ it as a technique in other trance situations, for instance when calling astrally to a prospective lover. When we are calling, for example, to the spirit of a stone, shell, or bone that will represent the garden on our list of divination pieces, we could invite them to draw closer to us by chanting something like:

> *Oh being that speaks of the soil,*
> *Of the sand beneath the stars,*
> *And of all that this means to me,*
> *Pray, show me where you are!*
> *Be you pebble or be you bone,*
> *Oh being that speaks of the land,*
> *I call to you alone,*
> *Pray, show me where you stand!*

It matters not how we call to each prospective piece, only that we do so with feeling and focused intent. If we do not have these, we have little hope of finding the right, most resonant representatives on a real beach full of hundreds of such bones and stones. We need to feel the magnetism of familiarity, which results from us connecting with the object beforehand, astrally, in trance. If we do this with a genuine desire to find what we need, then, when we actually walk on the beach, our eyes will be instinctively drawn to the piece we need to find. We may actually see, feel, or hear them calling back to us if we take our time and walk gently. The stones, bones, shells, etc., that we have called to us will shine for us to see, bringing the whole process alive.

Review: Finding Divination Tools

☐ We must find a place where our divination tools may reside and get to know that place physically

☐ We must gain a deeper understanding of the energies behind each divination piece that we seek

☐ We trance journey to "see" the place and feel the energetic representatives

☐ We physically journey to the place and find the representatives we seek

When we have collected our thirteen representatives we can then go about consecrating them (or dedicating them in a sacred manner) to our purpose. We can do this within a magical circle by "washing" (blessing) them in fragrant smoke as we burn an ethically gathered herb, one that is sacred to divination such as mugwort, wormwood, nutmeg, bay, or yarrow. Though these herbs are good representatives, we should still consult with our companion spirits to find the most suitable herb. A corresponding essential oil could also be used to anoint them as we name them and welcome them into our care. Then, holding them on our lap in a square of black velvet or another dark cloth, we can journey with them into the Otherworlds. Here we will bless them in the unseen worlds. And so they work on both levels, as do we.

To bless our divination set we will follow the normal procedures to undertake an otherworldly journey. Ask for the companion guides to be present and create a chant to sum up the purpose of the mission. Here is an example of what may happen next:

Trance Journey: Blessing Our Divination Set

I am standing on the slopes of a hill with the wind whipping round me. At my waist there is a pouch and inside it lie my thirteen representatives, my divination tools. I feel their reassuring weight and then I begin to walk uphill.

The clouds scud across a pallid sky, fragmenting as they go, dissolving into new forms, wisping into nothing. A buzzard's plaintive cry is heard, though he has gone too high for me to see now. This is a wild land, a moor of great desolate beauty; it sweeps down to meet the sea, one wild being racing to meet the passionate embrace of another. From where I stand on this rounded peak I can see the gunmetal grey waves pounding in the distance, tearing hungrily at a shoreline that is out of my view.

This land is scrubby, strewn with gorse and loose granite. Twisted, wind-blasted trees cower and crouch all around me. Behind me there is a dolmen, an ancient stone-lined mound that recedes into the hill itself. Its arched entrance is made of three granite blocks, fern covered and ringed with lichen; beyond it, passing into the hill itself, there is a fertile febrile darkness—a moist black cavern from which a faint echo of dripping can be heard as water seeps from above in an endless pitiless parody of weeping. The darkness beyond is alive and aware of me. I do not enter the darkness, rather look at the glyphs etched into the granite lintel and the two side pillars of the entrance. The glyphs are protective symbols carved by those who walked this way long ago, chevrons and cup-marks, a simple language that speaks plainly. They say, unequivocally, this place is sacred.

Sacred to who? It is sacred to me. And to she who belongs here.

Yet who would belong here? It is a harsh place, a land that eats its own shadows. It has jagged teeth and icy breath and a gaping maw. It is withered and scarred, pitted and as uninhabited as the hungry moon herself. But it welcomes me, and I embrace it, for it is built of old bones that hold the knowing. I come to know this place when I need to have a foretelling, for it is a place of sight and secrets revealed. It is the untamed domain of the hag, night's only begotten daughter. I seek her in the stagnant pools and yellowed moss. I know her by the creases in the land, their folds like those in leathery hide, hanging loose and mottled.

I sit at the entrance of this dolmen, on circle of dried flattened earth at its entrance, where a hundred old ones have sat before me, sat and called to her as I will, looking out to sea.

A single raven croaks overhead, with black-fingered wings as fierce as the bitter wind. The dull waves crash, I hear their sibilant hiss and fancy I can taste their spray even from this distance. Behind me more water seeps and drips into the dolmen cave. I begin to rock, my hands placed firmly on the dusty circle of soil, on this living land. I sing out:

> *I swear by damp in the darkness,*
> *By mildew on wet bark,*
> *That my intentions are as true*
> *As any who this way walk.*
> *I call by toad in her blind cave,*
> *By crevice and dust-dry crack,*
> *To she who rides on the last wave,*
> *May she bring the Sight I lack!*

With this I pound the ground, three by three, hearing the drumming beat of my fists echo into caverns, through chambers, down wells, and along submerged riverbeds. I hear the cry taken up by the ebony ones of sharp eye and sharper beak, ragged crow and time-ravaged rook:

> *May she come . . . craa-aak! May she come back! We lack!*

And toward me, up the moor's slope from the waves below, hurrying like an eager child, a child bound in flapping rags of sea-grey, she comes, closer; a face shrouded in layers of torn discoloured cloth, like memories.

I take the thirteen divination pieces from the pouch at my waist and I lay them out on their dark cloth before me. I whisper to them, "She will soon be here!"

And so she is, a vision, worn and shrivelled, yet shining like a dark star, pulling all light toward her, radiating shining wisdom.

I point, hating to do so but knowing that I must. I surround the fragile bird-form with blue-gold fire and I ask with as much authority as I can muster, "Show yourself truly, spirit!"

There is a flurry in the circle of flame, a blur of feathers, a river mist rising, the eyes of an owl staring at me unperturbed through whirling snowflakes, the wings of a bat stretching out. . . . And then there is a woman with faded lilac eyes and a shadow of a smile standing in the circle again. A ghost given form by dull old clothes, the most powerful woman I know. She has shown herself truly to be genuine.

She kneels before me and examines the treasure I have brought to show her. She likes treasure, this artful beachcomber. She holds each piece in turn, turning it over and over in her tiny palm lined with wrinkled skin. She sniffs it and kisses it, then she lays it back down on the cloth with gentle reverence and turns to the next one. She makes a circle of thirteen from them, a clock of life, for all life can be expressed by these divination tools. I introduce her to each one by name and she nods reverently. When I have finished their naming she puts both hands over them and they flutter like pale December moths. She says:

> *I bring them life that they may live,*
> *They show you life that you may live.*

I respond: "In your name I ask that they be blessed, in balance and beauty. May these tools of divination live! By your hands may they thrive! By your will may they be blessed!"

She makes a sweeping fluid motion, inscribing a sacred symbol in the air over these precious pieces. I see them shift a little, glowing with their own inner light.

She says: "It is done, it is so." She looks at me, expecting more.

"And I give you my word that each time I work with them, in the world, I will do so by your leave. And I pledge to do my best to see that your energy, and your imagery, are accepted back into human realms."

She nods again, a suggestion of a smile. I see a small smooth snake coiling around her wrist and then her hand is gone, tucked into her flowing, ripped garment. I look down at my tools and when I look up again she has vanished. I can sense where she once stood by a musty scent, the secret smell of the dark ones, of cool wet stone and the things that dwell beneath. I have vowed that I will speak up for those who walk in her image, in aged human form. My pledge is to display paintings or photographs that show the beauty in age, to challenge those who make remarks to denigrate age and to cease chasing and venerating youth in my own life, to the detriment of the elderly.

I fold my tools, my companions in divination, back into my dark cloth and place them so bound into my pouch. I lay my hands on the dolmen stones and whisper my goodbyes, for now. Then I slowly walk down the slope, past gorse and granite, back to ordinary reality.

Casting

With the divination tools so blessed and awoken we can now begin our work with them. We do this by asking a question and then "casting" (similar to throwing down dice) the representatives in order to receive guidance. This we may do when the moon is full to waning, aligning ourselves immediately with the correct energies. We should familiarise ourselves with all the possible meanings of each representative. Depending on both the question and how they are cast, the meaning of the stone or bone will be subtly different. For example, on one reading the cunning man may mean a magical influence and on another it may mean an elderly man in our life. It is up to us to attune with the various energetic messages contained within each representative piece and equate the most appropriate meaning to each individual reading. With repeated workings the stones and bones will sing to us, communicating flashes of insight and revealing associated images and feelings when we do a reading. Working with them is like learning to understand the subtle moods and inner thoughts of a lover or close companion, the more we align our energies with them, the closer we become, the better we can read them. It is a living way, after all!

Before we can cast the stones and bones we need to make ourselves a suitable pouch to hold them, a loose bag with a drawstring top, embroidered or painted in a way that suits our purpose in working with them. Seek suitable symbols, as ever, in trance journey with the companions.

Then work on a piece of dark cloth. Think of a suitable question that refers to the energies of a situation we wish to understand further. For example, rather than "Will I meet a nice man/woman at the party?" we can ask "What energetic influences will I be confronted with if I go to the party on Friday?" Another good question to ask ourselves is "What are the predominant energetic influences in my life for the next six months?" This is better than simply asking this: "What will happen to me from now until Christmas?" Our tools can show us the patterns involved and reveal the overall essence of what we seek but, like any divination tool, they cannot tell us what bus to catch or whether to buy the new shoes or not! As ever, we are working with symbolic resonances and energetic impressions, with fate and mystery, not hard facts and concrete.

Focusing on the chosen question we can shake the bag of stones and bones three times and then cast them (we may choose to shake them in our hands). How they fall will reveal a pattern, which we can interpret by simply looking at what lies where. Here are some guidelines.

- What lies on the periphery of the cloth? Such influences are not immediate to us.

- Has anything fallen outside the cloth? These energies are irrelevant.

- What lies in the centre? These energies are central to our issue.

- Do any representatives overlap or cluster together? These energies are interlinked or inseparable, depending on their proximity.

- Does any noticeable symbolic shape taken form? If so, what does it mean to us?

To enhance or advance a reading we can prescribe attributes to certain areas of our cloth before we begin. We can, for example, use our sacred wheel as a guideline—the north section of the cloth is for housing and work (manifest issues), the east for ideas and communication (airy issues), the south for creativity and passions (fire), the west for love and emotion (water), the centre for spiritual endeavour and development (ether). We can then have a double insight into our issue, for instance we may see two stones lying closely in the east and know that the energy of each piece, due to how it has been cast, links up with our thoughts or communications in the realm of air.

Once we are fluent in casting we can work confidently with the stones and bones for other people and be creative and intuitive in our readings. We can also think about adding further "secondary" representatives—stones, bones, and shells that are more descriptive than prescriptive. If we decide to do this, we must remember that if we include one feeling or description then we should really include it's opposite as well, for balance. Some examples: flow and its opposite, blockage; joy and grief; union and separation; illness and thriving; growth and stagnation; movement and stillness. It is best not to have too many of these or we will simply not be able to bond with them adequately nor work with them insightfully. Of course, with these secondary helpers we should follow the same process as we did with the primary representatives. And we can always ask the companion guides for their suggestions.

As with any organic growth process, our wild craft relies heavily on being fed and watered, in this instance by constant feedback from our guiding spirits. As they walk beside us, our divination technique, as with all of our practices, should evolve and become uniquely ours over time, transforming our lives as it in turn becomes transformed. All we have here is the suggestion of how to make a start on such practices, safely and hopefully with joy. The rest of it is part of our own Greening, the personal resurgence of an inherent wildness, that is uniquely ours by birthright, to express in the world. Our magic unfolds, a many-petalled wonder.

*   *   *

To conclude this chapter, and indeed this book, is there any final advice to be given to one seeking a fulfilling green-spirited existence, a life infused with mystical significance, steeped in deep enchantment? Well, yes, but as with all things in this book the answer may seem overly simplistic and naive. It is this:

Shine.

That is to say: "Be yourself. Your true magical self."

We must let our wild spirit be seen in our eyes. We know that our essence, that otherworldly being that we truly are, walks only for a time in this current human frame. Someday it will fly beyond it again. But while it walks within it, on Earth, it will tread lightly, in beauty, with integrity. Through the exercises and teachings we have shared, we are more aware of this eternal self and the vital part we have to play in the glistening web of fate, the brightly woven pattern of existence. Our own fears and the challenges that may lie ahead of us no longer render us powerless or hopeless, we know ourselves and the process more fully and that gives us strength. We have intimate knowledge and in-depth experiences that none can replicate; it is a unique and beautiful set of wonders to recall; wonders that can fortify us if our enthusiasm wanes in hard times. We have faith in our companion spirits, in the energetic beings that work with us and through us, and we are secure and protected in all that we practice. We see and know beyond that which is generally seen and known and we feel the bitter sweetness of each dying back and the joyous celebration of each sprouting.

Moreover, we not only know how to make magic come alive but we understand why we must actually live magic; we know that we have a choice but at the same time we have little say in the matter, for what we do in the world is what we *are*, it is naturally who we decide to *be* inside our human form. The world we experience is an enchanted place and we are a being of infinite potential, bound free.

Now is the time for us to put our knowledge into practice. To move beyond what is written here into what is truly ours and indelibly etched on our souls. We surrender ourselves to the wild like a brown buzzard riding a thermal, rising on the endless spiralling currents of existence, flowing with the tides of life, until we know both the brightest stars and the hidden treasures of Earth . . .

Fly on, shining ones, children of the Greening.

GLOSSARY

This guide is not in alphabetical order but instead follows the progression of the concepts in this book, explaining each term with reference to the next.

The Seen

The current plane on which we live. It appears solid to our human eyes. Also middle Earth.

The Unseen

Any aspect of existence that is not physical or manifestly visible. The unseen realms exist in tandem to the corporeal physical reality in which we currently dwell; these are the spiritual, ethereal dimensions that remain unseeable to most of humanity. The unseen is perceived or envisioned with the inner, or "third," eye using psychic sight rather than our human eyes.

The Otherworlds

These are the unseen realms, levels of existence that are less physically dense than the one we currently experience as reality. These are the etheric levels in which the spirits are able to move freely, expressing themselves without bodily restraints. Also the lower and upper worlds.

Spiritweaver

One who deliberately works with the denizens of the Otherworlds for the purpose of attaining deeper understanding and performing magic and healing. They will travel to the unseen levels where they may interact with spirits and effect positive change in the strands of fate that connect all beings. Thus they are a walker between that which is visible and that which is hidden and act as a weaver of the energies that connect the two.

Wildwitch

One who works as a spiritweaver for the good of all, having a direct and daily relationship with the unseen. This is done with the utmost respect for their current manifest home on Earth. This care for Earth and all her beings is creatively woven into otherworldly enchantments, bringing a new balance to the seen and the unseen. The wildwitch is a bridge between the spirits and the land so that their may be grater dialogue between the two for the sake of healing and wisdom. This is wild witchcraft, in essence.

Wild Witchcraft

An unsophisticated and wholesome way of expressing a love for nature and an empathy with the spiritual aspects of existence in a poetic, spontaneous, authentic, and highly individual way, which relies on a personal interaction with the unseen.

The Sight; the Seeing and the Knowing

This innate skill is employed by wildwitches or spiritweavers to enable him or her to witness the unseen more clearly. It is an inner wisdom that manifests in strong feelings, intuitions, and visions. Such psychic wisdom is referred to as the "seeing." It can be enhanced by working in a structured, disciplined way, making frequent journeys to the Otherworlds in trance. Once we know that we have "far seeing" (see definition below), we have the ability to gain deep insights that can lead us to further understanding of the greater whole of existence and consequently greater magical power—referred to as the "knowing." The knowing is an understanding—based on the psychic information gained in seeing—of energies.

Far Seeing

Using the gift of psychic sight to "look beyond" (toward the unseen realms and Otherworlds, the past and the future).

Inner Work

Anything we do to enhance our spiritual well-being and growth that is achieved in an other-worldly sense, through trance journey or otherwise. This is balanced or reflected in wild witchcraft by our outer work, i.e., our practical activities in the physical world.

Trance Journey

A route taken in a relaxed meditative state, which gives the greatest opportunity for communing effectively with the spirits connected with the particular matters we work for in the world. For instance, our companion spirits, the elemental spirits, or the Fey. The trance aspect does not denote being out of control or unaware, rather a deep state of relaxation facilitates inner vision.

Pathworking

A trance journey undertaken for a specific purpose, following a predetermined route.

The Fey

Collective term given to the Faery beings that dwell in the Otherworlds—particularly those realms on a level that overlaps our physical plane. To be "fey" is to share the attributes of this ancient unseen race, namely wild enchantment, deep poetic expression, enhanced psychic knowing, and a childlike joyful way of being that can show its flip side of unruly, sometimes cruel, misbehaviour. The Fey will protect Earth with a fierce passion, as they too dwell within her many layers of existence . . . theirs is just less opaque than ours.

Faerytide

A return to the enchantment that has been lost to humanity; the free-flowing lyrical magical eloquence of the Fey. It can also refer to the inspiration of the Fey in the life of the wildwitch.

Familiar/Companion/Guiding Spirit

The unseen beings who work along side us all; our most close nonphysical allies. We can contact these spirit friends through trance journey and other meditative, prayerful methods. They may be Fey or otherwise.

Earthwalk

The duration of a human incarnation on Earth; that which we, as essentially spiritual beings, undertake in a human form.

Green Mantle

That which the wildwitch symbolically takes on for an Earthwalk, an otherworldly cloak that can be felt but not seen by human eyes. Such a mantle stands as a gesture of allegiance to Earth and gives the wildwitch greater strength and courage to assist in her protection.

Green Spirituality

An unpretentious and Earth-honouring way of acknowledging the life force in ourselves and all fellow beings on a daily basis. A spirituality that is essentially wild, experiential, and without limiting religious affiliation.

The All

A way of describing the harmony of the seen and unseen worlds, a description that encompasses all beings, regardless of their status as spiritual or corporeal. This also applies to those who are nonhuman including celestial bodies, plants, creatures, etc.

The Creator/Source

The creative force behind all being; the mysterious initiating energy of creation. This is often referred to as God or Goddess but in wild witchcraft it is simply a driving, motivating force that is not humancentric.

Humancentric
Giving spiritual relevance to those only in human form.

Spellweaving
A spell can be said to be making our intent a reality through magical symbolism and focussed acts. These are carried out with reference to, and reverence for, the solar and lunar cycles and in harmony with the natural world. The weaving comes from the witch's careful, creative interactions between the unseen energetic levels and the manifest Earth level. All wild spells are a subtle blend of the ethereal and the corporeal.

Wild Enchantment
This is a poetic term that implies the use of chanting or repetition to fix a woven spell as well as the air of mystery and magic that pervades any spellweaving. The wild or natural aspect refers to the complete integration a spell has with the well-being of the land on which we live, as well as the joy and freedom of working in this way.

The Greening
A positive term used to suggest the return of Earth-honouring gratitude that is expressed in our lives and eventually the lives of everyone. We bring about the Greening by experiencing our connection with the land and working toward a resurgence of its energies. We blend the magical and the practical for this end, weaving healing magics as well as actively replenishing/recycling. The Greening is also a magical term which reflects our connection to the hidden denizens of Earth, the elemental spirits, and the Fey, and unites us in our mutual efforts to see the land green, unpolluted, and whole again.

Elemental Spirits
Those spirit beings inherently of the elements, the unseen energetic representatives of air, fire, water, and earth. They are both guardians and symbolic expressions.

Shining Ones/Children of the Greening
The ancient wise beings that once walked the Earth, now experienced by us in Otherworlds as the Fey. As wildwitches we can take on their attitudes and work toward our own Greening.

Enspirited/Ensouled/Spiritfull
To be possessed of an animating life force. This applies to all beings; again it is not humancentric. It also implies an inherent awareness of our own spirit nature beyond human flesh.

Prayer
To reveal ones intent with reverence for the All. An outpouring of individual will that honours the rest of creation.

Soul Song
The innate melodic vibration expressed by every unique spirit as part of the overall harmony of the universe.

Earth Dance/Dance of Life
The energetic ebb and flow of existence, which becomes tangible to the wildwitch.

Avatar
An energetic (unseen) representative of a particular principle such as peace or creativity.

Psychic Protection
A way of ensuring our spiritual safety as we travel through the Otherworlds in trance journey and otherwise.

Astral Safe Place
A place created in trance journey where secure and effective communication can be attained with the guiding spirits.

SUGGESTED READING LIST

Beth, Rae. *Hedge Witch*. London: Robert Hale, 1989.

————. *The Hedge Witch's Way*. London: Robert Hale, 2001.

————. *Reincarnation and the Dark Goddess*. London: Robert Hale, 2001.

————. *Spellcasting for Hedge Witches*. London: Robert Hale, 2004.

Baudino, Gael. *Maze of Moonlight*. London: Orbit, 1993.*

————. *Shroud of Shadow*. London: Orbit, 1995.*

————. *Spires of Spirit*. London: Orbit, 1997.*

————. *Strands of Starlight*. London: Orbit, 1991.*

Cooper, Susan. *The Dark is Rising Trilogy*. London: Puffin, 1968.*

De Bairacli Levy, Juliette. *Common Herbs for Natural Health*. Woodstock, NY: Ash Tree, 1997.

DeLint, Charles. *Yarrow*. London: Pan, 1992.*

Deveraux, Paul. *Fairy Paths and Spirit Roads*. London: Vega, 2003.

Dolan, Mia. *The Gift*. London: Element, 2003.

Evans-Wentz, W. Y. *The Fairy-Faith in Celtic Countries*. Franklin Lakes, NJ: New Page, 2004.

Feldman, Christina. *The Quest of the Warrior Woman*. London: Thorsons, 1994.

Figes, Kate. *Because of her Sex*. London: Pan, 1994.**

Fortune, Dion. *Avalon of the Heart*. Boston, MA: Weiser/Red Wheel, 2000.

Freke, Timothy. *The Wisdom of the Sufi Sages*. Hants, UK: Godsfield, 1999.

Franklin, Anna, and Susan Lavender. *Herbcraft*. Berkshire, UK: Capall Bann, 1996.

————. *Fairy Lore*. Berkshire, UK: Capall Bann, 1999.

————. *Familiars*. Berkshire, UK: Capall Bann, 1997.

Gibran, Khalil. *The Prophet.* Oxford, UK: Oneworld, 2000.

Gifford, Jane. *The Celtic Wisdom of Trees.* Hants, UK: Godsfield, 2000.

Gladstar, Rosemary. *Herbal Healing for Women.* London: Bantam, 1993.

Gould Davies, Elizabeth. *The First Sex.* London: Penguin, 1975.**

Greer, Germaine. *The Whole Woman.* London: Transworld, 1999.

Hawke, Elen. *In the Circle.* St. Paul, MN: Llewellyn, 2002.

Holdstock, Robert. *Mythago Wood.* London: Grafton, 1986.**

Hounsome, Steve. *Practical Spirituality.* Berkshire, UK: Capall Bann, 1997.

Kumar, Satish. *No Destination.* Devon, UK: Green Books, 1992.

———. *You Are, Therefore I Am.* Devon, UK: Green Books, 2002.

Lee, Patrick Jasper. *We Borrow the Earth.* London: Thorsons, 2000.

Llywelyn, Morgan. *The Bard.* London: Sphere, 1985.*

Newton, Michael. *Destiny of Souls.* St. Paul, MN: Llewellyn, 2001.

———. *Journey of Souls.* St. Paul, MN: Llewellyn, 1994.

Palin, Poppy. *The Greening.* Somerset, UK: Wild Spirit, 2005.*

———. *Season of Sorcery.* Berkshire, UK: Capall Bann, 1998.

———. *Soul Resurgence.* Berkshire, UK: Capall Bann, 2000.

———. *Waking the Wild Spirit Tarot.* St. Paul, MN: Llewellyn, 2002.

———. *Walking with Spirit.* Berkshire, UK: Capall Bann, 2000.

———. *Wildwitch.* Berkshire, UK: Capall Bann, 1999.

Richardson, Alan. *Spirits of the Stones.* London: Virgin, 2001.

Romani, Rosa. *Green Spirituality.* Somerset, UK: Green Magic, 2004.

Roney-Dougal, Serena. *The Faery Faith.* Somerset, UK: Green Magic, 2003.

Sams, Jamie. *Dancing the Dream.* New York: Harper Collins, 2000.

———. *Earth Medicine.* New York: Harper Collins, 1994.

Smith, Jill. *The Callanish Dance.* Berkshire, UK: Capall Bann, 2000.

Spink, Peter. *Beyond Belief.* Somerset, UK: Omega Trust, 2001.

Starhawk. *Walking to Mercury.* London: Thorsons, 1997.*

Summer Rain, Mary. *Phantoms Afoot.* Charlottesville, PA: Hampton Roads, 1989.

———. *Spirit Song.* Charlottesville, VA: Hampton Roads, 1985.

Weed, Susun S. *Healing Wise.* Woodstock, NY: Ash Tree, 1989.

Wood, Jan Morgan. *Easy to Use Shamanism.* London: Vega, 2002.

Wood, Nicholas. *Voices from the Earth.* London: Godsfield, 2000.

Wright, Machaelle Small. *Behaving as if the God in all Life Mattered.* Warrenton, VA: Perelandra, 1997.

* Denotes magical / inspirational fiction.

** Denotes works that may shed light on those considered "witches" in times past.

CPSIA information can be obtained at www.ICGtesting.com
Printed in the USA
LVOW09s0726240415

435810LV00003B/3/P

9 780738 705774